Enlightenment and Beyond

Enlightenment and Beyond

Political Economy Comes to Japan

Edited by
Chūhei Sugiyama and Hiroshi Mizuta

UNIVERSITY OF TOKYO PRESS

Publication of this volume was made possible by a translation grant from the Ministry of Education, Science, and Culture and from a publication grant from Kawai Institute of Cultural and Educational Research.

ISBN 0–86008–426–4
ISBN 4–13–047038–8

Printed in Japan

Contents

Contributors

Olive Checkland	University of Glasgow
A. W. Coats	University of Nottingham and Duke University
Hiroshi Mizuta	Faculty of Commerce, Meijō University
Tamotsu Nishizawa	Faculty of Economics, Osaka City University
Ikuo Ōmori	Faculty of Commerce, Waseda University
Shirō Sugihara	Professor Emeritus, Kōnan University
Chūhei Sugiyama	Faculty of Economics, Tokyo Keizai University
Mikihisa Suzuki	Faculty of Commerce, Meijō University
Norio Tamaki	Faculty of Commerce, Keiō University

Preface

Japan was a late-comer to modern world history primarily because of the extended period of isolationism under the Tokugawa Shogunate, from the seventeenth to mid-nineteenth century. Even then, Dutch merchants were able to enjoy a monopoly over foreign trade under the Shogunate, and as a by-product of the trade relations, Dutch studies (*rangaku*) in the natural sciences and engineering were transplanted to Japan. But Western philosophy and social sciences were almost totally ignored until the final days of the shogunate, when two students were sent to the Netherlands. They returned with the Dutch version of mid-Victorian liberalism, thus importing to Japan the first systematic knowledge of Western social sciences, including political economy.

But the Dutch monopoly on Western ideas ended even before the Meiji era. Intellectuals who travelled abroad realized that the Dutch played a less important role in the Western world than they had been led to believe. Henceforth, the centres for the study of social sciences abroad became New Haven, New Brunswick, Baltimore, London, Paris, and Vienna. And it was to the German universities that Japanese social scientists flocked, particularly after the Political Crisis of 1881, when the new government decided that Prussia would be its model for a modern state.

The year 1881 was a turning point in many ways, and for the future of higher education, it marked the decline of the liberalist tradition. The German Historical School, which had a large following among the earliest foreign and native teachers, became predominant in the newly established educational institutions, including the imperial universities and even such private schools as Fukuzawa Yukichi's Keiō Gijuku, which began with liberalist ideals. The government discouraged the teaching of democratic and liberal thought, but there were schools that continued to do so nonetheless. These were the private schools which were launched in the 1880s and 1890s—notably Tokyo School of Special Studies, later to become Waseda University—and attracted a number of dissenting scholars who taught liberalism and mild socialism. But the political climate was never conducive to this trend, and finally in 1910 with the High Treason Incident, the tide turned.

Besides the political trends which dictated educational policies of the Meiji state, one other factor should be noted here. This is the very early establishment of commercial training schools, such as Hitotsubashi, which supplied Japanese capitalism with future business leaders.

These are the general features of the topics discussed in the ensuing chapters. This book originated in an international research project called "The Institutionalization of Political Economy: Its Introduction and Acceptance into European, North American and Japanese Universities," which we joined in 1984, a year later than the rest of the component national working groups. Mizuta and Sugiyama, the joint convenors of the Japanese workshop, participated in the project preconference held in Paris in April 1985 and were also present, together with some workshop colleagues, at the conference organized at San Miniato in April 1986; at both these meetings we read our papers and exchanged views with the participants from other countries with their different experiences in the subject common to all.

The main part of the present book consists by and large of the papers we produced for the conference. We have, however, tried to enlarge the picture by placing our subject in a wider context in order to make our work of greater interest to the more general reader.

Instead of our own conclusion, we have had two Western colleagues write some afterthoughts, as it were, from their different points of view; these, we hope, illuminate our studies and broaden the objective outlook of the picture we have drawn.

The appendices to this volume were prepared by two members of our research team: The 'Chronological Table' by Ikuo Ōmori and 'Western Economics Books Translated into Japanese' by Shirō Sugihara.

Acknowledgments

This book would not have been realized had there been no international research project which we were invited to join, so that our thanks are first of all due to the international and to all the national convenors and to those who participated in the two successive conferences in 1985 and 1986. They gave us valuable encouragement and stimulation, across the round table, from the platform and from the floor, in the dining hall, at coffee, and even strolling in the garden—and, needless to say, through correspondence before and after the conference.

Professor A. W. Coats, with his usual assiduous interest, was willing to spare his time to write a chapter. Mrs Olive Checkland was also kind enough to give us useful advice and to contribute a paper to this book. Miss J. W. Taylor of Glasgow kindly took every trouble to go through our drafts to correct any linguistic shortcomings and thereby to improve our English style, though it is we who are responsible for any defects that may still remain.

We wish to acknowledge with gratitude the assistance of Messrs. Kazuo Ichijō of Hitotsubashi University and Jun'ichi Furukawa of Waseda for bibliographic research; and Miss Junko Fukuda, Miss Rieko Gomi, and Mrs. Yukiko Kubota from Keiō University and Mrs. Setsuko Tamaki for typing the manuscript.

Part 1

Historical Introduction

1

Historical Introduction

Hiroshi Mizuta

1. Traditional Economic Thought during the Tokugawa-period Isolation

Japan kept its doors closed to Western civilization until the middle of the nineteenth century, first as a natural result of its geographical location as an insular country at the edge of Asia, and second as a result of the policy taken in the seventeenth century by the feudal ruling classes for fear of the subversive influences of Christianity, which was thought to be incompatible with the traditional ancestor worship of Japan—the worship either of the emperor as a descendant of the Sun goddess or of the feudal lord as head of a clan or extended family.

In spite of this isolationist policy, it was impossible to keep the nation as a whole intact. In 1549, Francis Xavier, one of the founders of the Society of Jesus, landed on the southern end of Kyushu, and the missionary activities enjoyed relative freedom until the first violent suppression of 1596. The missionary activities of the Jesuits and Franciscans who followed were by no means fruitless. Repeated suppressions and martyrdoms could not uproot the tradition of hidden Christianity (*kakure kirishitan*), especially in the southwestern half of Japan including Kyushu. However, it is unlikely that this tradition had any considerable impact on the development of Western thought in Japan.[1]

Apart from the influence of Christianity, which was almost negligible during the period of isolation, there were some commercial and technological influences from Western civilization, even after the suppression of Christianity. Preceding Christianity, guns and gunpowder came to Japan in 1543 by means of a Portuguese shipwreck near an island off the southwest coast of Kyushu and revolutionized warfare among feudal lords. Technological development after that was rather inconsiderable mainly because of the policy of the Tokugawa Shogunate, which was the central government, de facto, from 1603 to 1867.[2] But after the suppression of Christianity, Dutch merchants were the exception in being allowed to stay to trade in Hirado and later in Nagasaki. It was exclusively through them that Western technology and its products flowed into Japan. Until the beginning of the Meiji era, all Western learning was called *rangaku*—that is to say, Dutch studies. The branch of Dutch studies which was considered most important was medicine. Some enlightened feudal lords were interested in chemistry and other sciences relating to industry. It was mainly from the clans of these enlightened lords that the leaders of modernization emerged in the Meiji era.

The transplantation of this Western learning gave birth to or promoted the rational way of thinking among Japanese intellectuals, not only about nature but also about society; however, political economy, as a branch of Western learning, was imported rather late compared with the natural sciences. Among the earliest Western books on political economy imported into Japan before the opening of its doors were *Untersuchungen über das Wesen und die Ursachen des National Reichthums* (a translation into German, by Max Stirner, of Adam Smith's *The Wealth of Nations*), 1846 (introduced by P. F. J. von Siebold, who came to Japan first in 1823 as a doctor and again in 1859); *Nederlandsch Handelsmagazijn of Algemeen Zamenvattend Woordenboek voor Handel en Nijverheid* (A General Dictionary of Commerce and Industry), 1843; A. Sandelin's *Répértoire Général d'Economie Politique Ancienne et Moderne*, 1846; and E. W. De Rooy's *Geschiedenis der Staathuishoudkunde in Europa van Vroegste Tijden tot Heden* (A History of the Ideas of State Householding in Europe from the Earliest Times to Today), 1851. Although there is no evidence that these books were brought into Japan immediately after their publication or that they were well read immediately after their arrival, at least we can say that in the mid-nineteenth century Western political economy was made accessible to Japanese intellectuals who could read Dutch. (Stirner's German translation of *The Wealth of Nations* might be more difficult for them.) In any case, until the 1840s or 1850s there was no direct or considerable influence of Western political economy on Japanese socioeconomic thought.

During the Tokugawa period, the official line of teaching in this field was that of the Chu Hsi sect of Confucianism with its paternalist overtones, which can be seen in the familial mythology applied to the emperor-subject relationship and the lord-warrior relationship. Under the Shogunate much more stress was put on the latter, whereas the scholars of *kokugaku* (national learning) stressed the emperor-subject relationship. Buddhism remained a popular religion—or, rather, a popular custom—but had nothing to say on socioeconomic thought. Almost all thinkers in the Tokugawa period tried to justify and explain feudalist clan society with the ruling warrior classes at the top, the merchants at the bottom, and the agricultural classes, including rural gentry and peasantry, in between. In spite of this hierarchical structure, it was inevitable that the role of money and merchants became more and more important.

One of the Tokugawa thinkers,[3] Nakae Tōju, represented the point of view of the rural gentry dealing with cultivation; his follower Kumazawa Banzan proposed replacing money with rice to strengthen the position of the gentry against the penetration of the money economy. Arai Hakuseki, who, as a higher official of the Shogunate, found himself confronted by monetary problems, maintained a sort of quantity theory of money and proposed to issue paper money without specie reserves, but this was only because he could not understand the increasing importance of money even in a feudal society. Ogyū Sorai tried to stop the liquidating effect of the monetary economy by returning warriors to the countryside to supervise peasants, binding peasants to the land, and forcibly sending urban vagrants back to rural areas. The consciousness of social crisis was so deep that he thought it necessary to have recourse to such artificial measures as these to stop the development, but Dazai Shundai, who was a follower of Sorai, reluctantly admitted the importance of commercial activities. From this time onwards industry and commerce were given their proper place in socioeconomic discussions. Honda Toshiaki and Sakuma Zōzan said that commerce and industry should be monopolized by feudal lords to prevent the exploitation of peasants by merchants and the resulting financial crisis of the lords. Zōzan, who had some knowledge of Western technology, found Japan's industrialization to be of urgent importance; he therefore declared that Japan should open its doors to the Western countries, but for this idea he was assassinated by a traditionalist. In spite of his advocacy of opening up the country, he was far from being a free-trader, but held that economic activities should be strictly controlled by the central government. Perhaps he may be defined as a forerunner of the bureaucrats of the Meiji absolute monarchy.

Of course there were some exceptions. Andō Shōeki was likened by E. Herbert Norman[4] to François Quesnay in his rational analysis of an agricultural economy, and to Gerrard Winstanley in his revolutionary aspiration. He criticized the feudal establishment and its apologists from the standpoint of the labouring peasants of northeast Japan, where he lived: living under harsh natural conditions, to make matters worse they suffered from double exploitation by feudal lords and merchants. Shōeki's social criticism was in contrast with Ogyū Sorai's ideas, and, in particular, his ideal classless society based on nature (agriculture) was against Sorai's artificial reinforcement of the feudal hierarchy. However, Shōeki was an isolated and forgotten thinker (as Norman put it). He practiced medicine in an underdeveloped rural district and had no significant influence in his age.

Miura Baien, who was an almost precise contemporary of Adam Smith, visited Nagasaki, which was a centre of Dutch studies. His knowledge of natural sciences, especially astronomy, was exceptional in eighteenth-century Japan, being, to all intents and purposes, rational and modern. In his *Kagen* (The Origin of the Price of Labour, 1773), he took an abstract point of view, applying the fiction of an isolated island to the nation's economy. The theory of money developed in this book has some similarity to Gresham's. However, Baien's nominalist or quantity theory of money did not differ very much from that of Arai Hakuseki: he said that money had no real value and hated the merchants who made their fortune by means of this fictitious value. The worship of Mammon accelerated the process of social differentiation between the rich and the poor, but the only remedy Baien proposed for this tendency was to re-establish Confucian morals as the basis of society. The only difference was that he did see the importance of material production as a result of his knowledge of natural philosophy.

Thus, in 1853, when Commodore Matthew C. Perry's American squadron came to Uraga, at the entrance of Tokyo Bay, to open ports to U.S. ships, there was no systematic knowledge of economics apart from the fragments mentioned above, and no system of higher education to propagate even those fragments. Those who might have been called economists of one degree or another were either advisers to feudal lords or teachers in tiny private schools. Although almost all the feudal clans had schools for the younger generation of samurai, their curricula were full of traditional moral teachings. Foreign studies were generally forbidden or discouraged until 1856, when the Shogunate established an institute for foreign studies two weeks before the conclusion of the Crimean War, but even then the very name of the institute denoted clearly the attitude of the government towards the work to be done there: Bansho Shirabesho, or 'Institute for the Study of Barbarian Books.' The institute started its work in Dutch studies, and later English, French, and German studies were added. In the additional three branches these languages were learned via Dutch. In none of these branches did the curriculum include social science subjects, though some of the students and teachers seem to have had some concept of political economy, learned perhaps in their private study. It is among them that we find the first students of social sciences to study abroad.

2. Study Abroad (1)—The End of Dutch Studies

In 1862, for the first time in Japanese history a group of fifteen Japanese was sent by the Shogunate to the Netherlands to study. The main members of the mission came from the Naval Training School of the Admiralty and their purpose was to observe the building of a warship ordered by the government from a Dutch shipyard in Dortrecht, and to sail it back to Japan. In addition to these five naval cadets, the mission included two medical students, two teachers from the Bansho Shirabesho, and six technicians and servants. The composition and reference of the mission tell us clearly that the government was interested in Western learning only from a military point of view. The two members from the Bansho Shirabesho, Nishi Amane and Tsuda Mamichi, had petitioned several times to be allowed to study abroad, but had been refused because the government was of the opinion that to study liberal arts and social sciences was of little value. At last they received permission, but the Admiralty ordered the mission strictly: that under no circumstances were they to change their religion, clothes, or any other ways of life into Western ones.

However, Nishi and Tsuda, and some higher officials of the government who arranged for them to go abroad, realized that the real foundation of national defence was not in warships or cannons but in industry and trade, education and learning. Before leaving Tokyo, Nishi wrote to a friend:

> Although I would say that Western studies are exceedingly popular throughout the capital, the Mito school theory of 'Revere the Emperor, expel the barbarians' has penetrated very deeply. Every day there are disturbances by the *rōnin* [masterless samurai], as they are obstinate and hard to change. . . . In any case, at present I think that we shall suffer more from the riots of conservatives than from incidents with foreign countries. It seems, I fear, that we are duplicating the mistakes of the Aisin Goro [the last of the Chinese

> emperors], partly because the policy of the imperial government is not decided yet and partly because those samurai, knowin gneither themselves nor foreigners, speak loudly the empty slogan of 'the land of gods and the country of emperors' and chauvinistically despise other countries. Recently I have read parts of Western philosophy and economics. I found them surprisingly just and fair, and quite different from Chinese thought. While Christianity is generally believed in the Western world, in Buddhism I found nothing to learn from its extreme vulgarity. The explanation of the principles of life offered by Western philosophy is better than in Confucianism. The principles of economic policy founded on natural laws are better than those of monarchical government. The civilization and institutions of the United States, Britain, and others seem to be superior to the best in China throughout their history. Indeed, by this new way of government why can the nation not become richer, why can its soldiers not become stronger, why can the welfare of people not improve, why can happiness not be procured by science, and why can arts not develop to their highest level?[5]

Apparently Nishi had some idea of Western philosophy and political economy before going abroad. It is impossible to find out what kind of information he extracted from what kind of sources. Presumably, as far as philosophy is concerned, one of his source books was George Henry Lewes's *Biographical History of Philosophy* (4 vols., 1845–46)[6] which was an attempt at showing Comte's positivism as an ultimate goal of philosophy, but it does not contain anything about economics. As to his knowledge about the United States and Britain, he undoubtedly learnt much from the members of the two diplomatic missions sent abroad by the Shogunate (one to Washington, the other to six European countries) before the naval mission, which included Tsuda and himself.

It took 215 days for the mission to arrive at Rotterdam on April 18, 1863. Nishi and Tsuda moved to Leiden and stayed there to the end of 1865. They had to start learning the Dutch language anew. For two years, refusing any fees, Professor Simon Vissering gave them lectures at his home twice a week on five subjects: Natuurregt (natural law), Volkenregt (international law), Staatsregt (constitutional law), Staathuishoudkunde (statehouseholding, i.e., political economy), and Statistiek (statistics). They took their work quite seriously as we can see from the notes they brought home. This was the first systematic study of the Western social sciences engaged in by the Japanese.

Nishi's notes on legal subjects and Tsuda's notes on statistics were translated and published from 1868 to 1874. But those on political economy did not appear, though it was said that Tsuda planned to translate them. Therefore, as far as political economy is concerned, the contents of their learning in Leiden can be gathered only from the economic thought of Vissering himself and from their own writings after returning home. While their writings must be a mixture of the ideas they learned in Leiden and those they developed later, the works of Vissering which were published about the time of their stay in Leiden may be more directly connected with his private lectures for them. In fact, Nishi wrote that Vissering's lectures on political economy were only a summary of his book, which was being published in four volumes.

In his inaugural lecture, 'Redevoering over Vrijheid, Grondbeginsel der Staathuishoudkunde' (Speech on Freedom, Fundamental Principle of Political Economy), given on March 23, 1850, Vissering criticized both 'the communism of our days with its bloody agitation' and the statism of 'the British Navigation Act, the Continental System, and German National Economics' and praised mankind's endeavours to achieve an harmonious balance through the struggle between self-love and love of neighbours.[7] He was described as 'the Dutch Bastiat',[8] but this was only true in the early stages of the development of his thought, perhaps up to 1851, when he wrote an article entitled 'Frédéric Bastiat'. In 1860 and 1861, one of his main works was published under the title *Handboek van Praktische Staathuishoudkunde* (Handbook of Practical Economics) in two volumes,[9] the first containing an introduction and part one, on Maatschappelijk Arbeid (social labour), and the second containing part two, on Maatschappelijk Welvaart (social welfare). In spite of the strange title, the first part included the main subjects of political economy from industry and agriculture to money and credit. The subjects discussed in the second part were population, poor relief, wages, and land-ownership. There was a third part, on public finance and education, but it was not published until after Nishi and Tsuda left Leiden.

We have to confine ourselves to a brief glance at this voluminous work of 1022 pages. A remarkable change compared with Vissering's earlier works is the shift of emphasis from French to British economists. Bastiat appears only once, as a critic of Ricardo's theory of rent, and Vissering does not agree with Bastiat. Instead, Adam Smith appears several times, and England is mentioned 'as a model of the sensible treatment of workers'.[10] According to I. H. Butter, 'Vissering was an eclectic of French and British economic doctrines, who was most susceptible to British economic thought during the later part of his life', and 'in later editions of the *Handboek*, references to Adam Smith became more frequent'.[11] What is more important for us is Vissering's criticism of the German Historical School and its conclusions. In his postscript to the *Handboek* he referred to the national economy of List, Roscher, Knies, and Hildebrand as opposed to the political economy of Quesnay and Adam Smith. According to Vissering, 'The Historical School came to the conclusion that in political economy one must not try to find general principles, but one must pose particular laws for each particular case, particular stage, particular time and particular nation'. In criticizing this idea, Vissering declared that there was no particular political economy for the East different from the one for the West: 'The point is explained by an example which is familiar to us Dutch. Once men come to understand the principles or natural laws which rule over the social life of any area, then they can no longer speak of an Eastern political economy distinct from our Western one and they will not repeat the foolish mistake we made in our East Indies, based on what we considered the difference [with regard to Western and Eastern political economy], and against all the principles of science'.[12] He did not refer to Japan, but no doubt he made no distinction between the Dutch East Indies and Japan and believed that his lectures to the two Japanese were applicable to Japan.

Thus we can be certain that the political economy which Nishi and Tsuda learned in Leiden was the Dutch version of the mid-nineteenth-century phase of the British classical school.

The next question is why only the notes on political economy from Vissering's lectures were not translated. The answer lies in a problem of translation. In spite of the belief of Vissering in the general validity of his principles, how was it possible for anybody to translate the Ricardian theory of differential rent into the language of a nation in which no one could find differential rent,[13] or to translate the Malthusian theory of population in a nation in which no one found an urgent problem of overpopulation, or to translate Smithian criticism of public debt in a nation in which nothing of this kind existed or could be thought of?[14]

The lectures on subjects concerning rights might be translated, but those concerning facts which did not actually exist could not be so easily translated. The translators were confronted with two kinds of difficulty in introducing entirely new ideas to Japan: they had to find appropriate vocabulary for the new ideas, sometimes even having to invent entirely new words, and they had to contend with cases where the new ideas were quite inconsistent with the old ones. For example, in the discussion about introducing the idea of civil law, a Japanese official of high rank is said to have asked a foreign adviser:

'What in the world does it mean, that people should have rights?' This was exactly the reason why the democratic movement of Meiji Japan began with the Jiyū Minken (Freedom and People's Rights) Movement, in which Nishi and Tsuda had a certain involvement. For the thinkers of the Japanese Enlightenment it must have been more difficult to translate economic terms than to translate legal terms concerning rights and law. While the latter did partly exist in Japanese reality and were partly understandable as pure ideas, the former could not be understood unless Japanese economic development provided instances of the matters being written about.

Nishi and Tsuda had returned home to inevitable frustration: the Tokugawa Shogunate had two more years of its long period of power remaining, and the attitudes of government leaders to Western studies had not changed. The new learning was encouraged only in the natural sciences and military engineering, so that they could teach only what they had learnt from Vissering in the Institute. The Meiji Restoration brought them more recognition, with ministerial posts, and later, seats in the parliament. They were also awarded the title of Baron and places in the Academy. Although their contributions to the Japanese Enlightenment were considerable, especially in *Meiroku Zasshi* (Meiji Six Journal), they were not radical enough to play any leading role in the Jiyū Minken Movement.

As far as political economy is concerned, we can conclude that Vissering's effort to transplant the discipline to Japan proved to be futile. It is true that his lectures were the first systematic education in social sciences which the Japanese had ever had, and as such contributed very much to the Japanese Enlightenment. However, once the Dutch monopoly of Japan's foreign trade had ended with the opening to other Western countries, the Dutch language ceased to be the only one transmitting Western thought. Even before Nishi and Tsuda left Japan, a member of a Japanese diplomatic mission had written from St. Petersburg to advise the government not to send them to the Netherlands: 'Even the Dutch people themselves read French and German books . . . therefore if somebody writes a book in Dutch, nobody will buy it. Naturally there are few books written in Dutch. The importance of Dutch affairs is less than a hundredth of those of Britain, France, or Germany. After returning home we shall never again advise our youth to study Dutch'.[15]

3. Reception of Western Thought

Although neither Vissering's course of lectures nor his book on political economy were translated, the first translation of a Western book on political economy was made from Dutch in 1867 by a great friend of Nishi and Tsuda, Kanda Takahira. This was H. Hooft Graafland's *Grondtrekken der Staathuishoudkunde* (1852), itself actually a Dutch translation of William Ellis's *Outlines of Social Economy* (1846). Therefore, this first translation of a Dutch book on political economy marked the turning point from Dutch to English influence in the process of transplanting Western economic thought. About the same time, another leader of the Japanese Enlightenment, Fukuzawa Yukichi, gave up his study of Dutch to start learning English with Kanda. From 1859 to 1867, he visited America twice and Europe once as a junior member of government missions, and, especially in 1867, he brought home a considerable number of American books including Noah Webster's *Dictionary* and Francis Wayland's *The Elements of Political Economy*. In his book, *Seiyō Jijō* (Conditions in the West) (1866–69), he largely relied on Wayland and on *Chambers's Educational Course: Political Economy for Use in Schools, and for Private Instruction*. He used Wayland's as a textbook in his school and a full translation was produced by one of his students from 1871 to 1877. In the first decade of the Meiji era (1868–77), we see quite a few translations of English and American books on political economy in addition to these—including those of A. L. Perry, R. Whately, J. S. Mill, M. G. Fawcett, F. A. Walker, J. E. T. Rogers, J. E. Cairnes, J. B. Byles, A. B. Mason, and J. J. Lalor, as well as *Chambers's Information for the People*. The fact that most of those books are for beginners is a precise reflection of the standard of learning in political economy in Japan during its emergence as a modern state.

In 1873, Nishi, Tsuda, Kanda, Fukuzawa, and other leading intellectuals formed a society for the enlightenment of the people. As it was the sixth year of the reign of the Emperor Meiji, the society was called Meiroku-sha (Meiji Six Society), and its journal was given the title *Meiroku Zasshi*. Both the society and its journal were rather short-lived (less than three years), and its membership did not much exceed thirty, but it represented the Enlightenment in Japan.

In his lectures to Nishi and Tsuda, Vissering taught the idea of natural law, or natural right. Starting from the Hobbesian idea of the right of self-preservation, Vissering proceeds to expound the principles of mutual preservation, the necessity of rules and laws, freedom of expression and action, and the limits of this freedom being the freedom of others, and the right of defence of one's own health and life against violence from others. He divorces the judgment of right and wrong in expression and action from jurisprudence, making it a matter of ethics, where he also places consideration of social problems such as relief for paupers and invalids. In his lectures on political economy he defends the freedom of business activities under the strange title of 'freedom of social labour', without properly understanding the labour problem or socialism.

In addition to Vissering's Dutch version of mid-Victorian liberalism, J. S. Mill's *On Liberty* and S. Smiles's *Self-Help* were translated from 1870 to 1872 by another member of the society, Nakamura Masanao. Nishi himself translated J. S. Mill's *Utilitarianism* in 1877. The principle of self-help for the common people is consistent with Vissering's attitude towards social problems. While people were left to themselves, the majority of the members of the Meiji Six Society quite willingly accepted Mill's intellectual elitism, together with his fear of mass democracy, even when there was no democracy at all in Japan. To the very extent to which they felt the importance of enlightenment, they felt contempt for the ignorance of the people, and, faced with the movement to establish a popularly elected parliament,[16] they declared that it was too early for ignorant, common people. Yet, by declaring that people were so ignorant as to be incapable of having their own parliament, the thinkers of the Japanese Enlightenment in fact denied enlightenment itself.

In spite of the fact that there were fragments of the Hobbesian idea of natural rights in Vissering's lectures,[17] the members of the Meirokusha did not understand or dare to accept the idea. Instead of the freeborn right of a human being, they assumed the rights of man to be granted by heaven. They thought that the Western idea of 'nature' was nothing but the Confucian idea of 'heaven'. However, in Japan, where the emperor was considered to be the son of heaven, 'heaven' could not be equivalent to 'nature'. Their heaven covered only Japan.

The controversy over human rights versus national rights (the individual versus the state) was the prelude to the controversy between free trade and protection. This sort of controversy is inevitable in the process of modernization of any underdeveloped country which has to catch up with advanced nations as models and rivals. To modernize a country, a considerable degree of individual freedom is necessary, even from the rulers' point of view—otherwise there can be no economic development. However, underdeveloped national industries cannot compete with those of advanced countries, even in the domestic market, unless they are protected by the government. Thus, quite apart from the nationalist and traditionalist inclination of the ruling classes, capitalism in underdeveloped countries is fated to have both liberal and nationalist tendencies at the same time. As was the case with many German thinkers from the time of the French Revolution to the middle of the nineteenth century (e.g., J. G. Fichte and F. List), so it was with Japanese thinkers from the Meiji era to 1945.

The Libel Act and the Press Code of June 1875 were enacted to suppress the popular movement, but threatened the continuation of even so mild a liberal group as the Meiroku-sha. Before the end of 1875 the Society decided to stop publication of its *Meiroku Zasshi*, and in effect the society itself ceased to exist. Later Nishi wrote a draft of the Imperial Message to Soldiers which was a backbone of Japanese militarism until the end of World War II.

However, the impact of Western enlightenment outlived the Meiroku-sha. Fukuzawa believed that the nation's future depended on the rise of a business middle class, and he devoted himself to developing such a class by way of education in his school, where courses on business and economics were considered most important. He refused to enter government service and expressed displeasure when any of his students did so. Broadly speaking, his school, which was to become Keiō University, and a commercial training school, which was to become Tokyo University of Commerce (later Hitotsubashi University), were the main sources of business leaders. Fukuzawa deplored the ignorance prevailing among the common people, but the more he deplored it the more he realized the importance of education, because he believed that the independence of individuals was an indispensable precondition for national independence.

Being aware of the international situation in the age of imperialism in East Asia, he had a deep consciousness of a crisis in national independence. He went so far as to say that Japan should 'go out of Asia into Europe', lest it follow in the steps of China and Korea as another victim of Western imperialism. Even though the independence of individuals inside the nation was one of the most important factors for Europeanizing or Westernizing Japan (under the critical conditions in the Far East) he felt he should reverse the order of reasoning by putting national independence as a precondition for the independence of individuals: 'There are no rights of man if there are no rights of state'. In this connection, the policy to have Japan enter into Europe meant that Japan should become an imperialist power.

Laissez-faire inside the nation and imperialist expansion outside was the most simplified feature of Fukuzawa's thought. No doubt he was the most important and interesting thinker of the Japanese Enlightenment, but at the same time nobody could deny that his ideas were full of contradictions and that he was a very debatable figure. His ideas fluctuated between individual and state, free trade and protection, liberalism and imperialism, and so on. According to Sugiyama, Fukuzawa's economic thought is 'a system of miserable contradictions'.[18] Nevertheless, a careful reader could not fail to read between the lines of Fukuzawa's works and see the figure of an intellectual who was trying hard to create an independent and modernized nation under siege from Western powers. Others who do not sense any contradiction might simply have missed or avoided the serious problems of an emergent nation.

Another way of evading the contradiction, as we tend to see it, in the Jiyū Minken Movement, in which some imported modern thought outlived the Meiroku-sha and its version of the Japanese Enlightenment, is to note that whereas the right wing of the Meiroku-sha enforced its position by relying on German Staatswissenschaft (science of state) as propounded, for example, by J. K. Bluntschli, the Jiyū Minken leaders relied heavily on Rousseau, and partly on J. S. Mill and H. Spencer. There was a well-known story about Kōno Hironaka, one of the influential leaders of the movements, who suddenly became converted as a direct result of his reading the translation of *On Liberty* while he was riding home from the prefectural office. This was early in 1873, that is to say, the year in which the Meiroku-sha was established. Immediately after this incident he established a local society for the promotion of people's rights and joined the national movement to demand, among other things, that the government should establish an elected parliament. Later he entered the parliament and was elected the chairman of the House of Commons.

The translator of Mill's *On Liberty* did not understand the exact meaning of 'society', especially as distinct from 'government'. In spite of, or perhaps because of, this kind of adaptation, the translation had a very wide range of readers among the leaders of the nascent Japanese democracy. The case of Spencer was more complicated. Some twenty translations of his works (including some duplications) were published during the decade from 1878 to 1887, in contrast to the twelve translations of J. S. Mill in the same period. His works had a much wider influence than Mill, but there were many more conflicting interpretations. While the translation of his *Social Statics* was called the textbook of the Jiyū Minken Movement, Spencer gave 'very conservative advice' to the Japanese ambassador when he was consulted about the Japanese constitution. He admitted in a letter that his advice was very conservative because of the people's immaturity for democracy and regretted that the advice was ignored by the Japanese government. However, as we have already learned, the perception of the people's immaturity was also held by the thinkers of the Meiroku-sha. Therefore Spencer's advice was by no means neglected. His advice was summarized in one of his letters. 'The proposed new institutions should be as much as possible grafted upon the existing institutions, so as to prevent breaking the continuity . . . that there should not be a replacing of old forms by new, but a modification of old forms to a gradually increasing extent.' He also advised: 'The ancient system of family organization . . . should be made use of in your new political system. These patriarchs or heads of groups should be made the sole electors of members of your representative body'.[19] From the wide range of his thought developed during his long life of eighty-three years, which coincided with the Victorian age, the individualist or anarchist elements were hailed by the left-wing democrats, while the organic elements were accepted by the conservative reformists including those in the government.

The first translation of Rousseau's *Du Contrat Social* was made in 1876 and published in 1882[20] by Nakae Chōmin, a left-wing leader of the Jiyū Minken Movement who came to be called 'an Oriental Rousseau'. He was the son of a samurai of inferior rank and was sent to Nagasaki to learn English and French. In 1871, as a member of the Ministry of Justice in the new government, he was sent to France. After two years, mainly in Lyons and Paris, he returned home in 1874. He worked for a short period for the Ministry of Justice and also served in the first parliament, but he spent most of his later life as a political journalist and an opposition leader of the Jiyū Minken Movement. As a follower of Rousseau he was a republican, but according to Rousseau, and also to Nakae, regardless of the forms of administration, any state which is governed by law should be called a republic.[21] In this sense, in spite of his republicanism, Nakae never denied the imperial regime, and even paid reverence to the emperor. However, he did not allow the emperor any political functions, even ceremonial ones. He praised the English and French revolutions against despotic governments and maintained that there was no need for a revolution in Japan insofar as it had such a lawful and liberal government. What is intended by this irony was that revolution is inevitable against any despotic government, even in Japan. As is the case with Fukuzawa, the relationship and balance between nationalism and republicanism or between emperor-worship and democracy in Nakae has long been a matter of discussion. We have to be content here with a tentative conclusion that even a left-wing leader of the Jiyū Minken Movement and follower of Rousseau like Nakae was not entirely free from the enchantment of the imperial regime. Nevertheless he played an important role as a left-winger under severe political persecution.

Nakae left no systematic work of political economy, but we can collect some fragments from his newspaper articles. He thought agriculture was the foundation of the nation's economy and, therefore, that the land tax should be decreased to promote modernization of agriculture. He did not agree with the idea of nationalization of landownership, nor with the equalization of land possession, as another left-winger, Ōi Kentarō, proposed. Instead, he insisted on agricultural improvement through the accumulation of capital by thrift and the application of science, and that industries should be developed in the same way.

Although he attacked severely the despotic and monopolistic tendencies of the government both in economic and political affairs, referring to Ricardo, Bastiat, and Rousseau, he did not agree with the laissez-faire doctrine of the Manchester School. In later years, when the results of the industrial revolution became obvious and Japan's precarious position in the international arena became a matter of great urgency, Nakae's thought gradually began to approach nationalism and protectionism. Actually, that was the fate of the Jiyū Minken Movement as a whole. After several armed risings and political assassinations, and correspondingly severe suppression, the participants in the movement were either domesticated by the government through promotion or condemned to death or imprisonment. Against the last remnant of the left wing, led by Kōtoku Shūsui, Nakae's most ardent follower, the government took recourse to a frame-up, whereby Kōtoku and his group were falsely accused and sentenced to death for an attempt on the life of the emperor.

Kōtoku was one of the first translators of the *Communist Manifesto*. Although we cannot divert our discussion to the development of socialist thought in Meiji Japan, a few lines of explanation are necessary. Socialist thought was fairly well understood by the end of the nineteenth century, which coincided with the middle of the period between the Sino-Japanese War of 1894–95 and the Russo-Japanese War of 1904–5, and the industrial revolution in Japan. Apart from the legacy of the left-wing Jiyū Minken Movement, socialist ideas came from the United States through American missionaries and Japanese students as early as about 1880. Richard Ely and Henry George were among other sources of Japanese knowledge of socialism, but it was only after Japan's victory in the Sino-Japanese War that socialism became a matter of practice, that is to say, a social movement. By this time the frequency of strikes had increased considerably, and in 1901 the Social Democratic Party was established, only to be banned on the same day. With the political execution of Kōtoku and his group in 1911, the Japanese socialist movement entered its ice age. This was one year after Japan's colonization of Korea.

4. Study Abroad (2)—Japanese Students in Britain and the United States

In 1863, one of the leading anti-Shogunate clans, Chōshū, sent five young samurai to England. Another leading clan, Satsuma, sent nineteen of its men to England in 1865. As government policy was to 'expel the barbarians', all those who were going to study under barbarians had to leave home secretly. Two days before the departure of the Chōshū group, the clan opened fire on Western ships in the Straits of Shimonoseki. Within a month, American and French naval forces made a counter-attack and occupied the Chōshū fortress. The news of this miserable defeat shocked the young Chōshū samurai, who had just arrived in London. The Satsuma group had a similar experience before they left home: as a result of an incident in Yokohama involving Satsuma samurai and British officials, the British fleet entered Kagoshima Bay and fired on Kagoshima, the capital city of the Satsuma domain. Although both groups included radical nationalists intent on expelling the foreigners, the shock of the military defeat and of the first impression of Western civilization in Shanghai forced them to change their opinion completely. The shock was so great that two members of the Chōshū group, Itō Hirobumi and Inoue Kaoru, curtailed their stay and hurried back to do their best to change the government's policy. Both of them became leading members in the new government.

At first, both the men who were sent abroad and those who sent them thought that the most urgent matter was to learn military engineering and related sciences to catch up with the Western powers, but those who were sent abroad did not fail to learn the lesson from living in Britain that the military engineering they so admired had a cultural background far broader than they had ever imagined. Many of them entered the University College London to learn natural and social sciences instead of practical engineering. After the Meiji Restoration of 1868, a stream of Japanese students followed them. Among these early students in London was Mori Arinori, who was to serve as the first minister to the United States and later became the first minister of education. He was one of the first Japanese to realize the urgent necessity for Japanese to learn political economy and business practice, and it was as a result of his planning that a commercial school came into being and later grew into Hitotsubashi University.

The professor of political economy in the University College London from 1876 to 1880 was W. S. Jevons. According to the records of the college, a total of seven Japanese students registered to attend his courses during this period.[22] In the academic year of 1878–79, there were four Japanese among the thirty-one students registered for his course. Since Jevons was not a good lecturer nor a kind teacher, it is difficult to trace what those Japanese students learned directly from him. No doubt his *magnum opus* was too difficult to become popular in Japan, and it was the last of his works to be introduced to Japan—the first full translation was not published until 1913.

However, his works for beginners and those on practical subjects began to be translated in 1878, and each went through several editions. *Money and the Mechanism of Exchange* was partially translated in 1878, and fully in 1883. The English text was used as a text in Imperial University in Tokyo and in Senshū School (a private law school, later Senshū University) in the 1880s. As the new government was trying hard to establish a modern monetary and banking system, they found Jevons's books very useful, together with those of H. D. Macleod. Four different translations of Jevons's textbook *Political Economy* were issued from 1882 to 1889, though the first attempt fell short of a full translation. In addition, a translation of the preface was published in a local journal. His works on logic were no less popular. *Logic* had four translations from 1879 to 1889, and the first one went through five printings. In an emergent modern state, where people felt it necessary to learn about the Western way of thinking as well as about Western institutions, Jevons enjoyed a sort of monopoly in logic textbooks. His *Elementary Lessons in Logic* was translated in 1883 by Soeda Juichi, to whom we shall refer later. It may be worthwhile mentioning here that even in the preface to this academic work the translator insisted on its practical use. *The State in Relation to Labour* was translated only once, in 1891, but it was introduced into Japan in the early 1880s and had a wide circulation, especially during the fierce controversy on factory legislation at the end of the decade.[23]

Not one of the seven Japanese students who attended Jevons's courses entered an academic career. The situation in Japan did not allow them to enter the ivory tower, but their learning was not entirely lost: Yamanobe Takeo, who became the president of Tōyō-bōseki (Oriental Spinning Co.), seems to have inherited Jevons's idea of social reform, and Kawakami Kin'ichi, who became a leading banker and businessman, taught at Tokyo Commercial School and wrote *Educa-*

tion of Commerce in Japan. These two examples give us a general idea of the career paths of these pioneers.

A similar case is that of Soeda Juichi, the first Japanese economist, known in the West as the first Japanese correspondent for the Royal Economic Society. Graduating from the University of Tokyo in 1884, he entered the Ministry of Finance, but soon after was asked to accompany one of his former lord's sons to study in Cambridge. It is said that Soeda had wanted to study under Henry Fawcett, but Fawcett died early in the month of Soeda's arrival, to be replaced by Alfred Marshall at the end of the academic year in May 1885.[24] Soeda's first teacher in political economy was probably Henry Sidgwick, a professor of moral philosophy, who nonetheless had a work entitled *Principles of Political Economy* published in 1883. Once Marshall took up his post Soeda studied under him. Soon after the establishment in 1890 of the British Economic Association (later the Royal Economic Society), Marshall appointed Soeda its correspondent for Japan. His first correspondence was published in *The Economic Journal* in 1893.

On returning home in 1887, Soeda rejoined the Ministry of Finance and was promoted to under-secretary in 1898. During his service in the ministry he played an important role in the controversies on the gold standard in 1893–97 and on factory legislation in 1896–98. In the first controversy he was one of the main advocates for the shift from the silver to the gold standard. In addition to his correspondence to *The Economic Journal* on the subject, he contributed to *A History of Banking in All the Leading Nations*, edited by W. G. Sumner (New York, 1896), and to *Political Science Quarterly* (1898). In the second controversy he was an exceptional government official, maintaining the necessity for factory legislation not only for the welfare of the working classes but also for the strength of the nation. It is said that he became interested in this problem when he was in Cambridge. Even before going abroad he knew of Fawcett, and perhaps he had some knowledge of Fawcett's ideas on social reform. Sidgwick advocated a sort of socialism, and Marshall started inviting labour leaders to his home from 1885 onwards.[25] It is quite understandable that Soeda took a similar line to theirs on social problems, though their movement towards women's emancipation (which Marshall later betrayed) might have been out of the question for him.

In his first article in *The Economic Journal*, entitled 'The Study of Political Economy in Japan' (vol. 3, 1893), Soeda classified twenty-six living Japanese economists into four categories—free traders, protectionists, state-socialists, and neutrals—and included himself in the last one. It is true that his attitude towards the labour problem made it difficult to put him into any of the other three categories. He participated in the establishment of the first nation-wide labour union, the Yūai-kai (Friendship Society), yet as a 'neutral' he promoted the establishment of the Federation of Businessmen (Jitsugyō Dōshikai), believing that both were necessary for social solidarity.

After the religious qualification for entrance to Oxford and Cambridge Universities was abolished, quite a few Japanese studied there, many of them the sons of former feudal lords. For example, I am the owner of a copy of M'Culloch's *Principles of Political Economy* (1870) with a book inscribed 'Kunimune Date, St. Peter's College, Cambridge, 1895'. There must have been a number of students of this sort, but nobody can deny the fact that Soeda was a good representative of the Japanese students who studied there before the end of the century. His activities as a part-time lecturer in Senshū School will be mentioned later.

Although there were those who studied in France and Germany, and the influence of the German Historical School was far from negligible in the long run, at the time when Soeda went abroad the United States was a much more popular place for the Japanese to go to study political economy. Perhaps it was through some missionary connections that many Japanese who studied in the United States went to New Brunswick. Naturally only a few of them entered Rutgers, and fewer still studied political economy. For political economy, Johns Hopkins and Yale were more important places of study, as illustrated by the example of Nitobe Inazō.

Nitobe went to Baltimore in October 1884 to study in the postgraduate school at Johns Hopkins. Early in 1887 he was appointed associate professor at his alma mater, Sapporo Nō Gakkō (Sapporo Agricultural College, later Hokkaido University), and ordered to study agricultural policy in Germany. He studied in Bonn, Berlin and Halle and completed his doctorate in Halle in 1890 with a dissertation entitled 'Über den Japanischen Grundbesitz, dessen Verteilung und landwirtschaftliche Verwertung' (On Japanese Landownership, and its Distribution and Agricultural Utilization). Then he returned to Baltimore to finish his thesis which he had started writing before going to Germany under the guidance of H. B. Adams. After finishing the thesis, which was published as *The Intercourse between the United States and Japan* (Johns Hopkins Press, 1891) he returned to Sapporo early in 1891 and was appointed to a full professorship immediately. We shall meet him again in a chapter on Sapporo Agricultural College, where he worked as a leading professor until

1898. His later career in the colonial administration of Taiwan, as a professor at Tokyo Imperial University, as president of Tokyo Women's Christian College, and as under-secretary general of the League of Nations does not belong to the period we are to consider.

At Johns Hopkins, he studied under H. B. Adams who 'organized teaching at Johns Hopkins on the model of the German seminars' and 'was a founder of the American Historical Association (1884)'.[26] Richard Ely was lecturing on political economy from 1881 to 1892 at Johns Hopkins, and his *An Introduction to Political Economy* (1889) had 'sold more than 30,000 copies in the course of the decade' and 'exercised a considerable influence on the thought of Americans'.[27] Nitobe took six of Ely's courses in the academic years 1884–85, 1885–86, 1886–87; history of politics, political economy, the history of political economy, administration, Germanic institutions, and finance.[28] Yet Ely's name appeared in Nitobe's lecture notes in Sapporo only twice, as a 'professorial socialist' and as the author of *French and German Socialism*, in addition to an incidental reference in the discussion of bimetallism. In the introduction, in which Nitobe mentioned some representative authors of the principles of political economy, Ely was not included.[29] It might be that either Nitobe in the years 1884–87 was not very keen on the subject, as we can guess from the book he started writing under Adams, or Ely was not a very impressive teacher, which is suggested by Thorstein Veblen who, after attending one of Ely's courses in 1881, noted that it contained nothing more than the works of German economists. However, this does not mean that Ely had no influence on his other Japanese students either at Johns Hopkins or in Wisconsin. On the contrary, his work was an important source of socialist thought in Japan.[30]

In any case, Nitobe began his study of political economy under Ely and developed it in Germany, first in Bonn under Ernst Nasse, then under Gustav Schmoller and Adolf Wagner in Berlin, under Adolf Meitzen in the Prussian Statistic Bureau, and under Johann Conrad in Halle. His article 'Bauernbefreiung in Japan' (Peasant-emancipation in Japan) appeared later in *Handwörterbuch der Staatswissenschaften* (Handbook of Sciences of State) (1909) edited by Conrad and others. Besides appreciating these German economists of the Historical School, or 'professorial socialists', Nitobe was much impressed by Emile de Laveleye when he visited Laveleye in Liege in 1888. Laveleye may also be included in the category of professorial socialists. Nitobe wrote that he knew of Laveleye's work before he left Japan, but did not mention his source.

The fact that he first intended to enter Schmoller's seminar to study agricultural policy, especially the peasant land-holding system in Germany (unfortunately Schmoller did not teach during that academic year), and the fact that he travelled east of the river Elbe and also in Canada to observe the agricultural conditions there, convince us that he was following List and Schmoller in an agricultural policy to create and maintain peasant farming by domestic colonization. This was the policy line which the Japanese government planned to take in its domestic colony, Hokkaido.

Nitobe, and an older friend, Satō, went to study in the United States on their own initiative. Later, the Imperial University of Tokyo, which was reorganized in 1886 from the Bansho Shirabesho and its successors, started sending its teaching staff abroad. Thus, studying social sciences abroad was institutionalized immediately after Nitobe. About the time when Nitobe started lecturing on political economy in Sapporo, those members of the Imperial University who had returned from their studies abroad began replacing their overseas teachers, e.g., Ernest Fenollosa from Harvard. Before examining the cases of particular institutions, we have to consider these overseas teachers in their role as the pioneers of the institutionalization of political economy in Japan.

5. Appointment in Japan: Overseas Teachers

From the establishment of the Bansho Shirabesho to the Imperial University Decree of 1886, there were several reshuffles in the system of higher education. As the government was trying hard to introduce Western learning for practical use in the emergent modern state, the Bansho Shirabesho and its immediate successors specialized in the study of foreign languages. A medical college was inherited from the Tokugawa government, a technical college was newly established, and a law school was attached to the Ministry of Justice. The arts and social sciences were introduced into higher education only when the University of Tokyo was established in 1877. The course on political economy in this new university was given first in the Faculty of Arts and later in the Faculty of Law in addition to the one in the Law School. The department of political economy came into existence in 1879 in the Faculty of Arts and moved into that of Law at the end of 1885, immediately before the establishment of the Imperial University.

In this early stage of the institutionalization of political economy, a number of overseas teachers played a very important role. By far the most important among them were Gustave Boissonade de Fontarabie, and Karl Hermann Roesler. Both of them came to Japan as legal advisers: Boissonade on civil law, for the period 1873 to 1895, and Roesler on constitutional law, from 1878 to 1893. While Boissonade gave lectures on political economy, not only in the law school of the Ministry of Justice but also in private law schools, Roesler was fully engaged in his advisory work, especially in preparing a draft of the Imperial Constitutional Law, but he was quite active outside his official work in propagating German thought, not only in law but also in the social sciences in general. The Franco-Prussian war was re-fought on the Japanese legal front, with France again suffering defeat. Boissonade's draft for the civil code was turned down, though his teaching activities were by no means fruitless.

Boissonade had experienced the February Revolution of 1848 as a law student in Paris and the 1871 Commune of Paris as an agrégé. The first course of lectures he gave in the University of Paris after 1870 was on political economy.[31] Almost a contemporary of Vissering, Boissonade was influenced by the liberal economists of France. Before he was promoted to his professorship, he was approached in 1872 by a Japanese legal mission that asked him to come to Japan as its legal adviser.[32] After his arrival in Japan he was asked to teach in the law school of the Ministry of Justice where, with his French colleagues, Georges Hilaire Bousquet and Victor Georges Appert, he gave several courses of lectures, including one on political economy. In the *Supplément de l'Echo du Japon* issued in Yokohama on January 13, 1876, we find the first part of his course of lectures under the title of 'L'Economie Politique au Japon'. Although the lecture was addressed to 'Messieurs les Sanghis [Imperial Councillors]', this was presumably the first of his lectures in the Law School. In his first lecture in the Faculty of Law of the University of Paris, Boissonade had made a long quotation from the preface of Bastiat's *Harmonies Economiques*, in which Bastiat expressed his faith in the creed that 'interests are harmonious, therefore the solution exists entirely in freedom', to which Boissonade added: 'If you admire these pages as much as I do, you will soon evaluate all the economists'. He seems to have maintained the same line in his lectures in Japan. He started with the explanation that political economy had nothing to do with any particular form of government nor any change in it. In the first section, on production, he said that it was Bastiat who had discovered the role of natural agents in production, while Adam Smith discovered the importance of human labour. By comparing the efficiency of freemen's [wage workers'] labour with that of slave labour, he concluded that slavery was abolished as a result of the development of political economy, which proved that justice and utility were always compatible with each other, that is to say, the replacement of slavery by the wage system was just and profitable at the same time. He had some reservations about free trade, especially the abolition of duties, and recommended the combination of both capital and labour: 'If workers organize themselves to raise their wages, and employers do the same against workers' demands, according to our French laws neither is considered a crime. The role of government in this case is only to protect the freedom to work of those workers who do not join the organization and want to work.' Apart from these, and some other minor reservations, he declared:

> Political economy discovered the principles of justice and reason which regulate the best distribution of the riches produced by those combined efforts. This is not to say that we have to appeal to legislative or administrative regulations. The public authority is asked only not to interfere with the matter. As it must not fix the way of exchange nor the price of commodities, so must it not deal with the decision of wages. If Japan reforms its civil and criminal laws following the laws of nature, and leaves its interests and development of riches to the economic laws, that is to say, if it gives honour and freedom to labour in any kind of application, if it encourages thrift in order to form capital, guarantees the civil rights and interests of individuals by the wisdom of its laws, keeps peace and concord without weakness, and maintains justice in everything, it will prepare for its longest and most brilliant place in history in the future.[33]

It may be of interest to note that the Japanese translator replaced the expression 'without weakness' (*sans faiblesse*) by a more nationalistic 'by increasing the national strength'.

In this course of lectures based on the principles of laissez-faire and the laws of nature, he devoted forty percent of the whole course (so far as we can gather from extant material) to land-ownership and land-tenure systems. Presumably he thought that discussion on differential rent was too premature for the Japanese. As a rule, he said, private and perpetual land-ownership proved to be best—the socialist idea of the nationalization of land-ownership will necessarily cause the nationalization of all economic activities and, consequently, unprecedented despotism and slavery. To make matters worse, under the common ownership of land, people would feel less encouraged to defend their country, because they will defend the country only to defend land which they own individually. 'Against this [socialist] theory the most learned economists of every country maintain that the government should keep away from private businesses as far as possible. This is the theory of self-government which is now on the way to being practised widely'.[34] He did not enter into the details of his idea of self-government, but the general outlines of his idea of laissez-faire are clear enough.

In a lecture he gave before the Society of French Literature in 1881, he said that free trade should be the basis for promotion of the public interest.[35] He went on to say that bimetallism would sooner or later become the sole important subject of economic discussion in Japan, and that the conflict between labour and capital would also become urgent as an inevitable result of Japan's industrial development in the near future. 'Someone among you may ask me why I do not explain to you why the system of private property is just, but is there anybody in your country who denounces it? Have you ever had anyone like Proudhon, who was bold enough to advocate such an indulgent and wrong theory as he did?'

As an adviser on modernizing the Japanese legal system, Boissonade participated first in the reformation of the criminal code and criminal-procedure laws. His advocation of the total abolition of the death penalty in the former and the introduction of a jury system in the latter were rejected by the Council of Senators, but most of his ideas were realized in two laws enacted in 1880—the first modern laws in Japan. Then he was asked to produce a draft for the civil code. He devoted the years from 1879 to 1892 to this important new work, but to his great disappointment, his draft was not adopted by the newly established Imperial Diet. A leading professor of law, Hozumi Nobushige, criticized his draft on the grounds that 'the civil law would destroy loyalty and filial duty'. After a few years of political and theoretical controversies, his draft was revised according to Germanic ideas, and the civil law enacted from 1896 to 1898 was a curious mixture of French and German legal thought, that is to say, the individualist thought of the former and the organic thought of the latter. Here again, German influence prevailed over French. Hermann Roesler contributed much to the victory, perhaps behind the scenes.[36]

German ideas did not win the battle single-handedly. The conservative political leaders had begun to fear an 'excess' of modernization. They thought that a model should not be sought in a republic such as France, but in a monarchy such as Germany or Austria. Itō Hirobumi, who undertook a study tour from 1882 to 1883 in preparation for drawing up the draft of the constitutional law, met Gneist, Mosse, and Lorenz von Stein in Berlin and Vienna. He and his colleagues thought Stein was the best choice as their legal adviser, but Stein did not accept the invitation because of his age. On the recommendation of someone in Berlin, Roesler was invited instead to serve as legal adviser on constitutional and commercial law.

Lorenz von Stein belonged to the Hegelian Left, and his earlier work *Der Sozialismus und Kommunismus des heutigen Frankreichs* (1841) is said to have had some influence on Marx and Engels in the early development of their socialist thought. Owing to his opposition to the Danish government in the conflict over his native Schleswig-Holstein, he lost his post as a professor at Kiel University in 1852. From 1855 to 1888 he was professor of Staatswissenschaft at the University of Vienna. Opinions are divided about his character and influence during the second half of his life. Karl Kautsky, who was to become a leader of the German social democrats, attended Stein's lectures in the 1870s and wrote that his lectures were designed for members of parliament and civil servants, stressing financial rather than economic subjects.[37] Thus Kautsky seems to have had no favourable impression of Stein, whereas Carl Grünberg, who was to become the first director of the Institute of Social Research of Frankfurt, wrote that Stein was 'a lecturer whose lectures were . . . most attractive for me at that time [1890s] and had an important influence on me'.[38] A Japanese professor said in a memorial lecture on Stein that Stein was not consistent in his opinion and spoke differently to different people.[39] Perhaps we have to leave it an open question as to what kind of development of thought made it possible for a thinker of the Hegelian Left to become an overseas adviser for the codification of an imperial consitution.

Stein gave lectures to several visitors from Japan, including the Imperial Councillor Kaieda Nobuyoshi and Prince Komatsu, and replied to some questions asked by Japanese political leaders. A full translation of his course of lectures for Kaieda was published in 1889. It contains five lectures on economic subjects and three on public finance and taxation. In these economic lectures he was rather liberal. He advised Kaieda to promote the 'science of wealth' and 'civil rights' and warned: 'Since the Restoration, your government has spent twenty years trying to get fruit from the branches without developing the roots of the economy'. The warning is still valid for Japan's economy today. In the political part of the course, he expressed his high opinion of the imperial regime of Japan and said: 'In the natural empire of Japan, the natural imperial regime stands firm between heaven and earth. I cannot understand the intention of those people who organize themselves into the Popular Rights Party, intending to change the constitution'. But in this part, too, he was rather more rational than the actual Japanese constitution could be with a demi-god emperor. For example, he noted that a Privy Council would not be compatible with a parliamentary system.[40]

Generally speaking, Roesler followed the line of Stein. However, since he came to Japan and was involved in the actual controversy on the legal system for imperial Japan, his political position could not remain ambiguous. By a curious coincidence, Roesler also was connected with Karl Marx, as the first academic reviewer of *Das Kapital* (1867), which he reviewed in *Jahrbücher für Nationalökonomie und Statistik* (1869). As a funny example, he wrote: 'Let us assume that the railways are under common ownership. If all the world can use the railways free of charge, what part of the total production is due to the workers who construct and maintain these railways?' However, Roesler was not as silly as we might be inclined to gather from this quotation:

> Yet we are by no means blind to the merits of the book. This is elaborately written and contains many appropriate descriptions. Readers will learn much from the statistical explanation of the English factory system which is the result of the author's full study of the reports of factory inspectors. . . . The author relentlessly draws an objective picture of the capitalist world and vulgar political economy which is by no means enviable. Yet his description is one-sided and therefore scientifically inaccurate. He sees only the suffering of the working classes without paying any attention to the enormous mental and physical progress brought about by the capitalist way of production. . . . The freedom of will which creates the multi-dimensional development of human nature is guaranteed only by laws. Therefore, social sciences should be legal sciences. . . . German [social] sciences have realized the fact recently, and they are trying to reorganize themselves in this direction. The work of Mr. Karl Marx should not be placed on the top of this development. Here we remember only the works of Stein on administrative laws and these are very important. . . . Lastly, according to our opinion, although there are many who categorically deny that Smithian concepts are the essential weapons of socialism, the book convinces them that they are wrong.

This passage from his review of Marx reveals his attitude towards Smith, Marx, Stein and the social sciences in general.

Roesler started his academic career as a lecturer at Erlangen University in 1861 and was promoted to ordinary professor of state science at Rostock University in the same year. He pioneered the typical German controversy on the Adam Smith problem[41] in his third book, *Über die Grundlehren der von Adam Smith Begründeten Volkswirtschaftstheorie* (Erlangen, 1868), and was the first of those to be called 'professorial socialists'.[42] Although he did not join the *Verein für Sozialpolitik*, he supported the Catholic social movement and was converted from Lutheranism to Catholicism. Although he was hostile to Adam Smith and Karl Marx, he was also hostile to Bismarck's Prussia. Johannes Siemes defined Roesler as a pioneer of the idea of the social state (welfare state), and Itō, to whom he reported as legal adviser, remarked that he had a certain liberal tendency and was opposed to Prussia. (Prussia was Itō's model of a new state.)

In one of his answers to Inoue Kowashi, Itō's assistant in drafting the constitution, Roesler attacked Manchesterism, though not directly its economic activities:

> I do not belong to those who insist on an extensive freedom of religious belief. . . . The government must try to unify religions as far as possible. . . . Since religious thought is the spiritual and economic foundation of the nation's life, wrong religions must not enjoy the same freedom which the orthodox one enjoys. . . . If they are given freedom of activity, your country will fall into the situation in which we find the United States now. In the United States, religion has become a business, and degrades the nation's life to a great extent. . . . I am of the same opinion about the freedom of education. . . . In Prussia, although academic freedom is admitted as a rule, there is no freedom of education. Even academic freedom is substantially limited through the administration of universities. All the excessive freedom already mentioned is founded on political Manchesterism which is not only very dubious in economic matters but also completely untenable in spiritual matters. . . . The government should be the supreme judge and legislator of the nation, representing moral and legal ideas and rejecting wrong ones. . . . This doctrine inspires in the people wrong ideas and sensual and material appetites. People cannot discover the truth by themselves.

Having rejected Manchesterism, it was quite natural for him to attack socialism when he referred to Bismarck's anti-socialist law

(Sozialistengesetz). 'Since the Socialist Party does not like to establish state or government, but attempts to deny the true god, to destroy religions, to destroy matrimonial and kindred relationships, and to abolish property and inheritance, . . . we cannot keep from suppressing it completely'.[43]

Unlike Boissonade, Roesler seems not to have written, or spoken on, economic subjects while he was in Japan. As he considered economics a branch of politics,[44] he seems to have felt no need to dwell on economic subjects separately. His name is not found in the list of overseas teachers of Tokyo University and the Imperial University, whereas Boissonade was listed as a teacher from 1890 to 1910, though probably on legal subjects. However, Roesler was quite active in promoting German studies, especially state sciences, through lectures and booklets outside the academic institutions. He joined the Society for German Studies (Doitsugaku Kyōkai) which was established by pro-German politicians and civil servants in 1881. In his speech before its general meeting of 1885, he criticized the English way of thinking because of its individualistic, anti-metaphysical, sensual and selfish tendencies. He went on to say that individualism would reduce society to a state of war and induce the discontented to overthrow the society by violence. As representative figures of this way of thinking, which he called the Common Sense School, he mentioned Bolingbroke, Locke, Adam Smith, J. S. Mill, Spencer, and Voltaire, Rousseau, and Helvétius as well, and added that such thinking must be quite alien to the mentality of Japanese people. Naturally, he emphasized the necessity of replacing English studies with German ones.[45] In a short article which he contributed to the society's journal in 1884, he gave an overall view of German social sciences, including political economy as a subdivision of political science.[46] He said that there were three schools of political economy—the first being the negative or natural law school, including Manchesterism; the second the positive or political school from Adam Müller to Adolf Wagner, including Stein and Roesler himself; and the third the radical school which included socialists, communists and social democrats, e.g., Marx, Dühring and Schäffle. As to the 'professorial socialists', he said that they were an ambiguous mixture of the political (positive) and the radical school denoting the transition of German political economy from the negative to the positive school. Of the works of these economists, he recommended the following three to Japanese readers:—List's *Das nationale System der politischen Ökonomie* (National System of Political Economy), his own *Vorlesungen über Volkswirtschaft* (Lectures on National Economy), and Wagner's *Finanzwissenschaft* (Science of Public Finance). All other works, except those of radicals, might be read, but only to cultivate the reader's critical thinking.[47]

Thus Roesler contributed considerably to the development of the pro-German currents in Japanese social science, but the turn of the tide from English (and French) studies to the German, from liberalism and individualism to protectionism and nationalism, had its own inherent cause in the political situation of the emergent modern state as a late-comer in the age of imperialism. We need not repeat the explanation for it, but it may be added that the turn of the tide was accelerated by American influence. Apart from the strong influence of H. C. Carey, some leading American economists of the 1880s, including R. T. Ely and H. C. Adams, studied in Germany and brought back German economic thought. Staatswissenschaft was also transplanted into America by T. D. Woolsey and others,[48] and Woolsey's *Political Science* (1877) was used as a text in the University of Tokyo and perhaps also in Sapporo Agricultural College. The currents of German thought came to Japan via both Western and Eastern routes.

In September 1878, a young American, Ernest Francisco Fenollosa, gave his first course of lectures on politics at the University of Tokyo based on Woolsey, Lieber (*On Civil Liberty and Self-government*, 1859), and Spencer. He was appointed professor of politics, but on his arrival in Japan he was asked to give courses on political economy and philosophy too. Until 1886, when the University of Tokyo was reorganized and became the Imperial University, he also taught sociology, ethics, logic, and aesthetics, in addition to politics and political economy.

In the annual report of the Ministry of Education for 1873, we read that the curriculum of the Department of English Law in Tokyo Kaisei Gakkō (Tokyo Kaisei School) included two political economy courses. As the school was one of the intermediate institutions between the Bansho Shirabesho and the University of Tokyo, we may consider these two courses to have been the beginning of political economy in the higher education of Japan, but all we know about their content is that the authors of works used as texts were Mill, Wayland, and Perry. Thus, apart from Fukuzawa's lectures at his school, Fenollosa's are the first lectures on political economy in a higher educational institution in Japan about which we have some detailed information, inadequate as it is. He started the course by using his own excerpts from J. S. Mill's *Principles* as a textbook. Then he summarized Carey and Cairnes before proceeding to the problems of money, banking, taxation, and foreign trade. Authors referred to in the course were Bagehot, Bastiat, Byles, Gossen, Jevons, Macleod, Ricardo, Roscher,

Smith, Thompson, Thornton, and Tooke, in addition to those already mentioned. The final examination questions show that Fenollosa stressed the problems which were urgent to Japan's economy. One of the questions required students to 'explain the relation between the protectionist theory and the [imperial] regime from the evolutionist point of view'. I myself could not answer this difficult question,[49] but apparently this and almost all the questions, on Bentham, J. S. Mill and Spencer, set during the course reflect the influence of his study at Harvard, which was a centre of Spencerism in America at that time.

Notes from his lectures, taken by Sakatani Yoshio while a student, are kept in the National Diet Library in Tokyo. Although Fenollosa was not a very original thinker, he was a very keen teacher and therefore very popular among the students. His contribution to the development of the social sciences in Japan does not derive from originality, but from the thoroughness of his knowledge of the learning he brought from Harvard. As he was twenty-five years old when he came to Japan, nobody could expect any original thinking from him. Students, who were not very much younger than he was, were at first excited about his lectures but soon became critical. The reasons are clear enough. Three or four courses of lectures at the same time are a heavy burden for a young graduate, however brilliant he may be. To make the situation worse, he soon became deeply interested in Japanese traditional arts, including ukiyo-e, and became famous in the West as a specialist in this field. However, as well as contributing to art history, he played a far-from-negligible role 'as a pioneer of Japanese [modern] thought'.[50]

In 1883, when the University of Tokyo was reorganized as the Imperial University, Fenollosa resigned from his post to devote himself to the study (and business) of Japanese fine arts. Actually, his role as a pioneer in the social sciences ended before his resignation. His place as a lecturer in political economy was taken over by one of his students, Wadagaki Kenzō, who had been sent by the University to study in Germany. This is another event which points to the beginning of the pro-German tendency in Japanese social science thought. After this, a stream of German teachers of political economy and related disciplines continually flowed in.[51] The last two were Emil Lederer and Alfred Amonn, who taught in Japan from 1923 to 1925 and from 1926 to 1929 respectively. The last candidate was Joseph Schumpeter. Charles Sumner Griffin, who came to Japan in 1899 to teach political economy and public finance at the Imperial University, was another Harvard graduate, but he came from Germany as part of the stream.

In spite of the change of tide in the government and the Imperial University, the transplanted liberal thought was not rooted out. As was the case with Boissonade and Appert, Fenollosa's liberal ideas had their successors in private schools. Fenollosa encouraged the democratic movement, at least in the first few years of his stay. The students thus encouraged would not, and could not, stay with their schools. When the opposition leader Ōkuma Shigenobu established Tokyo Senmon Gakkō (Tokyo School of Special Studies, later Waseda University) some of these students joined him as professors. The first translation of Shakespeare's *Julius Caesar* was made by one of them, Tsubouchi Shōyō, in 1884 under the title *Jiyū no Tachi Yoha no Eihō* (The Sword of Freedom in Excess of Sharpness). There were also some followers of Ely's Christian socialism among them.

In a Christian college in Kyoto, now Dōshisha University (literally, university of brethren of the same aspiration), in 1876 Dwight Whitney Learned started his course of lectures on the history of the Christian Church. He had graduated from Yale in 1870 and was invited to come to Japan as a missionary. As well as his missionary works and lectures on Church history, he lectured on political economy for fifteen years from 1879.[52] As to the origins of his economic thought we can mention that F. A. Walker was professor of political economy when he was a student, and his uncle, T. D. Woolsey, was a professor of politics.

His course on political economy was a mixture of orthodox liberalism with a slightly socialistic tendency: he denies that the introduction of machinery causes any serious unemployment and maintains that wages can be adjusted well by free competition; but he does not deny that trade unions are the natural result of the condition of the workers. He refers to a sort of social security system, but adds that it may be expensive and sometimes advantageous to the rich. In spite of this eclecticism or confusion, the fact which can not be denied is that his course was one of the first which introduced a sort of socialist thought, while falling short of Christian socialism. Although apparently influenced by German state science through Woolsey, Learned is by no means a nationalist statist. Following the tradition of Thomas Paine he defines the state as a means for securing the welfare of the people.[53] Even so mild a democraticism as this was a useful antidote to the imperialist and militarist tendency of the age. However, curiously enough, when Marxism was transplanted properly in the twentieth century, its stronghold was provided for by the Imperial universities. In Doshisha University where Learned taught, students expelled anti-militarist professors in 1937.

Part 2

Enlightenment and Political Economy: Some Pioneers

2

Fukuzawa Yukichi

Chūhei Sugiyama

1. Why a Book of Chambers?

Fukuzawa Yukichi, the founder of Keiō University, contributed more than anybody else to the introduction of the fruits and ideas of Western civilization to Japan and deserves the name of the champion of the Japanese Enlightenment. There were indeed many other economic writers among his contemporaries, but, at least during the first half of his career as a writer on economics and other subjects and consequently during the period of the Japanese Enlightenment, his figure was by far the greatest.

He has long been believed to be a liberalist in his economic, as well as political, thought. Some believe that he was a liberalist throughout his life. Others claim that he changed to being a nationalist in his writings published around 1880—such as *Tsūzoku Kokkenron* (Popular Theory of State's Rights) and *Jiji Shōgen* (Current Affairs Discussed)—but reverted to his earlier belief towards the later period of his activities. The aim of this chapter is to assess what Fukuzawa's economic thought really was.

A well-known episode from the period of political upheaval towards the end of the Tokugawa feudal regime relates how Fukuzawa, despite the sound of fighting not very far away, carried on his lecture on political economy at his private school in Tokyo, telling his students that the future of the country had already been settled, compared with which turmoil here and there was not worth bothering about. Indeed his was the first economic course ever given in any Japanese educational institution. The textbook he was using at that time was Francis Wayland's *The Elements of Political Economy* (1837). About the book he recollects some ten years later: 'It was one of those which I had never before come across. At first I found it hard even to follow the sentences, but after getting used to it by reading it twice or thrice, I was so deeply impressed by every chapter or even every phrase, with its arguments and expressions completely fresh to me, so much so that I often forgot about having meals'.[1]

Yet for some unknown reason, Fukuzawa's course of lectures in political economy lasted for only a year and was then taken over by his ex-student and colleague Obata Tokujirō, who later translated the Wayland textbook. Instead, Fukuzawa started lecturing on Wayland's *The Elements of Moral Science* in his class and never resumed lecturing in political economy.

Wayland belonged to the second generation of the liberalist school of economics, whereas Fukuzawa was, not only in his lecturing but also in his writing, one of the very first to introduce political economy of the liberal school into Japan. About the same time, i.e., a year before the Meiji Restoration, he published *Seiyō Jijō* (*Gaihen*) (Conditions in the West, vol. 2), a translation of a book published for popular use by the Edinburgh publisher William and Robert Chambers under the title *Chambers's Educational Course: Political Economy, for Use in Schools, and for Private Instruction*, of which neither the author nor the date of the first publication was stated.[2]

Fukuzawa notes that the latter half of the book is largely the same as an economics book translated into Japanese by his friend Kanda Takahira, so he does not translate that part, the elements of which had already become familiar to the reading public, preferring to apply the saved energy to offering newer and more useful information instead. Kanda's translation is from the Dutch version of William Ellis's *Outlines of Social Economy* (1846). Setting aside the question of the extent to which the Ellis book is similar to the latter half of Chambers's *Political Economy*, here we see Fukuzawa's attitude towards what he believed to be the needs of the day, an attitude which might well be characterized as that of the champion of the Japanese Enlightenment.[3]

In a like context, he says that when one translates a Western book, one ought not to concentrate on the elegance of style but on the plainness and readability of the translation—with the number of people able to read Western books believed to be very much on the increase, it was inevitable that the translation would soon prove to be no more than just rubbish. Fukuzawa was satisfied with serving the urgent necessity of the day, which was to enlighten people with the fruits of Western civilization.[4]

The first half of the book he translated is, he says, on social economy, whereas the second half, which he left alone, is on political economy. The translation covers the following chapters: Industry; social organization; The family circle; Individual rights and duties; Civilization; Equality and inequality: distinction of rank; Society: a competitive system; Objections to the competitive system considered; Divisions of mankind into nations; Intercourse of nations with each other; Origins of government; Laws and national institutions; Government functions and measures; The education of the people; The nature of political economy; Origin and nature of property; Protection of the profits or fruits of property.

In addition, Fukuzawa selected material from a few other sources and translated and added them to the text, but omitted the chapter on 'Objections to the competitive system considered'. One of the added chapters is one from Francis Wayland's *The Elements of Political Economy* entitled 'Different forms of human industry', in which the author refers to patent and copyright as a necessary protection for the results of mental labour which is different from manual labour, the latter being remunerated according to its quantity. As both patent and copyright were entirely unfamiliar to the Japanese reader, Fukuzawa believed that information about them should also be added from other sources. This is quite understandable, but what, then, is the reason for the omission of the original chapter? In that chapter the author refers to the assertion that 'a much better condition of society would be produced by doing away altogether with individual emulation and competition, and establishing in their stead an associative system',[5] as 'the principle of general competition and individual effort' is founded on 'the supposition that all men are sufficiently able by their mental and physical abilities . . . to realise the means of a comfortable livelihood', but such is far from being the case.[6] Although the source is not given, it was most probably taken from John Stuart Mill's *Principles of Political Economy*, Book 4, Chapter 7. In any case the argument corresponds with the content of a chapter named 'Effects of a partition of property', the chapter immediately after the one where Fukuzawa stopped translating, i.e., 'Protection of the profits or fruits of property', in which 'a French writer of celebrity' is referred to as one who 'proclaimed the principle that property is robbery'. Here again the name of that writer is not mentioned, but there is little doubt that it is Proudhon's assertion that is implied there. The author argues that such is simply 'empty speculation', for the partition of property can only be achieved by violence, which inevitably does away with capital, hence civilization.[7]

Thus one of the characteristics of this book lies in its advocacy of the capitalist regime of private property. To Fukuzawa, or rather to the Japan of his day, the capitalist society of the West seemed to represent a civilization which was the goal to be reached at any cost whatsoever. Consequently any kind of antithesis of capitalism had no practical meaning.

There is, however, one other reason for the omission, which is of interest. The author, in defence of the existing system against the 'objections to the competitive system', assumes that it has existed in its present form since the origin of human society and consequently must suit human nature:

> We are endowed with ambition, emulation, the desire to improve our circumstances, and to engage in enterprises suitable to our individual tastes and capacities. . . . Political economy has proved that these instincts are highly beneficial to the community as well as to the individual; that they stimulate the activity and industry which increase the general wealth, and supply motives for the defence and preservation of that which industry has realised; and this, as far as we can judge, much more effectively than would be the case if the interests were general instead of individual.[8]

This is nothing but a recitation of the old belief in natural freedom and pre-established harmony. One of the reasons why Fukuzawa saved himself the trouble of translating this chapter is very probably that he himself did not have any leanings towards these ideas, so he did not feel any urge to translate this essential part.

Therefore, this very lack of sympathy, or conviction, for such social philosophy must certainly have made his economic liberalism not as consistent as, for instance, Taguchi Ukichi's. Or, conversely, this very fact could make his economic thought far more realistic than Taguchi's.

In the chapter on 'The nature of political economy', which Fukuzawa did translate, the point is made that 'it is not a system for controlling men's actions, but for discovering how men are induced by their natural propensities to act',[9] or that 'certain propensities [are] implanted in mankind, which, when viewed alone, have a selfish, narrow, and almost degrading aspect, are, when contemplated in relation to each other, a wise provision for enabling man to advance his own welfare, happiness, and virtue.'[10] In the chapter on 'Government functions and measures' it is also said that 'it [the government] cannot provide for the subsistence of the people at large; for the extent of the remuneration which workers should receive for their labour, or the extent to which they should work for the wages they obtain; for the extent to which commodities of any kind—such as food, and clothing, &c. should be produced, the manner in which they should be sold, or the price that should be paid for them; generally speaking, government should not interfere with trade'.[11] These are, however, simple conclusive statements and as such are not quite as persuasive as the omitted material.

In this way, the greater part of political economy is omitted from *Seiyō Jijō* (*Gaihen*) and in what little is translated, the passage in which natural liberty and pre-established harmony were proclaimed is dropped. How, then, is it in Fukuzawa's own writings?

2. Independence, Individual and National

It is indeed true that Fukuzawa emphasized human equality. Particularly well known is the first paragraph of the first book of *Gakumon no Susume* (An Encouragement of Learning) to the effect that Heaven made men so that no one is over or under another or that no one is born nobler or meaner than another.[12] When this is compared with the opening passage of the chapter on 'Individual's rights and duties' in *Chambers's Educational Course*, the influence on Fukuzawa of this latter book is quite clear, for it runs: 'While God has given man the gift of life, he has also given him the capacity to support that life. . . . Accordingly, every human being, of whatever colour or country, has, by a law of nature, the property of his own person. . . . This freedom he is not at liberty to sell or assign'.[13] Starting from this point, *Seiyō Jijō* proceeds to men's equality before the law and ends by declaring that it is everybody's duty to obey the law. This same assertion about the duty to obey the law is also made in *Gakumon no Susume*, but what characterizes the book is that it encourages learning for the reason that the inequality in wealth and culture which exists among men in spite of their natural equality is caused by some being learned and others the very opposite (in Book I, 1872, and Book II, 1873). It also argues for the equality of nations, on the analogy of men's born equality (in Book III, 1873), in the following way:

> In Book II arguments have been put forward that all men, whether rich or poor, whether physically strong or weak, are born equal in their rights. Now in the present book [Book III] let us expand this to the discussion of the relation between nations.[14]

This is to say, as every individual is by nature equal with each other, so is every nation. Therefore, he argues, 'To defend our country against foreign countries it is essential to fill the country with the spirit of freedom and independence, and to let everyone, regardless of the difference in rank and wealth, think of his country as his own interest and do his duty to his own nation. . . . To sacrifice one's property or even one's life for the sake of one's country: such is real loyalty'.[15]

In Book X (1874) the independence of individuals is once again related to the independence of the nation by the same logic and on the same level:

> In the phrase freedom and independence is implied the concept of duty. Independence means not merely non-reliance on others for the subsistence of life. It is no more than an inner duty. There is an outer duty just as well, that is to say, the duty to exert oneself together with the rest of one's nation to make certain that one's country retains the state of freedom and independence. Only by so doing can it be said that one has performed one's duty in both ways.[16]

In a feudal society there was no freedom of choice of profession. But now 'it is up to everyone to choose whatever profession he wishes. One can be a farmer, or a trader, or a civil servant, or anything else according to one's choice. . . . All varieties of profession are open to free competition, but the competition is not for the sake of fighting against each other. On the contrary, the object of fighting, if not with one's sword but with one's best knowledge, is to confront foreigners. If we win in this intellectual fighting, then we have improved the station of our country. If we lose, then we have behaved in the opposite way'.[17] The purpose of civilization is thus said to be to fight an intellectual battle against foreigners and to help one's own country surpass foreign countries. 'Peace inside and emulation outside', formulated in later years in *Jiji Shōgen* (1881), is here expressed clearly before its time. Nationalism is evident throughout.

The same thing becomes even clearer when he claims in *Bunmeiron no Gairyaku* (An Outline of a Theory of Civilization) (1875) to make European civilization the object of all his arguments,[18] and yet without pursuing the object for its own sake, to make the independence of the country the ultimate value to which the civilization of the nation should be subservient.[19]

Such nationalism comes from his conception of the international circumstances of his times. Giving an example from India and Turkey in *Gakumon no Susume*, Book XII (1874), he says:

> Let us look at India and Turkey. The former is a country well known for its literature and the latter a great country of warriors. However, now the one has been possessed by Britain and its people are her slaves whose sole business is to grow opium . . . which British merchants sell with great profit. As for Turkey it is an independent country only by name, whose trade is governed by the British and French. Their natural growth is obliged to decay every day because of free trade . . . and for manufactured goods they entirely depend on imports from Britain and France. Their brave warriors in their poverty can hardly perform anything worthwhile. Why is it, then, that India's literature and Turkey's bravery have contributed little to their civilization? It is simply because their outlook does not reach beyond their own countries. They either enjoy peace at home or fight each other inside their own domain . . . while foreigners have been making a profit from them by means of business and trade. Western merchants have no opponents within Asia. If we are at the same time fearing and admiring their civilization, we have to exert ourselves, taking the circumstances inside and outside into consideration and comparing the one with the other.[20]

It is remarkable that the concept that developed countries control underdeveloped countries by means of free trade is clearly anticipated here. However, he is not discussing the theory or policies of free trade and protection here. In Book XV (1876) he writes, 'Most British economists favour free trade and maintain it as if it were a universal law, whereas some American economists argue for protection'.[21] But here again he is not contrasting one with the other in order to examine them both, because he continues to say simply that they are contradictory to the end. Instead, the purpose for his doing so is to point out by an example the difference between the people in Asiatic countries, who tend to stick to foolish prejudice, holding to the sayings of the ancient sages, and those in Western countries, who tend to seek the truth by arguments and discussions. To compare the rational with the irrational, the civilized with the uncivilized, is his aim. In *Gakumon no Susume* Fukuzawa's interest does not extend to political economy as such, and there is a marked similarity to his attitude in *Seiyō Jijō* (*Gaihen*), where he cuts out almost all the economic part.

Thus one of the main purposes of *Gakumon no Susume* is to stress the necessity of learning about Western civilization in order to confront Western countries. 'To fear a strong opponent and at the same time admire its civilization' is the attitude prevailing in many of his writings about that time. For example, in 'Nakatsu Ryūbetsu no Sho'

(Farewell to Nakatsu), written in the same year as *Seiyō Jijō*, vol. 3 (1870), one reads:

> Nowadays there are many among the foreigners, since our foreign trade has started, who by impoverishing us want to enrich themselves. Therefore it would only profit and rejoice foreigners if we continue to engage our interest in Japanese and Chinese classics, preferring old, rather than new, fashion, and thus falling into a state of poverty and stupidity without acquainting ourselves with the circumstances in the outer world. What they fear at this moment is our turning to Western studies. The way to achieve greatness for our country is to become accustomed to the world situation by reading as many books from the West as possible, . . . to achieve the people's independence and liberty inwardly by acquiring knowledge and virtue and to attain our nation's independence outwardly by keeping international laws.[22]

In *Keimō Tenarai no Bun* (Enlightening Penmanship) (1871) Fukuzawa also writes: 'Westerners are just the same human beings as we are, and so are the Americans. Nothing can contribute more to the wealth and strength of the country than to study while young'.[23] In the same year as *Gakumon no Susume*, i.e., 1873, when classes at Keiō School were divided into two different courses, regular and short, he wrote in his announcement the reason for establishing the latter course, which was to 'spread Western civilization rapidly by reading, lecturing, or translating the books of the West, and thereby to increase the national strength'.[24]

Although independence of the country was thus set as the main goal, it by no means meant that the independence of the individual was absorbed in the process as a mere means for achieving that goal. The sparkle of the spirit of enlightenment in its criticism of feudalism pervades the whole of *Gakumon no Susume* which asks in Book II: 'Men are equal with each other. . . . Is it not unreasonable that in feudal ages the division of classes between samurai and all other commoners was such that samurai treated the commoners as though the latter had been criminals?'[25] Or in Book III: 'A book called *Onna Daigaku* (The Greater Learning for Women) preaches three kinds of female obedience, firstly to parents, secondly to husband, and thirdly to children. Is this teaching not too partial and unfair?'[26] And the same question is raised in Book XIII: 'Once Confucius said in a grieving way that women and the small-minded are unmanageable. . . . But men and women are not different by nature. . . . The noble and the common are also born equal. Why is it that women and the small are particularly vulnerable? Is it not groundless to say that they are hopelessly vulnerable after teaching them nothing but obedience and binding them to the virtue of servitude?'[27]

What is characteristic of him in these arguments is that the independence of individuals is directly tied to the independence of the country. The following passage in Book I summarizes his logic:

> Both an individual and a country are free and independent by the law of nature. Therefore if there should ever be any who tries to interfere with the freedom of a country, that nation should be brave enough to fight against whatever country or countries in the world. Also if there should ever be any who tries to interfere with the freedom of a person, no one should fear any officer or officers of the government.[28]

The logic with which the freedom or independence of an individual and of a country is paralleled and combined on the same level is the same as that applied to civic and national rights. With Fukuzawa it is not necessarily the case that by civic right is meant the people's right against the state, or that by national right, the right of the state against its people, or the right on the part of the government to regulate people's inherent rights, and consequently that both kinds of right are on conflicting terms or at opposite poles. It is indeed true that Fukuzawa appeared to consent to the conflicting relationship between people's and state's rights by saying that he had postponed the publication of the already completed *Tsūzoku Minkenron* (Popular Theory of People's Right) until the completion of the *Tsūzoku Kokkenron*, fearing that, without thus recovering the balance between them, he might be misunderstood by the reading public.[29] Then again it was his belief that 'to maintain the people's right inside is in order to establish the national right outside' and that 'therefore the people's right and state's right are inseparable from each other'.[30] Here the state's right is its right against other states rather than against its own people,[31] so that the relation between the people's and the state's rights in this context is the same as that between personal independence and national independence developed in another context in *Gakumon no Susume*.

In *Tsūzoku Kokkenron*, Book II (1879), he says, 'Nothing is more urgent than letting the people understand what the international circumstances now are',[32] while in *Jiji Shōgen* he declares it to be his lifelong purpose 'to improve the national right'.[33]

In the meantime there was a heated controversy about the residence of foreigners in Japan. Some argued for the freedom of foreigners to reside wherever they liked. Others were against it and argued that they should be allowed to live only in a certain limited area, and Fukuzawa was among the latter. We shall return to the controversy itself later on. Referring to the problem, Fukuzawa later wrote, in *Bunkenron* (Decentralization of Power) (1877), that if the moment of their free residence should come, as he believed inevitable sooner or later, 'the Japanese could not fail to be placed under their control because the foreigners were skilled whereas the Japanese were not'.[34] Here too, he ascribes everything to the international circumstances in which Japan stopped its isolation policy and opened itself to the outside world. During the period of isolation, people had only to trust the government with everything and to obey its instructions, but 'once international communication started, we have had to fight against foreigners in trade and industry, in science and arts, and in all other spheres'. It is not a mere battle between governments. It is one between peoples. 'A step backward on our part means necessarily a step forward on their part'.[35] He discussed, in this context, the need for the decentralization of power, for the purpose of making people accustomed to public affairs. 'Decentralization of power is the way to train people for foreign intercourse. This is exactly why I claim that it is high time to tackle the decentralization of power'.[36] Thus even the decentralization of power is argued for from the viewpoint of the foreign relations situation, of which he is so very conscious.

An argument such as this, seen in *Bunkenron*, is clearly found as well in *Minkan Keizairoku* (Popular Political Economy), vol. 2, which appeared three years later, in 1880. There he refers to railways as an element of civilization: 'Civilization and culture consist in the control of nature by human art', and, 'convenience or inconvenience of transport depends on how skilfully or unskilfully the control of nature by art has been achieved'. Thus, talking about the significance of railways as an element of civilization, he maintains:

> There would have been no problems if it were the age of isolation now, just as it really was until twenty years ago. But the situation has changed. We have opened our country and have started competing with foreigners. We are no more than crawling worms, whereas they have wings to fly with. How can we equal them? . . . This is why the construction of railways is so imminent a necessity just now.[37]

Liberalists such as Taguchi would have argued in a different vein that railways, like all other things, should be left alone so that they would be constructed when the time was ready.[38] However, the main tenor of Fukuzawa's arguments is evident enough. Both volumes 1 and 2 of *Minkan Keizairoku* are no doubt written under the influence of the Chambers's and Wayland's books, which are popularized versions of classical political economy, and yet Fukuzawa's nationalism is so very clear.

Therefore when he asks, in *Jiji Shōgen*, on what we are to rely other than the power of arms in order to compete with Western nations in the present world arena, and says that the motto 'wealth and strength' does not imply the enrichment of the country first and the strengthening of arms next, but the other way round, because without strength there cannot be wealth,[39] his argument is simply a continuation of that about the railways. *Jiji Shōgen* proceeds a step further by saying, 'Among the Eastern countries there is only Japan which can be the centre of civilization to confront Western countries', and therefore one should be persuaded that 'the defence of Asian countries is Japan's responsibility'. He continues:

> It is like the spreading of fire when Western countries force themselves on us Eastern countries. These nations, particularly the Chinese and Koreans, are so slow and dull that they are no more capable of stopping them than wooden houses are able to withstand the force of fire. Therefore it is not for the sake of others but for our own sake that we help them with our arms. We must with every effort protect them and lead them in culture in order to let them follow suit with the object at entering the sphere of modern civilization. If ever no other alternative should be left, we may forcibly urge them to progress.

Indeed he goes as far as to affirm that to 'forcibly urge them to progress' is justified.[40]

In short, Fukuzawa regards international relations at large as consisting in 'the difference of magnitude and strength of financial and military power between the nations concerned',[41] and asserts that 'one ought to be convinced that the essence of foreign intercourse is power'.[42] 'Peace inside and emulation outside' is the only possible strategy. Here again he believes that 'the reason why Japan is in need of peace inside comes solely from the opening-up of the country some twenty years ago'.[43] The international circumstances in which Japan was forced to open itself to the outer world or, as one might put it, the imperialistic world situation of the time, characterized his thinking, and this applies to the ideas of the early Fukuzawa at least up to the period of *Jiji Shōgen*.

3. Protection and Laissez-faire

Thus Fukuzawa considers an individual not as an individual as such but always as a member of the nation. This was consistently his view, right from *Gakumon no Susume*. Consequently, he thinks of the self-love of a nation instead of the self-love of an individual. In *Bunmeiron no Gairyaku* he clarifies his ideas:

> Those who exert themselves to extend the right of their own nation, to enrich their own nation, to improve the wisdom and virtue of their own nation and to glorify the honour of their own nation are called people faithful to their country. . . . Their aim must be to distinguish their country from others, and to favour themselves in comparison to others, not necessarily to harm the latter, but to keep the independence of their country.[44]

This nationalism characterizes his views on foreign trade as well. As has already been seen, he maintained the view that the choice between free trade and protection 'is simply dependent on the interest of one's own country' before setting it out in *Jiji Shōgen*. What prevails in the real world is not 'natural freedom'. In the same section of *Bunmeiron no Gairyaku* he declares, 'The present world as it stands may suitably be called the world of business and war'.[45]

As early as 1869 he wrote, in 'Maruya Shōsha no Ki' (A Note on Maruya & Co.), 'Needless to say, the great aim of foreigners in meeting our brethren . . . is nothing other than seeking profit out of the latter by means of trade, so that it would be contrary to our duty if we idly see them keep the right of business and trade totally in their hands'.[46] This was expounded only a year after *Seiyō Jijō* (*Gaihen*). His view on foreign trade is exactly the same when he states next year in 'Nakatsu Ryūbetsu no Sho' that 'since the foreign trade has recently been opened, there are many among the foreigners . . . who want to make profit by making this country poor and this nation stupid'.[47] This view is carried through to *Bunmeiron no Gairyaku* via 'Shōgakkō o Tatsuru no Shui' (Prospectus of the School of Commerce) and 'Seitai Wagi no Enzetsu' (A Speech on the Peace of Taiwan) written four years later, in 1874, and also 'Ajia Shokoku to no Wasen' (Peace or War with Asian Countries) written five years later, in 1875.

In 'Shōgakkō o Tatsuru no Shui' he regards 'fighting the war of trade against foreign countries' as 'the public duty of merchants now' and says that 'in the age of fighting with swords one cannot go to the battlefield without previously learning the art of fencing', so, in the same way, 'in the age of fighting with trade one cannot compete with foreigners without previously learning the art of commerce'.[48] In 'Seitai Wagi no Enzetsu' he warns that although the reparations paid as a result of sending armies to Taiwan are welcome enough, one ought not to take into consideration only the two countries concerned. 'As to the profit or loss one must consider that there are other parties too . . . which are Western countries. Indeed they are not directly involved in the war or peace between Japan and China . . . but they are concerned in it by means of trade'. After the disputes both Japan and China are trying to be more properly armed, and the relationship is that the Westerners are the selling party and the Chinese and Japanese the buying part. 'Now, not only warships, guns and artillery are all foreign commodities but so are clothes, shoes, hats and the like. . . . Thus it is the Western merchants who always gain and never lose.' It is true enough that 'a war concerns honour or dishonour of a country so that it cannot be looked at from the point of view of mercenary gain or loss only', and yet 'care should be taken not to profit the Westerners by the disputes between us Asians'. Thus, 'our present difficulties lie in foreign affairs. Our powerful enemy now is the Western countries which are not an enemy in the military sense but in the trading sense.'[49]

Fukuzawa's argument in 'Ajia Shokoku to no Wasen' is very much to the same effect. He is opposed to the Korean War for the reason that 'it would hardly be worth rejoicing if Korea should bring tributes and become Japan's colony'. It would even be a loss to fight against the Koreans, for 'to win there would neither be honourable nor profitable, because to spend a huge sum of money to buy commodities, guns, and artillery of Western make would only amount to an increase in our foreign debt'. He continues that 'Japan will not achieve real independence unless it stands on an equal footing with Western countries', and that 'though there is foreign trade carried on in our major ports, all of it is in the hands of foreigners'. Indeed 'there are plans to start some manufacturing enterprises, but the Japanese are always the borrowing side of capital and never the lending side'.[50]

As though to formulate these discussions in a conclusion, he writes in *Bunmeiron no Gairyaku*:

> If one looks at the trade between Japan and foreign countries, one sees that Western countries are the manufacturers and Japan is the

> growers. . . . In economy the wealth of a nation depends far less on the plenitude of natural produce than on the skill of human arts. For example, there is India, on the one hand, where land is fertile and yet people are poor, and there is Holland, on the other, where there is scarcely any natural produce and yet people are rich. Therefore in trade between a manufacturing country and a growing country, the former makes use of unlimited human power and the latter the limited produce of land. . . . This is exactly the case with trade between Japan and foreign countries. We cannot but be on the losing side.[51]

In 'Bōeki Shōkai Kaigyō no Enzentsu' (Opening Speech at a Trading Company) he says: 'When I look at the foreigners who have come in their ships and who have been engaged in selling their commodities to us and then buying our products to export, I cannot help saying that they are the merchants and we are their customers'. He continues and asks: 'How do the foreigners live who reside in our trading ports? From where does their subsistence come? Riding beautiful horses, sitting in fabulous coaches, they spend millions or take them back to their home countries. That money . . . is nothing but the outcome of our toil and trouble. What else do we have to lament?' He even invokes the exclusionists' feelings: 'The exclusionists of old days wanted to expel by military force from Japan foreigners, whom they despised as lower creatures. The difference now from then . . . lies only in that we want to fight in business and trade'. Thus even calling upon the exclusionists whom he used to loathe so much, he says: 'Postponing a battle with weapons to some future day, at the moment we want to fight a battle of trade with foreigners'.[52] The reference to the exclusionists may sound extraordinary, but the analogy of an armed conflict does not, as must be clear enough already.

It would be strange if such a view of foreign trade did not bear the balance-of-trade theory or protectionism. Indeed, that kind of theory may be said to be implied in these arguments. In the same year as *Bunmeiron no Gairyaku*, i.e., in 1875, he wrote a periodical article, 'Gaikokujin no Naichi Zakkyo Yurusu Bekarazaru no Ron' (Foreigners Should Not Be Allowed to Live Freely among the Japanese), in which his theory on free trade is clearly revealed. On that subject there was, as mentioned already, a series of heated arguments between some leading writers. Free traders like Nishi Amane, Tsuda Mamichi, and others argued for freedom of residence for foreigners, while protectionists like Nishimura Shigeki and his friends argued against it.[53] Fukuzawa says: 'It is a great mistake to try to introduce Western civilization only by permitting foreigners to stay here freely, regardless of the unfavourable consequences it would obviously bring about. . . . It is all too early to permit it. . . . The immediate necessity now lies inside rather than outside ourselves. In other words we have, for the time being, to nourish our people's minds and spirits till we can make foreigners keep our laws on equal terms with ourselves, and only then ought their freedom of residence to be allowed'.[54] In fact, to be able to reside freely also meant free trade, so that this conclusion implies in itself an argument against free trade. But more clearly still, a conviction of anti-free trade and of the balance-of-trade is disclosed in the course of discussion: 'Foreigners come to Japan only for trade, not to bring knowledge and virtue to the people of Japan and thus to lead them to civilization'. Indeed since the opening of the country, 'we have gone so far as to overthrow the feudal government, making many striking changes, abolishing the old ways and seeking the new in every possible way', which is the outcome of our dealings with foreigners. As for the foreigners themselves, however, all this was 'by chance' and not by design.[55] 'Foreign trade means that those inside and outside the country fight for profit and that the ports are the place where that fighting takes place. When we look at the trade, we see that since the opening-up of the country, we have always been losers and they have been gainers. Therefore we have to say that the growth of foreign trade up to today has not brought about an increase but rather a decrease in our wealth'.[56] While arguing in this way he summarizes his ideas in a few points, of which the first two, in particular, express his views on trade:

1. When exports are small and imports are large in value, the balance cannot but be our debts.

2. Our imports are mostly manufactured commodities and our exports are goods of natural growth. For that reason our nation will be obliged to lose the advantages which accompany manufacturing industry and the skill with which to produce manufactured commodities.[57]

Here we see nothing other than the balance-of-trade theory. This is the antithesis of the views, to which Fukuzawa subscribed so earnestly, of Francis Wayland in his *The Elements of Political Economy*, for Wayland writes:

> We see how fallacious is the notion formerly entertained, that, by exchange, only one party is benefitted; and consequently, that what one party gains, the other party loses. Were this the case, no country could grow rich by exchange, unless by impoverishing every other

> country; and the gain of one nation would be nothing else than a transfer of the wealth of other countries to itself. On the contrary, precisely the reverse is the case.[58]

Fukuzawa's claim is exactly the reverse, for he states that in trade gain on one side is loss on the other, and that Japan has always been on the losing side. He says: 'What we lose must necessarily amount to what they gain. Therefore in trade foreigners have attained their objective to compete in order to make profit, and we have lost what they have gained'.[59]

He gives an example of the export of gold coins at the time of the opening-up of the country. If a merchant, he says, buys up gold coins worth 1,000 dollars for only 400 dollars, and then sells them to foreigners for 600 dollars, he may indeed gain the balance of 200 dollars, but from the standpoint of the nation as a whole, this transaction has caused the loss of 400 dollars. The same applies also to the case of silk and tea which were among the biggest items of contemporary export. If the production of silk and tea has increased and their price has gone up since the opening of the ports to foreigners, it cannot be regarded as the 'blessing of trade'. On the contrary, 'their price has only gone up in comparison to what it was previously', but seen from the viewpoint of the nation's foreign trade as a whole, that is to say, from Japan's relation to foreign merchants, the gain belongs to them and certainly not to Japan. Furthermore, 'our tea and silk are exported unmanufactured, whereas what we receive from them is their manufactured commodities. There are even cases in which they manufacture our raw silk and export that manufactured silk cloth back to Japan. . . . If in such a way our manufacturing trades should be taken away to the foreigners' profit, our nation's basic riches would daily go west, until the Japanese would eventually fall into the condition of labourers at their beck and call'.[60] Thus is described the influence of the exportation of raw materials and the importation of manufactured commodities on the balance of trade, and its effects on the outflow of capital and the loss of employment.

Needless to say, the assertion Fukuzawa makes, that by foreign trade Japan is a loser, does not mean that he denies the benefit of foreign trade as such. His attitude towards it has not changed since Tōjin Ōrai (Foreigners In and Out), written about 1865, when he stressed the need for the opening-up of the country and for foreign trade. This was the conviction which was to become the foundation of his later economic thought. He did not specify any particular trades as favourable or unfavourable. What he means here by foreign trade is simply trade with advanced countries at large. 'What foreign trade is to us is as nutrition to the human body', but 'though the benefit of nutrition cannot be denied, the physical conditions must first be questioned before it can be applied'. If the physical conditions are unsuitable, it might be dangerous to apply a good medicine. It is exactly the case with the country: 'Good medicine must be applied only little by little'.[61] In a like context he emphasizes the significance of foreign trade and at the same time asserts that free trade can hardly apply until foreign countries and Japan can stand on an equal footing.[62] In *Tsūzoku Kokkenron* written in 1878, he expresses his opinion even more explicitly:

> About foreign trade there is a theory that foreign commodities should freely be admitted so that anything that is inexpensive may be bought and consumed. Others, who are against this theory, claim that by importing manufactured commodities and exporting natural goods the nation cannot fail to lose profit that would otherwise be gained by manufacturing them and at the same time lose the manufacturing art itself. . . . Therefore they are of the opinion that these imports should either be restricted or heavily taxed. I, for one, agree with this latter opinion, but because of the unequal treaties there is no prospect yet for any restriction to be adopted.[63]

Also in *Jiji Shōgen* he says that just as the theory of natural civil rights applies only in the ideal state, in a state 'where all men are brothers and have equal access to the gifts of nature', whereas in reality it is only 'the theory of a government established in every country to keep peace inside' which applies, so, between the countries, the theory of 'mutual intercourse providing each other with each other's necessity', which is 'parallel to the above theory of natural freedom', is evidently in contrast with, and amazingly far from, real international intercourse.[64] This is much the same argument as that in *Bunmeiron no Gairyaku* six years earlier, in which he wrote: It is often asserted that 'international intercourse is based on the high way set by nature, so that free trade and free traffic should be observed. . . . But in order that this may be true, the first thing to be done is to abolish all the governments of the world in the same way as each clan in feudal Japan was abolished at the time of the Meiji Restoration. . . . If that cannot be expected, and if there continues to be a government in every country, then national feelings cannot be denied'.[65] In short he believes that free trade is good enough as an abstract theory but not applicable in reality.[66]

In *Jiji Shōgen* he repeats the same argument, that the international relationship really means 'fighting with weapons' in war and 'fighting with trade and industry' in peace.[67] In a similar vein, as in *Gakumon no Susume*, he refers to free trade and protection:

> In such a country as Britain where there is a plenitude of commodities manufactured by human arts and exported, with profit, to all over the world, free trade is defended and in such a country as America where there are plenty of goods of natural growth but few manufactured commodities, protection is defended. The discussion between both continues ad infinitum.[68]

The context here is not the comparison of superiority or inferiority between the two theories, but what is important is that he asserts that 'both free trade and protection are, after all, in the interest of their own country' and that protectionism in America had only been possible because it was backed by American military power, so that a country in Asia would not be allowed, even if it wanted to, to levy 'extraordinary customs duties'.[69] Fukuzawa's conception of trade, i.e., free trade for advanced countries and protection for underdeveloped countries, seems too clear to leave any room for doubt.

4. Conclusion

And yet it is hardly conceivable that in Fukuzawa's thought processes there is no element of economic liberalism apart from free trade. As early as 1871 he refers to political economy in *Keimō Tenarai no Bun*. Enumerating the 'subjects of Western studies', he points out political economy along with history, physics, and mathematics as 'the science which discusses the necessities of life, with the way to produce, exchange, . . . and increase them'. By defining it as 'a science to make clear that those who follow the law of nature are enriched and those who do not are impoverished',[70] he seems to imply economic liberalism, though what that 'law of nature' means is not very clear as yet.

However in *Bunkenron* (1877) there is a passage where he appears to defend the non-interference of government and freedom of competition:

> People who have positions in the government, regardless of their present rank and past careers, are now more advanced in their knowledge and faculties than the rest of the nation. That being so, the more advanced ought to lead the less advanced. . . . In this very

point the government in Japan is different from those in Western countries in that it has, as it were, a private task to carry out besides its own official task.

Therefore 'to assert the theory of natural freedom and accuse the government of performing its many tasks, listening to the abstract and vain theory of the West without considering the conditions of the country, is only idle speculation'. Yet, 'those who are in the government, however they may be advanced in abstract knowledge, are not as well acquainted with practical matters as the people at large'. Theory is one thing and practical application is another. Pathology and a clinic are not the same. A designer of a ship is not a shipwright or a pilot. 'If the government, not understanding this and mixing up theory with practice, should try to act on practical matters, the evils accruing from its action would be countless. The government officers who are all of them ex-samurai are least acquainted with industry and trade. If they should spend a vast amount of capital belonging to the government, capital larger by far than that of any other source, the result would very possibly be plunder and waste'.[71]

Thus Fukuzawa averred that the government must not be the agent of any economic activities. The present state of things as he saw it was that 'without depending on the government hardly any capital can be raised for trade and industry. In many fields trade and industry had already been started by the government'. There is the case, for example, of 'the cultivation of waste land or the opening of new mines'.[72]

It is true that in this argument only a denial that the government should directly operate a trade or industry is found. However, he also says that 'in an economy one spends only to gain by so doing'. In that point all men are the same, hence the competition among them all. 'They are all equally concerned with comparing expenditure with income, thus competing with each other with the prospect of being a winner'. The conduct of the government 'which spends without due consideration of gain' cannot only tend to be 'spendthrift and wasteful' but also to interfere with mutual competition between individuals, thus resulting in 'double losses'.[73]

In this way Fukuzawa rejects the idea of the government directly running business and at the same time presupposes the 'principle of competition'. The exclusion of the government from intervening in the economy by means of prohibition, permission and protection and the like can also be said to be implied. In fact he says, 'It would prove harmful and unprofitable for the government to intervene in practical affairs, or to prohibit or protect them'.[74]

This is in accordance with his definition of the duty of government, in a chapter of *Minkan Keizairoku* published in the same year, as 'jurisprudence, military affairs, taxation and foreign intercourse'.[75] It is true that the context in which this definition is stated deals directly with the division between central and local governments and does not positively limit the part to be played by the government, but it is also true that the duty of government is confined, though indirectly, to the above four items.

Something similar is also found in *Minkan Keizairoku*, vol. 2, published three years later. In the chapter on 'Public works' he writes that 'great public affairs', such as the railway, telegraph, gas and water supplies or 'what, like iron mines, does not directly relate to public affairs and yet cannot be run privately without loss and at the same time cannot be left undone', should been en trusted to the government. Then he continues to say:

> It would be a very great mistake to misunderstand this principle and believe that the government may do anything to enrich the country, running ordinary works and competing with people in trade and industry. Competition can only lead trade and industry to average prices and induce the parties concerned to every exertion. If there were someone who would do anything with no consideration of gain or loss, . . . the effect would only be disastrous.

He gives an example, saying that in the Tokugawa period, when clans ran businesses of their own, 'there grew no great businessmen at all'.[76] Thus Fukuzawa asserts that except that which is properly entrusted to the government, nothing ought to be run by the government. Everything concerning trade and industry should be carried out solely by competition.

Protection is likewise faulted. He goes on to say: 'If the government did not run businesses of its own, it sometimes protects some people by lending them some of its money under the pretext of encouraging trade and industry which are important to the economy. . . . But there can be no business whatsoever that is of no importance to the state'.[77]

Bunmeiron no Gairyaku also refers to government involvement: 'In attaining civilization each has to do his duty. The government deals with present necessities, scholars consider the future, and men of trade and industry enrich the country through their own private business, all thus participating in turn in civilization'. The main discussion in this passage is the relation between the government and scholars, and not the relation of the government to trade and industry.

Even so, it just as implicitly states that the government on the one hand, and trade and industry on the other, should fulfil their respective duties. About the relation between the government and people the book also says that 'government and people differ from each other, so that in private matters government ought never to be allowed to interfere', and that 'it would be totally groundless' for the government to levy taxes in order to 'regulate the matter of religion and education, order the rules of trade and industry, and even go as far as to meddle in the daily affairs of private families'.[78] Again, although the main theme is not the relation of the government to trade, industry and agriculture, it is clear that government interference in the economy is categorically rejected.

When it is said that 'men of trade and industry enrich the country through their own private business', the philosophy of natural liberty or laissez-faire might seem to be suggested. An extract from an article in *Minkan Zasshi* (Popular Magazine) two years later (1877) stating that 'private interest is the basis of public benefit, the latter of which can only be attained by those who pursue the former'[79] might seem to support such an interpretation. However, it must be pointed out that the phrase 'public benefit' as Fukuzawa uses it does not mean something in an abstract sense, but, on the contrary, quite clearly means national benefit. He says even more clearly in an article written two years later (1879), entitled 'Watakushi no Ri Itonamu Beki no Ichirei' (Private Profit Should Be Attained), that 'the private profit of each merchant will eventually be gathered and accumulated to contribute to the victory of Japan in the business world'.[80]

Thus it may safely be concluded that economic liberalism in the sense of non-interventionism or independence from the government is fairly clearly perceived in Fukuzawa's economic thought, and yet, at the same time, that that liberalism goes hand in hand with economic nationalism and, consequently, mercantilist protectionism.

3

Nishi Amane and Tsuda Mamichi

Chūhei Sugiyama

Those distinguished thinkers of the time of the Japanese Enlightenment, such as Nishi Amane and Tsuda Mamichi, with the exception of Fukuzawa Yukichi, left after them no systematic body of economic writing. Yet, not unlike many writers in the enlightenment movement in the West, they were interested in most phases of human intellect, and so, in economic matters as well. The economic thought of Nishi and Tsuda, exemplified in some of their articles, lecture notes and manuscripts, is of a liberalist kind, formed most probably under the influence of Simon Vissering, under whom both studied 'five subjects', including political economy, as described in Chapter 1. This chapter deals with both of them but with Nishi rather briefly and with Tsuda in more detail.

1. Nishi's Economic Thought

Like other thinkers of the Japanese Enlightenment, Nishi started his career as a thinker by denouncing the moral philosophy of Confucianism. In a manuscript titled *Shōhaku-Sakki* (1883) he writes that 'it is a loose theory for Confucians to teach that everything up from natural phenomena such as wind and rain, down to all human affairs is regulated by the everlasting and invariable law of heaven'.[1] In Confucianist thought an eclipse of the sun or of the moon, a bad harvest, floods, etc., are all attributed to the government and policy of the emperor—but to Nishi this was a groundless belief, based on sheer delusion.

'Physical law', as Nishi put it, is the law of nature which, like gravitation, is 'the necessity which must be obeyed regardless of any human will'. The Mongolian invasion of Japan in the thirteenth century failed not as a result, as was widely believed, of the prayers of some Buddhist priests such as Nichiren, but because of the typhoon which occurred in so timely a fashion, and ruined the entire Mongolian fleet.

Physical law and moral law are thus different from each other. 'Moral law is *a posteriori* but is far from being wilful or artificial. It is a law all the same'. The invariable identity of the law lies in the human propensity for love and hate, common to all human beings, and the propensity for love and hate is based on pleasure and pain. This Benthamite philosophy is the essence of Nishi's *Hyakuichi Shinron* (Uniformity of All Learning Reviewed) (1874).[2]

A series of articles entitled 'Jinsei Sanbō-setsu' (Three Treasures of Life) was written soon after the afore-mentioned book under the clear influence of J. S. Mill's *Utilitarianism* (1863), which Nishi admired as enlarging yet modifying greatly Bentham's theory. The ultimate state of well-being, or general welfare, was made the 'first and foremost aim of human life', and the means for realizing this state were 'first, health; second, knowledge; and third, wealth, which together constitute the 'three treasures of life'.[3] They are the essential basis of society and manifest the distinction between civilized and savage states. In the savage state they are hardly esteemed, whereas in the civilized state they are esteemed greatly.

What is characteristic of his argument is that people are deemed equal in the desire for those treasures so that everybody ought to be left free in his conduct, unless it destroys them. The second characteristic is that Nishi reduced them to private interest: 'If it did not benefit himself, who would strive for the sake of others?' Indeed, the aim of society is the 'public interest', in Nishi's terminology 'general welfare', but public interest is nothing but the 'aggregate of private interests'.[4]

All these discussions are moral and have little to do with economic matters. Yet if the pursuit of those 'three treasures' must be free, then the pursuit of material well-being, i.e., wealth, as one of the three, should also be free—a conviction which necessarily leads to economic liberalism.

In the economic part of his lectures, 'Hyakugaku Renkan' (All Learning Combined), Nishi defines political economy, saying that economy is a way by which a private person can attain wealth, whereas political economy is a science whereby a nation can attain wealth.[5] Starting from this definition, he then traces the history of political economy from Giovanni Botero to J. S. Mill. While doing so, he enumerates as untenable from the point of view of political economy, a number of items such as monopoly, guilds, protectionism, restrictive and prohibiting systems, mercantilism, usury law, restriction of luxury and interference of government. To these he adds more items just as untenable—socialism, communism and Fourierism.[6] Here the influence of economic thought then prevailing in Holland, where he had studied, is clear.[7] He thus subscribes to the system of laissez-faire by rejecting mercantilist and other restrictive systems on the one hand, and socialism on the other as another sort of state intervention in private property. Nishi inserts an English sentence into his Japanese text: 'When they [individuals] prosecute the branches of industry advantageous to themselves, they are necessarily also prosecuting such as are advantageous to [the] public'.[8]

In an article he contributed to *Meiroku Zasshi* (Meiji Six Journal) on the problem of whether foreigners should be allowed to travel freely inside Japan, he argues that just as only chemical analysis can reveal if an unknown fruit is or is not edible, so only logical reasoning can judge whether foreigners should be permitted to travel freely in the country. Logical analysis is composed of two kinds: deductive and inductive. The former is the method by which to know that a small curve, if extended, could not fail to make a circle. To apply this method to the problem concerned, it would follow that as the opposite of a curved line is a straight line, so the opposite of open ports and friendly intercourse is closed ports and an exclusionist policy. If the freedom of travel is part of the former, and if Japan has discarded the latter policy, then the answer to be given to the problem must be clear enough. The policy for freedom of travel ought by all means to be adopted.[9] To prohibit foreigners from travelling freely would be the same as pointing to the Bering Sea after deciding Australia was to be the destination. However, for such a practical problem as this, the inductive method may be more persuasive. As it is not possible to compare all the merits with all the demerits of the matter, it might be better to enumerate the negative points to consider whether they may be prevented or turned to positive effect.[10] Nishi thus enumerates some of the possible causes for complaint: that foreigners might trade not only in the open ports but also elsewhere, or that they might enter prohibited districts, or that the interpreters might sometimes be embarrassed at not understanding the foreigners, or that foreigners might be accompanied by dogs. He claims that all of these can be prevented beforehand by stipulating conditions, and that there will consequently be nothing negative and everything will become positive.[11] A true devotee of enlightenment, Nishi discusses much in this way, which may show how philosophically minded he is. However, his real intention here was to propose laissez-faire in one of the issues of the day. Tsuda also shared this view, though his approach to the matter was quite different, and more practical, as will be seen later. The characteristic feature of Nishi's argument may be made clearer, however, by comparison with Fukuzawa's opinion on the matter.

Fukuzawa contradicts Nishi with the same logic that Nishi has used. It is indeed true, he admits, that induction is the method by which to know the whole from its part. Just as Nishi says, one could easily presume the shapes of a cup, i.e., a circle, from a little piece of it, i.e., an arch. A small shift in the position of a star would suggest its orbit. However, the same method can be used to reach the opposite conclusion: 'If the international situation since the opening of our ports be regarded as a loss to our side, it can lead us to consideration of the whole that may be a great loss in the end'. The same thing applies to induction. Nishi enumerates a number of possible mischiefs but the policy he recommends seems far from being effective. Can a mere stipulation be of any use in a given state of things? The point is that we are not standing on an equal footing with foreigners. To permit freedom of travel will necessarily lead to allowing them to reside freely among the Japanese, which again will naturally lead to free trade, and free trade is a one-sided benefit to foreigners'.[12] Thus the confrontation between Fukuzawa and Nishi about the problem of foreigners' freedom of travel originated in their different views on the rights and wrongs of free trade. As Fukuzawa opposed it, so Nishi supported it. What was common to both of them, however, was the consideration of which would benefit the nation more. National interest always came first, national interest in the sense that what served the enlightenment and modernization of the nation most, ought to have priority.

2. Tsuda on Natural Freedom

Among the writers at the time of the Meiji Enlightenment, Tsuda may well be said to be among those who best personified the spirit of enlightenment. Even in commonplace matters he tried to spread a rational way of thinking, as is the case with, for example, his essays 'Fukushōron' (On Official Insignia), 'Kisetsu' (On Ghosts), or 'Fūfu Dōkenben' (On the Equal Rights of Husband and Wife).

In the essay 'Fukushōron' he argues that apart from the military officers whose duty it is to subdue violence by means of violence, civil servants are in no need of insignia or uniforms varying from rank to rank: 'Nowadays civil servants in European and American countries all wear the same formal clothes, from the emperor or president down to the commoner'. The reason is that, unlike military government, civil government is government by means of laws and morals and so needs no rank or robe. When he saw the Dutch consul in Hong Kong on his way back from studying in Holland, he was surprised to find him dressed in an ostentatious uniform. When Tsuda asked why, the consul smiled and replied that that was the only way to convince the Asian savage of the greatness of the Dutch consul.[13] Writing in this way, he no doubt implies that the Japanese, too, are among those 'Asian savages' who have by all means to be enlightened.

Referring in separate articles to belief in legendary beings such as long-nosed goblins (*tengu*) and the like, Tsuda states that it is only the Japanese who are so unenlightened as to believe in those mythical creatures, and that those who have reached a certain stage of civilization are free from all nonsensical beliefs. Here again the civilization of Europe is contrasted with the uncivilized savage state of Asians, or Japanese.[14]

Something quite similar is seen in his article 'Fūfu Dōkenben'. Distinguishing the equality of men and women from that between husband and wife, he denies the latter but approves of the former, again referring to the laws in European and American countries.[15]

Later he goes so far as to say that he supports materialism against spiritualism, believing that materialistic rationalism is the nucleus of Western civilization.[16] As to science and learning, he divides them into the 'real' and the 'vain'. By vain learning he implies theories based on Confucianism that had so long prevailed in Japan, and by real knowledge he means 'Western astronomy, chemistry, medicine, political economy, and Greek philosophy, all of which are based on ascertained realities'. To Tsuda, civilization seemed to be simply the state of affairs in which 'real studies prevail'. However, even Europe was not mature enough to have reached that stage, so that it would not be easy for 'south-eastern countries' to reach it.

Besides science, religion contributes to the general education of the people. There are varieties of religion such as Shintoism, Buddhism and so on in Japan, with Christianity, Islam, etc., in foreign countries. Of these, Tsuda claims Christianity generally, and Protestantism in particular, to be the best, for the latter is the richest in freedom and therefore the nearest to civilization. Thus he proposed to employ overseas Protestant missionaries in the same way as foreigners were employed for teaching science and technology.[17]

It might seem strange for Tsuda to promote religious belief—he who claims to prefer 'materialism' to 'spiritualism', and 'real' studies to 'vain' learning. For him, however, religion is no more than a means. In other words, as it takes time 'to achieve a civilized state by real learning prevailing among the general mass of people', for the time being there must be recourse to religion, in particular, its most liberal kind.[18]

Thus with Tsuda, enlightenment and freedom were inseparable. Discussing the freedom of the press he says that the difference between the civilized and uncivilized is the difference between the existence and non-existence of political restraint. 'Whether a nation is civilized or not depends on whether it enjoys freedom of speech and conduct'. Unlike the 'shameful politics of a barbarous government', suppressing its people by means of direct force, the despotic government of a half-civilized country is apt to control its people by laws and decrees. In Britain and America people enjoy complete freedom in what they do and say, unless they interfere with the freedom of others, whereas in other countries, such as France, there are regulations which forbid the publication of printed matter without the permission of the government. There, however, suppression of freedom had become the cause of political instability as was the case at the time of Napoleon III. In Japan, therefore, absolute freedom of the press should be proclaimed as soon as possible.[19]

The intervention of government should thus be done away with. 'Now is the time for the culture and civilization of the Japanese empire to start growing. When a tree is about to grow and stretch its branches, it should be given complete protection that it may be kept away from interference from outside. In the same way when people are about to develop their knowledge and culture, things ought to be left to their natural course'.[20] It is obvious that the aforesaid protection has nothing to do with so-called protectionism. But it is also true that, with Tsuda, freedom and enlightenment were not so much values to be pursued for their own sake as an indispensable means to achieve the wealth and strength of Japan as a modern nation. And this was also the case, as has already been expounded, with Nishi and other promoters of the Japanese Enlightenment. The flourishing of newspapers, Tsuda writes, 'nourishes, by contributing to the progress of civilization, the very root of the wealth and strength of the country'. The combination of enlightenment and nationalism is, more often than not, a characteristic trait of intellectuals in late-starting countries, and Tsuda and his friends are typical examples. For the advanced countries, having been enlightened, civilization is the state in which they exist, and barbarism or an uncivilized stage belonged to their past, whereas in underdeveloped countries their present state was nothing but the savage state, and their civilization belonged to the future state to be attained at any cost. 'National prestige' through modernization cannot but be what mattered there.

His argument on torture, a practice which Tsuda endeavoured to deal severely, has also to be taken into account. He says that 'nothing is more lamentable than torture', but he combines this argument with revision of the treaties. The reason why treaties between foreign nations and Japan are not equal in nature is that their respective laws differ. In the West, no crime is punished without evidence and there is a system of appeal to a higher court, whereas in Japan crimes are punished on confession only and there is no system of appeal. In the Western legal system, even if there were sufficient evidence, no crime is punished unless it is stated explicitly as a crime in law, whereas in Japan it is not necessary to have a relevant legal code for a crime to be punished. Thus it is not unreasonable that Western countries do not want their citizens in Japan to be placed under Japanese laws. Therefore 'if we want to make foreign residents in Japan keep our laws, we must abolish torture, and if we want to abolish torture, we must revise our criminal law'. It is true in this way that torture was regarded as an abuse, and it is an abuse that was to be abolished in order 'to stand on an equal footing with European and American contries'.[21] For Tsuda, enlightenment was a means to achieve the modernization of Japan, so that Japan could cope with advanced countries.

His argument on permitting foreigners to travel freely in the country is similar.[22] As has already been suggested, Tsuda argued differently, on the one hand, from Nishi who supported freedom and on the other, from Fukuzawa who objected to it. For Tsuda, it is not as easy as it might seem to be for Japan to acquire the 'two kinds of right, i.e., the right to try foreigners and the right to tax foreign goods', by revision of the treaties. The reason for the Japanese government's unwillingness to permit foreigners to travel freely anywhere in the country is that it feared that some Japanese might commit violence against them, on the one hand, and be cheated by them, on the other. Such lack of knowledge and enlightenment on the part of the Japanese should, properly, be removed by education, but the effects of school education could not be expected to be realized within a short time. The enlightenment of Europeans and Americans is due to the experience they have had, through world-wide trade and commerce. The best way might therefore be to let Japanese people in general travel abroad widely and thereby accumulate experience. This is, however, simply vain talk.

Consequently it must be regarded as a good chance for the Japanese nation to acquire experience, when foreigners residing here want to travel freely in the country. 'It is lucky for us that foreigners want to travel inside our country. They ought to be admitted promptly so that they might contribute by their communication and contact with our people to the progress of the people's knowledge and enlightenment'.

This is clear, Tsuda believes, from the experience they had at the time of opening the ports to foreign countries just ten years or so ago. At that time arguments were prevalent which regarded it as the greatest calamity the Japanese had ever undergone, but 'now it goes without saying which of the two policies, opening or closing the country to the outside world, has proved to be more beneficial'. The difference between 'enlightenment and civilization' as we see it now and the circumstances preceding it needs no explanation, and it was effected in such a small space of time.

If that is the case, then the same must apply to foreigners' travel in Japan. To claim that this ought not to be permitted before the right to tax and try foreigners has been secured is an argument standing on its head, because the real independence of the country can only be achieved by enlightening 'our people generally and those in the lower and middle ranks particularly', to which end the freedom of foreigners to associate with the people is of great assistance. Thus his ideas with regard to enlightenment for people in the middle and lower stations of life are very clear. What is to be noted at the same time is the fact that he made the realization of an 'independent free empire' the supreme objective to be attained, he believed, as a result of enlightenment, while he preferred the leaving of all affairs to their natural course' to 'the protecting of the people by the government'.

Thus he made the most of all possible opportunities to advocate freedom. For example, we may examine his article 'Jinzairon' (People of Talent). According to him, in ancient times Asia was rich in ability, whereas in modern times Europe and America are endowed with it. Within Japan, too, regions which produced distinguished people of talent have changed from age to age, for which the reason is not very clear, but might well be due to the difference in the degree of freedom: 'In Asian countries despotic monarchical governments are not favourable to the development of talent, whereas in European and American countries most governments favour people's freedom, which again contributes to the growth of talent'.[23]

Arguments to a similar effect are also seen in his article 'Seiron' (On Government): 'Our people have long been subject and accustomed to an oppressive system, so that their human nature has failed to develop itself'. Therefore what is essential is to 'let the government keep propriety in its policy and refrain from impeding the natural progress of enlightenment', for which purpose it is recommended that people should participate in national affairs through parliamentary elections. 'This unrestrained human nature is the source of national vigour, and where national vigour shrinks, national prestige cannot expand'. Here, too, we see that national prestige is directly connected with 'unrestrained human nature'.

In any case 'everything in the universe, be it physical or moral, is under the control of a rule free from human will', like a ball thrown up in the air which cannot help falling down. His conviction of the essential constancy of natural law is evident: 'Although civil laws are man-made institutions, they are subject to the necessary regulation of nature' and 'any deviation from the latter cannot fail to bring about mischievous results'. If any deviation from natural order cannot but effect mischief, the wilful intervention of the government in education and thought must also be harmful. 'To enact educational laws to appoint teachers is harmful to the freedom of education. To have a torture system in jurisprudence is harmful to the freedom of the people. To have decrees to control the press is harmful to the freedom of publication'.

Tsuda goes further than that. He claims that to widen municipal roads to obtain a beautiful view or for safety against fire is harmful because it is not the result of natural development. He refers to the contrast between Paris and London:

> To the south of Kyōbashi, Tokyo, roads have become wide enough to have a complete separation between pedestrian and other traffic, indeed as wide as the main streets in Paris, but they are government- and not popular-made. How can there be justification for spending huge sums of money levied on the people outside Tokyo in order to prosecute these extravagant works for the benefit of one particular part of the nation? . . . Beauty of outlook and protection from fire are all very well, but they are not justified unless they are the outcome of natural development. It is thus against the principle of equity.

The French, for their love of beauty, exploited their people to beautify Paris, and their government has often suffered popular revolts. The British, by contrast, are steady and faithful to the basic principles, so that their capital city, London, has long been free from civil war and popular turmoil and 'they are, in their wealth, second to none'.[24]

3. Tsuda's Economic Thought

Tsuda's economic thought is very much the same in nature as his political thought, being postulated on natural freedom. He did not publish books on economics, and he was even less inclined to express economic thought of his own than Nishi, who also left no specific writings on economic subjects. But the liberalistic character of his economic thought is clear enough in his writings. For him, economic freedom was also a means to achieve 'national prestige', in the sense of Japanese modernization. It is especially evident in his article 'Unsōron' (On Transportation).

In order to realize 'national prestige', Tsuda argues, it is as essential to develop transportation as to improve military forces and to expand education. Different countries produce different commodities, so that 'the wealth of the world can be commanded by collecting and making use of as many of those commodities as possible'. Therefore the richest country is the country whose transportation is most developed. What, then, is necessary for the development of transportation? He answers:

> It is generally assumed that no other country is so rich as Britain, as though there were no wealth in other parts of the world. Why is it that Britain has attained such wealth? It is simply because Britain enjoys the benefit of transportation more than any other country. The convenience of transportation in Britain is due to its favourable geographical position compared with any other country, but it is also due to its people, who compete with each other in intellect and labour. . . . That they can strive so hard is because their government secures for its people unrestricted freedom.

Thus it is asserted that in order to develop transportation and thereby to realize national wealth it is essential for 'the people to be provided with the unrestrained right to freedom', and that the best example of this is to be found in Britain.[25]

The liberalistic character of Tsuda's economic thought is even more apparent in his articles 'Hogozei o Hi tosuru Setsu' (Protective Duties Criticized) and 'Bōeki Kenkōron' (Balance of Trade).[26] For a more full-scale controversy on tariffs we must wait for the age of Taguchi Ukichi writing in *Tokyo Keizai Zasshi* (Tokyo Economist) and Inukai Tsuyoshi writing in *Tōkai Keizai Shinpō* (Tōkai Economist), but the controversy itself had been anticipated and Tsuda was one of the influential participants in the discussion. In 'Hogozei o Hi tosuru Setsu', he argues that according to those who advocate protection, imports have exceeded exports in recent years and consequently the outflow of bullion amounts to 17,000,000 yen, together with the salaries paid to the foreign employees and the interest on public loans. If things were to continue that way, 'the country's gold and silver must evaporate within some ten years'. He also counters the argument as untenable that in the old days European countries levied protective tariffs, and the United States still does so: 'Most Western economists, with hardly an exception, agree that protective duties do not protect but impoverish a nation'. It goes without saying that by 'most Western economists' he meant the orthodox free traders of the day. He continues that in the United States protective duties are advocated by many, but it is only because American industry is inferior to its European counterpart and for that reason, 'prices of manufactured goods cannot be as chcap in the United States as in Europe'. Even though it is harmful to the American people to levy high duties on imported goods, the aim is to develop their own industry, so that the benefit thereby gained may be returned to the people sooner or later. However, there can be no comparison between American and Japanese industries. The latter is far behind the former, and is next to nothing in comparison with European industry. This is exactly why we pay such an enormous amount of money to Western employees here.

Tsuda enumerates the points as to why he is opposed to the duties. First, under the current international treaties Japan has no right to tax imported goods; second, even in the case of such commodities as iron which incur enormous carriage expenses, imports are much cheaper; third, if there is a tax on Western wares which have already become necessities of life, there would be no home industry to protect by means adopted by the Americans; fourth, it is not proper to try to prevent Western commodities reaching the nation, because to love things Western is the necessity of the age; fifth, in the study of Western civilization Japan is in the stage equivalent to primary school, and the university stage is still far in the future. It is only too natural that Japan should pay a large sum for tuition fees without immediately gaining from it. The balance between imports and exports cannot but keep growing.

Will, then, the nation's gold and silver reserves drain away before too long, as some advocates of duties claim? Tsuda is confidently optimistic, answering, obviously quite unknowingly, in the same way Sir Dudley North did two centuries before him: 'Imports and exports are reciprocal. Sometimes the former may exceed the latter, but sometimes the balance goes the other way round. Just like heat and cold or ebb and flow, they fluctuate and thereby tend towards equilibrium'. No explanation is given as to why exports and imports tend to balance each other. Perhaps the meaning is implicit, in that, just like natural phenomena, economic affairs are regulated by one and the same principle of nature.

It may be reasonable to say that under the present conditions, with no autonomy in taxation, it is unrealistic to advocate protective duties, but it is certainly not logical to say that because Japan has no autonomy in taxation, free trade is tenable. Probably his main point was his belief in the naturalist view of the economy. He concludes:

> For a few years after opening our ports exports exceeded imports, and for the next few years imports have exceeded exports. No doubt for a few years to come, exports may be in excess. Imports and exports circulate according to the law of nature, so that there is nothing to worry about.

It is one thing, however, to say that in the long run imports and exports are regulated by the law of nature and tend towards equilibrium, but it is entirely another to state that Japan is at the stage of learning a great deal from the West and so is obliged to pay a 'tuition fee' and that 'the balance between imports and exports cannot but grow according to the growth of the nation's accumulation of knowledge'. It also contradicts his own assertion, already quoted, that 'for a few years to come exports may probably be in excess'.

Tsuda seems not to have realized this self-contradiction. In his article 'Bōeki Kenkōron', published in the following year, the arguments are essentially the same. The excess of imports is not to be worried about but rather something with which to be pleased. The situation is caused by a national trait, peculiar to the Japanese, to welcome and learn about novel things. 'Our nation is different from American or from African savages'. It is this alone that has caused the excess of importation over exportation'. Imports range from 'railways, the telegraph, lighthouses, mints, docks and all other apparatus' to 'tables, cake, and other like foods' of the West.

Tsuda's belief in enlightenment is evident when he thus contrasts civilized with uncivilized states and, from there on, claims that the imbalance between imports and exports is not to be lamented but to be welcomed. Repeating the same arguments propounded in the above article, that foreign trade is the same as the wind or the tide, which always tend to eventual equilibrium, he injects a more economic reasoning:

> Now the difference between imports and exports is too great and the imported foreign commodities exceed the purchasing power of the people. That is why Western commodities have fallen in price well below their original cost. Probably this year exports and imports will not fail to recover their natural balance or exports exceed imports to compensate for last year's imbalance. Unless exports and imports balance each other, foreign trade will not last long.

Thus he explains how the increase in imports has caused the excess of supply over demand and consequently the fall in the price of imported goods, which again would cause a decrease in supply, and consequently equilibrium between supply and demand or a change-over from an unfavourable to a favourable balance of trade. The afore-mentioned 'law of nature' would now appear to receive a theoretical economic endorsement.

Ushiba Takuzō at once took up his pen to contradict it, saying that what was to be worried about was not the imbalance between imports and exports as such but the outcome it must bring about. The imbalance would drain away gold and thereby make paper money 'a piece of wasted paper', the result being that business would stop, manufacturing would decay, farming would be deserted, mines would close . . . and the people would suffer most. Free traders claim, he continues, that imports and exports would come to balance each other in the long run and home industry would flourish without protection but, 'when does the time come?'[27] What Ushiba implies is that before the time really comes the national economy would be brought to ruin.

In this way Tsuda's attitude towards contemporary problems was, though within the inevitable bounds of the Meiji Enlightenment, fairly consistently, that of a liberalist political economist. His approach to practical policy problems was the same, because his thinking was supported by a firm conviction in natural liberty at a more general level. He writes: 'What is called law in the humanities originates mostly in the imagination. If a law clearly corresponds to the actual facts, then it is proved to be an inevitable law of nature. If not, it is simply a presumption'.[28] What, then, is that 'inevitable law of nature' in political economy? It is 'the nature of freedom' or 'self-interest'. Needless to say there are evils attached to freedom. 'The right of freedom is a right inherent to everyone, a right which is esteemed by all civilized nations. But no one is justified in abusing that right by injuring others'. It is because only its unfavourable consequences have been considered that for so long liberty has been regarded as a vice.

Likewise human love of profit has its merits as well as demerits.

'Self-interest' also has its positive as well as its negative side. 'Self-interest' is the propensity we have for increasing our physical well-being, but it has an evil tendency towards avarice and stinginess—faults which must be detested. It is wrong, however, to look only at the negative side without paying due attention to the positive side. Moral virtues have been taught, but not political economy, with the consequence that 'our people generally suffer poverty and lack physical happiness'. It was not understood that self-interest, too, belongs to the natural order of things.[29] Here we see that Tsuda's view of the traditional or orthodox conservative school of Confucianism is just like that of Fukuzawa and Nishi.

Thus to Tsuda, political economy was a science which could emancipate human nature from traditionally Confucian oppression. The background of all his thinking lay in the experience he had had of learning firsthand the systematic political economy of the West.

Part 3

The Institutionalization of Political Economy in Higher Education

4

The American Professors' Regime: Political Economy at Keiō University, 1890–1912

Norio Tamaki

1. Fukuzawa's Dream

In 1983, Keio University, the oldest private educational institution in Japan, celebrated with more than 24,000 students the 125th anniversary of its establishment. There were six students in 1858 when Fukuzawa opened a private school for young samurai on part of his clan's estate in Edo (Tokyo). His primary aim was to teach Dutch Studies which he had himself learned in the school of Ogata Kōan at Osaka. The number of students grew steadily. In 1867 a new site was bought and the school was renamed Keiō Gijuku.[1]

The first ten years of the life of Keiō Gijuku coincided with the most hectic and turbulent period in Japan's history. After the opening of the treaty ports to the West in 1859, Fukuzawa, who had a fairly good command of Dutch, visited the newly opened port of Yokohama. To his astonishment he found that the foreigners at Yokohama did not speak Dutch, as he had believed, and that all the signboards on their shops were written in English, which he could not understand at all. He started to learn English at once. Because of his increasing competence in the language and his enthusiasm, Fukuzawa was able to join the government missions first to the United States in 1860 (four months' stay), to Europe in 1862 (one year), and again to the United States in 1867 (five months). These three visits convinced Fukuzawa that Japan had to modernize and that it could never again close its ports and shut out the world. Fukuzawa's second visit to the United States was particularly important, for there he bought many books, including many copies of Francis Wayland's *The Elements of Political Economy* (first published in 1837).[2]

From the outset of teaching at the new premises in 1868, Fukuzawa took full advantage of numerous copies of the textbooks releasing his students from their traditional task of making handwritten copies of one single copy. Fukuzawa himself, together with his disciples Obata Tokujirō and his younger brother Obata Jinzaburō,[3] was in charge of the teaching of political economy. Fukuzawa and Obata Tokujirō repeatedly read Wayland's *Political Economy*, translating and explaining the text paragraph by paragraph. Books from the West, which were available to the students for the first time, must have been a source of wonder to them. The original Keiō Library catalogue gives a valuable insight into the textbooks used in this course, authors of which included F. Wayland, Nassau W. Senior, Henry Fawcett, J. T. Champlin, Francis Bowen, and Francis A. Walker.[4] Until 1890, when Keiō Gijuku entered a new stage as will be discussed later, political economy was taught as a subject called English economic literature'. Keiō's curriculum also included an 'introduction to economic doctrines'. This was taught by Obata Tokujirō for an hour every morning six days a week. No information remains as to what and how he taught.[5]

Wayland, the president of Brown University for 28 years, was a prolific writer in several fields, and his textbooks in moral philosophy, intellectual philosophy and political economy, some of which were translated into several languages, were widely used. Nassau Senior was the first holder of the Drummond Chair at the University of Oxford. Henry Fawcett was professor of political economy at the University of Cambridge, and a friend and disciple of John Stuart Mill. Francis Bowen was professor of natural religion, moral philosophy and civil polity at Harvard University for 36 years.

The Keiō teachers, however, were not satisfied with simply reading Western authors. They busied themselves with translation work and also decided to write textbooks themselves, as the list of Keiō publications in 1879 indicates.[6] One of Fukuzawa's first works, relating to the field of political economy in its wider sense, was *Chōai no Hō* (Bookkeeping) (Tokyo, 1873–74), a translation of H. B. Bryant, H. D. Stratton & S. S. Packard's *Bryant & Stratton's Common School Bookkeeping* (New York, 1871). He produced two other books of his own in the mid-1870s: *Minkan Keizairoku* (Popular Political Economy) (Tokyo, 1877) and *Tsūkaron* (On Currency) (Tokyo, 1878). The former was intended to be an introduction to economics for the beginner as well as for the non-academic reader. The topics ranged widely from 'prices' and 'wages' to 'transportation' and 'public utilities'. The latter was written as a response to monetary issues including the use of specie, currency, the quantity of money, and the exchange ratio between gold and silver. These examples were only part of Fukuzawa's extraordinarily wide-ranging works on matters pertaining to economic and social ideas.

Obata engaged himself exclusively in translation. He began with Wayland's *The Elements of Political Economy*, published in Japanese under the title *Eishi Keizairon* (Tokyo, 1870). Obata recommended that his readers first study another of his works, *Seisan Michiannai* (Introduction to Production) (Tokyo, 1870), which was composed of two parts. The first part was a translation of excerpts from Henry Mandeville's *The Fourth Reader for Common Schools and Academies* (New York). The excerpts, not quite five pages from the book, covered the topics of 'money' (pp. 39–40), 'commerce' (pp. 40–41), and 'exchange' (pp. 42–43). The second part was taken from Watanabe Ichirō's edition of *The Compendium of Political Economy: From the Lesson Book* (Numazu, 1869), which included a section, pp. 62–65, entitled 'Division of Labour: Adam Smith'.[7]

This extract was, in fact, pp. 13–15 of Smith's *The Wealth of Nations.* Obata's translation, incidentally, was the first introduction to Japan of Smith's famous work, if just a small portion of it. The remaining texts in *The Compendium* were from the works of Richard Whately, a successor to Senior at Oxford in the Drummond Professorship: *Easy Lessons on Money Matters* (Dublin, 1835) and *Introductory Lectures on Political Economy* (London, 1831). There were another two works in the 1879 list of Keiō publications: Morishita Iwakusu, *Rizai Zatsuron* (Miscellany of Economics) (Tokyo, n. d.) and Kai Orie & Mihara Kuniichirō, *Shōgyō Nyūmon* (Introduction to Commerce) (Tokyo, n.d.). The quality of these works does not compare with that of Fukuzawa's.

In spite of their enthusiasm in promoting the learning and teaching of the Western science of political economy, the work of these pioneers at this stage was no more than a duplication of Western ideas. In the late 1880s a way was found for them to do more original work.

2. A First for Keiō: Political Economy in a Private University

In 1886 the Imperial University Decree was promulgated, transforming the University of Tokyo into the Imperial University. Why not make Keiō a private university? This seemed to make sound sense, especially as the first president of the Imperial University was a Keiō graduate, Watanabe Kōki, but there were serious problems. The first and most pressing was that of finance. In the wake of the Satsuma Rebellion in 1877, Keiō Gijuku was facing grave pecuniary difficulties. Keiō decided to launch a fund-raising campaign. By the end of 1890 the magnificent sum of about ¥127,000 had been collected from Keiō graduates and their friends in the business world, including a contribution from the Emperor.[8]

What size should the 'university' be? How many departments or colleges should be established to make up 'Keiō University'? By 1890 the Imperial University had six colleges, each with its own graduate school with the authority to confer higher degrees.[9] A private institution like Keiō could not hope to emulate such an ambitious plan as that of the Imperial University which was allocated generous state funding. Keiō's founders had initially to be content with three tiny departments—arts, law, and political economy. Although Ernest F. Fenollosa had, between 1878 and 1884, taught political economy at the Imperial University, no department of political economy had been established. Indeed, the department of political economy at Keiō would, if successfully established, be the first of its kind. In the event, the Imperial University did not set up its department until 1919.[10]

Where then was Keiō to find good professors for the various chairs? After due deliberation 'Keiō University', though weak and vulnerable, decided to install professors from the Western academic world. They had from Fukuzawa himself a proud tradition of real and strong relationships with Western countries. This Keiō now determined to exploit. Arthur M. Knapp, head of the first Unitarian mission in Japan and a Harvard graduate, was a close friend of Fukuzawa and was staying near Keiō School. Their relationship led to an approach from Knapp, who disclosed to Reynolds, one of his colleagues at the American Unitarian Association, his intention with regard to Fukuzawa:

> The importance of the alliance with Mr. Fukuzawa can hardly be overestimated. You may find in Griffith's 'Mikado's Empire', p. 320, a description of his character and influence, and also, in Lanman's 'Leading Men of Japan' you will see that the longest chapter is devoted to him. But these accounts by no means give an adequate idea of the man, whose power has become so great during the past ten years as to make him the leader of the people. I have found a general consensus of opinion, even among those who do not sympathize with his thought that he is by far the most potent individual factor in the national life.[11]

Fukuzawa's request to search for three professors encouraged Knapp to develop an idea, which he disclosed again to Reynolds:

> Now in view of such needs, and I have by no means mentioned all of them, it seemed to me that Mr. Fukuzawa's request opened before us our opportunity for meeting some of them; and therefore I very frankly put before him my proposition, using in substance these words:
>
> 'While it is neither your desire nor my own to transform your college into a sectarian institution, or to bring it under sectarian influence, yet as you desire to employ these new professors only a portion of their time, and as the Unitarian Association will probably have in their field much incidental work for such men, and furthermore, as the additional salary which the Association might offer for such incidental work would, combined with your own offer, be likely to secure the service of first-class men, is there any objection on your part to cooperation with the Association in the selection to be made?'
>
> As I have mentioned above, his answer was a most cordial assent to the proposition, and the opportunity is now given to the Association to make an imposing beginning and to bring a strong Unitarian force upon the field at a comparatively trifling expense if only the men can be found.[12]

Although the Unitarian Association was taking advantage of Keiō's urgent needs, this connection was undoubtedly useful for Keiō, as later development was to prove. Knapp soon wrote to Charles W. Eliot, the president of Harvard University and 'the most influential leader in the educational activities of the country' (*Dictionary of American Biography*):

> It is because of the kindly interest which you have shown in my errand here that I venture to ask your help in a matter which may greatly affect the success of that errand. The situation is this: The Keiō Gijuku or Fukuzawa College is second only to the Imperial University and possesses many elements of strength which in the latter are lacking [some words illegible] friends have recently raised a fund to endow three new professorships and Mr. Fukuzawa had so far shown his appreciation of Unitarianism as to place in my hands the income of the endowments and to ask me to select the men to fill the chairs. Furthermore I have arrived at a frank understanding with him that if the A. U. A. wishes to engage the same

men for incidental work here in Tokyo, there would be no objection on his part to cooperation of that kind. As the object of the Endowment is to raise the standard of the college the men to be selected will be its new leaders and will exercise a moulding power over its whole life. The college now numbers more than a thousand students and with the addition of the new departments there will probably be an increase of three or four hundred next year. Mr. Fukuzawa himself is generally conceded to be the most powerful individual factor in the nation's life, and the proposed alliance is therefore greatly to be desired. . . . Now as the time at my disposal during my visit home this summer will be quite brief it will be very helpful to me in making the selection if the [one line illegible] candidates is [sic] ready for me on my arrival the last of May, and I therefore ask your kindly offices to put me, or Secretary Reynolds, into communication with such men as may seem to you to be suitable for the positions.

I will add that Mr. Fukuzawa greatly desires the establishment of friendly relations between his own institution and Harvard whereby the former may send its students and receive in return helpful suggestions as to methods of Education. I shall probably be the bearer of a message from him to yourself, looking forward to cooperation.[13]

As was predicted in the letter, Knapp brought Fukuzawa's message to Eliot, which read:

Having entrusted to Mr. Arthur May Knapp the selection of professors to fill recently endowed chairs in Keiō Gijuku and having instructed him to obtain such professors if possible from among the graduates of Harvard University, it is the further desire of the Authorities of our College to establish if possible more intimate relations between the chief seat of learning in America and the educational institutions of Japan. With this end in view I have therefore commissioned Mr. Knapp to confer with you upon the following points. . . . This plan has also suggested to me the question whether it may not be possible, by gradually filling our professors' chairs with Harvard graduates, and so far as may be, assimilating our courses and systems of instruction with those adopted by you, to carry such a method of examination so far as ultimately to apply it to the conferring of degrees, or in other words to make our institution, in some sense a Japanese branch of Harvard University. I am, of course, aware of the great difficulties in the way of bringing

> about so close an affiliation, but I have suggested it to Mr. Knapp as a subject of conference in the hope that some plan looking in that direction might commend itself to the consideration of your Honorable Board.[14]

Fukuzawa's plan of assimilating courses, systems, and degrees at Keiō to those at Harvard was indeed extraordinary, but may have been welcomed by the board at Harvard.[15] Could Fukuzawa's suggestion to make Keiō a 'Japanese branch of Harvard University' have come from Knapp? Fukuzawa's enthusiasm apparently moved the powerful Harvard president to conduct the selection process himself. Eliot's nominees were ready by the summer of 1889 and were, of course, welcomed by Keiō. The three professors were John H. Wigmore for the chair of law, William S. Liscomb for the chair of arts, and Garrett Droppers for the chair of political economy. Contrary to Fukuzawa's expectation, Liscomb was a graduate of Brown and not of Harvard University.

It was therefore by Unitarian initiative that the first chair of a political economy department of a university in Japan was filled. Harvard University was developing remarkably under its first Unitarian president, Charles Eliot.[16] Fukuzawa, himself non-religious, was favourable to the Unitarian cause, contributing articles to *Unitarian*, a Japanese-language periodical issued by the Unitarian mission.[17] The three professors and their families accompanied by Arthur Knapp arrived in Japan at the end of October 1889. The three professors set to work on their curricula and were soon ready for lectures. The first entrance examination was held in the middle of January 1890 and 59 students were admitted to the newly born Keiō Gijuku University.[18]

The Department of Political Economy was the largest of the three departments, with 30 students enrolled in a three-year course. From the outset, Keiō adopted the Harvard system of elective subjects. There were seven compulsory subjects and three electives in the first grade, five compulsory and ten electives in the second grade, and seven compulsory and four electives in the final grade. All subjects relating to the field of political economy were compulsory: principles of political economy, and modern economic history in the first grade; the science of finance, and history of protectionism and free trade in the second grade; and an introduction to various schools of political economy, statistics, and tutorials for economic subjects in the final grade.[19] The dominant figure in this hard-working department was, of course, Garrett Droppers.

3. The American Professors' Regime

Garrett Droppers was born in Milwaukee and brought up in the faith of the Dutch Reformed Church. Leaving a high school in Milwaukee, Droppers found a job as an assistant teacher of Latin and Greek in an unknown school where he was engaged for six years from 1878 to 1884. During these years he devoted much of his time to reading the works of Herbert Spencer and John Stuart Mill. His enjoyment of the works of these men encouraged him to look for further education. He enrolled himself as a BA candidate at Harvard University in 1884. The staff at the Department of Economics included several distinguished men, among others, C. F. Dunbar, monetary economist and editor of *Quarterly Journal of Economics* (1886–96), J. L. Laughlin, monetary economist and editor of *Journal of Political Economy* (1892–1933), and F. W. Taussig, an economist who succeeded Dunbar as editor (1896–1936) of the *Quarterly Journal.* Droppers graduated with a BA degree and, after some delay, was offered a job as principal at a high school in New Jersey. The high school generously gave him a year off for his own research from the summer of 1888. He took this opportunity to proceed to Germany where he undertook research at Berlin University under professors such as A. H. G. Wagner and G. von Schmoller. In July 1889, Droppers received a letter from Eliot enquiring whether he was willing to accept an offer of a professorship at a college in Tokyo. Droppers accepted immediately, returned to Massachusetts to marry his fiancée, Cora Augusta, in September 1889, before leaving for Tokyo.[20]

Droppers taught for eight years in the Department of Political Economy at Keiō, teaching the principles of political economy, modern economic history, the science of finance, and history of protectionism and free trade. The textbook for his lectures on the principles of political economy was J. S. Mill's *Principles of Political Economy with Some of Their Applications to Social Philosophy.*[21] Why did he choose this text? Droppers attempted to answer this question at a meeting of the Asiatic Society of Japan held on the 11th of March 1896, presided over by Sir Ernest Satow.[22] Droppers argued,

> You cannot define man wholly as a wealth producing animal, because he constantly sacrifices wealth for other objects, better or worse, and therefore the whole idea of the narrow orthodox school of basing economic laws on certain rigid hypotheses is an emasculating process which can only redound to the injury of economics and society. It is important to note at this point that the greatest writers

> on political economy have never in fact confined themselves to the narrow point of views here described. Almost without exception all the leaders of economic science, Adam Smith, Malthus, Jean-Baptiste Say, even Ricardo, discussed practical matters in their scientific books. John Stuart Mill in his great work on Political Economy goes out of his way to examine all sorts of questions not directly concerned with the increase or decrease of wealth; land tenure in various countries, the moral foundations of private property, poor laws, education, emigration etc.[23]

Droppers' admiration for Mill's broader view certainly influenced his selection. However, it must also be remembered that Mill's *Principles* was set for Harvard students during the late 1880s and early 1890s. Droppers himself had been reared on it. Laughlin, Droppers' tutor at Harvard, wrote in his preface to the edition of Mill's *Principles* published in New York in 1892:

> An experience of five years with Mill's treatise in the class-room not only convinced me of the great usefulness of what still remains one of the most lucid and systematic books yet published which cover the whole range of the study.[24]

It was therefore natural for Droppers to use Mill's *Principles* as a textbook when he himself came to teach at Keiō in Tokyo.

Modern economic history was another compulsory subject in the first grade. Although William Ashley's textbook on economic history *An Introduction to English Economic History and Theory* (Oxford, 1889) had already appeared, it was of little help to Droppers. Ashley's work was concerned with the medieval period, and in any case Ashley's examples were drawn from England. Droppers chose to develop his own syllabus, as he himself explained that 'the topics suggest the principal ideas connected with the various lines of economic development while the references mention the best authorities to guide the student in his research'.[25] The syllabus had more than 40 pages and the headlines of the topics are as follows:

> Commercial world in 1763—rise of cotton manufacture—rise of woollen manufacture—rise of iron manufacture—invention of the steam engine—banks in the XVIII century—effects of American Independence—France before her Revolution—effects of the Revolution upon France—England during the war with Napoleon—reforms in Prussia—development of American commerce and in-

> dustry—the adjustment of supply—labour and the factory system—migration of labour—improved transportation—advance of liberal ideas of commerce—the Zollverein—adoption of free trade by England—the (discovery of) new gold (mines)—France under the second empire—effect of investment in India—decline of American navigation—effect of the Civil War—American wheat in the European markets—the Suez Canal—general effect of improved communications—unification of Germany and Italy—the war of 1870–71—payment of the French indemnity—revolution of 1873—specie payment and the revival of industry—commercial crises—bank and public debt—the present trade of the world.

Droppers also prepared a comprehensive bibliography including Smith's *The Wealth of Nations*, J. S. Mill's *British India*, J. Steuart's *Political Economy*, H. D. Macleod's *Dictionary of Political Economy*, W. Bagehot's *Lombard Street*, and Josiah Tucker's *Four Tracts*. The syllabus must have been tremendously helpful for the students attending Droppers's lectures, as we shall discuss later. The syllabus afterwards grew to be Droppers's only book entitled *Outlines of Economic History in the Nineteenth Century* (New York, 1923). Clearly Droppers regarded himself as responsible for teaching economic history as well as political economy. Keiō was thus well ahead of its older model, Harvard University, where the chair of economic history was not established until 1892.

Droppers also worked hard on two other compulsory second-grade subjects, the science of finance and the history of protectionism and free trade. The course on the science of finance was taught under seven headings: preliminary remarks, literature and history of finance, general characteristics of government expenditure and income, domains, industrial domains, taxation and national debt.[26] Although Droppers defined the science of finance as political economy, he devoted 60 percent of the lecture time to explaining taxation.

For the lecture on the history of protectionism and free trade he prepared two notes, entitled 'Tariff History' and 'The Present Position of the European Tariff System'.[27] He discussed the events chronologically, but it was in this lecture that he made clear his own opinion on trade policy:

> From the dangers which practically beset in the policy of protection as well as to the peaceful development of the resources of all nations which human nature naturally looks forward to it follows that free trade must be the rule or at least the ideal to which we should look

> forward while protection is exception that is a temporary measure which is expedient in certain times and conditions . . . whenever duties on foreign articles can save home industries from real dangers. There is no reason why the protective measure should not be applied.[28]

Droppers's argument for conditional and temporary protectionism bore some relation to Mill's view:

> In countries in which the system of Protection is declining, but not yet wholly given up, such as the United States, a doctrine has come into notice which is a sort of compromise between free trade and restriction. . . . The only case in which, on mere principles of political economy, protecting duties can be defensible, is when they are imposed temporarily (especially in a young and rising nation) in hopes of naturalizing a foreign industry, in itself perfectly suitable to the circumstances of the country.[29]

Although there were many writers at this time who argued in a similar vein, perhaps Droppers was encouraged by these authoritative passages.

Droppers of course gave lectures in English. How did he manage to communicate with his Japanese students? Though they had taken elementary English courses, few students had experience in attending lectures given entirely in English. In these circumstances, he had no choice but to use written material to communicate himself to the students. Indeed, he read, aloud and slowly, Mill's *Principles of Political Economy* to the students, from time to time repeating and summarizing paragraphs. This style of lecturing was followed by his successor too.[30] A copy of Mill's *Principles of Political Economy*, published in 1891 as a volume of the series Sir John Lubbock's Hundred Books, has been preserved by Keiō Library, and this is the actual copy used by Horie Kiichi, one of Droppers's earliest students. Horie wrote in the margins numerous notes on the paragraphs and sometimes even criticisms suggested by Droppers. For instance, on page 368, we find this note: 'Mr. Droppers said that metals were ornamental and demands for them could not change rapidly according to people's taste, and therefore that Mill's argument was an exaggeration'. He also wrote down one of his teacher's comments, 'Mr. Droppers said that, if the value of money is constant, Mill's argument is correct'.

In teaching modern economic history, the science of finance and the history of protectionism and free trade, Droppers was obliged to be on his own. There were no adequate textbooks. Even in Western universities, lectures on these subjects had barely started and no standard textbooks had yet appeared. For the lectures on modern economic history, Droppers's own syllabus was undoubtedly useful. For the rest, all he could do was to speak slowly and clearly so that the students would not feel lost. The students on their part also had to work hard, or even harder than their teacher, taking notes as he lectured. They occupied every short break exchanging notebooks to fill in blanks.[31] Nevertheless, there were excellent students such as Horie Kiichi, whose fine notebooks prove his brilliance.

In the last three years of the nineteenth century, Keiō University made two notable changes in its system. In 1898, it introduced a five-grade system, in which students of all departments were offered a common course in the first and second grades and thereafter could specialize in either political economy, arts, law or in the newly established politics department. In 1900, the departmental system was abandoned and the students were instructed to select their subjects under the supervision of teachers. This system lasted only one year. Students, and indeed the public, found this confusing. The five-grade system continued until 1918 when the University Order was promulgated and Keiō, together with other private universities, first acquired recognized legal status.[32]

While Keiō University was undergoing major changes, the curriculum of the Department of Political Economy remained basically the same as before, with several specialized subjects being added. The choice of elective subjects broadened: in 1898, money and currency in the third grade; the history of economic thought and banking in the fourth grade; social problems, statistics, applied political economy and Japanese finance in the fifth grade; and lastly, in 1900, industrial economics, foreign trade, and transport were offered in the fifth grade.[33]

At the end of 1898, when Keiō was in the process of reform, Droppers left to take an appointment as president of the University of South Dakota.[34] Many gathered at the farewell party to give him thanks for his nine years of dedicated service and to wish him godspeed.

Eliot at Harvard was again asked to recommend a successor to the chair. Eliot wrote to Kamada Eikichi, the then president of Keiō, as follows:

> The person I have selected is Mr. Enoch Howard Vickers, who received from Harvard University in June 1893 the degree of Bachelor of Arts with honorable mention in Economics, and in June

> 1894, the degree of Master of Arts with highest honors in Political Economy. He subsequently held for one year an Assistantship in Political Science at the University, and was then appointed to a travelling fellowship in Social Science. This fellowship enabled him to reside three years in Europe, where he studied at both Berlin and Paris, travelled in Belgium, Holland, Germany, Austria, Hungary, Switzerland and France. He reads and speaks both French and German with ease and accuracy. He was born in Maryland in 1869, and his first degree was taken at West Virginia University in 1890. He was a resident student at Harvard University from 1892–95 in the department of Economics, History, Political Science and Sociology. He is an alert, refined and conscientious person of good health, quick intelligence and high character, capable of sustained and enthusiastic labour. He will leave home in time to teach in Tokyo by the middle of December.[35]

Vickers started teaching in January 1899. His duties were certainly heavier than Droppers's, partly because there were so many more specialized subjects to teach. Over long periods, he taught seven subjects, i.e., principles of political economy, economic history, the history of economic thought, science of finance, tariff history, social problems, and commercial policy. In addition he was responsible for several tutorials for senior students.[36]

In giving lectures on the principles of political economy, Vickers followed the method pioneered by his predecessor. However, Vickers, who was familiar with French, chose a French work on political economy as his textbook, i.e., the English version of Charles Gide's *Principes d'Economie Politique,* namely *Principles of Political Economy* (Boston, 1898), translated by E. P. Jacobson of the University College London.[37] Preserved in the Keiō University Library is a copy of *Principles*, actually used by one of Vickers' first students, which has many notes and insertions in the margins, though far fewer than those found in Horie's textbook.

For the rest of the subjects, a notebook copied by Masui Yukio, afterwards professor of French economic thought at Keiō and translator of F. Quesnay's *Tableau Economique*, reveals some aspects of Vickers' lectures. The notebook refers to a lecture on the history of economic thought.[38] Apparently Vickers dealt with ancient Greece through the Middle Ages to the Physiocrats and Adam Smith. The notes end suddenly here, though there remains a bibliography including L. L. Price's *A Short History of Political Economy in England from A. Smith to A. Toynbee*.[39] The bibliography suggests that Vickers may have brought his lecture up to date and also that his lecture was based upon a wide range of sources covering German and French literature. This was the first recorded lecture on the history of economic thought in modern Japan. Vickers's ability to use a wide range of sources aroused much interest among the students. Indeed, Keiō became one of the strongholds in this subject. Professor Masui Yukio himself was the evidence of this.

Vickers also applied the principles of political economy to Japan. He stressed that

> [Japan] should utilize to her own great advantage, every invention, every discovery, every scientific result obtained by the long labours of the Western people. Among the sciences which may be made to contribute to the substantial welfare and to the continuous progress of this nation, not one is of more value than political economy.[40]

He was also critical of the classical economists' writings:

> The scope of political economy has been vastly extended. The methods of accumulating wealth have been scrutinized more closely. The intervention of the state has been invoked and secured to prevent many methods which are recognized to be in flagrant conflict with general interests.[41]

Closing his argument, he recommended that in order to act intelligently, in order to accomplish these ends, *history* and its *theories* must be studied.[42] His arguments for state intervention and historical study were perhaps borrowed from the German Historical School by which he had been influenced during his stay in Berlin.

Vickers was very enthusiastic—always ready to give lectures and supervise his students. Takahashi Seiichirō, one of his students and later professor of the history of economic thought at Keiō, commented:

> I have never seen such a good and dedicated person. He lived on Mita Hill [the site of Keiō University] and devoted his whole time to giving lectures and marking exams, and so he did not have enough time for his own research. His intense dedication sometimes intimidated poorer students.[43]

His dedication and determination resulted in a difference of opinion between himself and one of his colleagues in the supervision of some examinations in 1909. Vickers resented a colleague because he had ignored his strict instructions. This may have accelerated his departure from Keiō. He left Japan in 1910 and was soon appointed to the Chair of Economics at West Virginia University. In 1938 he retired from West Virginia University, as an emeritus professor. He also became a life member of the Asiatic Society of Japan. He died in 1958, the year in which Keiō celebrated the hundredth anniversary of its establishment.[44] No obituary appeared in any Keiō publication.

4. Japanese Economists at Keiō: The Disciples of the American Professors

In 1899, on returning from a trip round European Continental countries, Britain and the United States, Kadono Ikunoshin, a teacher and councillor at Keiō, determined to reform the university. A new campaign for raising funds was launched. Money was needed to build a dormitory to accommodate more students and to pay to send teaching staff abroad. Keiō was in urgent need of conducting as economic a management as possible, and this resulted in the abandonment of the four-department system in 1899. As Kadono put it, Keiō faculty feared that the university would economize on the number of teachers required, by consolidating the four departments into one.[45]

A glimpse at the new curriculum gives us a remarkable insight into the new Keiō. Students were offered 46 subjects in all, of which 20 were compulsory and 26 elective. Of the 20 compulsory subjects, 11 were specialized subjects in political economy and law, and the rest were in language and history.[46] Indeed, all students were required to take nine subjects from the field of political economy. The balance in the curricula of the former four departments was lost, and Keiō University became almost 'a college of political economy'. Some of the graduates complained about the excessive emphasis on political economy.[47] According to its regulations, Keiō aimed to produce economists, businessmen, government officials, politicians and journalists,[48] but it is clear that Keiō deliberately chose to characterize itself as an institution specializing in educating economists and businessmen. Keiō's attitude undoubtedly reflected Japan's rapidly growing economy in the wake of the victory in the Sino-Japanese War of 1894–95 and also the fact that other institutions such as the Imperial University and Tokyo School of Special Studies (Waseda) still attached more importance to law and politics.

Responding to the changes in the structure of studies given in Keiō University, the students themselves, who majored in political economy, positively defended its policy for promoting and spreading the science. Yokoyama Rokusuke, later the founder of Tokyo Commercial Inquiry Agency, wrote:

> There are roughly two species of science, that is to say, concrete and business-related sciences on the one hand and metaphysical sciences on the other. In other words, the former is the sciences related to commerce, manufacture, agriculture, and so on, whereas the latter is those related to politics, law, philosophy, and so on.[49]

How, then, did he see the situation of Japan?

> In its present circumstances Japan has no choice but to base itself on trade and industry. To regard the prosperity of the liberal arts as the accomplishment of cultural education is no more than the false opinions of scholars who overlook the reality.[50]

He concludes with these strong words:

> I suspect that those who are responsible for education are making their policies with the view I have already shown. If their policies should become increasingly separated from trade and industry, and aim—in vain—at an undue expansion of metaphysical theory and literary education, I definitely raise objection, from the economic viewpoint, to that sort of policy.[51]

We can easily see in his argument the American professors' influence that 'the whole idea of the narrow orthodox school of basing economic laws on certain rigid hypotheses is an emasculating process which can only redound to the injury of economics and society'.[52] The American professors' regime was coming to fruition.

Another student, Mano Shunji, later a successful businessman, produced a more solid argument in a paper entitled 'Keizaigaku Fukyū no Kyūmu' (An Urgent Need for the Spread of Political Economy). Opening his argument, he notes,

> Those who discuss the economy of today are a small number of specialists and businessmen. Many people in society are alike in that they do not understand what the science of political economy is. Furthermore, if you look more closely into the economic knowledge of so-called specialists and practical men, you cannot help feeling dissatisfied. Their arguments may hit the mark, but, if people do not

> understand and use them, it is just like reading to the deaf, and will be useless.[53]

Then Mano discusses two possible social obstacles to the spread of political economy. In the first place, the science of political economy has been neglected by businessmen as well as by the majority of the members of society, partly due to the feudalistic residue which could be found in every layer of the society. More important, this neglect resulted in a shortage of enlightened businessmen. In the second place, the science of political economy is, Mano stresses, misunderstood, and those who speak as economists indulge in merely academic discussions. Political economy must be, Mano says, construed to explain production and distribution, as Sismondi argued, and as such give people a basis to help them understand economic phenomena. Next he turns to certain technical obstacles to the spread of the science: a shortage of economic literature, and a lack of consistency in the use of economic terms. The technical obstacles, Mano avers, could easily be removed. Thus he comes to the conclusion that,

> All in all, it is most deplorable for the development of a national economy that the Japanese people in general lack economic ideas. The most important and useful remedy consists in promoting the spread of the science of political economy. This is an urgent task.[54]

Here again we encounter the idea of applying political economy to real world problems, which was perfectly in line with Yokoyama's and the two American professors', as well as with Fukuzawa's, views. The changes in Keiō University's structure on the one hand and the two students' arguments on the other provide indisputable evidence that political economy was being firmly institutionalized in Keiō in the last decade of the nineteenth century.

Indeed, *Keiō Gijuku Gakuhō* (Keiō School Bulletin), which commenced in March 1898, published forty-seven economic articles in its first three years. The range of subjects is shown in Table 1. Their topics indicate that Keiō economists were most interested in the institutional development of the advanced countries, especially the United States and Britain. Their interests in the domestic economy were well balanced among its various branches.

Table 2 discloses that 25 out of 33 authors who wrote in the *Keiō Gijuku Gakuhō* were Keiō graduates, and of these probably 21 were taught by Droppers or Vickers. It is likely that they were all substantially influenced by the American professors' emphasis on the

Table 1. Economic Topics in *Keiō Gijuku Gakuhō*

A.	On foreign countries, mainly United States, Great Britain, and other European countries:	
	1. Institutions and recent developments	12
	2. Economic thought and history	8
	3. Free trade and protectionism	3
	4. Labour and social problems	3
		26
B.	On Japan:	
	1. Economy in general	5
	2. Transport	4
	3. Trade	3
	4. Agriculture	3
	5. Census	2
	6. History	1
		18
C.	On teaching the science of political economy:	
		3

Source: *Keiō Gijuku Gakuhō*, 1898, 1899, 1900.

importance of concrete science. By looking at the distribution of their occupations we can also sense the strength of that influence. The occupations of these 25 Keiō graduates were: businessmen, including bankers, 14; journalists, 4; Keiō lecturers, 4; politicians, 2; and government officials, 1. Thus, the occupational distribution of Keiō economists, remarkably, coincides with the purposes described in the regulations of Keiō University, though, of course, businessmen, especially bankers, made up the largest group. Keiō was perhaps the most notable supplier, among higher educational institutions, of businessmen, particularly bankers, at the turn of the century when the Japanese economy was greatly strengthening itself. It should also be noted that this was undoubtedly due partly to the fact that, through Fukuzawa, Keiō had strong connections with the House of Mitsui and its finance house, the Mitsui Bank.[55] The House of Mitsui was a most formidable concern, to which no other *zaibatsu* (financial group) could aspire, right up to the eve of the Pacific War. Many ambitious Keiō graduates of ability went into Mitsui. Keiō was not only a supplier of graduates for Mitsui, but certainly had some influence there. For instance, the reorganization and reconstruction, in 1891, of the Mitsui Bank, which had been suffering from bad debts during the 1880s, were conducted by a new management led by Keiō graduates who were appointed at the suggestion of Fukuzawa.

During the decade commencing in December 1892, when the first graduation ceremony was held, Keiō University sent out 217 graduates,

Table 2. Contributors to *Keiō Gijuku Gakuhō*

	Keiō Graduate	Taught by American Professors	Occupation	Topics of papers	Number of papers
1.	K	P	businessman	A1	1
2.	K	P	businessman	A1	1
3.			journalist	B4	1
4.	K		journalist	A4	1
5.	K		lecturer	A2	1
6.	K		politician	A1	2
7.	K	P	govt. official	A1	2
8.	K	P	businessman	B1 C	2
9.	K	P	lecturer	C	1
10.	K	P	businessman	B2	1
11.	K		lecturer	B5	1
12.	K	T	businessman	B1 B3	2
13.	K	P	businessman	A4	1
14.			politician	B1	2
15.			lecturer	A2	1
16.	K	P	banker	B1	1
17.			lecturer	A2	1
18.	K	P	banker	B3	1
19.	K	P	banker	B6	1
20.				A2	1
21.	K	P	banker	A1	1
22.	K	P	journalist	A1	1
23.	K	P	businessman	B2	1
24.	K	T	journalist	A2 B2 B4	4
25.	K		banker	B4	1
26.			banker	A1	1
27.	K	P	politician	A2 A4	2
28.	K	T	lecturer	A1 A2 A3	3
29.	K	P		A1	1
30.	K	P	businessman	B3	1
31.	K	P		A1	1
32.	K		banker	A3 B2	3
33.			lecturer	B5	1
34.	K	T		C	1

Notes: K = Keiō graduate; T = taught; P = probably taught; lecturer = Keiō lecturer. Symbols A1–C are keyed from Table 1.
Source: *Keiō Gijuku Gakuhō*, 1898, 1899, 1900.

of whom 132 were from the Department of Political Economy, 46 from Arts and 39 from Law.[56] This fact was evidence that, though Keiō called itself a university, it was effectively 'a political economy college', but, as such, Keiō could claim to be in the forefront of the institutions teaching the science of political economy at the turn of the century.

In 1899, Keiō decided to send six of its teaching staff overseas: two to the United States of America and four to Germany. Horie Kiichi was one of the two destined for Harvard University. As a student Horie had been a regular contributor to *Keiō Gijuku Gakuhō*. He wrote in favour of bimetallism, while in another paper he argued that for Japan free trade might be theoretically correct but that there must be freedom to have recourse to protectionism from time to time. On both bimetallism and protectionism, Horie appears to have been influenced by Garrett Droppers. Horie also instituted book reviews on Western scholars' works in *Keiō Gijuku Gakuhō*, reviewing seven books in the issue of May 1899.[57] This was an important innovation and must have been very hard work—Horie's dedication during his earlier career as a journalist as well as in his scholarly life is well known.[58]

Horie, together with fellow faculty members, left Japan in August 1899, arriving in Cambridge, Massachusetts, in September. On Droppers's recommendation he enrolled as an 'occasional' or 'graduate student' at Harvard. Horie stayed there for eleven months and then continued his studies at the University College of London, and at Berlin University. He returned to Tokyo in July 1902 and immediately embarked upon a writing programme that resulted in the publication of *Kahei Seidoron Gaiyō* (An Outline of the Monetary System) (Tokyo, 1902), *Ginkō Seidoron* (The Banking Systems) (Tokyo, 1903), *Saishin Kaheiron* (Money) (Tokyo, 1904), *Saishin Ginkōron* (Banking) (Tokyo, 1904), and *Zaiseigaku* (Public Finance) (Tokyo, 1908). In 1908 he was appointed Head of the Department of Political Economy. This effectively marked the end of the American professors' regime.

The last days of the Meiji era witnessed a drama at Keiō in which Japanese political economists took the place of the American professors. In 1909, *Mita Gakkai Zasshi* (Journal of Mita Society) was launched. Vickers contributed to the first issue a short paper on 'Some aspects of charity and providence'. This was the last appearance of Vickers in a contemporary Keiō publication. Vickers' relationships with the rest of the staff at the department had been deteriorating, and the situation came to its lowest ebb at the examination time of 1909, as we have already learned. He left Tokyo for a new job in the United States.

A year later, after Vickers' departure, the *Mita Gakkai Zasshi* issued a special number on Adam Smith.[59] The issue took up every aspect of Adam Smith, including a brief biography, the differences among various editions of *The Wealth of Nations*, the theory of politics, the theory of value, issues of colonization and public finance. There were seven contributors to the issue; four from the Political Economy Department, two from the Law Department and one a German visitor.

The most distinguished of them was Kiga Kanjū. Kiga was a member of the group despatched to America and Europe in 1899. He stayed in Germany and studied at the Universities of Leipzig, Göttingen, and Berlin. Before returning to Japan in 1903, he submitted a Ph.D. thesis, 'Die Bankwesen Japans', which was accepted by the University of Leipzig in 1904. He was a reserved man and his activities and abilities were eclipsed by those of Horie, but he did some remarkable work. Kiga's first work on his return to Japan was the translation of Eugen Philippovich's *Grundriss der Politischen Ökonomie* (1893–1907). The introduction of Austrian political economy certainly infused new blood into the Department of Political Economy at Keio, which had long been under the influence of English and American political economy through the American professors. Through Kiga's works, Keiō political economy had decisively entered a new era.

5

His Majesty's University: Tokyo Imperial University

Hiroshi Mizuta and Mikihisa Suzuki

1. Changes in the Higher Educational System after the Restoration

The University of Tokyo came into existence in 1877 with four faculties, of law, science, arts, and medicine. We will not enter into a discussion of the very complicated process of the changes which occurred in the higher educational system from the Tokugawa period to the Meiji era. Suffice it to say that the university was the successor to the Bansho Shirabesho (Institute for the Study of Barbarian Books) and the Igakukan (Medical Institute). The Bansho Shirabesho survived the political changes of the times, being reorganized first as the Kaiseijo (Kaisei Institute), and then into Kaisei Gakkō (Kaisei School), concentrating on Western learning. Quite independently, an institution called Daigakkō was established in 1869 as a stronghold of national studies (*kokugaku*), but proved to be a failure. In addition to the University of Tokyo, three schools of higher education were established for more urgent and practical purposes. These were the Technical College (Kōbu Daigakkō), headed by Henry Dyer of the Royal Technical College of Glasgow, the Law School, where Boissonade was a leading teacher, and Sapporo Nō Gakkō (Sapporo Agricultural College). Political economy was taught in Kaisei Gakkō, but the only information we have about the course in Kaisei School is that the texts used were those of Mill, Wayland and Perry.

With the Imperial University Decree of 1886, despite some opposition, the University of Tokyo was amalgamated with other higher educational institutions and reorganized as the Imperial University, with faculties of law, medicine, technology, arts, science, and agriculture. In 1897, when Kyoto Imperial University was established, the Imperial University was renamed Tokyo Imperial University. Political economy was first taught in the Faculty of Arts, following the British model, and later in the Faculty of Law, following the continental model. An independent Faculty of Economics was not established until 1919.

The first professor of political economy at the University of Tokyo was Ernest F. Fenollosa. He was assisted by Tajiri Inajirō, an employee of the Ministry of Finance, who lectured on public finance. Tajiri had been sent by the Admiralty to America in 1871, where he studied political economy at Yale University from 1875 to 1879. On returning home, he was appointed a junior clerk in the Ministry of Finance. Tajiri went on to become one of the founders of Senshū School, and his work is discussed more fully in that chapter. Here, we will only mention that his course on public finance at the University of Tokyo was based on the work of Paul Leroy-Beaulieu.

In the later years of his professorship, Fenollosa tried to reduce his teaching load to concentrate more on philosophy and fine arts. First he abandoned the course on politics, and then that on political economy. In 1884 his place was taken by Wadagaki Kenzō, one of the first graduates of the University of Tokyo and who had been sent by the Ministry of Education to study political economy in Germany. Although Udo Eggert and other German teachers occupied posts in the faculty at various times, they were by no means leading members, so that the appointment of Wadagaki marks the full institutionalization of political economy in Japan.

In addition to the courses on political economy given by Fenollosa and Wadagaki, other related courses, such as public finance or money and banking, were also taught by professors such as Udo Eggert, Karl Rathgen, and others. In 1908, the Department of Political Economy was established in the Faculty of Law. It comprised four chairs in political economy and two additional chairs for public finance and statistics. The course on public finance seems to have been considered as having special importance, not only because the Department of Political Economy in particular, but also the Faculty of Law as a whole, were the sole suppliers of human resources for the higher stratum of civil servants in the new government. Statistics was also appreciated as an essential source of numerical information about the nation, as is reflected in the original term applied to this discipline, *seihyō* (political tables). Unlike the four chairs in political economy, these latter two fulfilled a service role more characteristically expected of His Majesty's university.

Table 1. Graduates of the Faculty of Law, University of Tokyo, 1878–1918.

Year of Graduation	Univ. of Tokyo Faculty of Law	Department of Law	Department of Politics	Department of Economics	Department of Commerce
1878–1885	62	–	–	–	–
1886	–	10	1	–	–
1887	–	3	8	–	–
1888	–	46	13	–	–
1889	–	28	11	–	–
1890	–	55	28	–	–
1891	–	38	5	–	–
1892	–	61	9	–	–
1893	–	54	24	–	–
1894	–	40	34	–	–
1895	–	57	30	–	–
1896	–	61	36	–	–
1897	–	43	24	–	–
1898	–	64	43	–	–
1899	–	108	47	–	–
1900	–	73	56	–	–
1901	–	68	38	–	–
1902	–	83	58	–	–
1903	–	81	64	–	–
1904	–	75	78	–	–
1905	–	105	63	–	–
1906	–	152	84	–	–
1907	–	103	69	–	–
1908	–	206	78	–	–
1909	–	205	158	–	–
1910	–	199	131	–	–
1911	–	244	142	–	–
1912	–	226	134	73	–
1913	–	214	114	62	15
1914	–	286	128	53	11
1915	–	320	165	62	10
1916	–	262	223	55	13
1917	–	560	183	123	37
1918	–	321	133	30	26

Source: *Tokyo Teikoku Daigaku Gakujutsu Taikan* (Outline of the Sciences in Tokyo Imperial University), ed. by the University (Tokyo, 1942), p. 500.

Table 1 shows the number of graduates from the Faculty of Law in the period 1878 to 1918. Statistics on the professions entered by the graduates up to 1893 clearly show the role played by the Faculty of Law in the process of building a modern state: of 455 graduates,

139 entered the Ministry of Justice (including judges, prosecutors, etc.), 130 took up administrative posts in the civil service, 45 became advocates, and 12 were teachers, with only 22 going into business or banking (others include those who went on for further studies and those who died). Thus supply of the upper echelon of civil servants in the Meiji government was monopolized by the University of Tokyo's Faculty of Law, whereas the lower ranks were provided by the private schools. The business world recruited its people from commercial schools and Fukuzawa's Keiō School. Of the 317 graduates of the Higher Commercial School up to 1903, 172 entered business, 47 became teachers, with only 39 entering the civil service.[1]

2. Native Professors

The first native professor, Wadagaki Kenzō, did not publish anything on economics. His articles in the *Kokka Gakkai Zasshi* (Journal of the Society for State Sciences) introduced the outlines of the German *Finanzwissenschaft* (science of public finance) according to Luigi Cossa, and of the schools of political economy in Germany, especially that of 'Kathedersozialismus' (professorial socialism).[2] Although there was nothing original in his work, it confirmed the transplantation of German political economy to Japan. He translated Cossa's book on public finance, which was very influential at the time, from the German translation. The lectures given by Rathgen, even though they were not on public finance, also helped to strengthen the current. The final step in the shift to German thought on public finance is represented by the translation in 1904 of Adolf Wagner's *Finanzwissenschaft* (1871–72), and an original work by the Japanese economist Matsuzaki Kuranosuke with his *Saishin Zaiseigaku* (Modern Public Finance, 1912). Under the influence of these German ideas, Japanese studies on public finance began to consider the social implications of the taxation system.

From the end of the 1880s, two financial issues occupied Japanese economists, including the professors of the Imperial universities. The first was whether or not the land tax should be lowered to protect small-scale farmers, the majority of the Japanese rural population. This issue was the Japanese counterpart of the German discussion of a customs policy to protect its domestic industries. As early as 1891, Matsuzaki Kuranosuke, professor of public finance at the Imperial University, declared that there was a war of interests between the agricultural and commercial classes, and within the agricultural class, the interests of the small-scale independent farmers represented the public interest. These farmers were considered the foundations of the imperial regime.

The second issue was whether or not the taxation policy should provide a remedy for the inequality in income and property by the introduction of progressive instead of proportional taxation. Tajima Kinji, who became a professor at the Imperial University of Kyoto, first raised the point in his article 'Ruishinzeiron' (On Progressive Taxation) in *Kokka Gakkai Zasshi* (1895), in which he advocated progressive taxation as the remedy for the unequal distribution of wealth, because he keenly felt the increasing urgency of this social problem. Others, however, tended to be more or less ambiguous on the relative advantages of the two systems, depending on the degree of their sensitivity towards social problems.

Wadagaki was a pioneer, if not an original thinker, in public finance and the historical study of political economy. His interest in the history of economic thought made the subject mandatory in the curricula of political economy courses in Japanese universities.

Following Wadagaki, a number of his students were appointed to professorships in the faculty: Kanai Noburu graduated in 1885, and received his appointment in 1890; Matsuzaki Kuranosuke graduated in 1888, and was appointed associate professor in the Faculty of Agriculture in 1890, transferring to the Faculty of Law in 1898; Takano Iwasaburō graduated in 1895 and was appointed to a professorship in 1906, along with Yamazaki Kakujirō who had graduated in 1889; Yahagi Eizō graduated in 1895 and was appointed professor in 1907. They had all been sent to study in Europe, in Germany in particular, by the Ministry of Education, returning to teach subjects such as social policy, public finance, statistics, money and banking, commercial policy and agricultural policy. By the end of this period, the study of political economy in the Imperial University was virtually self-contained, though under strong influence from the German Historical School, especially professorial socialism.

3. Kanai Noburu and the Learned Societies

As the number of social scientists or socially minded intellectuals increased, they tended to organize themselves into societies. The Doitsugaku Kyōkai (Society for German Studies) was the first of these. The second was possibly the Kokka Gakkai (Society for State Science) which was established in 1887. The first article in the first issue of its journal *Kokka Gakkai Zasshi* was Wadagaki's 'Zaiseigaku Taii' (Outlines of the Science of Public Finance). The Hōgaku Kyōkai

(Society for Legal Studies) also published its own journal. As far as political economy is concerned, a third society, the Shakaiseisaku Gakkai (Society for Social Policy), was established in 1896, apparently in imitation of the German Verein für Sozialpolitik established in 1872.

Kanai Noburu was the first president of this society. After graduating from the Faculty of Arts of the University of Tokyo, he studied in Germany from 1886 to 1889, under Karl Knies, Joseph Conrad, Gustav Schmoller, and Adolf Wagner. In 1890, after visiting England, he returned to Japan. Although he had been sent to study public finance, he actually studied social problems. Given the situation in Europe at the time, his change of field is quite understandable, but when Kanai began to study social problems the subject was not recognized in the Japanese academic world—in fact, the University of Tokyo did not establish a chair in social policy until 1923. In Germany he studied the activities of the Verein für Sozialpolitik, and in England he stayed in Toynbee Hall and investigated the conditions of the poor in the East End district of London. During his stay in Toynbee Hall he met Alfred Marshall several times. He also studied the history of factory legislation in the British Museum, and was most impressed by Charles Booth's *Life and Labour of People in London* (1889–91).

He returned home just before the opening of the Imperial Parliament. Formally at least, Japan had become a modern state. Substantially, too, Japan's economy was moving toward an industrial revolution, a situation fully realized by the time of the victory in the Sino-Japanese War (1894–95). Inevitably, labour and socialist movements began to appear. Suppressing the socialist movement, on the one hand, the government started to consider the enactment of factory laws, on the other. In 1896 the government set up the Higher Conference on Agriculture, Trade and Industry and consulted its members on the problem. There were two types of opposition to factory legislation: the first came from the traditional employers, who said that the relation between employers and employees in Japan was almost the same as the relation between fathers and sons, so that it would be no use regulating the relationship by laws, since legal interference would destroy the traditional, good family-like relations in their factories; the second group of opponents were liberal journalists, who thought that factory legislation amounted to state intervention which violated the principle of laissez-faire. Kanai did not belong to either group. He thought that the interest of the state as a whole made it essential to improve the standard of life of the working class. Soeda Juichi, who participated in the conference as an under-secretary of the Ministry of Finance, joined Kanai in saying that factory legislation was ultimately profitable to the employers too. Although the opposition lost ground little by little, it took twenty years to get factory legislation enacted.[3]

In the meantime, a group of professors and graduates of the university was moving to organize themselves into a society to discuss social problems. In 1895, Yamazaki Kakujirō, who had graduated from the university in 1889, returned home from five years' study in Europe, bringing with him fresh knowledge about the German professorial socialism. Although he later specialized in monetary problems, as a young intellectual he could not keep from being interested in social problems while he was in Europe. In 1896, Yamazaki and some younger friends in the university set up a debating society on social problems. In their first meeting they discussed the relation between freedom of business activities and labour legislation, as exemplified by the German act on business (*Gewerbeordnung*). Later in the same year Kanai was asked to become de facto president and, with some members from outside the campus, the group was reorganized to become the Society for Social Policy. Following its German model, the society declared its opposition to both liberalism and socialism, its belief in the ethical mission of the state to guide the people, and that it was its aim to maintain an economic system based on private property and the realization of social harmony within this system, through the initiative of individuals and the power of the state. In 1907, the society expanded its role, opening its doors to increase the membership, and by so doing it became the gateway to an academic career for young economists. The later activities of the society, especially in the first two decades of the twentieth century, will be discussed later.

Returning to Kanai, two other areas of his activities should be noted. The first is his failure to have his plan for the amalgamation of the economics and politics sections into a faculty of political economy adopted. A Department of Economics was set up in 1908, in addition to the departments of law and politics, in the Faculty of Law, and a Department of Commerce was established in 1909—apparently a reflection of the development of capitalism in Japan. Kanai's intention was not to isolate economic and commercial studies in the narrow sense of the terms, but to achieve a unification of politics and economics as a science of state in a faculty of politics or political economy, in the strict sense of the word. His plan was not realized because of the strong opposition of the law professors, and, after that, the separation of politics and economics was regarded almost as a rule in Japanese universities. Politics remained in the minority in the law faculty, while economics tended to become non-political, pure economics or business studies. Incidentally, the situation of sociology was worse, for it remained, as it still does, a sub-department in the arts faculties.

The second is his promotion of a tough policy towards Russia. After the suppression of the Boxer Rebellion in 1900, the Russian army continued to occupy Manchuria. Kanai, with some fellow professors and some right-wing politicians, formed a debate society for discussion of Japanese policy towards Russia. At first their movement had little significance, but when it became known that Russia had not withdrawn its army as promised, seven professors, including Kanai, called on the prime minister and handed him a letter setting out their advice—which included the declaration of war against Russia. The government accepted the advice, and the group came to be called 'the seven doctors', a reference to the fact that under the old Japanese degree system the status of a holder of a doctorate was higher than that of a professor. Although there were changes in the membership, the group continued to be active, even after the war had begun, discussing, for example, the conditions for concluding the war. As a matter of fact, Japan had no strength left to continue the war after the victory in the Japan Sea in May 1905. The government asked the president of the United States of America to mediate, and agreed to rather unfavourable conditions for peace. When the conditions were published, meetings of discontented citizens erupted into revolt, and protesters set fire to several parts of Tokyo, resulting in the declaration of martial law. The seven doctors petitioned the Emperor not to ratify the peace treaty.

One of the group, Tomizu Hirondo, was militant enough to write that Japan should occupy East Siberia, and that it should not seek peace too early. In 1905 the minister of education suspended Tomizu from his post, without stating any specific reason. A meeting of the Faculty of Law denounced the action as a violation of academic freedom, and 191 professors, including faculty members from the Kyoto Imperial University, signed a letter of protest and threatened to resign unless the minister of education cancelled the order against Tomizu and resigned himself. The seven doctors eventually won the battle. Some historians celebrate their victory, recorded in Japanese academic history as the 'Shichi Hakase Jiken' (Seven Doctors Incident), as one of academic freedom over a despotic government, and compare the seven doctors with the seven professors of Göttingen. It must be noted, however, that the fight in Göttingen was in support of a democratic constitution, whilst that in Tokyo was in support of a war.

4. The Society for Social Policy

Confronted with social problems as a result of the Industrial Revolution, the professors studied solutions based on the German model. The economic and social thought of the German Historical School was first introduced to Japan through Nakagawa Tsunejirō's *Keizai Jitsugaku Kōgi* (Lectures in Practical Political Economy),[4] while Satō and Nitobe were attending the lectures of Richard Ely, who was trying to introduce the same ideas to the United States. Two years later, in 1888, the Ministry of Agriculture and Trade (later MITI) published its *Ōbei Junkai Torishirabesho* (Report of the Study Tour through Europe and America), and Wadagaki Kenzō published his 'Kōdan Shakaitō' (Professorial Socialists) in *Kokka Gakkai Zasshi.* In all of these introductory works the German Historical School was identified with the Verein für Sozialpolitik, and especially with its activities for social legislation. Its historical methodology and studies were almost ignored. In contrast with the individualism and materialism of the British School since Adam Smith, the nationalism and moralism of the German School were highly evaluated.

According to Nakagawa:

> The British School, since Adam Smith, has always constructed its theory on the principles of self-interest and competition. As a result, individualism prevails in political economy, and the contrast between the rich and the poor is especially apparent. However, a new school, called 'professorial socialism', has appeared recently in Germany. It is trying hard to improve the conditions of the poor and to decrease the difference between the upper and lower classes to a reasonable extent. The policy of the Prince of Bismarck also inclines towards this idea.

With this in mind, he foresees the necessity for factory legislation, for,

> although the conflict between capital and labour is still unknown in our country, thanks to the negligible difference between the rich and the poor, any careful observer of the situation in European countries cannot fail to see the fact that capitalists always fully control the legislation of the country—the workers are forced to remain in their miserable conditions for life, and long suppressed indignation explodes at last into socialist or communist parties which subvert the peace and order of the state. This is entirely the result of a political economy which has preached self-interest exclusively,

> without any reference to moral problems. However, happily enough, recently [in those European countries] the authorities have realized the importance of the matter, and are moving towards legislation to emancipate the poor from the bridle of capitalists and entrepreneurs, and to improve the conditions of female and child workers in factories.[5]

The Ministry of Agriculture and Trade's report explicitly includes Friedrich List as a professorial socialist:

> A man called Friedrich List founded Historicism, and introduced a proper way of solving social problems. This school, which rejects Smith's ideas, insists on paying special attention to the particular economic conditions of each country. Government should not leave matters to natural progress, but should help the weak and promote the idea of mutual benefit. It should not make the right of individuals the sole principle of the economy, but should cultivate a moral and patriotic mentality. This is a midway principle rejecting both oppression and laissez-faire.[6]

The report proceeds further to give an outline of German social policy and details of *Gewerbeordnung* (regulation of business), including factory law. From the point of view of administration officials, the report clearly anticipated academic discussion in the necessity of factory law.

Only a month later Wadagaki's article 'Kōdan Shakaitō' appeared. According to Wadagaki, there had so far been two major ideas put forward to deal with the inequality of the distribution of wealth. One was liberalism, from Rousseau to Ricardo, and the other socialism, from Plato to Marx. A third banner was being raised by the professorial socialists. The Society for Social Policy (of Germany) was chiefly against socialism and then averse to laissez-faire, and had proposed a third, new, principle. In contrast with the British School, which made the increase of products through free competition the supreme objective of human life, the society considered wealth as nothing more than the material means for the ethical ideal of life. It believed that human beings do not exist for the sake of production, but rather that they produce to live. It therefore gave priority to the welfare of the nation as a whole over the profit-making activities of individuals. Contrary to the British School's sole belief in the existence of a universally valid law of nature in a complicated economic world, the society believed that the first important step to be taken in dealing with the economic problems of a country was to consider the situation of that country and examine its historical and statistical data. While the British School was so narrow-minded as to confine itself to a particular feature of human nature, forgetting to see life as a whole, the society tried to see any matter with an open mind and a sense of justice. Whereas the British School saw only the importance of production, the society paid due attention to distribution, and the role of the government in the economic activities of the people and insisted on the total renewal of the fundamental structure of the national economy. Thus the society sought to protect the weak of a nation, to increase its productive forces, and to raise public spirit among the people. The society refused to accept the principles of atomism, individualism, and the laissez-faire of the British national economy. In short, the society gave priority to a country over its individuals, to public benefit over private profit, and to social over private economy.

In this outline of the Society for Social Policy, Wadagaki refers to its historical methodology, but in Japanese studies based on this school of thought the history of Japanese capitalism was ignored, with the exception of Fukuda Tokuzō's *Die Gesellschaftliche und Wirtschaftliche Entwickelung in Japan* (1900), which was written in German at the suggestion, and with the encouragement, of Lujo Brentano. The subject was to be taken up later by Marxists, with brilliant results.

After giving some examples of policy and legislation based on these principles, Wadagaki concluded that the formation of the society's ideas did not come about by accident, but rather as a direct result of the situation in Europe at the time. He left to his disciples the task of tackling the corresponding problems in Japan. Towards the end of his article he described the respect and status commanded by German scholars: 'Even prime ministers listen to their warnings and advice, as if they were oracles descending from the clouds. . . . Their contribution to social happiness and state policy-making is comparable with that of the parliament. . . . Happy is the country rich in scholars of this kind'. Here again, he foretold the future of his disciples, such as the 'seven doctors' who urged the government to take a tougher line on Russia.

Kanai, Wadagaki's first student, returned from abroad to a professorship in 1890. In December of that year, he gave a lecture entitled 'Genkon no Shakaiteki Mondai' (Social Problems of Today) before the Society for State Science. According to Kanai, social problems, especially labour problems, had not yet arisen in Japan, but were already serious in Europe. He reported on the work of Knies, Wagner, and Schmoller in Germany, and of Booth and Webb in England. 'What is the labour problem?' he asked. 'Socially speaking, as there is a formidable gap between the rich and the poor, when workers become conscious of this gap their new consciousness plays an important role in the labour problem'. Social problems, in this sense, are more serious in Germany than in England, and 'do not exist in Japan'. However, they would appear in Japan much sooner than generally expected. 'Therefore', he concluded, 'we have to be well prepared for their appearance, first of all by the enactment of factory regulations'.[7] He had clearly seen that social problems of this type are not so much simply the result of the unequal distribution of wealth, as the result of the birth of a class consciousness among the workers and their social movements.

In another article, 'Boissonade-shi no Keizairon o Hyōsu' (A Critique of the Economic Theory of Mr. Boissonade), *Hōgaku Kyōkai Zasshi* (Journal of the Society for Legal Studies), 1892–93, he criticised Boissonade's opposition to factory legislation from the point of view of liberal political economy.

According to Kanai:

> The principles of free trade and laissez-faire which prevail in the business society of England curiously have not much influence over the workers. The social policy of protection and state intervention has been developed instead. In strange contrast to Britain's general economic policy as a whole, the factory legislation introduced there has become a model for other countries. . . . So-called natural harmony can be seen only among those who are equal to each other in social and economic position, without much difference in power and wealth. On the contrary, between the workers and capitalists, free competition will destroy the harmony of the economy and their peaceful relations. Absolute freedom will result in practical inconvenience.

It was after these theoretical preludes that, in 1896, the establishment of a society to study social problems was proposed immediately after the Sino-Japanese War. At first it was a small debate society within the Imperial University, but, as mentioned above, it was reorganized in the following year as the Society for Social Policy, with Kanai Noburu as president, and a number of members from outside the university. Of the four initial members of the reorganized society, three were graduates of the university, and another was from the universities of Halle and Freiburg; three were in their twenties; and by profession they included a professor, a rural landlord, a leading businessman, and a senior official of the Ministry of Agriculture and Trade.

Thus the Society for Social Policy was established in the final stage of Japan's industrial revolution. As foretold by Kanai, social and labour problems appeared in Japan much earlier than generally expected. In 1889, Yokoyama Gennosuke wrote in his *Nihon no Kasō Shakai* (Lower Social Strata of Japan),[8] that the Sino-Japanese War had begun an epoch in the history of labour problems. The society continued its activities until 1924 as the only organization of economists, theoretical or practical, in Japan. During its heyday, membership reached over two hundred, including amongst them even some labour leaders, such as Katayama Sen.[9] For academic economists, membership of the society was an essential qualification to practice their profession. However, the historical studies which distinguished its German model were entirely neglected under the influence of the many practical economists among its members from business and government.

5. Movement Towards Factory Law

The first subject of study and discussion taken up by the Society for Social Policy was, naturally enough, factory law. This problem had first been addressed in the late 1870s by the Department of Hygiene of the Ministry of Home Affairs. The leaders of the Meiji government were well aware of the need for healthy soldiers and workers to maintain the growth of their newly emerging modern state. In 1881, the Ministry of Agriculture and Trade was set up to take over economic affairs from the Ministry of Home Affairs. Starting with a preliminary survey in the following year, the new ministry drew up the first drafts of the Workers' Act and Apprentices' Act in 1887, perhaps on the model of the British Factory Consolidation Act of 1878. The drafts contained the following protective clauses on child and female labour: no factory may employ a child less than ten years old as a labourer, and even apprentices may not be younger than eight years old; the workday for those younger than fourteen may not exceed ten hours; and female and younger [i.e., those less than fourteen] labourers may not be put to work during the night. These regulations were rather advanced for their time, and therefore failed to obtain the consensus needed within the ministry. In contrast to this abortive attempt to introduce protective legislation, in the same year the Security Act was enacted to suppress the growing social movements, including trade unionism.

In 1891, the ministry consulted the National Federation of the Chambers of Commerce on the Workers' Act, but again met with no success. It was only after the end of the Sino-Japanese War that tolerable progress towards actual legislation was finally made. It was in that year that the Society for Social Policy was established, and the ministry looked to it for public support. The ministry established the Higher Conference on Agriculture, Trade and Industry, and brought up the issue of the Workers' Act at its first meeting in 1896. The representatives of the ministry explained how essential it was that factory legislation, modelled on the British law, should be enacted as soon as possible because labour was the prime mover of industry. Businessmen in the conference were generally unhappy with the proposal. Representative of their concern was Shibusawa Eiichi, an outstanding business and industrial leader: 'I am not opposed to the law itself, but if you intend to simply copy the European model based on pure theory, then I cannot agree with you, by any means. . . . We should start by investigating the actual situation in this country'. Although no records survive from the second meeting, at the third meeting of the conference, which took place in 1898, the ministry produced a draft of the factory law, prefaced, 'Kōjōhō Seitei Riyūsho' (Reasons for the Enactment of the Factory Law), which pressed for the legislation:

> We see that in the relations between factory owners and workers, the old sense of father and children, or teacher and pupil, is finally fading away, and being replaced by the awareness of class differences. This is an inevitable result of industrialization, and a universal phenomenon in the history of the world. Attachments have passed away, but legal relations have not yet become established to take their place. . . . The most urgent policy for the sound development of our industries is to set up a legal framework to regulate the relations between the two parties. Such legislation will stabilize business management for factory owners, on the one hand, and secure a healthy labour force, on the other.[10]

The conference accepted the ministry's draft for the factory law by the narrow margin of fifteen to thirteen, after considerable revision—such as the extension of the maximum workday for female and child labourers from ten to twelve hours, and the dropping of the prohibition on night work. One of the dissenting liberal economists, Taguchi Ukichi, opposed the law on the grounds that, with free competition, capital and labour were already in harmony, and that political interference was against the logic of the economy.

Under Shibusawa's chairmanship, the third conference adopted a resolution calling on the government to conduct a special investigation on the current conditions of factory labour. In 1900 an extraordinary budget was allocated to the study, and its report, *Shokkō Jijō* (The Condition of Labourers), was published in five volumes from 1901 to 1903. Kuwata Kumazō, one of the founding members of the Society for Social Policy, was commissioned to conduct the study. The eldest son of a great rural landlord, he had first graduated from the Imperial University, and then studied in Europe at his own expense. Although in the following decades Marxism was embraced by many of the sons of the rural gentry, whose studies at the Imperial University revealed the parasitic nature of their position in society, Kuwata stayed firm in his role as an enlightened landlord all his life. While he and his collaborators worked on the report, the discussions on factory law continued in the meetings of the Society for Social Policy, yet despite the agreement and support built up for the legislation, it was another decade before the factory law was actually enacted, in 1911, and brought into force, in 1916.

In 1902 the ministry had prepared a draft to be brought before Parliament, but the critical situation on the brink of the Russo-Japanese War prevented its introduction. It was the conspicuous increase in the number and scale of labour conflicts after the war, which shocked even the business managers and entrepreneurs, that at last made measures for the stabilization of labour-capital relations seem desirable. In 1906–7, there were frequent strikes in national munitions factories, at the Mitsubishi Dockyard in Nagasaki, and in the mines—the army was called in to suppress the striking miners. In this climate, which seemed to favour the introduction of their legislation, the ministry sent a draft to Parliament, but it was rejected following the impasse on the clause prohibiting night work for female labourers: the Central Federation of Hygienic Workers insisted on the clause, and the industrialists were just as adamantly opposed to it. In the following year, a revised version was presented for discussion by the Committee on the Investigation of Production. Asked whether it was intended to protect the workers or the industries, the ministry replied that factory law was not only for the protection of the workers, but was also necessary for the sound development of industry. Revised again, the legislation finally passed through Parliament in early 1911, after a year of major political events, such as the annexation of Korea as Japan's second colony, and the frame-up of Kōtoku Shūsui and other anarchists in the High Treason Incident. The final revisions to the law show some compromise—the maximum workday was twelve hours rather than ten, the age limit applying to child labour was ten rather than twelve, and the application of the clause prohibiting night work for female labourers was suspended for fifteen years.

6. His Majesty's Professors off Campus

In 1899, the Society for Social Policy issued its statement, 'Shakaiseisaku Gakkai Shuisho' (The Statement Establishing the Society for Social Policy), which was reprinted in the *Kokka Gakkai Zasshi*:

> It is our great pleasure to see an extensive development in our industry and trade, and an evident increase in national wealth. However, as a result of this, the difference between the rich and the poor tends to increase, and there seem to be symptoms of social discord. For instance, the conflict between capitalists and workers has already appeared in embryonic form. Whenever we think about this, we cannot keep from trembling with fear. The examples of possible results are not so far from us, in Europe. If we do not prepare a remedy now, it will be too late for regrets later. Therefore we would like to organize ourselves into a society to discuss the problem. We oppose the principles of laissez-faire, because self-interest in its extreme, and free competition without limit, will result in widening the gap between the rich and the poor. We also oppose socialism, because the destruction of the present economic structure and the annihilation of capitalists would be hurtful to the development of the nation. Our conviction is that we should maintain the present economic system based on private ownership, and prevent class conflict within its own framework through individual action and the power of the state, and so realize harmony in society. The main aim of our society is to study social problems in the light of these principles, examining actual cases within and without the country, and referring to scientific theory. We dare appeal to the public through this statement.

Evidently the first target of the society was the principle of laissez-faire. However, as we have already seen, while Kanai had said in 1890 that social problems did not exist in Japan, the discussion of factory regulations had been going on in the Ministry of Agriculture and Trade since 1881, perhaps even since the 1870s. Civil servants were more sensitive than academics to the actual state of society, and it was only after the Sino-Japanese War that the society began to consider the matter seriously. When the government hesitated over taking to parliament the draft law agreed on by the third meeting of the Higher Conference on Agriculture, Trade and Industry, the society moved to promote the law. Its leading members lobbied members of parliament and businessmen, but the influence of the liberalism of economists such as J. S. Mill was too strong and their attempts at persuasion fell on deaf ears. The society decided to appeal to the public in open lectures.

In 1898, Kanai wrote an article, 'Kōjōhōan ni Taisuru Rōryokusha no Iken o Terasubeshi' (The Workers' Opinion of the Draft Factory Law Must Be Heard) (*Kokka Gakkai Zasshi*), in which he maintains that the aim of social policy is to keep or create balance or harmony between capital and labour:

> To be fair to the general trend in public opinion on the matter, we have to listen to the voice of the workers, who form one of the interested parties. . . . The government asked for the opinion of the National Federation of the Chambers of Commerce, and later consulted the Higher Conference, . . . but Chambers of Commerce consist exclusively of capitalists and businessmen, who are one of the parties involved, and the Higher Conference, even though it includes some neutral members, also consists mainly of the same interests. There is hardly anybody representing the workers. It is not fair to listen only to the voices of these two parties and ignore the workers. There are orderly organizations of workers, such as the Tokyo Industrial Society, the Union of Iron Workers, and the Society for the Promotion of Trade Unions, and there would be no inconvenience in consulting them. . . . It is clearly wrong to decide the principles of factory law, the first step in our social policy legislation, by consulting only one side of the concerned parties, and ignoring the other.

Kanai is promoting fair consultations, but he is by no means advocating the cause of the workers. On the contrary, in the following year he emerged as a fierce opponent of the socialist Katayama Sen.

For a time after this, the factory law lost its prominence in the society's activities, partly because its leading members were involved in the debate over policy towards Russia which led up to the 'Seven Doctors Incident', and partly because of the society's attitude towards socialism. At the time, both the government and public opinion were fully occupied with problems relating to the Russo-Japanese War. However, with the war over, the society took the matter up again in 1907 as the main subject of the lectures at its first general meeting, 'to draw the attention of the public to the necessity of preparing factory legislation through discussion on the matter and examination of the articles of the law, if necessary'. The meeting was open to the public, and attracted an audience of seven or eight hundred, gathered to hear twenty speakers and two guests of honour address the matter. In his introductory lecture, Kanai told the audience that

> factory legislation is a necessary product of the industrial revolution, or innovation. As Japan has reached this stage of development, the legislation is a matter of necessity, but we should not take a straight translation of the Western model. The government must make it a Japanese law. The aim of social policy is not only to protect the workers, but to achieve harmony in the state by protection. First of all we have to have the law enacted.[11]

The second lecturer was Tajima Kinji, a professor at the newly established Kyoto Imperial University. According to him, since the Meiji Restoration, the government had never adopted the principles of laissez-faire. From the major areas of production to the railways and banking, the government had provided everything for private enterprise. The policy had been along protectionist lines, but only to protect capital. The only protection in the interest of workers that we might find is a discount on railway fares for emigrants.

Next was Kuwata Kumazō, editor of the survey of working conditions mentioned earlier, who based his lecture on that investigation. He admitted that the government report was rather reserved on many points, and evasive on the description of the actual situation. He therefore undertook to explain the situation of the workers as he himself saw it. According to him, the number of workers to whom factory law would apply was half a million, whereas the British law covered four million workers. Of those half a million Japanese workers, ten percent was younger than fourteen, including some no more than six or seven, and seventy percent was female, ninety percent of whom worked in the silk industry for twelve to fifteen hours a day. In such factories, workers were ordered to take no more than five minutes for meals, and although night work was usually done in shifts, sometimes workers were forced to work twenty-four or thirty-six hours continuously. After observing such conditions, and knowing that there were many others who could confirm his observations, he had no doubt about the necessity for factory law. However, he also conceded that allowance needed to be made for the stage of Japanese industrial and political development, and regretfully proposed a compromise by which the age limit would be twelve, the workday would be twelve hours long, including an hour or more for meals, and night work would generally be forbidden, and when permitted, would be only in shifts. His political stance in the discussion of factory legislation was his conviction of the need both to resolve social problems within the country, and to maintain strong forces overseas—he believed that a strong army could not be maintained without the introduction of factory legislation to prevent the rise of socialism.

As a guest of honour, Shibusawa Eiichi (by then, Baron Shibusawa) told the meeting that he was a midwife attending the birth of a factory law which he did not want to be born. He had studied only traditional Chinese learning, but if every member of the business world would follow the teachings of Confucius, there would be no need to trouble the Society for Social Policy with their discussion. Although, he concluded, he dared not say that it was still too early for factory law, he urged those present to study the actual situation in the textile and other industries carefully.

The speeches of two other speakers also deserve mention. Soeda Juichi, the other guest of honour, who had studied at Cambridge University, particularly with Alfred Marshall, raised the following three points: first, if socialism were transplanted to Japan, it would not take a moderate form like that in Britain because of the national character of the Japanese, who would need the control of a factory law to prevent their socialism from becoming radical and violent; second, factory legislation should include clauses covering the responsibilities of employers for the working conditions, and the establishment of factory inspectors; third, when confronted with the practices of foreign countries, Japanese political economy should be proud of the traditional good relationship between its capital and its labour, that is to say, the master-servant relationship as an inheritance from feudalism. This last point was severely criticized by many, but it remains typical of the thinking of many of the leaders of Meiji Japan, however much knowledge they had acquired, directly or indirectly, of Western learning.

A sharp rejoinder came from Fukuda Tokuzō, a professor at Tokyo Higher Commercial School who had studied under Lujo Brentano. He pointed out that it was that very master-servant relationship which prevented improvement in the conditions of the workers. Fukuda asked those opponents of factory law who argued that imitation of Western legislation was not suited to the Japanese situation why imitation of the Western factory system had been adopted? He saw no reason for the liberal opposition to factory law, to say nothing of the socialist opposition, because factory law was intended to help those who could not help themselves within the principles of 'self-help'. Takano Iwasaburō, who after World War II published a draft of a constitution for the Japanese Republic, also criticized Soeda's praise of the master-servant relationship as a feudalist utopianism, which was just as utopian in its ideas as socialism. He argued that the workday should be eight hours, instead of the twelve suggested by Kuwata, and that the trade unions must also be inspected to avoid their manipulation by capitalists.

In 1908, the Ministry of Agriculture and Trade asked the society for advice on the drafting of the factory legislation. Minor improvements were proposed, but rejected.

7. Social Policy versus Socialism

As we have already learned, the Society for Social Policy was first opposed to the principle of laissez-faire. Socialism was its second target. However, as Soeda pointed out, state protection of industries was firmly established before the society came into existence. The issue on which the society opposed laissez-faire was the arbitrary and despotic exploitation of workers. It seemed therefore that the society accepted state intervention in industry in order to protect the workers; yet, as was the case with its German model, the protection of workers advocated by the society was actually the protection of capital through the expedient of the peaceful co-existence of capital and labour. The protection of labour from arbitrary and excessive exploitation was thought to be the best means of preventing the labour movement from becoming revolutionary and dangerous. Social policy was indeed the regulation of capital, but it was regulation to protect it from the danger of socialism. The difference between the German model and its Japanese version was that the socialist movement had existed before the formation of the German society, whereas it had been only an idea in Japan before the establishment of its society.

The idea of socialism was first introduced to Japanese readers by an article published in a Unitarian journal in 1881. The name of Karl Marx first appeared, in connection with Bakunin and Kropotkin, in 1882 in a book on the Russian Nihilists. In 1897, an abridged translation of Ely's *French and German Socialism in Modern Times* (1880) brought to Japanese readers a general introduction to Marx and his ideas, perhaps for the first time. In the meantime, trade unionism was becoming a reality. In 1890, in San Francisco, some forty Japanese labourers, including Takano Fusatarō, organized themselves into the Shokkō Giyū Kai (Friendly Society of Working Men of Justice) to study the actual situation of the labour problem in Europe and America, to prepare solutions for problems anticipated for Japan. Most of them returned home in 1896, the year of the foundation of the Society for Social Policy, and established an identical friendly society in Japan. They sent a circular, 'An appeal to working friends', to factories encouraging the labourers to organize themselves into trade unions. Their efforts resulted in the formation of Rōdō Kumiai Kiseikai (Society for the Promotion of Trade Unions), which in turn gave birth to the Union of Iron Workers before the end of the year. Early the following year there was a massive railway strike, out of which came the establishment of a union of engine-drivers, the Society to Remedy Japan Railways. The Friendly Society of Printing Workers followed. All of these organizations aimed primarily at mutual financial help for workers. For the Union of Iron Workers, this very aim brought dissolution, through a failure in financial administration. At the same time, the government sought to suppress the trade unions through the enactment of the Security Police Act in 1900, and in 1901, on the grounds that it advocated socialism and universal suffrage, the Society to Remedy Japan Railways was disbanded.

Ironically enough, the suppression and decline of trade unions led some of the leaders to further involvement in socialist movements in search of an outlet for their concerns. In October 1898, the Society for the Study of Socialism was established. Its name was changed to Socialist Society in 1900, and in the following year six members of the society, five Christians and an anarchist, founded the Social Democratic Party. Although the party was immediately suppressed, its Manifesto was published in several newspapers. The manifesto called for, among other demands, municipal ownership of street trams, the outlawing of night work for juvenile and female labourers, an eight-hour workday, and the enactment of trade union law. The party presented itself as an organization trying to interweave socialism and democracy under the conspicuous standard of socialism. Katayama Sen, who was responsible for the publication of the manifesto in a labour journal, *Rōdō Sekai* (World of Labour), was accused of a breach of the Newspaper Act, but the District Court of Tokyo dismissed the case on the grounds that the publication of the manifesto could not be considered a subversion of social order.

Observing these developments in socialist thought and movements, the leading members of the Society for Social Policy felt it necessary to make clear that, although there was some similarity in ideas, the society was by no means a socialist one. In 1901, they rushed into print their statement, 'Social Policy and Socialism', more generally known as the 'Apologia of the Society for Social Policy'. Signed by

Wadagaki, Kanai, and Kuwata, it contained the following statements:

> We are quite happy with the manifesto which made the idea of socialism in this country quite distinct, so that the public can readily distinguish between socialism and social policy. . . . We are trying to maintain the present social structure, based on free competition and private property. No doubt we can solve social problems within this framework. . . . If the similarity of our policy with that of socialists should make us socialists, even Bismarck and the German Emperor can be called socialists, because of their workers' insurance and factory law. . . . On the contrary, the very fact that the socialists follow our lead, by taking up the issue of factory law as part of their programme, proves that they have realized that socialism is not feasible.

Although the statement directly criticized the manifesto, it implicitly criticized left-wing members of the Society for Social Policy itself. Kanai's main opponent within the society was Katayama Sen, whose application to join the society had been approved only with difficulty. Although he had said, in a meeting of the society in 1899, that he had no doubt that the Japanese labour movement would develop peacefully and achieve the ideal harmony between capital and labour, a few months later he declared in a lecture sponsored by the Printing Workers Union:

> Harmony between capital and labour is indeed necessary. But under today's conditions, it is not at all possible to achieve such harmony. The so-called harmony of today is not harmony at all. . . . It is the master-slave relationship. . . . True harmony will be achieved by labourers under the standard of socialism, and we must lead them towards it. . . . Socialism is not only for labourers, it is for mankind.

Following Katayama as a speaker at the same meeting, Kanai criticized Katayama vehemently:

> The reason for the present success of trade unionism is its refusal of political relations and its concentration on economic activities. . . . We must make it clear before the trade unions that we oppose socialism, as advocated by Mr. Katayama. . . . As members of the Japanese nation, we cannot agree with it, because it will destroy the present structure of the state.

It was ten days after this exchange that the society issued its 'Apologia'. Kanai's diary reveals that, even before their public clash, Katayama had been asked to resign from the society. It must be noted that Kanai's fundamental objection to socialism was the damage it was feared to cause to the state. According to him, the German Social Democratic Party inherited its extreme individualism from the revolutionary theory of the French Revolution.[12] In this sense, his criticism of socialism was in line with his criticism of laissez-faire, and is evidence that he shared the general view of the problem of the individual versus the state as an inevitable one for a nation deemed to be a late-comer to the capitalist world.

It was only natural that the rejoinders to the society's statement came from two fronts, socialist and liberalist. A Christian socialist, Abe Isoo, who later became president of the Socialist Popular Party, wrote that although he did not think that socialism and social policy were the same thing, he did not see any contradiction between them: 'According to our socialist point of view, social policy is a step to socialism. Therefore we are by no means hostile to it. We rather welcome it. Our only point of disagreement with you is that we do not consider social policy the last means for solutions to social problems'.[13] The stubborn liberalist, Taguchi Ukichi, then wrote criticizing both the Society for Social Policy and the Social Democratic Party. According to him, both had in common the hatred of despotic factory owners, sympathy for labourers, and the idea of legal control of the workday. The only difference between these two groups was that whereas the socialists thought it impossible to remedy abuses without the public control of capital, the members of the Society for Social Policy believed it possible without recourse to such measures. He proceeded to state that socialists insisted on the public ownership of capital only because of their ignorance of political economy, that is to say, of the theory of harmony between capital and labour, and that 'the Society for Social Policy has the leading economists of this country for its members, and they should understand that labour and capital are already in harmony under free competition. Therefore I am puzzled as to why they view them as being in disharmony, and try to interfere in them by law'.[14]

This triangular controversy continued for a while, but the high treason case of 1911 dealt a heavy blow to socialist and labour movements, and business leaders, as Soeda put it, took it for granted that they enjoyed the protection of the government in both internal and external affairs. Under such conditions, the Society for Social Policy began to lose its raison d'être. It had not only played a role in promoting social legislation, but, as the first nation-wide learned society of economists, it contributed considerably to the establishment of political economy as a discipline independent of political and legal studies, though it was still political enough to hamper theoretical and historical studies in economics.[15] The Meiji era ended in 1912. In 1919 the Faculty of Economics was established in Tokyo Imperial University, marking the end of the academic role of the society, which finally disbanded in 1924. The time had become ripe for 'Taishō democracy', maimed as it was, and the revival of socialism especially under the impact of the Russian Revolution, developments which are beyond the horizon of this survey.

6

For Domestic Colonization: Political Economy in Sapporo Agricultural College

Hiroshi Mizuta

1. American Teachers in Hokkaido, a Domestic Colony

On July 31, 1876, the ninth year of the Meiji Restoration, four Americans galloped under the cloudy sky into the main street of Sapporo, the capital of Hokkaido. Early that morning they had left the port of Otaru where they had arrived by boat from Tokyo. Among them was William Smith Clark who had been appointed the first president of Sapporo Nō Gakkō, Sapporo Agricultural College.

Hokkaido is the northernmost island of Japan, and the name literally means 'the northern sea road' or 'coastal road'. Until the end of the Tokugawa period, Japanese habitation was limited to the southern end of the island, leaving the rest to the original population, the Ainu. Immediately after the Restoration, in 1869, the government established the Hokkaido Development Authority. They thought this thinly populated island quite a suitable place for the migration of the poverty-stricken peasants from the north-eastern district of the mainland, and for samurai who had lost their stipends as a result of the dissolution of the feudal regime but would not, or could not, find posts in the new government. As it was thinly populated, the first president of the Development Authority, Kuroda Kiyotaka, planned to develop a large-scale landownership scheme for farmers, based on what he had learned during his study tour in the United States. The establishment of Sapporo Agricultural College was the first step towards carrying the plan into reality.

W. S. Clark was the president of Massachusetts Agricultural College when he was approached by Mori Arinori, the Japanese acting minister in Washington, who asked him to accept some Japanese students. When Mori visited the college, he had seen the students in military training, and perhaps Clark had told him of some of his experiences during the Civil War, in which he had served as a colonel. The combination of agriculture and military training seems to have made a strong impression on Mori who, as a future minister of education, was studying the educational system of the United States. Perhaps he thought that colonies of farmer-soldiers would be useful to defend the thinly populated island against Russian invasion or Ainu revolt. It may be on Mori's recommendation that Kuroda appointed Clark the first president of his college.[1]

As Clark was a mineral and agricultural scientist he had nothing to do with the introduction of political economy, but as president he decided or approved the curriculum which included political economy in the latter half of the fourth year. Since he was on special leave from the Massachusetts Agricultural College, he actually stayed only half a year in his position in Sapporo to lay the foundation of the Agricultural College. Therefore he did not have the opportunity of seeing the effect of his curriculum. Neither do we have the opportunity to assess its political economy content: in the annual reports of the college for the first ten years we find political economy as a course but no name of a professor or lecturer is listed.[2] All we can guess is that until the appointment of Satō Shōsuke and Nitobe Inazō there was no proper teacher of political economy. Since during this period one professor gave courses on anatomy and on English literature, political economy might have been taught in the same way.

2. A Course on Political Economy: Nitobe Inazō

Satō Shōsuke was one of the first fourteen students of Sapporo Agricultural College and Nitobe Inazō was one of the seventeen students in the second class. Both of them had decided to study in the United States, and, arriving by different routes, they met in Baltimore and studied under Richard Ely and Herbert Baxter Adams. In the same year in which Satō matriculated, that is to say in 1883, so, too, did Woodrow Wilson. Nitobe arrived during the following year. When the League of Nations was established by the initiative of Wilson as President of the United States, Nitobe was appointed its under-secretary general, perhaps as a result of their youthful friendship.

While studying at Johns Hopkins, Nitobe was appointed associate professor of his alma mater and ordered to study in Germany owing to the turn of the tide in the Japanese political and academic world to a pro-German direction. He studied agricultural economics under Gustav Schmoller and other economists of the Historical School. He returned to Sapporo in 1891 and was appointed professor of the college where he taught until 1898. Although his course of lectures on political economy was not the first one in Japanese higher education, it represents one of the first streams which flowed into Japan from various origins and through various routes.

According to lecture notes taken by an unidentified student, Nitobe's course on political economy consisted of some prefatory comments on certain economists famous in Europe and America at that time (Walker, Laveleye, Mill, Fawcett, Roscher, Hermann, Cohn, Cossa, Wagner, Jevons),[3] followed by three parts, the first being a general introduction, the second on the principles, and the third on the history of political economy. Unfortunately the extant notes have no third part, but a historical chapter is included in the first part. The chapters of the introductory part are: 1. Wants or desires; 2. Classification of wants or desires; 3. Standards of living in different nations; 4. Commodities; 5. Utility and value; 6. Character of value and wealth; 7. Economy; 8. Political economy; 9. Boundaries of political economy; 10. Divisions of political economy; 11. How to study political economy; 12. Historical outlines of political economy.

The second part contains: 1. Production; 2. Labour; 3. Division of labour; 4. Population; 5. Capital; 6. Organization of labour, or industries; 7. Exchange and circulation of wealth; 8. Money; 9. Legal tender system or monetary system; 10. Distribution (rent, interest, and wages); 11. Relief for the working class; 12. Socialism. At the end of each chapter he recommends some books on the subject. He mentions Böhm-Bawerk's *Positive Theory of Capital*, Marx's *Das Kapital*, Jevons's *Political Economy*, and Dietzel's *Theoretische Socialökonomik* in the chapter on utility and value.

Among the schools of political economy of his day, he rejects the mathematical school as an impractical desk theory and mentions the Historical School as a prevailing one:

> A living member of the Historical School is Schmoller of Berlin University. The Historical School was born in Germany and spread to England, America, France, and Japan. It developed extensively in the United States of America where new theories are always welcomed, but not so in Britain where people are conservative. In France it is developing rapidly thanks to Laveleye's advocacy.

In the historical chapter he lists some sixty economists with short remarks, for example: 'Mr. Adam Smith was Mr. Quesnay's friend, . . . In a Scottish university he said that the key to human relations was moral sentiment, that is to say, sympathy. However, man is self-interested and this is the origin of economic activity, so he resigned from the chair to study it'; 'Ely is a passionate person and is to be called a socialist'; 'Von Stein was a friend of Roscher and died five years ago. He was a man of talent, very talkative, and active as well. He was so eloquent that he could convince our ministers of state'; 'Marx is famous for his socialism, and is the author of *Das Kapital.* Lassalle is a destructive politician rather than a scholar. He is an eloquent speaker. He has written no book but has published a collection of his speeches. He made socialism a matter of politics.' Of the contemporary English economists, Toynbee is mentioned as a man of respectable character, and Marshall is mentioned but without remark. The fact that about a half of the economists he mentioned here are German is evidence of Nitobe's familiarity with the German economists.

In the final chapter on socialism, he sees that socialism is an inevitable result of the victory of democracy and individualism over feudalism, and avers that Rousseau was ambivalent about private property with regard to social reform. Relying on Laveleye, he explains the process of the development of socialism among the working class as an ironical result of the expansion of armament. However, almost as a conclusion, he declares that it is useless to express feelings of sympathy and pity towards the members of the lower classes because they do not have the intelligence to accept it. He says that he saw a poor woman who emigrated from the mainland to Hokkaido and landed at Port Otaru, barefoot in the cold rain, and also a native Ainu walking barefoot in snow. In both cases he considered it was not worthwhile expressing sympathy, because they had no intelligence. Therefore, according to Nitobe, so long as they have no consciousness of human dignity and of their miserable life, socialism is impracticable. Although he adds that the first thing to do is to give them education to develop their intelligence, his contempt for the masses and their ignorance is a characteristic common to the men of the Meiji Enlightenment.

In 1898 he resigned from his post owing to illness. From 1901 to 1903 he worked for the Commissioner of Taiwan, a newly acquired colony of Japan. He contributed very much to the development of the sugar industry there. In 1903, on the forceful recommendation of Commissioner Gotō, he was appointed a professor at the newly established Kyoto Imperial University. He started a course on colonial policy together with one on agricultural economics. The following year he was appointed head master of Dai-Ichi Kōtō Gakkō (First High

School) in Tokyo, and in 1909 the chair of colonial policy was established in Tokyo Imperial University especially for him. As may be gathered from his attitude towards the working class, his lectures on colonial policy contain some justification of colonialism and imperialism based on the idea of the survival of the fittest through natural selection and that of the mission of civilized nations to bring development to underdeveloped peoples. On the other hand he opposed the use of military force to conquer the native tribes of Taiwan, who were living peacefully in the mountains. Even in his lectures he said that colonialism was a temporary phenomenon or a sort of sickness. It is quite consistent with his idea of the mission of civilized nations that colonies should be emancipated as a result of their cultural development. However, except for an incident in 1932, he had no open conflict with the military authorities. He died the following year in Vancouver after attending a conference of the Institute of Pacific Relations.[4] Yanaihara Tadao who succeeded Nitobe as professor of colonial policy was forced to resign from the chair in 1937 owing to his criticism of Japanese imperialism and colonialism in Taiwan and Manchuria.

As for Sapporo Agricultural College after Nitobe left it in 1898, it was reorganized in 1907 as the Faculty of Agriculture of the newly established Tōhoku Imperial University (with administration and other faculties in Sendai), and in 1918 it became Hokkaido Imperial University. As it had neither faculty of arts nor social sciences, the department of agricultural economics in the Faculty of Agriculture was the only department in which political economy was taught until the post-war educational reform of 1948.

Whereas Nitobe taught in his alma mater only seven years, Satō Shōsuke remained there for forty years until 1930, as a professor and, eventually, as president of Hokkaido Imperial University after its reorganization. As already mentioned, he went to Baltimore before Nitobe, and was in Johns Hopkins from 1883 to 1886. He studied under Adams and Ely, perhaps as the first Japanese student in political economy. On returning home the same year as Nitobe, he also started teaching in his alma mater. When he translated Ely's *Introduction to Political Economy*, he wrote to the author: 'The work is the very kind we need in Japan. I have no doubt that it will do a great deal of good in Japan'. However, in spite of his long study under Ely, and of his letter saying that 'the public got tired to hear the dry explanations of the Manchester School for vital economic problems of today',[5] he had no idea of Ely's thoughts on social reform.[6] He used the term imperialism without any critical sense, and identified it with the imperial regime which awarded him a baronage.

Takaoka Kumao was a student of Satō and Nitobe in Sapporo Agricultural College. Immediately after graduation he was appointed a lecturer in agricultural economics in an agricultural training school attached to the college. In 1898 when Nitobe resigned, he took his place as an associate professor in charge of the course on political economy. In 1900 he was ordered to study agricultural policy and agricultural economics in Germany, especially under von der Goltz and Sering of the University of Bonn. On his return home before the end of 1904, he was appointed professor in charge of agricultural policy and colonial policy. Before studying abroad he published *Hokkaidō no Nōgyō* (Agriculture of Hokkaido, 1899) and translated *Vorlesungen über Agrarwesen und Agrarpolitik* (Lectures on Agriculture and Agricultural Policy) of von der Goltz in 1901. The former was the first scientific book on the subject, and the latter was very influential on the studies of the subject in Japan.

A result of his study in Bonn was his book in German entitled *Die innere Kolonisation Japans* (The Inner Colonization of Japan, 1904). Later he contributed to the government's policy on colonization in Taiwan, Manchuria, Sakhalin, the tropical Pacific islands, and Brazil. It may be correct to summarize his idea on the subject as follows: the best policy to resolve the economic difficulty of the small-scale peasant farming which prevails on the mainland, especially in the northeast, of Japan, is the promotion of colonization, first of Hokkaido, then outside the country.

In 1942, when the Japanese invasion of China and South-East Asia was in progress, he was elected president of the newly established Shokumin Seisaku Gakkai (Society for Colonial Studies). He loved to quote Mommsen's words, 'The things acquired by war may be lost by war, but this is not the case with the things acquired by the plough'. He seems to have made a clear distinction between military invasion and 'peaceful' colonization, but actually the effect was that by supporting the latter he supported the former too, however unintentionally. He could not see that military invasion was made under the disguise of peaceful colonization.

7

Pioneer Economics Department: Senshū School

Chūhei Sugiyama

There were in the beginning five private law schools in Meiji Japan: Senshū School (Senshū Gakkō), Meiji Law School (Meiji Hōritsu Gakkō), Tokyo School of Special Studies (Tokyo Senmon Gakkō), Tokyo Law School (Tokyo Hō Gakkō), and the School of English Law (Igirisu Hōritsu Gakkō). These were the predecessors of five well-known private universities in Tokyo: Senshū, Meiji, Waseda, Hōsei, and Chūō universities, respectively. The oldest of these five is Senshū School, which was established in 1880, amalgamating with two informal private schools and the evening course in law attached to Keiō School. 'Senshū' means specialization. Why, then, a specialization school? The prospectus published at the time of its establishment says:

> The range of sciences is so wide as to cover political economy, law, astromomy, geography, technology, physics, etc. Human faculties are limited in such a way that we cannot pursue them all at one time. . . . Now that our knowledge and learning have been remarkably widened since we began to communicate with overseas nations, we are unable to reach the highest standard of learning without specializing in one particular subject. This is why a 'senshū' school is needed today.

A characteristic of the school is that unlike other law schools, or even the Law Faculty of the University of Tokyo, it had an independent department of political economy from the very beginning. In that sense it was really a pioneer. How did this come to pass? The inauguration notice of the school was signed by eight people, among them two economists, i.e., Tajiri Inajirō and Komai Shigetada, who had studied at Yale University and Rutgers College, respectively. Some of the rest shared the experience of studying at Yale and Rutgers, though their subjects were not political economy, but law. Possibly while they were studying abroad together, they had discussed and agreed on the launching of a private school in Japan where law and political economy should be taught side by side.

Another feature is that all lectures in the school were given in Japanese from the beginning. The other private law schools established later followed suit. The prospectus also says:

> In government-established institutions only those who are acquainted with Western languages and Western books are admitted [because the lectures there are as a rule delivered in Western languages].
>
> . . . Now we want to establish a school for specialized studies where lectures are to be given in Japanese. . . . It will probably enable those who cannot enter the government-established schools to realize their wish to study.

Thus Senshū School was unique in two ways. First, although it started as a law school, it had, from the onset, an independent department for teaching political economy exclusively, whereas in the University of Tokyo political economy was taught only as part of the subjects of the Faculty of Law, there being no independent economics faculty.[1] Secondly, unlike the University of Tokyo, lectures at the school were given in Japanese. When the first graduation ceremony was held in 1881, the eleven graduates (nine in law, and two in political economy) were joined by a large number of distinguished guests, including such well-known economists as Kanda Takahira, Fukuzawa Yukichi, Tsuda Mamichi, Nakamura Masanao, Sugi Kōji, Nakamigawa Hikojirō, Obata Tokujirō, Ushijima Tokuzō, and the like.

What kind of subjects were taught in this earliest department of political economy and by whom?

The curriculum ranged over two years, each year consisting of two terms. Some subjects were taught only for a term but others for two or even three successive terms. There were three lecturers to teach all these subjects: Tajiri Inajirō, Nakakuma Keizō, and Komai Shigetada. The subjects were: history, money, principles of money, outlines of political economy, principles of political economy, history of political economy, economic history, British history of commerce, banking, history of banking, foreign exchange, government budget, taxation, government loans, applied political economy.

In the second year of its establishment the school added a course on statistics given by Sugi Kōji, who was to be the founder of the science of statistics in Japan. Sugi was the only lecturer who was not a civil servant.

By today's standards they were no more than part-time lecturers, but in those days all government offices, and the offices of the major private firms, are believed to have closed every day at three P.M., which made it possible for teachers and students to come to the school early enough for lectures. Even so, it is amazing that people such as Tajiri, Komai, and Nakakuma were so energetically devoted to the running of the school. Until 1905 when the day course was opened, the lectures of the department of political economy were given daily from 3.30 P.M to 5.30 P.M., and the department of law from 6.15 P.M. to 8.30 P.M. The number of graduates in the second year was five from the department of political economy as against sixteen from the department of law, and in the third year eleven from the department of political economy as against fourteen from the department of law. From then on the number steadily increased.

Besides teaching at the school, Tajiri started lecturing at the University of Tokyo as early as 1881. Soon there came to be a number of lecturers at the school who had been Tajiri's students at the University of Tokyo. Therefore, although Senshū School was a private institution, its relationship with a government-established institution such as the University of Tokyo was not entirely adversary.

In 1883 the school reorganized and instituted a three-year course, offering the following subjects: first year, first term: principles of political economy, money and history; second term: principles of political economy, outline of political economy, foreign trade, money, finance and history; second year, first term: economic history and banking; second term: economic history, foreign trade, applied political economy, banking and the history of banking; third year, first term: government loans, the government budget, history of commerce, history of banking, social conditions and politics; second term: the government budget, government properties, government loans, history of commerce, taxation, economic history, history of banking, politics, social conditions and speech.

To these, three more subjects were added in 1886: economic harmony for the first year, logics and bookkeeping for the second year, and bookkeeping again for the third year. Meanwhile the number of lecturers also increased, and in 1887 there were ten additional names listed: Murakami Tasuku, Hamada Kenjirō, Tsuchiko Kinshirō, Katō Akiyasu, Nagasaki Gōjūrō, Horiuchi Masayoshi, Aikawa Masamichi,

Sakatani Yoshio, Kure Ayatoshi, and Soeda Juichi. They were mostly graduates of the University of Tokyo and government officers at the Ministry of Finance with the exception of Tsuchiko, who had been transferred from the ministry to Tokyo Commercial School (the predecessor of Hitotsubashi University).

The curriculum, and the lecturers who taught the courses, were as follows: (1) first year (in two terms): outline of political economy with Tajiri, principles of political economy with Nakakuma, money with Murakami, bookkeeping with Horiuchi, banking with Tajiri, elements of political economy with Hamada, economic harmony with Tsuchiko, principles of foreign trade with Komai, applied political economy with Katō, method of political economy with Nagasaki; (2) second year (in two terms): economic harmony with Tsuchiko, banking with Tajiri, history of political economy with Sakatani, foreign exchange with Nagasaki, government loans with Tajiri, economic history with Komai, bank bookkeeping with Horiuchi, theoretical statistics with Kure, practical statistics with Kure; (3) third year: public loans with Tajiri, politics with Aikawa, commercial history with Tsuchiko, commercial history with Soeda, statistics with Kure, taxation with Katō, economic history with Komai, practical statistics with Kure, accountancy law with Sakatani, government budget with Soeda; (4) extraordinary lectures: Imperial Constitution with Aikawa, history of political economy with Sakatani, monetary system in China with Komai, monetary system in Austria with Nagasaki, banking in America with Sakatani, history of statistics with Kure, vital statistics with Kure.

One thing to be noted is that in the period between 1885 and 1887 five private law schools, Tokyo Law, English Law, Senshū, Tokyo Senmon and Meiji Law schools, introduced three-year extramural or correspondence courses with specially prepared textbooks. Tokyo Law and English Law schools were the earliest (1885), Senshū School was the second (1886) and the other two followed a year later. The subjects and the lecturers for the correspondence course of the department of political economy of Senshū School were as follows: (1) first year: outline of political economy, principles of political economy, elements of political economy, economic harmony, money, applied political economy, banking, finance, bookkeeping; (2) second year: banking, foreign exchange, economic history, foreign trade, history of banking, economic traditions, commercial history; (3) third year: taxation, government loans, government budget, government-owned property, commercial history, social conditions, logics.

These were taught by Tajiri, Komai, Nakakuma, Wadagaki Kenzō, Sakatani, Tsuboi Kumezō, Nagasaki, Tsuchiko, Murakami, and Katō.

Four of the regular-course lecturers—Aikawa, Hamada, Kure, and Soeda—are not included, and instead two others, Wadagaki and Tsuboi, are added. Although the reason for this difference is not clear, in later years those excluded names reappeared whilst those added were dropped. The extramural course was a success, and in 1890 the number of students enrolled grew to 179, though it declined for some unknown reason for some years thereafter.

The textbooks were distributed regularly. Those for the years from 1888 to 1889, for example, were as follows:

(1) first year: *Keizai Taii* (Outline of Political Economy), by Tajiri Inajirō, 194p.; *Keizai Genron* (Principles of Political Economy), by Nakakuma Keizō, 382p.; *Kaheiron* (On Money), by Murakami Tasuku, 358p.; *Bokigaku* (Bookkeeping), by Horiuchi Masayoshi, 256p.; *Ginkōron* (On Banking), by Tajiri, 652p; *Keizai Yōron* (Elements of Political Economy), by Hamada Kenjirō, 118p.; *Ronri Bokigaku* (Theoretical Bookkeeping), by Horiuchi, 144p.; *Keizai Chōwaron* (Economic Harmony), by Tsuchiko Kinshirō, 432p.; *Gaikoku Bōeki Genri* (Principles of Foreign Trade), by Komai Shigetada, 58p.; *Keizai Ronpō* (Methods of Political Economy), by Nagasaki Gōjūrō, 101p.;

(2) second year: *Keizai Chōwaron* (Economic Harmony), by Tsuchiko, 432p.; *Ginkōron* (On Banking), by Tajiri, 652p.; *Keizaigakushi* (History of Political Economy), by Sakatani Yoshirō, 228p.; *Gaikoku Kawaseron* (On Foreign Exchange), by Nagasaki, 166p.; *Kōsairon* (On Government Loans), vol. 1, by Tajiri, 412p.; *Keizai Kōchō* (Historical Political Economy), by Komai, 432p.; *Ginkō Bokigaku* (Bank Bookkeeping), by Horiuchi, 106p.; *Riron Tōkeigaku* (Theoretical Statistics), by Kure Ayatoshi, 185p.; *Jissai Tōkeigaku* (Practical Statistics), by Kure, 351p.;

(3) third year: *Kōsairon* (Government Loans), vol. 2, by Tajiri, 316p.; *Seijigaku* (Politics), by Aikawa Masamichi, 222p.; *Shōgyōshi* (Commercial History), by Tsuchiko, 180p.; *Shōgyōshi*, (Commercial History), by Soeda Juichi, 186p.; *Tōkeigaku* (Statistics), by Kure, 232p.; *Sozeiron* (On Taxation), by Katō Akiyasu, 58p.; *Keizai Kōchō* (Historical Political Economy), by Komai, 587p.; *Jissai Tōkeigaku* (Practical Statistics), by Kure, 224p.; *Kaikeihō* (Accountancy), by Sakatani, 144p.; *Saikeiron* (Government Budget), by Soeda, 346p.;

(4) Extraordinary lectures: *Teikoku Kenpō* (Imperial Constitution), by Aikawa, 122p.; *Keizaigakushi* (History of Political Economy), by Sakatani, 228p.; *Shina Kaheikō* (Monetary System in China), by Komai, 157p.; *Ōkoku Kahei Seidō no Zeikaku* (Outline of the Monetary System in Austria), by Nagasaki, 21p.; *Beikoku Ginkō Enkakuron* (Outlines of American Banking), by Sakatani, 16p.; *Statistics Rekishi*

(History of Statistics), by Kure, 42p.; *Jinsei Tōkeigaku* (Life Statistics), by Kure, 142p.

The lectures, and the textbooks were mostly, if not wholly, translations of, or extracts from, Western books. Tajiri's *Keizai Taii* is something of an exception, for he lectured in his own terms. He divides his lecture into four chapters: (1) General considerations, (2) Production, (3) Distribution, (4) Consumption. The opening passage of the first chapter reads:

> Political economy is a science that discusses from the point of view of commodities the relations between people in associating themselves into a society. . . . Where there are people, there must be demands for the necessities of life. Once society is composed of people, there must be ways to supply those demands. In demanding and supplying there must be mutual relationships. This is what is meant by material relations. There are various aspects of human relationships, social, moral, legal, and so on. The relationship political economy discusses is only the material one. It does not deal with other kinds of human relationships.

This passage might already suggest that Tajiri is exceptional. As for the others, Nakakuma's definition, for example, follows Wilhelm Roscher:

> Political economy deals, first of all, with goods and there are four aspects to be considered: production of goods, distribution of goods, exchange of goods, and consumption of goods.
>
> Secondly, political economy deals with trade. Trade is divided into agriculture, industry and commerce.
>
> Thirdly, it deals with government economy or public finance, which is divided into budget, treasury, annual expenditure, and annual revenue (mainly from taxes, government loans, paper money, etc.).
>
> Fourthly, it deals with the exchequer.
>
> At this school, the lecturers share these topics. I, for one, lecture, for the first year students, on the first of these divisions, relying mainly on Henry Fawcett's *Manual of Political Economy* (1863).

Komai's *Keizai Yōron* (Elements of Political Economy) depends on John Elliot Cairnes, for he says:

> What I am about to lecture on is taken solely from Professor

> Cairnes's book *Some Leading Principles of Political Economy* and not from my own publication. However, the book discusses basic theories of political economy for those who have already learned elementary points.
>
> Therefore if I lecture on the outline of the book straight away to beginners, they would probably stumble at the very starting point. For this reason I shall sometimes refer the reader to what the author does not mention for the sake of easier understanding for the beginners. The lecture might sometimes look superficial but this cannot be helped.

Tsuchiko's *Keizai Chōwaron* is, as the title itself suggests, taken from Frédéric Bastiat's *Harmonie Economique* (1850). He says in the introduction:

> Economic harmony, about which I am going to lecture, depends on the French scholar Frédéric Bastiat's book. The first ten chapters were published during the author's lifetime, and the rest was published posthumously. The reason why the book is entitled economic harmony is that, according to the author, the fair interests of human society at large do not contradict each other but are wholly in harmony.

Katō Akiyasu's *Ōyō Keizai* (Applied Political Economy) is taken from John Stuart Mill's *Principles of Political Economy* (1848). He says:

> Mr. Mill divides his book *Principles of Political Economy* into two parts of which the first is genuine or purely theoretical political economy and the second is applied political economy. What I am to lecture on is this second one. The science of political economy, whether theoretical or applied, deals with the law that regulates economic phenomena. . . . The difference lies in that the former considers society to be in a stable state whereas the latter does not. Society never stands still but is always in progress. Population grows, wealth increases, human knowledge develops. Politics and laws are often connected with the economy. The science of political economy, therefore, cannot be complete without taking this progress and change into consideration. It is in applied political economy that these factors are discussed.

Apart from whether J. S. Mill really divides his *Principles* into theoretical and applied parts, it is clear enough from the above that

Katō's lecture depends on Books IV and V of Mill's *Principles*, 'Influence of the Progress of Society on Production and Distribution' and 'On the Influence of Government', respectively. It is indeed true that Mill mentions the difference between the 'dynamics' and 'statics' of political economy in the opening passage of Book IV.

Nagasaki's *Keizai Ronpō* (Method of Political Economy) is taken from J. E. Cairnes: 'The method of political economy concerns whether discussion of political economy should be dealt with by induction or deduction. I want to lecture mainly following Dr. Cairnes's book *The Character and Logical Method of Political Economy*'.

Similarly, *Shōgyōshi* (Commercial History) by Tsuchiko and Soeda is the translation of Leone Levi's *History of British Commerce* (1872), or more precisely of Books I and II (Tsuchiko) and III (Soeda), respectively. Likewise *Kaheiron* (On Money) by Murakami is taken from Jevons's and Chevalier's works on currency: William Stanley Jevons, *Investigations in Currency and Finance*, (Herbert Foxwell, ed., 1884); Michel Chevalier, *La Monnaie* (1850) (English translation by Richard Cobden under the title *M. Chevalier's Treatise on the Probable Fall in the Value of Gold* (1859).

Further examples are not necessary. There is, however, an example of a different kind which might be of interest. Komai's *Keizai Kōchō* is, as the title of his lecture would suggest, the translation of the abridged English version of John Joseph Lalor's *Principles of Political Economy* (1879) and of Wilhelm Roscher's *Grundlagen der Nationalökonomie* (1854). Translating the introduction, Komai writes that in the sciences of society there are two different methods, the historical and the idealistic, of which the former is preferable. Why a textbook such as this, belonging to the German Historical School, is taken up along with the Anglo-French school of economic liberalism is not quite clear. If it anticipates the switch-over in the general trend of economic thought in Meiji Japan to German historicism or the social policy school that was to take place before long, it would certainly deserve notice. Incidentally, Sakatani's *Keizaigakushi* is a translation of Luigi Cossa's *Guida allo Studio dell'Economica Politica* (1876), made from the second half of the English edition *Guide to the Study of Political Economy* (1880), which also belongs to the historical school, though not German in nationality.[2]

These are, as mentioned above, just examples of the lecture titles, and of the accompanying textbooks for the extramural course students. But it may safely be presumed that at least most, if not all, of them were at the same time the textbooks used for the lectures given to the regular course students. Senshū University has preserved a number of the books from those early days, with covers on which are printed the words 'Senshū School Textbook' along with the title, author's name or, in the case of the many translations, the author's and translator's names.

It is well known that, during his visit to America as a junior member of a diplomatic mission, Fukuzawa Yukichi, the founder of Keiō School, the predecessor of Keiō University, purchased a great many English and American books to be used by his students. The practice of lending such books to students continued at Keiō until 1898. The lending of textbooks and other books, all written in Western languages, was also the practice at the University of Tokyo.[3] So the use of Japanese books, whether original or in translation, at Senshū School was epoch-making as well as toilsome work, toilsome at any rate for the lecturers.

To mention just a few other important translations, in 1882 Tajiri translated George Joachim Goschen's *The Theory of Foreign Exchange* (1861) and Henry Dunning Macleod's *The Theory and Practice of Banking* (1855), and also, in 1883, Paul Leroy-Beaulieu's *Traité de la Science des Finances* (1877). In 1883 Nakakuma translated Henry Fawcett's *Manual of Political Economy* (1863), and in 1884 Komai translated Henry Fawcett's *Free Trade and Protection* (1863). In the preface to his translation Komai writes:

> It has been twenty years since we opened our ports to overseas countries and started mutal communication, during which period foreign trade has increased month after month and year after year. Therefore foreign trade must by all means be studied. There are indeed many books which consider foreign trade, and yet some are absorbed in idle talk and others are concerned with its mere utilities. I find that Mr. Fawcett's work on free trade and protection, unlike most other works on the subject, uncovers the truth of foreign trade. This is why I have translated it and offer it to the public.

Not that serious arguments on the advantage or disadvantage of foreign trade subsided, but here one sees an early appearance of observation from a more reserved or objective point of view.

Now we leave the teaching side, the lectures and lecturers, the textbooks and translations, and move to the learning side, the students. Out of the twenty-five in all who graduated from the Economics Department in the early period of its establishment up to 1886, eleven were either non-professional or unspecified. Of the other fourteen one was in business, seven were in the civil service, two were schoolmasters and three went abroad for further study. Compared with these, the graduates from the Law Department are rather more clearly classified. Out of 103 in all, 33 were either unspecified or unemployed. Among the other 70, those in the legal profession—such as judges, advocates, etc.—numbered 30, in the civil service 12, and the other 28 were scattered in various occupations. It is quite natural that the students of the law department tended to take up legal professions; alternatively it is possible that those already engaged in legal offices wanted to pursue legal studies in the evening course, that is, in the Department of Law, Regrettably, we cannot ascertain which was the case. Whichever the case, the fact remains that in both departments together, there is no particular characteristic pattern in the professions to which the students of the school, as a non-governmental institution, proceeded after graduation.

The most notable feature, if any, lay more in the ease of entrance for students. In 1883 the number of students enrolled in the first year of the school suddenly increased to 95 in the Economics Department. By 1888, there were 219 in the Law Department and 173 in the Economics Department, and in 1889 there were 202 in Law and 269 in Economics. Thereafter the pattern changed, and in 1890 there were 167 in the Law Department and 232 in Economics. The change in the comparative numbers of students in the Law and Economics departments, already recognizable in 1888 and 1889, was dramatic in 1891, when there were 60 Law Department students as against 237 in the Economics Department. The reason for this is again unascertainable, but most probably the privilege so far given to law students allowing them to proceed to higher posts in the civil service without sitting for a special examination was already being questioned. The privilege was withdrawn in 1893, and the school decided to abolish its Law Department that same year.

Accordingly, the courses taught in the Economics Department were modified to a large extent, resulting in the following list of subjects at about that time:

> Principles of political economy, money, historical political economy, law and statutes, administration, personal crime laws, social problems, politics, Imperial Constitution, civil law, property (civil law), property (part II), commercial law (general), commercial law (company), commercial law (bills), commercial law (insolvency), legal testimony, social policy, agricultural economy, practical statistics, economic history, the new theory of industry, bank bookkeeping and history.

One of the reasons for this restructuring must have been that some of the lecturers from the abolished Department of Law had to be re-assigned to the Department of Political Economy. Even so, the modification was a step, a great step forward at that, towards attaining college status according to the decree for establishing colleges, and then towards university status also according to the new decree establishing universities in 1903 and 1918 respectively.

Before closing the history of Senshū School it should be added that the year 1905 marked two memorable events, in that the college opened a day course and at the same time established the Department of Commerce, thus creating one of the first private commercial colleges in Japan, a move which corresponded with the rise and spread of the world-wide movement towards commercial education.[4]

8

In the Schools of Law: Hōsei, Meiji and Chūō

Shirō Sugihara

In May 1888 some 1,500 students from the five major law schools in Tokyo gathered together for a debate. Those five schools were Senshū Gakkō (Senshū School, later Senshū University, established July 1880), Tokyo Hō Gakkō (Tokyo Law School, later Hōsei University, established September 1880), Meiji Hōritsu Gakkō (Meiji Law School, later Meiji University, established January 1881), Tokyo Senmon Gakkō (Tokyo School of Special Studies, later Waseda University, established October 1882), and Igirisu Hōritsu Gakkō (School of English Law, later Chūō University, established September 1885). The meeting attracted the interest of a wide circle of people, resulting in the proceedings being published by the publishing house Hakubunkan.

After such an auspicious start, the meeting was held once every two months, and a periodical for the specific purpose of reporting the proceedings was launched.[1] It was, in a way, a campaign to impress on the public at large that these were the leading law schools, not only in Tokyo but also in the whole country. Indeed, there were quite a number of law schools competing with each other to answer the needs of the new social structure. Of the major five, separate chapters in this book are devoted to the first and fourth, Senshū and Waseda. This chapter deals with the other three, Tokyo Law School, Meiji Law School, and the School of English Law in particular with their relation to political economy, though the legal teaching side of the story cannot be left out.

Before looking at the schools individually, however, it would be useful to have a glance at the circumstances surrounding the law schools in general. A large number of private schools were set up around the

Meiji Restoration of 1868 and thereafter, most of which were for foreign language, especially English, teaching. But in and after the 1880s, private schools for teaching specialized knowledge or skills rather than just language were on the increase, and among these, law schools were particularly conspicuous. In order to achieve the amendment of the so-called unequal treaties then applying to Japan, an institutional reorganization of the whole system seemed essential to gain Japan's recognition as a nation governed by law. The birth of many law schools was apparently in response to this need.

In the second half of the 1880s, two factors brought about a new phase in the development of the law schools. Firstly, many of the existing law schools were in fact not schools in the proper sense of the word. As well as teaching law, they ran legal consultation businesses at the same time. Running a school was not necessarily profitable, and recruiting enough teachers sufficiently qualified to give specialized lectures was not easy. In other words the law was mostly practised by *daigennin*, or legal agent and not modern advocate that was then in existence. Legal knowledge was believed to be necessary only for winning a lawsuit. Those who were engaged in the legal business were more often than not of indifferent skill and character, and there were some who were accused, with reason, of being pettifoggers. Thus, to gain the trust of society at large, the law schools needed to disassociate themselves from legal practice. In 1880 the government revised the *daigennin* regulations, prohibiting the law schools from engaging in legal business.

Secondly, the leaders of the private law schools were mostly, though to different degrees, connected with political movements opposing the government. For example, many of them were involved in Numa Morikazu's Ōmeisha or Ono Azusa's Kyōson Dōshū (organized in 1877 and 1874, respectively), both of which were actively engaged in the political movement for liberty and popular rights. Tanaka Kentarō, one of the founders of Senshū School, belonged to both organizations; the founder of Senshū and English Law schools, Takahashi Kazukatsu, belonged to Kyōson Dōshū; the founder of Tokyo Law School, Kanamaru Tetsu, to Ōmeisha; Hatoyama Kazuo, who was concerned with Meiji Law and Tokyo Law schools, also belonged to Kyōson Dōshū.[2] Thus the schools had friendly personal, relationships with each other through their members' mutual involvement in political societies. The government, naturally, did not view this tendency favourably. In particular, since the political reshuffle in 1881 the government was resolutely determined to have national policy follow the German style of political system and social sciences, and so it was not inclined to leave unchecked the development of law schools which openly promoted French- or English-style legal systems. The government thus promulgated a decree for the supervision of the private law schools. Its aim was to place the leading private law schools in Tokyo under the supervision of the president of the University of Tokyo or more accurately the Imperial University (renamed so earlier the same year). According to the Imperial University Decree, among the five colleges—of law, medicine, technology, literature, and science—composing the Imperial University, the deanship of the Law College was to be held by the president of the university. This signified, no doubt, that the study of law, and so the college for legal studies, were deemed to be of special significance. In the Law College new curricula had already been planned, based on the German system of jurisprudence and state science, so that for the private law schools to be placed under the supervision of the Imperial University's president it implied that the French and English legal studies, which had so far been prevalent there, could not but be checked or transformed. On the other hand, by placing themselves under the Law College of the Imperial University, the law schools could enjoy some benefits in that their graduates would then be exempted from the examination for the lower ranks of the civil service, and would become eligible to sit for the examination to enter the higher ranks of the civil service. In this way the five leading private law schools gradually, if not drastically, lost their independent non-establishment, if not anti-establishment, character and needed to look for any possible way of preserving their respective individuality within the framework of the prevailing statism.[3]

1. Boissonade's School: Wafutsu Hōritsu Gakkō, the Franco-Japanese Law School

There were three private law schools in Meiji Japan with which Boissonade was connected: the Kansai, Franco-Japanese, and Meiji Law schools. He did not lecture at the first of these, but did so in the other two, and even became the deputy principal of the Franco-Japanese Law School.

The Franco-Japanese Law School was founded in September 1880 as the law-teaching section of Tokyo Hōgakusha (Tokyo Law Society), which had been established in April that same year. Lectures in law were given by four teachers. The society had also founded another section, the *Daigen-kyoku* (Legal Advisory Section), but this was soon to be abolished, for the reason already explained above. The law-teaching section was reorganized as Tokyo Law School in May 1881, when

Boissonade and Appert started lecturing there. Soon after being placed under the supervision of the Imperial University, the school was involved in negotiations for the amalgamation of three private schools: Tokyo Law School, Meiji Law School, and Tokyo School of French (Tokyo Futsu Gakkō). The last of them, incidentally, was a school established in 1886 for the purpose of teaching French, and had added a law department in 1888 with Boissonade, Appert, Kishimoto Tatsuo, etc., as lecturers. Now Tokyo Law School and this last school agreed to amalgamate to become the Franco-Japanese Law School, which became Hōsei University after the Specialized School Decree of 1903.

The central figures in the process leading to the inauguration of the Franco-Japanese Law School are Satta Masakuni and Ume Kenjirō. Ume, a graduate from the law school attached to the Ministry of Justice later became a professor at Tokyo Imperial University and is known for his part in the drafting of the Civil Law bill. By comparison, Satta is not widely known, and so detailed reference to him may be of use.[4]

Satta was born in Kyoto and, after studying French at a French school established by the Kyoto prefectural government, went to Tokyo. While continuing his study of French, he became acquainted with Boissonade through whom he came to help in the work of drafting the Civil Law bill then under way at the Ministry of Justice. It was at about that time that he, together with Kanamaru Tetsu and some others, established Tokyo Law School.

In an article on the inauguration of the school, 'The purpose of the establishment of Tokyo Law School', Satta wrote to the effect that

> the reason why ancient Greece and modern Spain had to decay is that they had a system of slavery, which fact shows that they ignored the 'principle of human equality' taught by jurisprudence and the 'principle of free labour as the basis of wealth' taught by political economy. Moral science such as ethics, jurisprudence, and political economy, unlike physical science such as the natural sciences, has its significance in that it contributes to human happiness and to social prosperity. It has to be studied by people of their own accord. 'This is an age of law, and not of physical force, in which we live.' The spread of legal knowledge has thus become essential and it is for this reason that we are resolved to inaugurate the school.[5]

What is significant here is, firstly, that the study of law is claimed to be necessary not only for those who are engaged in the legal profession, but also for people in general, in order for them to attain equality. Only by spreading legal knowledge to as wide a circle as possible, could society be improved to a state worthy of the name of modern society. Secondly, the study of political economy is claimed to be important for the student of law. A young man like Satta, at the age of twenty-four, could proclaim such a statement only against the historical background, with the Jiyū Minken (Freedom and People's Rights) Movement at its height, but it may also be reasonable to presume that he developed these ideas under the influence of the liberal jurist Boissonade, who attached importance to the relationship between law and socio-economic realities.

However, the first curriculum of the Tokyo Law School contained no lectures on political economy. These made their first appearance only in October 1881 when, under the leadership of Satta, the curriculum was reorganized. This coincided with the time when Boissonade and Appert started lecturing there. There were to be lectures on political economy for the third-year students. In April 1884 the first article of the new rules and regulations of the school stated that the aim of the school was to teach law in the main, and political economy in addition. The first lecture in political economy, which started in September of the same year, was delivered by Tajiri Inajirō. Incidentally, Appert, who lectured on the public and administrative laws of France, referred in his lectures to 'direct and indirect taxes', thereby extending his teaching to include part of public finance.[6]

Just as Tokyo Law School attached importance to political economy along with jurisprudence, so too did Satta and some of his colleagues in the monthly open lectures from 1885 to 1887, under the title of 'learned lectures on jurisprudence and political economy'. In 1886, when the school was put under the supervision of the president of the Imperial University, the curriculum was greatly remodelled. Besides French law, taught by Boissonade and Appert, and the outline of jurisprudence and criminal law, taught by Satta, there were to be weekly lectures on public finance and political economy, taught by Sagane Fujirō. Sagane was a graduate of the University of Tokyo, who had studied economic subjects under Wadagaki Kenzō and others. He lectured on political economy and public finance at Tokyo Law School and Senshū School while at the same time doing post-graduate studies. His own books, *Keizai Genri* (Principles of Political Economy, 1890); *Zaiseigaku* (Public Finance, 1889) and his translations from R. T. Ely and F. A. Walker (cf. the separate list of translated books) suggest that his economic views were a mixture of the liberalist and historical schools.

In contrast to Meiji Law School, where Appert taught the course, and Kansai Law School, where one of Boissonade's students lectured, political economy at Tokyo Law School was taught by Sagane, a graduate of the University of Tokyo. It may well be that for a lecturer in economic subjects at a school under the supervision of the Imperial University, where the German style of state science was encouraged, a person such as Sagane, who was free from the influence of the French scholars and who was a contributor to the periodical *Gakurin*, connected with the Society for German Studies, was considered more suitable.

About the time when Sagane started lecturing there, Satta left his managerial post at the school and retired to Kyoto. With his departure, those close to Boissonade lost their influence. After that the school became known as the Franco-Japanese Law School and followed a somewhat different line, under the leadership of Ume Kenjirō. The aims espoused by Satta in his article 'The Purpose of the Establishment of Tokyo Law School'—to give lectures in jurisprudence and political economy in order to defend people's liberty, equality, and happiness—were not necessarily adhered to in the school's later development. In 1903, the Franco-Japanese Law School was upgraded, and renamed Hōsei University. In the university section, lectures in political economy (by Kanai Noburu and Yamazaki Kakujirō, both of the Imperial University) and in public finance (by Oka Minoru of the Ministry of Agriculture and Trade) were added, and in the specialized school section a department of business (later renamed the department of commerce) was established. Thus the school seemed to change its character from being an institution for educating students solely, or mainly, in law. This development was not so much a result of the basic educational principles as a policy to enroll a larger number of students and to pass them on to the business world to meet the needs of the growing capitalist age.

2. Another 'Boissonade' School: Meiji Law School

In January 1881, three of the first graduates of the law school attached to the Ministry of Justice, Kishimoto Tatsuo, Miyagi Senzō and Yashiro Misao, founded Meiji Law School. They had all studied under Boissonade. Yashiro, who had been the deputy principal of a small private law school named Kōhō Gakusha (Law Teaching School, opened in 1877), was dissatisfied with its small size, and when Kishimoto and Miyagi returned from study abroad in France, he organized with them the opening of a law school of a more satisfactory size under the name of Meiji Law School. The declaration at the opening of the new school stated that the aims of the school were to contribute to the correction of the prevailing views which regarded law as simply the means to win a lawsuit, and to the strengthening of the views which regarded law as the means to attain the liberty and rights of the individual in society—aims quite similar to what had been stated in the inaugural declaration of Tokyo Law School.[7]

Originally, the three founders gave lectures on Japanese and French laws, but in due course the progressive peer Saionji Kinmochi, Appert, and Boissonade's student Inoue Misao joined them as lecturers.[8] It was not until 1887 that Boissonade himself joined, the delay being due to some troubles between the school and Tokyo Law School, to which Boissonade had been giving his support.

An official document of the school published in 1883 stated that its aim was 'to teach two subjects: jurisprudence and political economy', from which it is clear that from the very outset the school attached as much importance to political economy as to jurisprudence. The first lecturer in political economy was Georges Appert, who lectured on that subject from February to September of 1881, before he proceeded to give lectures on public finance. The Japanese translations, by Ugawa Morisaburō, of these lectures were published in 1883, entitled *Keizaigaku Kōgi* (Lectures in Political Economy) and *Rizaigaku Kōgi* (Lectures in Public Finance). Based on J.-B. Say's and J. S. Mill's liberalist theories, the lectures were divided into sections on production, circulation, distribution, and consumption. The section dealing with distribution criticizes socialism. By and large these were the most detailed among economic lectures delivered in contemporary Japan. Referring from time to time to affairs in Japan, he spoke in plain terms for easier understanding. The translated versions were reprinted in 1885 and 1886.

Appert's lectures on political economy were taken over by Noritake Kōtarō, and on public finance by Koike Seiichi. About these successors Fukui Atsushi draws attention to the fact that the translator Ugawa was also a member of the political group Kyōson Dōshū headed by Ono Azusa, and also that Koike and Noritake were fellow members of another political group, Ōmeisha. Thus Fukui presumes that through Ugawa, Koike came to succeed Appert in giving lectures, and that Noritake was then introduced to the school by Koike.[9] Fukui also points out that both Koike and Noritake belonged to a society for the study of political economy led by the liberalist Taguchi Ukichi. Taguchi was the editor of *Tokyo Keizai Zasshi* (Tokyo Economist) and the organizer of a society for economic studies, whose members published Japanese translations of a number of European and American economic and other related writings. For one of these issues of

Tokyo Keizai Zasshi Koike translated Walter Bagehot's *Lombard Street* (1873), and Noritake contributed translations of H. D. Macleod's *The Theory and Practice of Banking* (1855–56) and Herbert Spencer's *The Principles of Sociology* (1855). Noritake and Koike were among the most knowledgeable in British political economy and they were liberalists associated with the Jiyū Minken (Freedom and People's Rights) Movement. Meiji Law School engaged them to give lectures on political economy and public finance, thus complementing the curriculum for legal education based on liberalist ideas.

In 1887 the school started issuing textbooks of lectures for students unable to attend full time. Incidentally, Boissonade's lectures in national law were among these publications. Noritake's lectures in political economy were divided into four separate parts: history, principles, money, and banking. Koike also divided his lectures into three different parts: public loans, taxation, and budgets. Noritake's lectures were later published in two volumes: *Keizaigaku Kōgi* (Lectures in Political Economy): *Genrihen* (Theoretical Part) and *Rekishihen* (Historical Part).

In 1888 Noritake joined the Yokohama Specie Bank, and his place was taken by Aruga Osabumi the following year. Aruga's lectures were also issued in a series of transcripts, or textbooks, and were also published later in independent book form, entitled *Kokumin Keizaigaku Kōgi* (Lectures in National Economy, n.d.). He was a graduate of the University of Tokyo, and, as the above title suggests, his lectures were not of the English or French Liberalist School but of the German Historical School, coinciding with the arrangement whereby the school was under the supervision of the president of the Imperial University.

Under the provisions of the Specialized School Decree of 1903 the school became a university in 1904. Meiji University, as it was renamed, had a Faculty of Commerce along with three other faculties: law, politics, and literature. The establishment of the Faculty of Commerce was to answer the needs of the business world for people endowed with higher professional knowledge. The lectures, centring on accountancy, management, and commerce, were mostly given by the teaching staff of Tokyo Higher Commercial School at Hitotsubashi and of Tokyo Imperial University. Lectures in political economy were given by Kanai Noburu of the latter university.

3. A Private Law School of the Tokyo University Line: The School of English Law

Igirisu Hōritsu Gakkō, or the School of English Law, was founded by a group of eighteen people in September 1885 on the campus site of Meiji Gijuku Hōritsu Gakkō (Meiji Private Law School). Most of the founders, including the first principal, Masujima Rokuichirō, were graduates of the Faculty of Law at the University of Tokyo, and three in particular, Masujima, Okamura Teruhiko, and Hozumi Shigenobu, had become barristers after studying jurisprudence in Britain. They were either lecturing at the University of Tokyo or doing advocate business during the day and lecturing on English law at the school in the evening.[10]

By this time the law curriculum at the University of Tokyo had already been Germanicized and the Society for German Studies had already been organized with the support of the government. Why is it, then, that a private school for teaching English law was established by those who were connected with the university? The announcement printed in the newspapers of July 30, 1885, stated, 'The school is now established with the aim of teaching the entirety of English and American laws by a large number of experts, of publishing relevant books and of instituting a law library'. On September 19 the inaugural ceremony was held, with Masujima giving a speech in English very much to the same effect, saying that the aim was to teach English law 'in a scientific way'. The school, as has already been said, succeeded Meiji Private Law School, on its campus and in the building where Masujima had been a lecturer. Unlike Meiji Private Law School, which had amongst its members people such as Baba Tatsui, who were closely associated with the Jiyū Minken Movement, the School of English Law had no political link of any kind, a fact made clear by the above announcement and also by comparison with the statements issued by the above two schools on similar occasions.

The reason for the announcement about the systematic teaching of English (and American) laws, the publication of related books and the setting-up of a law library was to stress that, though there were schools teaching English and American laws, this school claimed to teach them in fuller content and in better facilities. Tokyo Senmon Gakkō already had a reputation for its teaching of English law in particular, but its location in the outlying suburb of Waseda was inconvenient, leaving room for the newly started school to announce that there would be lectures on English law by a better staff, in Kanda, a convenient central location in Tokyo.

What may be noted in that respect is that among the founders of the school there were two people who had been teaching staff at Waseda: Yamada Kinosuke and Okayama Kanekichi. It is even suspected by some that Tokyo Senmon Gakkō (Waseda) was not a very desirable school from the government point of view with regard to the circumstances which had led to its inception, and that the government had recourse to various means in order to suppress it. That the School of English Law was instituted by a group connected with the University of Tokyo was also thought to be related to government action directed at Waseda. It may even have been a tactic aimed at forcing Waseda, or its law department, into liquidation.[11] Regardless of whether this was really the case or not, the establishment of the school was doubtless a great menace to Waseda.[12]

At first the school's curriculum had no other subjects than law throughout the whole three-year course. The only exception was logic; political economy was not taught. In the curriculum of 1887 to each grade the subject of English was added, and Samuel Smiles's *Self-Help* (1859) and M. G. Fawcett's *Political Economy for Beginners* (1870) for the second grade and the English version of F. P. G. Guizot's *History of Civilization in Europe* and J. S. Mill's *Considerations on Representative Government* (1861) were assigned as reading material for third-year students. It was not until 1894 that the school remodelled the curriculum to include two hours a week of political economy for the second-year students, and two hours a week of public finance in the third year. According to the records of the teaching staff in 1897, there were lectures in political economy by Kanai Noburu and in public finance by Takano Iwasaburō. In the same records, though with no list of the subjects with which they dealt, the names of Wadagaki Kenzō and Tajima Kinji are also listed.[13] Thus we see that the teaching staff were all from the Imperial University.

The school had from its outset a course for extramural students, for whom it published a series of textbooks, though for some time at first only on law subjects. Political economy appeared for the first time in the textbooks in connection with Wadagaki's lectures for the third year students in 1893. Therefore it may be that the appearance of political economy in the curriculum was a little before 1894. Also, Tajima's political economy (1898) and Takano's public finance (1899) were also published in the series.

The school was renamed Tokyo Law University in 1903 in keeping with the Specialized School Decree, and later Chūō University in 1905. As is stated in the first article of the new rules and regulations of the university, the higher and specialized subjects of jurisprudence, political science, and political economy were taught, and independent departments of political economy were formally organized along with the department of law both in the university section and in the specialized school section. The curriculum of the department of political economy of the university section shows that applied fields such as agricultural policy, commercial policy, colonial policy, social and industrial policy, and insurance policy are particularly conspicuous and that a number of commercial subjects such as bookkeeping, commercial history, commodity products and commercial geography are also listed. This set the stage for future reform, and in 1909 rules and regulations were announced, setting up the department of commerce separately from that of political economy.

A look at the list of lecturers in charge of the subjects listed in the extramural textbooks in 1912 reveals that Kanai Noburu, Kawazu Susumu, Yanagita Kunio, Yamazaki Kakujirō, and Kuwata Kumazō were respectively responsible for political economy, commerical policy, agricultural policy, credit and banking, and social and industrial policy. Fukuda Tokuzō is also among the lecturers, though he was not responsible for any subject that year. Clearly prevalent are names from the Imperial University of Tokyo, whose standpoint was of the German Historical, or Social Policy, School which formed the main-stream of political economy at that time in Japan. It may not be so unexpected that political economy in Chūō University was characterized by German historicism, because it was two of the school's founders, Masujima Rokuichirō and Hozumi Shigenobu, who introduced to Japan Sir H. J. Maine's legal theories, in particular his book *Ancient Law* (1861), and Maine's doctrine had been formulated under the influence of German historical jurisprudence.[14]

9

'Captain of Industry': Tokyo Commercial School at Hitotsubashi

Chūhei Sugiyama and Tamotsu Nishizawa

1. The Birth of Commercial Education

'Captain of Industry' was a common expression much heard in prewar Hitotsubashi University, and a phrase almost synonymous with the 'Hitotsubashi spirit' as it was fondly known. The expression as such is doubtless taken from Thomas Carlyle's *Past and Present* (1843), though the author himself seems not to have meant anything particularly admirable, and perhaps even something despicable, by it.[1] Apparently it was first used in an enthusiastic way in addresses to students by young professors like Fukuda Tokuzō, Kanda Naibu, and others who had just returned from study abroad in Europe around 1901, but it is not quite clear when it became so fashionable among the professors and students of Hitotsubashi. What is clear, however, is that in the period under consideration the emergence of any 'captains of industry' was a process still barely begun.

By examining the roots of commercial, or business education, and something of economics education, as it developed at Hitotsubashi University, we will see the thinking behind that process, if not actually any of its products.

Our story starts with Mori Arinori, the first Japanese diplomatic representative to Washington, D.C. He is generally believed to have been a progressive liberal, another champion of the Japanese Enlightenment, though he became, as did many others, a reactionary nationalist in his later years. To us it seems, however, that reactionary or not, he was a nationalist from the beginning of his career. We shall return to this point later. As to his enlightenment, he even believed that his mother tongue was not suitable for the reception of Western civilization, so that English, or rather a simplified version of English, should be adopted as the new national language. During his posting first minister, he wrote to a number of prominent Americans asking for their advice about what line Japan should follow in the matter of education:

> . . . In a general way, I wish to have your views in reference to the elevation of the education of Japan, intellectually, morally, and physically, but the particular points to which I invite your attention are as follows:
> The effect of education—
> 1. Upon the material prosperity of a country
> 2. Upon its commerce
> 3. Upon its agricultural and industrial interests
> 4. Upon the social, moral, and physical condition of the people; and—
> 5. The influences upon the laws and government.
>
> Information on any one, if not all, of these points, will be gratefully received and appreciated. . .[2]

To this some answered in a brief way, but others in detail. One impressive example is the advice with regard to civil liberty. Mark Hopkins, president of Williams College, for example, advised that 'freedom be allowed that is compatible with order, especially freedom of opinion and religious worship',[3] and G. S. Boutwell wrote that 'a system of education should not include the teaching of any particular dogmas or opinions in religion, and experience is calculated to strengthen this opinion'.[4]

Also interesting is the answer of a Peter Cooper of New York, who stressed the need for polytechnic or adult schools where mechanics could acquire useful knowledge. But more interesting still for our present purposes is reference to political economy and commerce. Professor J. H. Syeele of Amherst College pointed out:

> The production and accumulation of wealth follow great laws as exactly as do the movements of the tide and the planets. There is a science of public economy, that is, a science of wealth, as true and as beautiful as the science of astronomy. All the mistakes which governments have ever made in their financial legislation, or which individuals make in their business transactions, come from ignorance of the fundamental truths of this science. Knowledge of this, therefore, is all-important for any nation, but such knowledge is not

> easily gained. The science, though now in its main principles well established, is very intricate, and demands well-trained intellects to master it. . . .[5]

Syeele's conviction is no doubt that of natural freedom in classical political economy. He seems to be proposing the establishment of schools where 'well-trained intellects' can be fostered. He proceeded to suggest:

> From what I have already said, the bearing of education upon commerce will appear. Education implies a knowledge of ourselves and of others. This implies a knowledge of our wants and how to supply them, and this is the foundation of trade. . . . It is always a healthy sign of individual or national growth, when we feel our wants, and thus recognize our dependence on others. Industry and commerce and wealth grow out of this, and therefore for the sake of commerce I would say, make education thorough and universal.[6]

James McCosh, president of Princeton University, referred to commerce too, saying that 'commerce can be extensively carried on only in nations in which there is a body of enlightened mercantile men, who know the wants of the country, and the products to be had in other countries'.[7]

Joseph Henry also referred to political economy and commerce, saying that an important subject which ought to occupy the attention of Japanese statesmen, and of which the basic principles ought to be taught in higher institutions of learning, is political economy. He continued:

> Although there is scarcely any department of human thought which has been more obscured with sophism, there is in it a basis of established truths which is of the greatest value, especially to those who are to make laws which regulate the commerce of your country.[8]

The reply Professor David Murray wrote on behalf of W. H. Campbell, president of Rutgers University, is perhaps the most noteworthy. Doubtless implying political economy, he touched on the first of Mori's points:

> National prosperity is held to consist in the accumulation of wealth in the hands of the inhabitants, in the general activity of trade and exchange, in the increase of the productions of a country, and in its

> general growth in population. These circumstances, which constitute material growth, are sure evidence also of the existence of happiness and contentment among the people, and have no small share in producing them. . . . It [education] stimulates in the mind of the individual a desire to improve its present condition, and aids him in devising ways and means to do so.[9]

As to the effect of education on commerce he said:

> Commerce brings nations into relations with each other. The seclusion of an empire from the rest of the world not only narrows and represses the national character, but, by its effect upon commercial relations, cuts it off from one of the chief sources of national wealth. In order that these relations be mutually satisfactory and mutually advantageous, a common ground of intelligence and culture must exist between them. . . . It is, however, the work of time, and in that work education must be a principal instrument. It is that which must stimulate the national mind to strive after the advantages of commerce; and it is that alone which can train up a body of men fitted by knowledge, skill, and enterprise, to carry on its vast and far-reaching schemes.[10]

No doubt Mori was deeply impressed by these answers. It may also be that he felt his conviction of the necessity of commercial education confirmed and strengthened. He had already known that there was a system of commercial education in the United States of America, for in September 1871, in an English preface to a book published under the title *Life and Resources in America*, he referred to the Bryant and Stratton College established in Chicago in 1856 and a number of its branch colleges established thereafter in various places. The passage runs:

> In none of the public schools of America are the foundation principles of commerce taught, and hence there have been established by private individuals what is called a 'Chain of Commercial Colleges';—they number not less than forty, and extend from Maine to Louisiana; their course of instruction is very complete, and covers all that is necessary for a commercial life.[11]

Mori became convinced that the wealth and strength of America were not merely due to its richness in natural resources but also to that in human resources. Among the differences between America and

Japan, one thing particularly conspicuous seemed to him to be the fact that in America men of ability were willingly engaged in business, whereas in Japan education in trade and commerce had for so long been neglected or even despised. Thus convinced of the imminent necessity of modernization in general, and of commercial education in particular, he returned to Japan in July 1873 and immediately initiated the enlightenment movement by, for instance, organizing the Meiroku-sha (Meiji Six Society) with its journal *Meiroku Zasshi* (Meiji Six Journal). The establishment of a commercial school had priority as one of his modernizing activities.

He applied to the Tokyo Council (formerly Tokyo Reconstruction Council) for financial help to employ a suitable American as a teacher, and also for a plot of rent-free land for the campus of his intended school. After a successful application to Tokyo prefectural government, the Council acceded to Mori's request. Meanwhile, on the recommendation of the acting Japanese Consul in New York, Tomita Tetsunosuke, an ex-student of the Bryant-Stratton-Whitney College at Newark, Mori invited Dr. W. C. Whitney to teach at his school. Whitney arrived in Japan in August 1875 together with his family to take up the post. There seems to have been some misunderstanding between Mori and Whitney over commercial education in Japan, but we shall come back to that later.

Construction of the school, to be named Shōhō Kōshūjo (Commercial Training School) was begun, but without waiting for the completion of the building, the school started in temporary premises in September 1875. This marked the beginning of commercial, or business, education in Japan generally and, in particular, the inauguration of a school which was eventually to develop into Hitotsubashi University. Fukuzawa, one of the three trustees of the school (with colleagues Mori Arinori and Mitsukuri Shūhei) wrote in the prospectus:

> . . . In the past when Japan closed itself to the outer world its merchants had only to be acquainted with inland trade, and it was sufficient for them to be smart enough not to miss any business chance there. . . . Now that foreign trade has begun, things have changed drastically. So far the wealth or skill of a merchant has only been a private matter. He should now know the public side of his affairs, which is how to deal with Western merchants. . . . The civilization of the country as a whole is such that backwardness in business and trade only is not to blame. Nothing can be improved all of a sudden. . . . In every Western country it has been recognized that where there are merchants, there are also commercial schools.

> It is as though where there were samurai in the feudal ages, there were fencing schools. In fighting one another by means of the sword one cannot go to the battlefield without learning the art of fencing beforehand. Likewise, in the age of battles by means of business, one cannot confront foreigners without learning the art of business.[12]

To claim that the object of a commercial training school is to teach the would-be merchant how to fight against foreigners is nothing but nationalism, or, one might even call it, mercantilism.

Two incidents, one involving Tomita, the acting consul in New York, and another involving Mori, illustrate this point. Tomita had been sent by his clan to study at the private school of Katsu Rintarō, who later achieved fame for his role representing the Shogunate in the negotiations which led successfully to the peaceful transfer of political power that became known as the Meiji Restoration. Katsu sent Tomita to America to accompany his son who intended to enter the Naval Academy at Annapolis. When Tomita heard the news of the collapse of the Shogunate regime, he hastened back to Tokyo, worried about his master, Katsu, and the lord of his own clan at Sendai, who had joined the local revolt against the new regime. When Tomita met Katsu, he was amazed to find the latter furious with him. Katsu told him to consider why he had been in the United States of America. According to Katsu it was not for the sake of a mere clan, or of the Shogunate government, or for Katsu himself. Those were all minor considerations in comparison with the future of the nation at large. It was the nation that mattered. Katsu sent Tomita back to America.

Once Katsu's son had succeeded in entering the academy, Tomita became a student at Whitney's commercial college. But why particularly a commercial college? A very likely answer is that what Katsu had in mind was to prepare capable persons who could contribute to the modernization of the country to the point where Japan could compete with Western countries. Tomita got to know Whitney, and later recommended him to Mori as the most suitable person to be a teacher in the school Mori was then so determined to establish in Tokyo.

With this background it seems quite natural that, later in 1875, when Tomita met the protectionist H. C. Carey he promised to translate his *Principles of Social Science* (1858–59) into Japanese. Although Tomita became too busy to do it himself, in the preface to the fourth edition of the Japanese version prepared by a friend of his, Inukai Tsuyoshi, he states that Carey had told him to be careful about what the Westerners had done and were still doing to the Asiatic nations. It would seem natural, too, that he also wrote a preface to the Japanese translation of *Das nationale System* by Friedrich List, in which he stressed that Japan ought not to follow the way proposed by Adam Smith.

The second illustration comes from the rather mysterious attitude Mori had towards Whitney. Soon after Whitney's arrival in Japan, Mori wrote in one of his letters to a friend that he was much disappointed in Whitney's person and calibre. Although other people concerned, such as Fukuzawa, Mitsukuri, and others, received Whitney warmly, quite suddenly Mori appeared to have lost his enthusiasm for a commercial school.[13]

It was only with the persistent persuasion of the other supporters and the offer of a substantial sum of money from Katsu that Mori was finally convinced to open the school. The reason for his disappointment and loss of enthusiasm is still unknown. It is quite likely that Mori had in mind a school for future merchants who could compete with, and protect the country's interests from, overseas merchants, whereas Whitney simply had in mind commercial education in the technical sense of the term, just as he had taught it at his own college at Newark.

If that was the case, we may safely conclude that Mori's disappointment with Whitney, Katsu's fury with Tomita, and the spirit in which Fukuzawa wrote that prospectus—all these came from the same root: nationalism or, as it may be more proper to say, nationalism and enlightenment combined, an ideal basis for the first Japanese commercial school, and the same spirit characterized by the economic thought of Fukuzawa Yukichi.

What were the subjects actually taught at the earliest stage of the school's existence? Regrettably, hardly anything is left to use as evidence. There is only a simplified version of the rules and regulations of the evening course at the school, according to which lectures were to be delivered from seven to nine every evening, except for Saturdays and Sundays. Subjects to be taught were from *Bryant & Stratton's Common School Book-Keeping*, translated into Japanese by Fukuzawa: English conversation, grammar and penmanship, mathematics, and geography.[14] It may be presumed that at least the same subjects, and perhaps some more, were taught in the regular day course.

Another document, dated December 1875, entitled 'The Simplified Regulations of the Commercial Training School',[15] reveals that to be admitted students should be at least fifteen years old, and that the subjects to be taught in the regular two-year course were: English (reading and pronunciation), mathematics, dictation, calligraphy, commercial mathematics, promissory-notes, bookkeeping, deed-writing, catalogue-making, bills of exchange, receipts, bank bills, invoices, transport by sea and by land for the first-year students; and for the second-year students English commercial correspondence, political economy, banking, brokerage, insurance companies, the post office, retail, wholesale, bookkeeping. By 1883, a total of 716 students had been admitted, whereas only 30 had managed to finish their studies by that year.

Just two months after the launching of the school, Mori was appointed Minister to Peking. His request for the Tokyo Council to take over the school was accepted. Then in September the following year, the school was once again transferred from the council to Tokyo prefectural government, thus completing the transition from a private to a public institution. In 1878 the prefectural government decided that it could no longer afford to pay the high salary Whitney received, and discharged him, though the contract between him and his former employer Mori had not yet expired. Two other American teachers of commercial subjects (F. A. Meyer and A. J. Hare) were employed in his place.

In 1880 the school offered students aged at least fifteen a three-year course, in six terms. The first to third terms were devoted to theory, the fourth and fifth to theory and practice, and the sixth to practice only.

In 1881 the school again changed its regulations, moving from a three-year to a five-year course. To be admitted students had to be thirteen years old and to have finished primary school education. The five years were divided into ten terms, and the subjects to be taught in each term were as follows:

First term: calligraphy, mathematics, bookkeeping, commercial practice, commercial geography, political economy, natural and artificial commodities, composition, dictation, commercial bargaining, English (spelling, reading, penmanship); second term: continuation of first term; third and fourth terms: continuation of above, with some modifications; fifth term: commercial composition, commercial dictation, customs regulations (national and foreign), international treaties, commercial law (national and foreign), national decrees (bank, public loan, telegraph, post office), commercial bargaining, practice (retailer, wholesaler, broker), English (geography, world history, penmanship, conversation, etc.).

Sixth term: continuation of above, with slight modifications; seventh term: Fawcett's short political economy, Bryant and Stratton's bookkeeping, Bryant and Stratton's commercial arithmetic, Brown's goods and commodities, bookkeeping practice, commercial bargaining; eighth term: continuation of seventh-term subjects; ninth term: F. A.

Walker, *Science of Wealth* (1871), A. L. Perry, *Elements of Political Economy* (1865), English, French, telegraphic code, English commercial correspondence, commercial bargaining, practice (retailer, broker, wholesaler, manufacturer); tenth term: continuation of above, with a few modifications, particularly in practice (bank, insurance company, shipping company, post office, customs office, etc.).

We see that political economy is at last defined. What had been listed simply as political economy without further description, is now more clearly described, though it is uncertain whether 'Fawcett's short political economy' means Henry Fawcett's *Manual of Political Economy* (1863) or M. G. Fawcett's (his wife) *Political Economy for Beginners* (1870). Even so, together with Walker and Perry in the ninth and tenth terms, there can be no doubt that the political economy taught in the Commercial Training School was nothing but the popularized version of classical political economy, in spite of the nationalist spirit that lay at the basis of the school. The English textbooks were lent to the students, following the practice of Keiō, Senshū and other schools.

The number of students steadily increased and in the same year (1881) the enrolment was as high as 200. But the school encountered a serious crisis when the prefectural government decided that it could not afford to support it any longer, and planned to close the school after the end of the financial year, i.e., July 1881. The then minister of education reminded the governor of Tokyo Prefecture of the use and benefit that the school had proved to have so far. A substantial sum of financial aid was offered by the minister of agriculture and trade. Three years later, in March 1884, the school was transferred to that ministry, thus becoming a national institution, renamed Tokyo Commercial School (Tokyo Shōgyō Gakkō). Most of the graduates proceeded to the business world, though whether they were to become nationalist-minded businessmen or 'captains of industry' is a matter for conjecture.

2. Further Developments

In 1902, Tokyo Commercial School, with a new structure and a new name, Tokyo Kōtō Shōgyō Gakkō (Tokyo Higher Commercial School), became established as the first collegiate school of commerce in Japan. In this section we examine the development of commercial education at this institution ensuing its early history up to 1884, showing the evolution from the original practical basis founded by W. C. Whitney to a college of higher commercial and economic education. The demand for collegiate training for future businessmen appears to have reflected the rapid development of Japanese capitalism during this period. The Japanese economy entered into self-sustained growth after two successful wars, with China in 1894–95 and with Russia in 1904–5.[16]

The development of commercial education in Japan runs parallel to the movement towards a collegiate commercial education in Europe and America. In America, the Wharton School of Finance and Economy in Pennsylvania was established in 1881, then in 1898 the College of Commerce was set up in Chicago and California, both of which were fundamentally different from the 'Chain of Commercial Colleges' of the 1860s. In Germany a Handelshochschule was founded in Leipzig in 1898, then in 1901 in Cologne. In England, too, the Faculty of Commerce was created in Birmingham in 1902. With the rise of large-scale industries towards the end of the nineteenth century, the business community in the capitalist countries obviously felt the need for higher commercial or business education for future officials, for 'officers' (as opposed to clerks) of the mercantile and industrial army. It came to be realized that the training of businessmen was as important for the community as the training of lawyers and doctors, and that the art of commerce was just as much in need of an adequate and organized education in a college or university as law and medicine.[17] Japan, however much a late-comer, seemed never to be far behind in this world-wide development. Especially after the Sino-Japanese War in 1894–95 the teachers and students at Hitotsubashi united in a campaign for improved arrangements for education in commercial science. This early history of the school can be conveniently divided into two parts: the period under the headmastership of Yano Jirō, 1884–93, and the period after the appointment of Koyama Kenzō as headmaster in 1895.

The Shōhō Kōshūjo (Commercial Training School) was transferred to the Ministry of Agriculture and Trade in 1884, and renamed Tokyo Shōgyō Gakkō (Tokyo Commercial School). Succeeding Kawakami Kin'ichi, Yano Jirō, the school's former director, was appointed headmaster, and held this position until his dismissal from office in 1893. Under his leadership, American-style, practical commercial education dominated the school. Bookkeeping and commercial practice were the two major subjects, with the aim of training commercial clerks for employment in the traditional merchant houses.[18] In January 1884, the Ministry of Education issued the 'General Regulations for Commercial Schools', the first governmental regulations concerning commercial education in Japan.[19] Then several commercial schools renewed their regulations and some five more commercial schools were founded by the local governments as schools of middle rank. When Tokyo Commercial School opened in March of the same year, the Ministry of Education established its own school, Kōtō Shōgyō Gakkō (Higher Commercial School), affiliated with the Tokyo Foreign Language School, which had been operating since 1873. The Higher Commercial School is believed to have been the first higher commercial education institution in Japan, though it survived in its original form for only one and a half years.[20]

The school followed the Belgian model of higher commercial education, based on the highly successful Institut Supérieur de Commerce d'Anvers, which was, towards the end of the nineteenth century, perhaps one of the most advanced commercial education institutions in the world. It attracted students from all over the world, literally speaking, 'from China to Peru'. William Layton, professor of English at the Institut, deplored the decline of English commerce and the backwardness in the English commercial education, writing that 'not only France, Germany, Switzerland, and Italy, but also Japan in the Far East, followed the Belgian example in founding higher commercial schools'.[21]

In 1885, Julian van Stappen, a graduate of the Institut Supérieur de Commerce d'Anvers, was invited to teach at the Higher Commercial School. In May of the same year Tokyo Commercial School, under the leadership of Yano, was finally placed under the control of the Ministry of Education. In September it was amalgamated with the Higher Commercial School and with Tokyo School of Foreign Languages, and this united Tokyo Commercial School reopened in the place called Hitotsubashi, with Yano Jirō as its headmaster and Viscount Mori of the Ministry of Education as its superintendent. However, as has often been remarked, the amalgamation, initiated by Mori and Yano, did not proceed smoothly: there arose a great deal of opposition against this reorganization among the students of the original Higher Commercial School, and Julian van Stappen is said to have left the school because of his dissatisfaction. These feelings of dissatisfaction and opposition do not seem to have subsided and were the main reason for the later agitation for the expulsion of the headmaster Yano.[22]

According to the revised regulations issued in July 1886, the new Tokyo Commercial School was to be the 'place where the future administrators and managers of commercial affairs, or the future directors of and teachers in the commercial schools are to be trained'. In December of the same year, Arthur Marischal was invited from Belgium to teach at the school. In October 1887, after the educational standard had been raised and the course had been divided into a one-year preparatory course and a four-year principal course, it was renamed Kōtō Shōgyō Gakkō or the Higher Commercial School. It remained the only governmental higher commercial school until 1902, when Kobe Higher Commercial School was opened. Thus the Higher Commercial School at Hitotsubashi was to become one of the two main sources, the other being Keiō Gijuku, of the supply of teachers for the intermediate-level commercial schools and of business leaders.[23]

As far as political economy is concerned, an outline was taught in the first year; money, banking, and foreign trade in the second year; taxation, national debt, accounting, and administration in the third year; and statistics was taught in the second year. The principal teacher for political economy was Tsuchiko Kinshirō, who had been transferred from the Ministry of Finance.[24] The subjects taught at the Higher Commercial School differed considerably from those at Keiō. The Higher Commercial School at that time had neither economists of the stature of Keiō's Garrett Droppers and E. H. Vickers, nor the economic teaching of Tokyo Imperial University's E. F. Fenollosa.

They did have Arthur Marischal, who during his six years at the Higher Commercial School taught all the main subjects in commercial science, such as merchandise, commercial history, commercial geography and commercial practice. He was 'the most important person in transplanting European commercial science' into the Higher Commercial School in Tokyo.[25] Undoubtedly it was commercial science, not political economy, which characterized the curriculum of the school in its early days. Marischal also introduced commercial education to the people of Japan, lecturing for the Dainihon Kyōikukai (Educational Society of Japan) on the education of the merchant in Europe.[26] A farewell article, 'Good-bye, Mr. Arthur Marischal', testifies to his meritorious service to the school in its early days.[27]

In 1892, E. J. Blockhuys, who was qualified as a Licencié en Sciences Commerciales from Antwerp in 1879, came as the successor to Marischal. For forty years Blockhuys taught the practice of foreign trade, commercial geography, commerical arithmetic, and commercial English. He remained with the school, and subsequently with Tokyo University of Commerce until March 1930 and died on Feburary 24, 1931, in Japan.[28] No other foreign teachers of specialized subjects (except those for foreign languages) came to Hitotsubashi until 1897, when Ernest Foxwell, a Cambridge graduate and brother of H. S. Foxwell, came as a lecturer in commercial economics.

A number of the students and staff of the school went to Belgium to study at the Institut Supérieur de Commerce d'Anvers. Iida Hatarō, probably the first of them, went in 1887; Harada Sadanosuke in 1888; Murase Haruo, later the authority on insurance science in Japan, and Nagatomi Yūkichi in 1889; then the eminent practical economist, Seki Hajime, went there in 1898.[29]

Iida Hatarō, who had studied under Julian van Stappen, left Tokyo Commercial School without finishing the course, and went to Belgium in February 1887 and was taken into the institute by Stappen. After the preparatory course and the two-year principal course, Iida received the degree of Licencié en Sciences Commerciales and came back to Tokyo.[30] Although it was only after its reorganization in 1897 that the Institut awarded the degree of 'Licencié du degré supérieur en sciences commerciales et consulaires', the institute had often been called the 'Consular School' while Iida was there. In his article, 'Ryōji-ron' (On the Consul), he attached great importance to the consular report for a prosperous commercial nation.[31] According to his article 'Belgie-koku Shōgyō Gakkō no Hanashi' (On the Commercial School in Belgium), while commercial geography, merchandise and commercial practice were the three major subjects in the institute, commercial practice was properly called 'the primary subject'. The 'Report on Higher Commercial Education in Belgium' by the Consul-General, Gerald de Courcy Perry, also says that the course of practical commercial instruction in the 'commercial bureau' or 'commercial office', where the students would carry on imaginary business operations of all kinds, was one of the most important features of the institute.[32] What was essential in this establishment seems to have been the collaboration or coordination of commercial science and commercial practice, in short, practical commercial science.

In November 1889, Murase Haruo, a founder of the tradition of *jitsugaku* (practical science) at Hitotsubashi,[33] and his friend Nagatomi Yūkichi, also went to Belgium before finishing their courses at the school. According to Itani Zen'ichi, they left the Higher Commercial School, dissatisfied with Yano's American-style, strictly practical commercial education.[34] Murase, who had received the degree of Licencié en Sciences Commerciales in 1892 and had spent another six months in Leipzig to study insurance, came back to the Higher Commercial School in April 1893, then entered the business community, becoming the vice-president of Imperial Marine Insurance in 1895. While working in the business world, Murase also lectured in commercial science at Hitotsubashi. He was a great authority on marine and fire insurance, and his *Murase Hoken Zenshū* (Murase's Collected Works on Insurance) was published in 1926.[35]

3. Towards University Status

Towards the end of the 1880s, two streams of thought had currency among the students of the Higher Commercial School: on the one hand 'Kaikakuha', or the reformist group; and on the other 'Maedareha', or the conservative group. The latter, whose members were the sons of merchant families, was inclined to learn practical commerce only, and to concentrate on their own benefit and their families' prosperity. They were willing to obey blindly the policy of their schoolmaster, Yano Jirō, whereas the students who were anxious for reform were indignant at the miserable situation of Japan's foreign trade, which had been taken in the hands of foreign merchants in the settlements under the unequal treaties.[36] They were eager to pursue the new and advanced arts of commerce and foreign languages, in order to confront and compete with the foreign merchants. At the beginning of the 1890s those 'Kaikakuha' students came to be profoundly conscious of the need for the Higher Commercial School to become the seat of education for the new arts of commerce, and the institution for the training of the leaders of commerce and industry. However, its headmaster, Yano, doggedly stuck to his educational policy of producing only clerks. Consequently the reformist students clashed with Yano over his educational policy, culminating in a student movement to have him dismissed.[37] In 1893, Headmaster Yano was finally relieved of his position.

About two years after the dismissal of Yano, Koyama Kenzō, a secretary to the Minister of Education, was appointed headmaster of the Higher Commercial School in August 1895. He held office until May 1898. The period under Koyama's headmastership was a time of great transition in the Japanese economy after the Sino-Japanese War of 1894–95. As part of its industrial policies the Meiji government gradually paid more attention to efficient industrial education, and Koyama had given distinguished service in that field together with Teshima Seiichi of Tokyo Technical School.[38] In July 1897, addressing the audience at the graduation ceremony, Koyama said: 'In these days of great commercial and industrial enterprise the necessity for commercial education is particularly urgent'. He also remarked that the Higher Commercial School should exert every effort and use every means in order to supply the country with men qualified to withstand the strong competition in this field of the world's commerce.[39] It was actually 'the time of commercial renovation' in Japan, as the prospectus of *Shōgyō Sekai* (Commercial World) noted, in November 1898.[40]

During his term of office, Koyama revised the curriculum to a large extent, and improved and enlarged the membership of the teaching staff, taking in some specialists from business circles and sending young teaching staff to Europe and America to study.[41] The main points in his revision of the curriculum were: (1) establishment of the subject of mechanical engineering, exchanging the professors with Tokyo Technical School; (2) introduction of the subject of commercial morality, to foster a high integrity befitting the modern businessman; (3) improvement of the lectures on political economy and law so that these two subjects along with the science of commerce would become the school's educational core, and further subdivision of the courses on political economy and statistics, into political economy, statistics and finance; and (4) setting up the science of commerce as a subject.

Koyama thought it essential to nurture trustworthiness in each individual's character, or to foster 'business habits', so as to make men morally blameless and worthy of the reputation of good businessmen.[42] Commercial morality was taught by Nakajima Rikizō. Political economy was taught mainly by Yamazaki Kakujirō from the University of Tokyo, while Takahashi Jirō of the Statistical Bureau of the Cabinet taught statistics; and the theory and practice of finance were taught by Soeda Juichi, Chief of the Supervisory Office of the Ministry of Finance. There was a very large staff to teach the science of commerce: Soyama Shōzō, who had studied at the Ecole Supérieure de Commerce de Paris for three years; Mizushima Tetsuya, recruited from Yokohama Specie Bank by Koyama; E. J. Blockhuys, Murase Haruo, and others. In addition, Ishikawa Iwao lectured on merchandise, Nasa Tadayuki on commercial and industrial geography, Yokoi Tokifuyu and Wadagaki Kenzō on commercial and industrial history, Seki Hajime and Sano Zensaku on the practice of commerce and bookkeeping, Ishikawa Bungo on the practice of commerce and English, and Shida Kōtarō on commercial law.[43]

In 1879, under the leadership of Koyama, Senkō-bu (Department of Special Studies) was instituted in the Higher Commercial School, for the benefit of graduates who desired to pursue their studies further in particular subjects or to be engaged in the consular service. The term of study was at first one year, but was extended to two years in 1899 under the headmastership of Komai Shigetada, who was in office from March 1899 until his death at the age of forty-nine in December 1901. The graduates of the Department of Special Studies were granted the degree of Shōgyōgakushi, later Shōgakushi (B. Comm.).[44] It seems to have been about this time that the teaching of political economy was greatly extended in the Higher Commercial School at Hitotsubashi. In 1897 Foxwell had arrived as a lecturer in commercial economics.

From 1898 Baron Tajiri Inajirō, Under-Secretary to the Minister of Finance, also joined the Higher Commercial School as a lecturer in commercial economics.

After the turn of the century, Sano Zensaku, Seki Hajime, and Fukuda Tokuzō, who had just come back from Europe, began to teach political economy as well as the practice of commerce at the newly named Tokyo Higher Commercial School. In April 1902, owing to the establishment of the Higher Commercial School in Kobe, the Higher Commercial School at Hitotsubashi was renamed Tokyo Higher Commercial School. In 1903 Charles Sumner Griffin was appointed as professor of political economy. In 1905 O. M. W. Sprague, who had been C. F. Dunbar's assistant during the last years of his activity as teacher, and had edited Dunbar's *Economic Essays* (1904), came to Hitotsubashi to teach political economy and finance.[45]

The impressive strengthening of the Higher Commercial School undertaken by Koyama Kenzō and Komai Shigetada attracted attention in Germany, where, according to Fukuda Tokuzō who was then studying there, the urgency of a truly university-level education for future businessmen was earnestly being advocated.[46] Towards the very end of the nineteenth century a genuinely higher commercial education movement, initiated in Germany and in America, seems to have developed. The 'big spurt' in these movements in Europe was reported in detail by Fukuda Tokuzō, Seki Hajime, and Ishikawa Bungo, who had all been sent by Koyama to Germany and Belgium.[47]

R. Beigel in Strassburg, then in Germany, highly praised the Higher Commercial School in Tokyo in his book, *Der Kampf um die Handelshochschule* (The Struggle for a Higher Commercial School), a part of which Fukuda translated and sent to Koyama, together with a long letter from Munich, dated May 31, 1898.[48] After reading the English edition of the *Calendar of the Higher Commercial School for the Year 1896–1897*, Beigel wrote that the Higher Commercial School was 'most nearly allied to what the German people tried to establish as Handelshochschule or Fakultät für Handelswissenschaft'. Since the Handelshochschule at Leipzig, the first Handelshochschule in Germany, had not yet been established, Beigel thought that Japan was more advanced than Germany in the higher commercial education movement, and that the German intelligentsia should therefore follow the Japanese example.[49] According to Fukuda's report on the 'Recent Situation of Commercial Education in Europe and America', when the Handelshochschule at Leipzig was inaugurated in April 1898, the *Zeitschrift für das gesamte Kaufmännische Unterrichtswesen* (Journal for Commercial Education System) also reported that 'thus the German idea of

Handelshochschule has now reached the east coast of the Pacific Ocean, whereas it had already existed on the west coast of the Pacific Ocean, i.e., in Japan'.[50]

The Handelshochschule at Leipzig was founded in close alliance with the University of Leipzig, where the famous economist Karl Bücher was playing a leading role. In Fukuda's opinion Leipzig Handelshochschule was 'the first higher commercial education institute of genuine university rank in the world'.[51] In October 1898, the Department of Commercial Science was established as part of the Royal Technical High School at Aachen; in 1901 Handelshochschulen were established both at Cologne and at Frankfurt am Main. The avowed object of these Handelshochschulen was the training of future business leaders or a 'business elite', but their curricula seem to have centred on political economy rather than business subjects, and emphasis was laid upon general education rather than specialist training. In their early years these Handelshochschulen apparently aimed both to raise the social status of businessmen and to broaden the outlook of future businessmen, but they did not provide thorough training in business techniques and business administration. All this gives the essence of the movement for higher commercial education around the turn of the century, before the foundation of the Berlin School of Business Administration in 1906 and of the Harvard Business School in 1908.[52] Until these institutions for professional business education were developed, political economists were in the key positions, and economic subjects rather dominated the Handelshochschulen. What Fukuda wanted to transfer from Europe to Japan seems to have been this type of general education rather than professional training. In the case of the Leipzig Handelshochschule most of the subject, such as political economy, statistics, finance and law, except for the proper commercial subjects, were taught at the University of Leipzig.[53]

Richard Ehrenberg, an economics professor from Göttingen who was responsible for the inauguration of the Leipzig Handelshochschule, seems to have emphasized the role of economics in the teaching of future businessmen. He considered the curriculum of the London School of Economics and Political Science to be the model for the soon-to-be-established German Handelshochschulen.[54] Seki Hajime, then in Belgium, also admired the higher commercial education at the London School of Economics, which had been founded in October 1895 with W. A. S. Hewins as its director. Hewins was one of the pioneer economists of the English Historical School at the turn of the century, together with W. J. Ashley, an economic historian with direct ties to the German Historical School who organized the Faculty of

Commerce at Birmingham University in 1902, at the instance of Joseph Chamberlain and the Birmingham Chamber of Commerce.[55] In the organization of the commercial department, the London School of Economics enjoyed the co-operation and support of the London Chamber of Commerce and the Technical Education Board of the London County Council. The 'Report of the Special Sub-Committee on Commercial Education' by the Technical Education Board in 1899 was translated in an abridged form by Seki Hajime in the same year and sent back to Japan to be published by the Ministry of Education.[56] Sano Zensaku, who was probably studying at London School of Economics then, gave a lecture on commercial education there, a part of which was printed in the 'Special Reports on Educational Subjects' by the Board of Education as 'Commercial Education in Japan' in 1902.[57]

In 1898 an International Congress on Commercial Education was held at Antwerp. Referring to this, E. J. Blockhuys of the Higher Commercial School wrote: 'It is most gratifying to see that Japan is not lagging behind in the promotion of this most useful branch of technical education'.[58] The next International Congress was held in May 1899 in Venice, where Fukuda received courteous treatment as a guest of honour, and the Higher Commercial School in Tokyo was highly praised, as reported in *Gazzetta di Venezia* of May 7, 1899.[59] In 1900, the Paris International Exhibition was made an occasion on which to hold the First International Congress of the Alumni Association of the Higher Commercial Schools. Seki Hajime attended this meeting as a delegate of the Alumni Association of the Higher Commercial School in Tokyo and presented a paper in French about the 'Association des anciens élèves de l'Ecole Supérieure de Commerce à Tôkiô, Japon'.[60] Fukuda was a member of the organizing committee of the International Society for the Encouragement of Commercial Education founded in June 1901 in Zurich.[61] In the same year, when writing about the Handelshochschule at Cologne, Seki concluded with the words of Eberhard Gothein, Professor of Economics at the Cologne Handelshochschule: 'The age of mere debates is over and the age of action has come'.[62] In this way both Fukuda and Seki continued their efforts to ensure that the Higher Commercial School in Tokyo never slipped behind the international commercial education movement at the turn of the century.

In addition, an event of particular importance was a meeting of the teaching staff of Hitotsubashi in Berlin in January 1901. On this day eight professors, who were studying abroad, gathered in Berlin; after five days' discussion, they drafted a statement on the 'urgent necessity of establishing a university of commerce', along with a detailed 'Curriculum for a university of commerce', signed by Ishikawa Iwao, Ishikawa Bungo, Kanda Naibu, Takimoto Yoshio, Tsumura Hidematsu, Fukuda Tokuzō, Shida Kōtarō, and Seki Hajime. This statement has become widely known as the 'Berlin Declaration'.[63] In 1900 Sano Zensaku came back to Japan, and in 1901 both Fukuda and Seki returned. At Hitotsubashi they spoke enthusiastically to the students about commercial education in Europe and the necessity of securing the commercial predominance of Japan by means of training educated businessmen. It was in this way that the need for the creation of 'Captains of Industry' was proclaimed far and wide.[64]

10

For Diffusing Economic Knowledge: Tokyo Senmon Gakkō (Waseda)

Ikuo Ōmori

1. Introduction

In 1982, Waseda University celebrated its centenary, counting from the birth of its predecessor Tokyo Senmon Gakkō (Tokyo School of Special Studies). In the early stage of its history, Waseda, or Tokyo School of Special Studies, suffered oppression by the government as will be described in this chapter. This experience gave the school a characteristic spirit, i.e., a critical spirit of the authorities. Tokyo Senmon Gakkō, therefore, contributed greatly to the development of various activities in politics and journalism, although it had less influence upon business activities during the Meiji era (1868–1912) than other universities or colleges. Even so, it may be said that Waseda University has played its part in the institutionalization of political economy.

There were four outstanding features in the education and study of political economy in Tokyo School of Special Studies. The first three are the separation of political economy from jurisprudence or the science of state shown both in departmental organization and in curricula; the introduction of J. S. Mill's political economy into Japan; and the influence of American political economy upon some early economists who graduated from the school. In the first part of this chapter, we shall make a survey of the development of the courses in political economy in relationship to the organizational arrangements between 1882 and 1902. We shall next examine the impact of Western economic thought upon the school in the light of some textbooks, including many lecture notes, published for the extramural or correspondence courses. Our further task will be devoted to some characteristics of the thoughts on political economy held by three distinguished members of the staff of the school in its early days: Amano Tameyuki, Abe Isoo, and Shiozawa Masasada. Finally, the fourth feature deserving attention is that Waseda University has continued to promote the school's emphasis on the diffusion and utilization of political economy through the popularization of economic education. This idea is stated distinctly in the third clause of the university's 'Declaration of Aims', which implies not only the practical utilization of knowledge but also the diffusion of it through education. In the last part of this chapter, we shall consider, therefore, how the school put this idea into practice.

2. The Birth of Tokyo School of Special Studies

The forerunner of Waseda University, Tokyo Senmon Gakkō, was established in 1882 by Ōkuma Shigenobu, who later assumed the premiership. The school owes its existence to Ōkuma's generosity. Between 1878 and 1881 Ōkuma was at the height of his political power as the head of the Sangi (member of the council of state) of the Meiji government. Then, in October 1881, a serious political crisis developed both from the problem of the disposal of government-owned property in Hokkaido and from the controversy over the introduction of a parliamentary system. Ōkuma, who had advocated democracy, in opposition to the Satsuma and Chōshū clans in the government, was suspected of conspiring with others against the government and was consequently dismissed from the office in what was called the 'Political Crisis of Meiji 14 (1881)'. Immediately after his dismissal he launched into a plan to establish an institution of higher education with his own funds. From its very inception, the school was, therefore, regarded as Ōkuma's private school against the government, which is why the government subjected it to various kinds of pressure.

Ōkuma's plans for the school were carried out by Ono Azusa who was his right-hand man both in political and educational activities. After studying jurisprudence and banking in the United States and Britain between 1871 and 1874, Ono became a government official as a legal and financial expert. Following the 'Political Crisis of 1881', he resigned his post of auditor in the government and devoted the remainder of his life to Tokyo School of Special Studies. The school would have never been instituted without his strenuous exertions which, incidentally, hastened his own death. Ono stated his critical view on the state of Japanese education in his days, as follows: 'We have not enjoyed academic independence for a long time because of the fatal defects in our traditional system of education. I am firmly convinced that independence in learning can lay the foundation of the independence of a state'.[1]

Ono's conviction was eventually realized in the first two clauses of the 'Declaration of Aims at Waseda University' issued in 1912: 'Waseda University aims to uphold the independence of learning, to promote the practical utilization of knowledge, and to create good citizenship. / To uphold the independence of learning, the university will strive to emphasize freedom of research and investigation, and to encourage original and creative studies, thereby contributing to the advancement of knowledge'.[2] Thus, one of the most important features implicit in the 'Declaration of Aims' was the freedom of investigation. Ono and others of the school were firmly convinced that freedom of investigation would lead, by exerting a stimulating influence upon government institutions, to sound progress in civilization.

Furthermore, Ono had the conviction that the independence, in its true sense, of a nation must be based upon education given in its own language. Thus, another characteristic of the new school was the training of students in the new learning of the West in Japanese. This seems to be one of the most significant achievements which was attributable to Ono and Tokyo School of Special Studies in the history of higher education in Japan.[3]

It does not mean, however, that Ono overlooked the significance of studying foreign languages. From his own experience he required students to learn foreign languages, in particular English, in order to study various branches of learning in Europe and the United States. Ono seems to have encouraged his students to learn English from a kind of pragmatic standpoint: 'Learning in Germany, I think, has not yet reached its zenith nor has that in France. Thus, I cannot but appreciate the character of English people because of their attempt to cultivate the spirit of self-government and to enhance their pride in nationhood'.[4]

This appreciation of British civilization is also evident in the influence of classical political economy in Britain on the early economics teaching at the school.

Another feature of the institutionalization of political economy at Tokyo School of Special Studies was that, from the beginning, political economy was taught not so much in the Department of Law as in the Department of Political Science and Economics. Generally speaking, in most other schools in those days courses in political economy belonged to a branch of jurisprudence, following Continental models. One of the few exceptions was the Department of Political Economy at Senshū School (later Senshū University) founded in 1880.[5] Among those who gathered around Ono as lecturers at Tokyo School of Special Studies were graduates from the University of Tokyo who had left their alma mater unhappy with its pro-German tendency. Takata Sanae and Tsubouchi Yūzō (Shōyō) were, along with Amano Tameyuki, to become known as the greatest teachers at the school. While Tsubouchi was considered 'the father of modern Japanese literature' rather than an economist, Takata was very much the successor to Ono. Takata, as a political scientist and university administrator, reflected on the early days of the school as follows:

> What may be said (from this fact) is that the University of Tokyo first included political science and political economy in its university curricula. Yet it is our Tokyo Senmon Gakkō (now Waseda University) which was the first to regard political science and political economy as subjects independent of each other and to separate them from law and others.[6]

In the Faculty of Arts at the University of Tokyo, Takata, Amano, and others had taken some courses in political economy taught by E. F. Fenollosa. According to Takata, Fenollosa introduced J. S. Mill and M. G. Fawcett on economic theory, W. S. Jevons and F. A. Walker on money, and H. D. Macleod on banking in his lectures in political economy.[7] The ideas of those Western economists in association with the utilitarian philosophy of Anglo-American origin were, thus, offered to the students of Tokyo School of Special Studies through Fenollosa's disciples.

The idea for the organization of the Department of Political Science and Economics to be independent from the Law Department also stems from the experience of Takata and other graduates at the University of Tokyo. When they studied, the economic education there seems to have followed the British academic tradition. The Department of Political Science and Political Economy, one of the three departments in the Faculty of Arts, provided some courses not only in politics and political economy but also in public law. Only private law was then dealt with in the Faculty of Law. Takata, Amano, Tsubouchi, and others—the founding members of Tokyo School of Special Studies—could be said to have brought with them the basic idea of the University of Tokyo's departmental system into the new institution.

Tokyo School of Special Studies, therefore, opened with three departments: the Department of Political Science (including Political Economy), the Department of Law, and the Department of Science (discontinued after 1885). In 1885, an idea of Ono's was realized with the establishment of the Department of English Studies, which was a sort of department of general education with the subjects taught in English. When, in 1888, the departments of Political Science in English, Law in English, and Public Administration in English opened, the existing departments added the words, 'in Japanese' to their titles. In the 'departments in English' students were required to read a number of textbooks or reference books written in English. Furthermore, graduate courses were inaugurated in the departments three years after the Department of Literature was established in 1890, with Tsubouchi as its head. The school was licensed under the new decree governing private schools in 1899, and at the same time the Higher Preparatory School was opened. In 1902 when the school celebrated the twentieth anniversary of its founding, it acquired the new name of Waseda University. This institution was composed of the Faculties of Political Science and Economics, Law, and Literature, Senmon-bu (Junior Colleges), the Higher Preparatory School, and the Graduate School. In 1904 the Faculty of Commerce was opened.[8] From its establishment in 1882, the number of students increased steadily: the enrolment in 1882 was 65; in 1891, 514; in 1899, 846; in 1900, 1010; and in 1904, 4078.[9]

In short, the history of the school in its early days is full of repeated trials of its founders in improving the organizational arrangements and curricula.

3. Political Economy in the Classroom

Although the founders' attempt at establishing the Department of Political Science reflects their conviction that politics should be independent of law, many courses prepared by them covered political economy rather than politics. It may be remarked, therefore, that political economy also became independent of law. The official records of the university reveal some confusion about what the department itself was formally named:[10] it should not be called the 'Department of Political Science' but correctly the 'Department of Political Science and Economics'. We may assume that the department covered a wide area of what is now called the comprehensive and interdisciplinary study in social sciences.

According to the announcement of the opening of the school in the newspaper *Yūbin Hōchi Shinbun*, the founders planned to provide various courses of study: history, political economy, logic, Japanese and Chinese literature, jurisprudence, constitutional law, psychology, composition, Japanese public finance, social studies, administrative law, theory of law, diplomatic science, political philosophy, and statistics. Among them, the subjects concerned with political economy were as follows.[11] For first-year students: principles of political economy (full-year course). For second-year students: economic history (autumn term), taxation (autumn term), public finance today (autumn term), money (spring term), international trade (spring term), public finance under the Tokugawa (spring term). For third-year students: statistics, an outline (spring term). A peculiar point in this arrangement of subjects is that it appears based on our interpretation of a newspaper report that politics even in a broad sense occupied a smaller pari of the curricula prepared by the founder-members than political economy did. The official record of the university shows a little modification in the political economy courses in the next academic year 1883–84. Economic history, which seems to have been cancelled, was replaced with economic reasoning, banking, national debt and exchange.[12] Some subjects concerned with politics such as principles of politics, general theory of government, constitutional government and political philosophy were also prepared at that time.

Unfortunately, no official records about the teachers in charge of these subjects in the earliest days are available. It seems that the founders took charge of political economy courses; for example, principles of political economy was taught by Amano, money and taxation by Takata, Japanese public finance by Ono, and so on. Before 1897, fifteen people had given a considerable number of lectures in political economy as full- or part-time lecturers.[13] Among them, Amano, Soeda, and Uchida occupied rather influential positions in the development of political economy in Japan. As the economic thought of Amano will be examined later in this chapter and Soeda has been mentioned in the introduction, here we will take notice of Uchida Ginzō.

Uchida Ginzō graduated from both Tokyo School of Special Studies and Tokyo Imperial University, and later became a professor at Kyoto Imperial University. He is said to have been one of the founders of scientific research in Japanese economic history. He began to give lectures in economic history at Tokyo School of Special Studies as a part-time lecturer in 1898. The remarkable feature of his lectures is that Uchida first systematized Japanese economic history including agricultural history, whereas most economic historians before him had not dealt with the production process but only with the circulation process of an economy. The contents of his lectures at the school were presented in book form as *Keizaishi* (Economic History, 1898–99) and *Nihon Keizaishi* (Japanese Economic History, 1902). According to the former work, political economy is divided into three parts: economic history, principles of political economy, and applied political economy.

He also laid stress upon the distinction between economic history and other histories, particularly commercial history or monetary history. In 1899, Uchida held the first chair of Japanese economic history at Tokyo Imperial University, and left Japan four years later to study economic history at the University of Oxford, where he was greatly influenced by British historiography.

Incidentally, it might appear quite peculiar that unlike Tokyo Imperial University and Keiō Gijuku (later Keiō University), Tokyo School of Special Studies employed no foreign economists on its teaching staff. In fact some university records reveal that there were some sixteen foreigners employed as part-time lecturers in the years between 1882 and 1902, nine from the United States, three from Britain, one from Canada, one from Italy, one from China, and one from an unknown country,[14] but, with the exception of two lecturers in law all were simply teachers of foreign languages, and of English conversation in particular. There seem to have been two reasons for this. One was Ono's policy of teaching most subjects in Japanese, a policy shared by Senshū School and other private law schools. The other was of a more practical nature. The school could not afford to spend enough money for the very high salaries then paid to foreign teachers. The founding staff members, represented by Takata, thought that continued dependence on Ōkuma for financial aid would weaken their spirit of independence and that the best way to repay their benefactor would be to place the school on a self-supporting basis. With this end in view, they introduced many reforms and made fair headway towards that goal by their commendable self-sacrifice. After twenty years, Takata recollected that they had had to work hard for a pittance.[15] The school was not, however, yet in a condition that would allow anything like an immediate execution of their plan for the school's future.

An outline of the curriculum of the course in political economy and public finance in the last academic year of Tokyo School of Special Studies (1901–2) shows us the contents of economic subjects in a little more detail:[16] in the first year: principles of political economy (full-year course) covers general remarks, production, distribution, and exchange; economic history (autumn term); history of political economy (spring term) covers history of economic doctrines and critical comments on major economists; in the second year: money (full-year course) covers the nature of money, principle of circulation, single and double standards of money, paper money, and credit; applied political economy (full-year course) covers economic policy, agricultural economy, social problems, and commercial and industrial economy;

public finance (full-year course) covers general remarks and annual expenditure; in the third year: international trade (full-year course) covers international prices, trade policy, and foreign exchange; banking and financing (full-year course) covers use of banks, policy and financial institutions in several countries, financial control, and a brief history; public finance (full-year course) covers annual revenue, taxation, fiscal budget, and public debt.

What should be pointed out in the above is that Amano adopted the so-called trichotomy in principles of political economy: production, distribution, and exchange. Generally speaking, it seems to be proof of the significant influence of Millian methodology upon political economy at Tokyo School of Special Studies. Mill stated in the 'Preliminary Remarks' of his *Principles of Political Economy* (1848) that 'the subject with which its enquiries are conversant has in all ages necessarily constituted one of the chief practical interests of mankind, and, in some, a most unduly engrossing one. / That subject is wealth. Writers on Political Economy profess to teach, or to investigate, the nature of wealth, and the laws of its production and distribution: including, directly or indirectly, the operation of all the causes by which the condition of mankind, or of any society of human beings, in respect of this universal object of human desire, is made prosperous or the reverse'.[17] We shall later examine his influence on the economic thought of Amano.

Some examination questions set by Amano on the principles of political economy show us that his lectures (1886–87) went into an extensive range of economic subjects:

1. Give a definition of the following terms: production, land, consumption, and rent.
2. Point out some factors which increase or decrease the productivity of labour.
3. Discuss the law of diminishing returns and explain why a rent is a sort of residual.
4. Discuss whether or not cultivation proceeds from fertile to less fertile land.

However, Amano began to give his students more practical questions in the academic year 1898–99:

1. What conditions are required in order that a commodity may be converted into money?
2. Explain the following terms: bill of exchange, cheque for withdrawal, and convertible paper currency.
3. How is a price in international trade determined?[18]

The change in these questions was not caused so much by a change of his views on political economy as by his own approach to a practical utilization of it. The idea of practical utilization of economic knowledge would be regarded as one of the most important features of the economic investigation and education at Tokyo School of Special Studies and Waseda University.

4. The Popularization of Economic Education through Publications

We shall now turn to some textbooks, or reference books, used in the classroom. Those books elucidate the influence of the Western political economy upon the school. The founding members clearly recognized that students should read foreign literature extensively, even though they had placed great emphasis on lectures in Japanese. That is why the Department of Political Science and Economics in English was established in 1888. Based on a table of the curriculum in that year and the Library Catalogue first issued in 1903,[19] the reading assignments in the course of political economy and public finance can be guessed to have been as follows: In the first year, J. S. Mill (ed. and abridged by J. L. Laughlin), *Principles of Political Economy*, 1886; L. Cossa, *Guide to the Study of Political Economy*, 1880 (English version of *Guida allo studio dell'Economia Politica*, 1876). In the second year, W. S. Jevons, *Money and the Mechanism of Exchange*, 1882 (1st ed. 1875); H. D. Macleod, *The Elements of Banking*, 1876; W. G. F. Roscher, *Principles of Political Economy* (English translation by J. J. Lalor in 1878, possibly of *System der Volkswirtschaft*, Bd. 1: *Grundlagen der Nationalökonomie*, 1854). In the third year, G. J. Goschen, *The Theory of Foreign Exchange*, 1883; H. C. Adams, *Public Debts*, 1887. Going back to the school's opening days, we also find the following titles listed for reference: J. E. Cairnes, *The Character and Logical Method of Political Economy*, 1870 (1st ed. 1857); F. A. Walker, *Money*, 1878; J. R. McCulloch, *A Treatise on the Principles and Practical Influence of Taxation and the Funding System*, 1865; W. T. Thornton, *On Labour*: *Its Wrongful Claims and Rightful Dues, Its Actual Present and Possible Future*, 1869.

Another document containing Amano's report on his own lectures in the academic year 1882–83 indirectly supports the above guess concerning his assignment of reference books. He wrote:

> I spent four hours a week giving lectures in political economy over two terms. The course ranged from theories of production and distribution during the first term to theory of exchange and methods

> in economic studies during the second term. It was Cairnes both on political economy and on its method [i.e., *Some Leading Principles of Political Economy*, newly expounded ed., 1874], Mill on principles of political economy, Jevons on principles of political economy [probably, *The Theory of Political Economy*, 1871],[20] Walker on wages [i.e., *The Wage Question*, 1876], Thornton on labour, and Walker on money, which I used as reference books.[21]

It is also noted that Amano's lectures were fairly similar to those of his American teacher Fenollosa at the University of Tokyo. The books they recommended were mainly the writings of the Classical (Liberalist) School and its followers in Britain and America, although the names of W. S. Jevons of the Marginal Utility School and W. Roscher of the German Historical School also appeared in the list of references quoted above. Classical political economy represented by such economists as J. S. Mill, the Fawcetts, and Cairnes occupied a dominant position in the academic world of political economy in Britain roughly up to the middle of the 1880s. In the newer work in the field, Jevons had begun to influence H. S. Foxwell and F. Y. Edgeworth. Jevons's version of economic theory was not fully appreciated by Japanese economists at that time. He was then not known as an economic theorist of revolutionary mind, breaking new horizons, but as an applied economist in the field of money, foreign exchange, or labour problems.

One of the most outstanding contributions to the educational system in Meiji Japan attributable to Tokyo School of Special Studies was its publication of numerous transcripts of lectures for the school's correspondence courses. This was of great importance in promoting the extension and utilization of knowledge as well as of popularizing higher education all over Japan. The system of teaching by correspondence, which was inaugurated in 1886, owed its foundation to the foresight of Takata Sanae, and a few years later the school press was established to take charge of the extension course. The school was, thus, estimated to be one of the pioneers in Japan in university extension by means of correspondence. Its success gave stimulus to other institutions so that similar systems were also launched by them. In the field of political economy, Amano contributed to the development of correspondence instruction by publishing many lecture notes. He took charge of a wide range of economic courses here as well as in the classroom. According to Sugihara Shirō's research,[22] Amano's published notes are as follows: *Keizaigaku no Seishitsu* (The Nature of Political Economy) and *Keizaishi* (Economic History), which were in fact the translation of the general and historical parts, respectively, of Cossa's *Guide*, *Beikoku Sozeiron* (Taxation in the United States), *Kokusairon* (National Debt), *Keizaigaku Kenkyū no Hōhō / Keizai Genron* (Methods in Economic Studies / Principles of Political Economy), which is supposed to have been a compilation of H. Fawcett's *Manual of Political Economy*, 1863 (5th ed. 1876); *Gaikoku Bōekiron* (Foreign Trade); *Kaheiron* (On Money), and so on. Another important example is Hiranuma Yoshirō's *Tsūshin Kyōiku Keizaigaku* (Political Economy for Correspondence Courses, 1886), in which a peculiar mixture of Mill's political economy and of the economic thought of the new German Historical School is to be found. This book consists of six parts (general remarks, production, consumption, distribution, exchange, and taxation) with numerous tables and diagrams.[23] These publications were undoubtedly welcomed by miscellaneous classes of people, particularly those living far from large cities such as Tokyo, who had little access to higher education, and we may interpret this as an illustration of the development of the school's aim to promote the diffusion and utilization of learning.

With the establishment of correspondence courses, the school mapped out another kind of publishing plan. In 1884, this plan was coordinated with the movement to found an academic association (*dōkōkai*) including teachers, students and other concerned people from outside the campus. The association planned two kinds of projects: a series of open lectures, and the issuing of an academic periodical, *Chūō Gakujutsu Zasshi* (Central Academic Journal), which was the forerunner of *Waseda Gakuhō* (Waseda Journal), now issued by the Alumni Association of the university. Several papers on political economy appeared in each issue of the journal. In particular, the first two issues (March 10 and 25, 1885) are noteworthy for the following two articles: Amano Tameyuki, 'Ri-shi Chidai Ron' (Mr. Ricardo's Theory of Rent), and W. S. Jevons (tr. by Maebashi Takayoshi), 'On the Measure of Pleasure and Pain in Political Economy'. The second article was a rather free translation of Jevons's 'Theory of Pleasure and Pain', chapter two of his *Theory of Political Economy* (1871), including the two famous diagrams illustrating the law of diminishing marginal utility. This implies that early economists at the school had already started paying attention to economic theories other than those of classical political economy.[24]

The founders drew up a plan to send some of their top graduates abroad to study. In 1900, the school sent off the first of its teachers under the newly established faculty scholarship for study abroad, and then three graduates received scholarships in the following year.

Two of these graduates, Tanaka Hozumi and Shiozawa Masasada, later became professors of political economy at Waseda University. The former received an M.A. degree from Columbia University, the latter studied political economy under Richard T. Ely at Wisconsin, and then at Halle and Berlin. Furthermore, the school record indicates that in the period between 1885 and 1902 fifty-three graduates went abroad to study, of whom twenty-eight (53% of the total) had graduated from the Department of Political Science and Economics, and thirty-eight of them (72%) studied in American universities or institutions.[25] No doubt the educational policy of the school was orientated partly towards the American-style pragmatic education.

There are three important aspects in the influence of American political economy upon the school. First, Fenollosa academically influenced the early teaching staff, such as Amano and Takata, as did Dwight W. Learned, an American teacher at Dōshisha School in Kyoto (later Dōshisha University), who had a tremendous impact upon two students who later became professors at Waseda University, namely, Abe Isoo and Ukita Kazutami.[26] Ukita was known as a sociologist and political scientist. Learned's Christian spirit enlightened them not only with his academic views, but also with his belief in humanism and liberalism. Second, these teachers assigned as textbooks or reference books much of the American economic literature that had been written under the dual influence of the late Classical School in Britain and the early German Historical School represented in particular by Roscher. Third, the school preferred to send its faculty and graduates to study in the United States rather than in Germany during this period. This tradition was kept alive as some second-generation economists of the school (then Waseda University)—such as Inomata Tsunao and Kitazawa Shinjirō—studied economics in American universities during the Taishō period (1912–26).

5. Three Major Economists at Waseda in Its Early Days

(1) The Economic Thought of Amano Tameyuki: A Pioneer in the Study of Political Economy in Japan

Amano Tameyuki towered brilliantly over the other early economists at Waseda University, or even in Japan generally. Besides translating a few foreign books, such as J. S. Mill (J. L. Laughlin ed.), *Principles of Political Economy* (1886; *Kōtō Keizai Genron*, 1891), J. N. Keynes, *The Scope and Method of Political Economy* (1891; *Keizaigaku Kenkyūhō*, 1897), and H. C. Adams, *Public Debts* (1887; *Kōsairon*, 1900), Amano was also an active writer: *Keizai Genron* (The Theory of

Political Economy, 1886), *Shōseihyōjun* (Principles of Commercial Legislation, 1886), *Ginkōron* (On Banking, 1890), *Keizaigaku Kenkyūhō* (Methods in Economic Studies, 1894), *Keizaigakushi* (History of Political Economy, 1898), *Keizaigaku Kōyō* (Elements of Political Economy, 1902), and *Keizaisakuron* (Essays on Economic Policies, 1910). As S. Kirby argued, the acceptance of the Millian political economy into the East was due partly to Mill's integral social theories including political economy, 'which in turn', Kirby said, 'merged into the broader current that also embraced Darwin, Spencer, Buckle, and others. Besides being satisfactorily comprehensive, Mill's treatment was found in the East to be entirely realistic'.[27] Amano doubtless studied economic theory under the influence of Millian political economy through Fenollosa's lectures at the University of Tokyo, although he was always interested in different doctrines, for example, those of J. N. Keynes and W. S. Jevons.

The most important of his works, *Keizai Genron*, was widely acclaimed and by 1896 had run to twenty-one editions, selling, it is said, more than thirty thousand copies.[28] Amano quoted J. E. Cairnes in English, 'It teaches us the conditions of our power in relation to the facts of economic existence, the means by which, in the domain of material well-being, to attain our ends. It is by such knowledge that man becomes the minister and interpreter of Nature and learns to control Nature by obeying her'. The book consists of four parts: general remarks, production, distribution, and exchange. Amano shared with J. S. Mill the concept of separating distribution theory from production theory, though his student, Shiozawa Masasada, attributed the idea to the influence of the Fawcetts. Although Amano essentially just repeated his Western predecessors' theories in his book, his work seems to have been appreciated as the first systematic treatise of political economy in Japan, in spite of its naive interpretation in economic theory.

In the 'General Remarks', Amano distinguished the science of political economy from the art of it:

> By what measure should we distinguish the science of political economy from the art? Generally speaking, the ultimate aim of the science is to inquire into natural laws, whereas the aim of the art is the application of natural laws in order to achieve our practical goals.[29]

Amano clearly believed that political economy as a science must draw a sharp line between itself and the applied field of this science. Accordingly, he had a deep interest in the methodology of political economy and dealt with some methodological questions through the works of Cossa, Cairnes, and J. N. Keynes. It does not mean, however, that he disregarded the art of political economy. On the contrary, in his methodology he seems to have stood on the other side, as is clearly perceived in his writings, such as *Shōseihyōjun* and *Keizaisakuron*. Amano's idea of the 'harmony of science with practice'[30] is implicit in the following remarks on the academic climate at Waseda University:

> It would be wholly wrong if Waseda School were to provide knowledge of just the applied sciences. I really hope that anyone with different aims—to pursue applied studies on the one hand, and to learn the genuine sciences on the other hand—will come and study here.[31]

Amano's second book, *Shōseihyōjun*, is a product of his applied study, a sort of case study undertaken from the viewpoint of the Smithian doctrine of free trade, concerning the comparative effects of laissez-faire and protective policies upon an economy.[32] His aim to promote the diffusion and utilization of economic knowledge was also realized in two other areas, both in higher and secondary business education, and in journalism. The former was given form with the establishment of Waseda Jitsugyō Gakkō (Waseda Middle School of Business) in 1901 for secondary-level education and of the Faculty of Commerce at Waseda University in 1904 for higher commercial education. As to the latter, although his first attempt to publish and edit *Nihon Rizai Zasshi* (Japan Economist) in 1889 failed within only a year,[33] he trained a considerable number of would-be economists in journalism as the manager and executive editor (1897–1907) of *Tōyō Keizai Shinpō* (Oriental Economist).

As a journalist, Amano took a stand for free trade in the controversy over the Japanese trade policy, which had arisen from discussion over how to industrialize the Japanese economy. He was regarded as a 'moderate' adherent of free trade, and was opposed to the 'radical' free trader, Taguchi Ukichi of *Tokyo Keizai Zasshi* (Tokyo Economist) first issued in 1879.[34] This conflict is apparent in their different interpretations of Mill's view of the Smithian doctrine of laissez-faire. Amano considered Mill as an orthodox and realistic successor to Smith, whereas Taguchi regarded him as deviating from the Smithian doctrines.

(2) The Influence of American and German Political Economy on Two Economists at Waseda

Of the two economists who represented the second generation of Waseda University, Abe Isoo left his mark both on the history of the university and on the political history in modern Japan, as a professor of the 'social problem' and socialism and as a leading social democrat in politics. Abe's social and economic thought stems from Learned's lectures at Dōshisha Eigakkō. He was converted during his stay at a theological school in the United States to Christian socialism under the influence of Edward Bellamy's *Looking Backward 2000–1887* (1888), and then became a lecturer at Tokyo School of Special Studies in 1899. Abe's first famous book, *Shakai Mondai Kaishakuhō* (Methods for the Interpretation of the Social Problem) (1901) was widely accepted against the background of rising socialist thought at the turn of the century. Abe urged against the use of the expression 'social problems' which, in a broader sense, included labour problems, land problems, educational problems, and so on. In contrast, he took a narrow view of it and said:

> I believe that the expression 'Social Problems' should correctly be replaced by 'the Social Problem'. No matter how extensive the study of the social problem may be, it must after all contribute to the relief of the poor, the filling of the tremendous gap between the rich and the poor, and a complete removal from society of the antagonism caused by poverty. The ultimate aim of my study in the social problem lies there.[35]

Abe continued to teach at Waseda University and to devote time to political and social activities until his death. Abe approved of the private ownership of consumption goods, though he strenuously argued for the nationalization of the means of production, such as capital and land.[36] His idea of socialism is said to have hardly changed in either theory or practice throughout his life. He earned, therefore, the esteem not only of the students of Waseda University as a sincere teacher, but also of the public at large as a moderate socialist and, in particular, a faithful pacifist.

Shiozawa Masasada was another influential economist at Waseda University. As mentioned before, he had studied at the University of Wisconsin in 1896 as one of the first recipients of the Tokyo School of Special Studies's graduate scholarship for study abroad. Shiozawa wrote his doctoral dissertation, 'A study of social and economic institutions of ancient Japan', under the tutorial guidance of R. Ely.

After receiving his doctorate, he moved to Germany and took some courses of lectures by Johannes Conrad, Gustav von Schmoller, and Adolf Wagner at the universities of Halle and Berlin. This enables us to assume that he was definitely receptive to the economic philosophy of the German Historical School, both in America and in Germany, then regarded in the Japanese academic world as 'a new political economy'. It is, therefore, natural that he should be strongly interested in labour problems, and, indeed, he became an influential member of the Society for Social Policy (Shakai Seisaku Gakkai). This indicates his intellectual independence from the tradition of economic thought of Mill (and, in a sense, of Roscher) which had been followed in Amano's lectures since the opening of Tokyo School of Special Studies.

Shiozawa did not publish any major books, and so we do not have sufficient sources to draw conclusions with regard to what the whole picture of Shiozawa's political economy was or would have been, and yet we have certain clues in a 1913 paper entitled 'Keizai to Rinri no Kankei ni Tsuite' (On the Relationship between Economy and Ethics). From the ethical point of view, he argued that human beings should not be dependent upon the material world.[37] This is based upon his own interpretation of Knies's and Ely's basic ideas of economy, which emphasized the essential role of non-economic factors, i.e., the so-called heteronomy of economy.[38] Shiozawa's original views on economic theory and social and labour problems were developed in terms of this basic principle. We can see it, for example, on the one hand, in his economic theory which laid stress on the structural and realistic analysis of the capitalist economy in the long run, and in his assertion of respect for the labourers' humanity in labour problems on the other. He thus represents the beginning of a new epoch in the study and teaching of political economy at Waseda University, freed from Amano's influence.

6. Concluding Remarks

To summarize, we may simply say that political economy at Tokyo School of Special Studies and Waseda University had a particularly strong bias, through education, towards the practical and the popular. It owed much, needless to say, to the school's initial aim of promoting the practical utilization of knowledge. In the third clause of the 'Declaration of Aims' of the school, there is a clear statement: 'To promote the practical utilization of knowledge, the university shall endeavour to foster ways and means of utilizing knowledge side by side with the continuation of academic research and learning, thereby contributing to the progress of civilization'.

The reorganization of the school in 1902 was not merely a change of name from Tokyo School of Special Studies to Waseda University. It was the realization of Ono Azusa's heartfelt wishes to establish a practical university, as opposed to Tokyo Imperial University, whose primary aim was the pursuit of purely academic or administrative interests. As mentioned before, this stress on practical knowledge led Waseda University to open the Faculty of Commerce in 1904, and furthermore to establish the Faculty of Science and Engineering in 1909, thus making it a university in the true sense of the term. As to the popularization of political economy which was another aim of the school, the efforts to make knowledge available to the public at large were already seen in the days of Tokyo School of Special Studies with the introduction of correspondence courses and lecture tours. After the school became a full-fledged university, a course of public lectures was inaugurated. The establishment of the Department of Extramural Education in 1910 is symbolic of the movement for the extension of university education.[39]

The history of the study and teaching of political economy at the school is also that of its efforts to make a gradual advance towards that 'Aim'. The early economists there devoted themselves not to training the elite of society such as the Imperial bureaucracy, but to fostering a well-educated middle class and popular opinion-leaders, who made a singular contribution to the development of Japanese capitalism. To distinguish, very clearly, political economy at Waseda from that in other institutions we need only look at the field of journalism. Some graduates from the school played active parts in economic journalism: for instance, Masuda Giichi, who first issued an economic magazine, *Jitsugyō no Nihon* (Quality Magazine for Business Pioneers) in 1877; Ishibashi Tanzan, who was called a 'statesman economist'[40] and assumed the premiership in 1956 following a long career as a liberal journalist at *Tōyō Keizai Shinpō*; Takahashi Kamekichi, an independent economist and journalist; Obama Toshie, an economic journalist in the newspaper world; and so on. All of them, except for Masuda, participated actively in the debate on the lifting of the gold embargo in 1930, and their arguments then are valued by the economists of today. Thus, the school's aim to promote the diffusion and utilization of economic knowledge found shape in their activities in journalism.

11

In the 'Commercial Metropolis' Osaka: Schools of Commerce and Law

Shirō Sugihara and Tamotsu Nishizawa

In the Tokugawa period (1603–1867), Osaka was, with Edo (Tokyo) and Kyoto, one of the three largest cities in Japan. While Edo was the political centre of Japan and Kyoto the cultural, Osaka was the economic and commercial one, that is, a trading centre for such staple commodities as rice. By 1867, Osaka's population was as large as four hundred thousand. After the Meiji Restoration, it became, besides being a commercial and financial centre, one of the great industrial centres. A representative industry in Osaka was the textile, especially the cotton, industry. A great many of its products were exported to China and other Asian countries. The cotton industry of Osaka has been one of the key industries in the development of modern Japanese economy. By the end of the last century, Osaka was the second largest city, next only to Tokyo, and was aptly called the 'Manchester of the East'.

Before 1945, there were three universities in Osaka: Osaka Imperial University (national), Osaka University of Commerce (municipal), and Kansai University (private). The first had only two faculties (science and medicine), so it had no connection with political economy. Osaka University of Commerce (now Osaka City University) celebrated its centenary in 1980, counting the years since the birth of its predecessor, Osaka Commercial Training School, and Kansai University celebrated its centenary in November 1986, also since the birth of its mother school.

1. Godai Tomoatsu and the Reconstruction of Osaka

In 1985, Osaka City University, whose predecessor was Osaka Commercial School, celebrated the centennial of the death of Godai Tomoatsu, to whom Osaka owes, in a great measure, its development after the Meiji Restoration. It was even said, 'There was no big business in early Meiji Osaka which was not the concern of Godai'.[1] In the beginning of the Meiji era, Osaka lost its prosperity it enjoyed before and its people became depressed. Seriously worried about the economic decline of Osaka caused by the Restoration, Godai was to prepare the road which would restore its declining fortunes and transform it from an old mercantile metropolis to a prosperous modern industrious city.

Godai's role in the economic development in Japan seems to have been quite similar to Shibusawa Eiichi's. They have often been referred to as 'Shibusawa in the east and Godai in the west', though Godai did not live long enough to see, the rapid development of Japanese economy after the Sino-Japanese War of 1894–95, in contrast to Shibusawa, who saw the development right up to the age of Japanese imperialism. They both went to Europe to be enlightened by its advanced capitalism towards the end of the Tokugawa Shogunate. They attended the Great Exhibition in Paris in 1867. They were both high-ranking civil servants in the Meiji government, which was in need of their new knowledge. After having worked in governmental service for a few years, they entered business, yet keeping close connections with the government. They both made invaluable contributions to the development of Japanese capitalism in private circles. But they exhibited a fairly different style from such great entrepreneurs as Iwasaki Yatarō of Mitsubishi, Yasuda Zenjirō, or Masuda Takashi of Mitsui and Hirose Saihei of Sumitomo, all of whom founded *zaibatsu*. While engaged in economic activity, Godai and Shibusawa made a point of pursuing national benefit rather than working for their own private interest. This was particularly the case with Godai, who was not as successful a businessman as Shibusawa and even left a debt of one million yen after his death. 'Godai was not a genuine businessman, nor a venturer . . . or a "captain of industry". He was rather a bureaucrat or an administrator . . . who was in non-governmental circles. . . . However, at a time when Japan was making rapid but primitive accumulation under the strong state direction, a man like Godai who served as go-between for the government and the private circles was indispensable'.[2]

Perhaps the most significant contribution of Godai and Shibusawa to the economic development was their leadership in organizing and sponsoring the business community. Godai established the Osaka Stock Exchange and Shibusawa the Tokyo Chamber of Commerce.

They initiated and promoted the institutionalization of commercial and economic education in order to transplant the new discipline of commerce and to cultivate human resources for modern economic growth. Osaka Commercial School and Tokyo Commercial School are considerably indebted for their formation and development to Godai and Shibusawa, respectively. Godai was especially orientated to the pursuit of economic activity from the viewpoint of national interest, and he expedited the national enrichment policy for the rapid industrialization and modernization of Japan in the face of pressure from advanced capitalist countries. Thus, according to Miyamoto Mataji, Godai 'took an entrepreneurial attitude in a backward country, as Alexander Gerschenkron says'.[3]

A glance at Godai's experience in his early days is of some help in understanding his later career. He was born in 1835 in the clan of Satsuma, which was under the enlightened lord Shimazu Nariakira. Satsuma was situated at the south-east end of the Japanese islands and had been vulnerable to foreign ships. It is said that Satsuma started its policy of coastal defence in the 1840s.[4] Godai studied at the Naval Training School in Nagasaki, where he became close to Thomas Glover, a well-known Scottish merchant. His experience during the British bombardment of Kagoshima in 1863 inspired him with a policy of national enrichment by means of Westernization.

Godai initiated the sending of Satsuma students to England with the object of introducing modern industries to their own clan. Fifteen students led by Godai and Matsuki Kōan arrived at Southampton on June 21, 1865: among them was Mori Arinori, who was to become the first Japanese minister to the United States and the first minister of education. Most of the students were put under the kind auspices of Alexander Williamson, professor of chemistry at the University College London. Laurence Oliphant, M.P., who had been a secretary to the British minister in Japan and a friend of Thomas Glover, was also helpful.[5] Godai became acquainted with the Comte des Cantons de Montblanc, a Belgian aristocrat who had strong interests in Japan, and they entered into negotiations in order to establish a trading company and also for Satsuma's products to be on show at the Great Exhibition in Paris, which Shibusawa also attended. Godai and Niiro Nakazō made tours of such English industrial cities as Manchester and Birmingham, purchasing spinning machines in Manchester and guns in Birmingham for Satsuma. Godai wrote, 'There were two salient features in the European countries, namely, those of "industry" and "commerce" '. The images of Manchester and Birmingham were probably imprinted on his mind. Later Godai 'came to believe that it was his mission to make Osaka into a prosperous industrial city like Birmingham'.[6]

Osaka had long been the commercial metropolis of Japan. As the liberal Meiji economist, Taguchi Ukichi, wrote, 'Whatever commodities were gathering in the market of Osaka and priced there were then sent and sold out everywhere in Japan: it was as if every commodity of Europe and America was going to the London market, to be priced there and exported everywhere'.[7] Such commercial prosperity in Osaka had been largely dependent on the commercial system called *kabunakama*, or traders' guilds, and on the financial convenience of the exchange bill, using silver as the standard. *Kabunakama*, though monopolistic, had kept the commercial community in order. However, the Meiji Restoration radically changed the traditional customs of commerce by dissolving *kabunakama*, by abolishing the silver standard and by many other means. Thus it undermined not only the basis of Osaka's commercial prosperity but also the order of Osaka's commercial community itself, thus occasioning the decline of Osaka in the beginning of the Meiji era. Yet the merchants of Osaka, who had been accustomed to the time-honoured commercial customs and credit system, could not easily find ways to meet the changing times, or, rather, they were conservative and turned their backs on the modern methods of commerce.[8]

The development of the 'new Osaka' was initiated by someone from outside Osaka. In February 1868 (the first year of the Meiji era), Godai Tomoatsu came to Osaka as a supervisor for the Foreign Affairs Office. This was the starting point of Godai's active part in the industrialization of Osaka. While he served the interests of foreign affairs in Osaka, he was also working, together with Mioka Hachirō, for the foundation of the Mint. After being engaged in government service, Godai entered business to assume leadership in modernizing Osaka's commercial world and to prepare the basis for the industrialization of the city.

As Miyamoto remarked, 'Godai persuaded the old merchants, who were doubtful about new enterprises, to participate in industrial investment, and displayed his great ability in coordinating the entrepreneurs, whose interests were conflicting; he contributed a great deal to creating new economic rules and institutions, and thereby to forming business corporations'. Godai made his greatest efforts in founding the future Rice Exchange in Dōjima and the Osaka Stock Exchange'.[9]

Godai and a few other influential men of business, who were concerned about the decline of Osaka, presented a petition to the government of Osaka Prefecture in July 1877 for establishing a chamber of commerce following the Western example. The petition was signed by fifteen leading men of business in Osaka who were prepared to accept the new ideas of industrialization and the industrial policies of the Meiji government, nine of whom were originally from outside Osaka. The petition was accepted, and in August the Osaka Chamber of Commerce was inaugurated under Godai's presidency; Nakano Goichi and Hirose Saihei were elected vice-presidents, and Katō Yūichi and Shibakawa Matahei directors. Hirose, who was born in the district of Ōmi and provided the basis for Sumitomo's development as *zaibatsu*, was also a great benefactor for commercial education in Osaka. Katō, who had worked as Godai's lieutenant in the Foreign Affairs Office, was a great intellectual who had enlightened the people in Osaka and provided Godai with new knowledge. He wrote many books, advocating the new ideas of a new age. Thus he is said to have been the 'greatest exponent of the new knowledge in Osaka, comparable with Fukuzawa Yukichi in Tokyo'.[10]

2. The Early Development of Osaka Commercial School

Besides Osaka Chamber of Commerce and other commercial organizations, Godai advocated creating a well-organized commercial school in Osaka for the purpose of educating the sons of merchants, and more generally for the purpose of cultivating human resources for Osaka's modernization and industrialization.[11] Since the first commercial school in Japan, Shōhō Kōshūjo (Commercial Training School), was founded in Tokyo in 1875, schools of the like kind grew apace: Kobe Shōgyō Kōshūjo (Kobe Commercial Training School) was founded in 1878, while Osaka Shōgyō Kōshūjo (Osaka Commercial Training School) and Okayama Shōgyō Kōshūjo (Okayama Commercial Training School) were founded in 1880. The formation and development of these commercial schools seem to have been influenced by and benefited from Fukuzawa and Keiō School in various ways.[12] Godai might have read Fukuzawa's 'Shōgakkō o Tatsuru no Shui' (Prospectus of the School of Commerce), written by Fukuzawa Yukichi at the time of the Commercial Training School's establishment, since a copy of it was found among Godai's papers kept in the Osaka Chamber of Commerce and also because they had been acquainted with each other.[13] In the summer of 1879, Katō Masanosuke, a young journalist who had been educated at Keiō School, came to Osaka to take the position of chief editor of the *Osaka Shinpō*, a leading paper in Osaka of which Godai had become owner. Katō had brought with him a letter of recommendation from Fukuzawa to Godai. Katō's first article appeared in *Osaka Shinpō* on August 14, 1879: it was entitled 'Shōhō Gakkō Mōkezaru Bekarazu?' (Why Shouldn't a Commercial School Be Established?). In this article he insisted that a commercial school should be established as soon as possible so that the arts of commerce would be improved, old commercial customs revised, and bookkeeping methods altered. In his opinion, Japanese merchants can fulfil their responsibilities only when they are able to carry on trade with foreigners on an equal footing and are competitive with foreign merchants in both domestic and foreign markets.[14] Katō's arguments seem to be very similar to Fukuzawa's in his 'Prospectus'. Presumably Katō wrote this article for Godai and the people of Osaka under the influence of Fukuzawa. According to Mōri, Godai had wanted to bring Fukuzawa's arguments for a commercial school to Osaka.[15] Kadota Saburobei, a very wealthy timber merchant, and Kawaguchi Jun were highly sympathetic with Katō's arguments: Sumitomo, Kōnoike, and Fujita, the largest merchant families in Osaka, were also involved in this movement. In November 1880, Osaka Commercial Training School thus came into being as a private school, thanks to the efforts of Godai, Kadota, Hirose Saihei, and some thirteen others. Kirihara Sutezō, who was also educated under Fukuzawa, was appointed the first headmaster.[16]

Though details on the subjects taught at Osaka Commercial Training School cannot be found, they were apparently of a very practical nature, just as those at Kobe Shōgyō Kōshūjo.[17] A list of books transferred from Osaka Commercial Training School (dated August 11, 1881) tells us something about the instruction there. Of the number of books kept there, by far the most were those concerning bookkeeping, followed by those on political economy, and then on arithmetic. The following seem to have been used as textbooks: *Boki Kaitei* (Steps in Bookkeeping); *Bokigaku Reidai* (Exercises in Bookkeeping); *Ginkō Boki Reidai* (Exercises in Bank Bookkeeping); H. Fawcett (tr. by Nagata Kensuke), *Manual of Political Economy*; *Nihon Keizairon* (On the Japanese Economy); L. Levi (tr. by Taguchi Ukichi), *The History of British Commerce*; and Fukuzawa Yukichi, *Minkan Keizairoku* (Popular Political Economy). The list also includes: H. B. Bryant, *Bookkeeping*; *What Is Free Trade?* and probably F. List, *The National System of Political Economy*. Great improtance appears to have been attached to commercial practice. The list includes various commercial instruments such as imitation bank notes, cheques, stamps, bills of exchange, and bonds of debt used in the commercial bureau.[18]

Owing to financial difficulties, Osaka Commercial Training School was placed under the supervision of Osaka prefectural government in July 1881. Then, in the following year, under the leadership of Iba Sadatake of Sumitomo and Yamamoto Tatsuo, a future governor of the Bank of Japan, the school regulations and curriculum were revised. Yamamoto, who had received his education at Keiō School and Mitsubishi Commercial School (Mitsubishi Shōgyō Gakkō) and had just retired from Okayama Commercial Training School, gave the address at the opening ceremony of this municipal school, as the head-teacher: 'We should make our greatest efforts to cultivate able and successful merchants for the purpose of restoring the declining fortunes of Osaka and reviving our commercial independence lest foreign merchants monopolize the East Asian market. Then we should increasingly promote our commercial prosperity and make our country wealthy and competitive'.

Under the new regulations two courses were prescribed: a main course and a short course for evening classes. The main course, which took over three years to complete, taught ten subjects: bookkeeping, arithmetic, ethics, political economy, Japanese and Chinese literature, geography and merchandise, commercial law, calligraphy, English and Chinese languages, and commercial practice. Political economy was taught by Yamamoto, using the Japanese translations of the following books as textbooks: H. Fawcett, *Manual of Political Economy*, and Francis Wayland (tr. by Obata Tokujirō), *The Elements of Political Economy*, Bookkeeping and arithmetic were much in request among commercial circles. Yamamoto also wrote a textbook entitled *Shinsen Jitchi Shōgyō San* (Practical Commercial Arithmetic, Osaka, n.d.) with Yamaoka Kiyonao, who was also a teacher at the school. It seems that particular importance was placed on the Chinese language, probably because of the strong interest in the Chinese market among the commercial circles of Osaka. The short course was especially designed for the pupils who worked during the day, in other words, those who were employed by the merchant families and others. The short course was one and half years long, and bookkeeping, arithmetic, and commercial practice were taught. Commercial practice, to which particular importance was attached, appears to have been very successful and effective.[19]

In March 1885 the newly named Osaka Shōgyō Gakkō, or Osaka Commercial School, started under renewed regulations in accordance with Class I of the general regulations for commercial schools issued by the Ministry of Education in January 1884. Before then the curriculum of commercial schools was virtually left to the founders. This issue of general regulations by the Ministry of Education, which was the first governmental regulations relating to commercial education in

Japan, was to effect a division of commercial education into two classes: the schools belonging to Class I were to be of a practical nature with the object of training those destined for a commercial career, and the schools coming under Class II were intended to give instruction in such higher branches of commerce as were necessary to train people for the management of commercial affairs. The subjects of study under Class I were ethics, reading, writing, arithmetic, bookkeeping, commercial correspondence, commercial geography, merchandise, commercial economy, and commercial practice. Besides Osaka Commercial School, four existing commercial schools renewed their regulations in accordance with Class I of the general regulations: they were Kobe Commercial School, Yokohama Commercial School, Niigata Commercial School, and Akamagaseki (Shimonoseki) Commercial School. In addition five commercial schools were newly founded by the local governments in accordance with Class I, or the commercial schools of the middle rank. They were Nagoya Commercial School, Shiga Commercial School, Nagasaki Commercial School, Kyoto Prefectural Commercial School, Hakodate Commercial School. The Commercial Training School in Tokyo was renamed Tokyo Commercial School in 1884, and it was transformed into the Higher Commercial School in 1887, which was the only higher commercial educational institution in Japan before the turn of the century.[20]

Osaka Commercial School was to instruct the subjects necessary for commercial affairs and train pupils in commercial practice. The course of study extended over three years and the subjects, which were of a practical nature, were thirteen in number: drawing, physics, and English were added to the subjects under Class I of the general regulations. Among the subjects, commercial economy was regarded as the most important, since 'the men with commercial careers should be familiar with the laws of economy in general'.[21]

Between 1885 and 1889 Osaka Commercial School seems to have experienced a great transformation, thus providing a basis for its later development as a well-organized commercial school. The renovations, particularly those after 1888, were carried out by Naruse Ryūzō, then the head-teacher of the Higher Commercial School in Tokyo, by order of Minister of Education Mori Arinori who visited Osaka Commercial School in 1885 and in 1887. In 1888, Naruse came to Osaka Commercial School accompanied by Mizushima Tetsuya, also a teacher of the Higher Commercial School. Mizushima, later the first principal of Kobe Higher Commercial School (Kobe Kōtō Shōgyō Gakkō), was to take charge of the school affairs in Osaka as the acting headmaster up to September 1889, when he left the school and entered a leading business firm, Fujita-gumi. Naruse also appointed the deliberative council of Osaka Commercial School, which consisted of three great business leaders in Osaka: Fujita Denzaburō, Tamate Hiromichi, and Hirose Saihei of Sumitomo. Sumitomo's contribution to the early development of Osaka Commercial School seems to have been considerable. Iba Sadatake had been the headmaster again from 1888 to 1891. In September 1889, Osaka Prefectural Commercial School (Osaka Furitsu Shōgyō Gakkō) was transferred to the control of the city of Osaka and renamed the Osaka Municipal Commercial School (Osaka Shiritsu Shōgyō Gakkō).[22] Since then the development of Osaka Commercial School, i.e., to Osaka Higher Commercial School (Osaka Kōtō Shōgyō Gakkō) in 1901, then to Osaka University of Commerce (Osaka Shōka Daigaku) in 1928, and finally to the present Osaka City University (Osaka Shiritsu Daigaku), has been under the auspices of the city of Osaka.

Naruse-Mizushima's manoeuvring came to fruition in the renewed regulations of 1888, which stated that the school was to provide the education necessary for domestic and foreign commercial affairs and for the training of future administrators and managers in commercial affairs. The course of study was to extend to over four years, which were to be divided into a two-year preparatory course and a two-year main course. The subjects to be taught in the preparatory course were English, Japanese and Chinese literature, calligraphy, composition, bookkeeping, mathematics, geography, history, drawing, physics and chemistry, and gymnastics. The subjects for the main course were English, commercial correspondence, commercial arithmetic, bookkeeping, commercial history, commercial geography, political economy, merchandise, statistics, law, commercial practice, and gymnastics.

Concerning political economy the following books were used: Fukuzawa Yukichi, *Minkan Keizairoku* (Popular Political Economy), 1877; Kawamoto Seiichi, *Rizai Genron* (a translation of A. L. Perry's *Elements of Political Economy*), 1878; Amano Tameyuki, *Keizai Genron* (The Theory of Political Economy), 1886; Tsuchiko Kinshirō, *Keizaigaku Taii* (Outlines of Political Economy), 1887; Morishita Iwakusu, *Keizai Genron* (Principles of Political Economy), 1883. In addition, Mizushima Tetsuya taught the following books in English: Henry Fawcett, *Manual of Political Economy*, 1863; and Henry D. Macleod, *The Elements of Banking*, 1876. For bookkeeping, besides *Bryant and Stratton's Commercial Bookkeeping* (1871), the following textbooks were used: E. G. Forsom, *The Logic of Accounts*, 1873; Takeda Hitoshi, *Shōyō Bokigaku* (Commercial Bookkeeping), 1882;

the Department of Banking Studies in the Ministry of Finance ed., *Ginkō Boki Reidai* (Excrcises in Bank Bookkeeping), 1879; Fujio Rokurō, *Ginkō Boki Seikai* (Solutions in Bank Bookkeeping). For commercial history, Leone Levi's *History of British Commerce* (translation by Taguchi Ukichi) was extensively used. There were some English teachers such as Edward Hawken and Edward Lambert teaching Thomas Macaulay's *Life of Clive, Life of Hastings*, and Herbert Spencer's 'Representative Government'.[23]

In March 1892, Naruse Ryūzō, who had travelled to the United States and Europe from 1889 to 1890 in order to observe commercial education there, came to Osaka to take up office as the headmaster of Osaka Commercial School. In October 1892, Osaka Commercial School moved into new buildings in Dōjima, where the Osaka Chamber of Commerce and Osaka Commercial Museum were situated. At the opening ceremony to mark this new beginning of the school, Nishimura Sutezō, the under-secretary of the Ministry of Agriculture and Trade who had once been governor of Osaka Prefecture, addressed the audience: 'Osaka Commercial School has produced only twenty-seven graduates since 1885. Among them a mere five are from Osaka'. Regretting this situation, he continued: 'Unlike the older days, we are in a civilized world. Instead of training for military conquest, we should be trained in various types of technology in order to carry on trade with every country and to attempt a commercial and industrial war with them'. Then Nishimura said he wished that the merchants and manufacturers of Osaka, who numbered almost four thousand, would send their sons to an industrial school to be trained in industrial and commercial technology.[24]

Naruse revised the regulations, which were carried into effect from April 1, 1893. The major points of revision were: to rename the affiliated course as a supplementary course for educating the pupils who would enter the preparatory course; and to set up a new and superior course after the main course for students wishing to pursue their studies further. In particular, the superior course was founded to improve the knowledge of those who would be engaged in foreign trade. Concerning political economy: in the main course, starting from the definition of political economy, production, distribution, exchange, and consumption were taught; and in the next stage money, banking, foreign trade, and foreign exchange were instructed; furthermore a course on statistics in theory and practice was compulsory. In the superior course, there were lectures on commercial economy, in particular with regard to the fluctuation of prices and financial affairs, and public finance was also taught. The principal teacher of political economy was Suzuki Shigeo. After three and half years' service, Naruse retired from Osaka Commercial School in September 1895, and entered business as manager of Shanghai Textile Company.[25]

During the first two or three decades of the Meiji era, the recovery of commercial independence was a sort of ideology in commercial circles in Japan. Most foreign trade had been monopolized by the foreign merchants of the settlements in Yokohama and Kobe, and before the turn of the century there were very few, with the exception of Mitsui Trading Company, that did not rely on those foreign merchants. In the 'settlements trade', Japanese merchandise had to be beaten down, whereas foreign merchandise had to be accepted according to the prices they offered. The merchants of Osaka were anxious to put an end to this situation and to carry on trade directly with overseas countries. However, at that time they did not even know how to sign an invoice. They had to go to the commercial museum for translation services for their foreign correspondence. In order to avoid these inexpediencies, the leading merchants of Osaka increasingly sent their sons to the commercial school to be trained for future business. The urgent need for training future merchants in commercial practice in order to carry on trade on an equal footing with foreign merchants and thus to recover commercial independence was becoming more understood not only in Osaka but in many commercial cities.[26]

Since 1892 under the directorship of Naruse, promising men of business were trained in large numbers. Among them was Nomura Shinnosuke, who studied there from 1892 to 1895 and was to be the founder of the future Nomura Shōken (Nomura Securities Company). Thus, according to *Osaka Shōka Daigaku 60 Nenshi* (Sixty Years of Osaka University of Commerce), the cultivation of human resources was effected to meet the needs occasioned by an epoch-making development in Japanese capitalism after the Sino-Japanese War of 1894–95. The number of graduates in 1893 was twenty-six, equivalent to the total number of graduates since its establishment in 1880. After 1893 the number of graduates steadily increased: in 1894 it was twenty eight and in 1895 thirty-six. They were to assume the industrial and commercial leadership of the country and also contribute to the industrial revolution of Japan. Towards the turn of the century, the students of the school who took pride in being engaged in their fathers' business had, on the whole, been decreasing, whereas the number of enterprising and innovative graduates from outside Osaka were increasing.[27] It was around this time that the cotton industry of Osaka made great strides due to the efforts of Yamanobe Takeo and Kikuchi Kyōzō, who once studied at the University College London and at Manchester Technical College, respectively. We might say that the graduates of Osaka Commercial School were to make, though not directly, some contribution to the transformation of Osaka from an ancient commercial metropolis to a modern 'cottonopolis', or the 'Manchester of the East'.

In order to supply human resources for the rapid development of Japanese capitalism after the Sino-Japanese War, there were great social demands for industrial and commercial education. In Osaka there had already appeared, in 1892, a proposal for higher commercial education. As the number of graduates from Osaka Commercial School increased, the alumni association grew and became active.[28] On July 28, 1891, the first issue of *Osaka Shōgyō Gakkō Dōsōkai Shūshi* (Magazine of the Alumni Association) was published, for the people 'to navigate the wildly raging commercial sea and to traverse the complex and tangled commercial world'. The magazine was to be instrumental in the promotion of the higher commercial education movement in Osaka. An article entitled 'Kōtō Shōgyō Gakkō o Osaka ni Setchi Suru Gi' (A Proposal to Establish a Higher Commercial School in Osaka) appeared in it in July 1900.[29] In September of the same year a conference of principals of commercial schools carried a motion for establishing a higher commercial school in Osaka. However, a motion to a similar effect which was actually presented to Parliament in January 1900 was rejected by a majority of only one: seventy ayes and seventy-one noes. Then it was decided that the second national higher commercial school was scheduled to be built in Kobe instead. Therefore the headmaster of Osaka Commercial School, Katō Akikane, collaborating with the deputy mayor, Hiranuma Yoshirō, the immediate predecessor of Katō, attempted to promote Osaka Municipal Commercial School into Osaka Municipal Higher Commercial School. On April 11, 1901, Osaka Higher Commercial School came into being as an institution to conduct higher education concerning domestic and foreign commercial affairs. This was one year before the formal foundation of Kobe Higher Commercial School in 1902.[30]

3. Political Economy and Kansai Law School

Kansai University began as Kansai Law School (Kansai Hōritsu Gakkō), then situated in the centre of Osaka city, in 1886. Kansai means the 'western side of the barrier', that is, the western half of Japan, in contrast to Kantō, the 'eastern half of Japan'. Many lawyers were needed for the new constitutional state about to be formed. The

Meiji government established the Law School (Meihōryō) in the Ministry of Justice in 1874 (which was to be absorbed afterwards into the Faculty of Law of Tokyo Imperial University), but having only one law school was evidently insufficient to meet the demand for lawyers and civil servants, so many private law schools were opened in the 1880s, and later developed into universities. They were all situated in Tokyo except for one, Kansai Law School.

There are three points worth mentioning about Kansai Law School.[31] Firstly, it was organized not by one great figure, but by the cooperation of several young judges, most of whom had been students of Boissonade and Appert in the law school of the Ministry of Justice. These able judges were transferred to Osaka Court, initially to deal with the 1885 Osaka Incident (the disclosure of Ōi Kentarō's scheme which attempted to support a coup d'état by the Independent Party of Korea), but when they came to Osaka, they saw the need to establish a law school in this economically important city. Secondly, a man named Doi Michio subscribed 100 yen to this school for its foundation fund. He was a friend of Godai Tomaotsu. Doi proved to be one of the leading business figures in Osaka after Godai's death in 1885. Thirdly, the curriculum of this school was, of course, organized around various subjects relating to law, but it attached great importance to political economy as well, and this is the point on which I wish to elaborate on here.

According to a newspaper advertisement calling for students, dated October 21, 1886, Kansai Law School announced that it would give lectures on domestic and foreign laws and political economy. As advertised, the lectures on political economy were given twice a week by Tezuka Tarō and Nomura Shinkichi. We know the contents of their lectures from students' notes now preserved in Kansai University Library.

Tezuka, a graduate of the law school of the Ministry of Justice, lectured on political economy, and in addition gave courses on an introduction to jurisprudence and French civil law. In his lecture on political economy he was responsible for a general outline and production. Distribution and exchange were covered by Nomura Shinkichi, who had graduated from the Faculty of Law of the University of Tokyo in 1878, specializing in English law. Both lecturers were the public prosecutors in the court of Osaka.

While Tezuka's lectures on political economy were based on the French School which had been introduced into Japan by Boissonade and Appert, the lectures by Nomura followed M. G. Fawcett's textbook *Political Economy for Beginners*, which was then in wide circulation in Japan. However, both lectures shared the liberal tradition represented by such figures as J. B. Say, N. Senior, J. S. Mill and the Fawcetts, who constituted the main current of Western political economy circa 1830 to 1880.

The title of the chapters in their lectures are as follows:[32] Introduction (Tezuka); 1. Definition of political economy, 2. The relation between political economy, law, and politics, 3. Political economy as a science which people must study, 4. Outline of economic history and history of economic thought, 5. Comments on some technical terms. Book I Production (Tezuka): 1. Introduction, 2. Land and other natural forces, 3. Labour, 4. Capital, 5. Effect of the cooperation of the three elements (mining and agriculture, industry, commerce and transporation). Book II Distribution (Nomura): 1. Introduction, 2. Rent, 3. Wages, 4. Profits. Book III Exchange (Nomura): 1. Introduction, 2. Value and price, 3. Credit, 4. Foreign trade.

The characteristics of political economy in Kansai Law School can be summarized in the following three points. 1. The value theory is not the labour theory of value but the theory of costs of production.

2. According to the theory of distribution, the product is to be distributed among the proprietors of the three elements of production, i.e., land, capital, and labour. Mutual cooperation of these three elements makes it possible to produce wealth, and the product is distributed among the proprietors in proportion to the contribution of each element of production.

3. It subscribes to liberalism, which criticizes the mercantilistic state intervention on the one hand, and rejects socialism and communism on the other. In the section entitled 'over-regulated society', for example, Tezuka emphasized the evil of absolutism as an economic policy, while Nomura criticized protectionism when discussing foreign trade. Meanwhile, in writing the chapter on production, Tezuka protested against the radical ideas which had appeared some thirty years previously and had attacked the capitalist class. In discussing profit, Nomura rejected the exploitation theory and justified capitalists' income by supporting the abstinence theory.

It is very significant from the following two points of view that such a lecture on political economy was delivered in Kansai Law School as early as the 1880s:

1. The task of Japanese lawyers was not to interpret the provisions of ready-made codes and apply them to respective cases, but to understand the fundamental meaning of modern civil law in general and recognize its function in civil society as a whole. To perform this task it was necessary to master political economy, because this science

came into being with the important mission of establishing a theoretical system for the analysis of the economic structure in modern society. This system was founded by Adam Smith and developed by David Ricardo, and political economy in Kansai Law School was nothing but a popularized form of classical political economy. Teachers of the school lectured on this science in the same way as it was taught by Boissonade and Appert. However, since 1881, the government undertook a new course of modernization of the state modelled after Germany, and it made an effort to introduce German 'state sciences' into Japan, so the nationalism and historicism of the German Historical School were introduced gradually in place of the liberalism of the classical school. Therefore it is worth noting that political economy in the Kansai Law School in 1886 was still in the liberal tradition.

2. At that time it was rather easy to attend lectures on political economy in Tokyo. In other districts, however, there were few schools in which political economy was taught. It is true that there were small private schools in various prefectures in the 1870s, in which Western liberal thought was taught, and sometimes the Japanese editions of M. G. Fawcett's work were adopted as a textbook. But almost all of these schools had disappeared by 1886. The advance of deflation and the suppression of the democratic movement of the Liberal Party by the government struck a hard blow against those schools.

Compared with the capitalists in Tokyo who had a chance to establish connections with the state power or bureaucracy, the capitalists in Osaka were generally liberalistic, and were strongly opposed to any state intervention. This contrast continued until long afterwards, so it is interesting that lectures on political economy in Osaka in those days were of a liberal character.

According to the curriculum of this school, a course on political economy was to be given to first-year students once a week and to second-year students twice a week. The course on public finance was to be given in the third (last) year once a week, but regrettably no information is available about this lecture.

In 1894, Hamada Kenjirō was appointed a lecturer. Hamada graduated from Tokyo University in 1884 together with Soeda Juichi and lectured on political economy in Senshū Gakkō with him. He returned to his native city of Osaka in 1893 and was installed as the chief secretary of the Osaka Chamber of Commerce. We have no record on his lectures, but in view of his writings they would have been closer to the German Historical School than Tezuka's and Nomura's.[33]

In 1905, Kansai Law School was reorganized into Kansai University, which had three faculties: law, political economy, and commerce.

The subjects relating to political economy were taught by the staff members of Kyoto Imperial University, such as Tajima Kinji and Kawakami Hajime.

There are two more points on political economy in Kansai Law School that should be mentioned here. Firstly, the director of the school from 1886 to 1889, Yoshida Isshi, published a textbook periodically for students taking his correspondence course. Some of the law schools in Tokyo published similar textbooks, and Yoshida modelled his on these. He had spent some years in Tokyo, where he had studied the social sciences, supported the Liberal Party, and for a short time had run a school (Meiji Private Law School), before he moved to Osaka. After the decline of the liberal political movement, many young men changed their field of activities from politics to journalism or education. Yoshida was one of them.

Secondly, Yoshida published a monthly journal *Keizai Kōwa* (Lectures on Political Economy) from November 1887 in Osaka. The journal was devoted to the introduction of political economy. The contributors were teachers of Kansai Law School, and Yoshida also wrote some papers. He did not lecture in the school, but considering his writings, his political economy must also have been of a liberalistic nature.[34] Two other journals, *Keiseihōri* (Economics, Politics, and Law) and *Bunmei no Hō* (The Law of Civilization), were published by graduates from Kansai Law School from January 1890 onwards. In them we read papers on law and political economy written by teachers of the school. The first graduates from Kansai Law School numbered only seventeen, but the political economy taught in the school spread extensively not only through the textbooks for the students of the correspondence course but also through these journals.

4. Political Economy in Kobe and Kyoto

There are two major cities near Osaka: Kyoto, the old capital located about fifty kilometers north-east of Osaka, and Kobe, about thirty-three kilometers south-west of Osaka, which is one of the largest ports in Japan. At present there are four universities in these cities which have their origins in the latter half of the Meiji era: the University of Kobe in Kobe, and Dōshisha University, the University of Kyoto, and Ritsumeikan University in Kyoto. The following is a brief sketch of the state of lectures on political economy in these institutions during the period of their foundation.

The University of Kobe evolved from Kobe University of Commerce (Kobe Shōgyō Daigaku), which was founded in 1929.[35] There were three commercial universities in pre-war Japan: Tokyo University of Commerce and Kobe University of Commerce, both of which were national universities, and Osaka University of Commerce, which was run by the city of Osaka. Like Tokyo and Osaka, Kobe University of Commerce evolved from a higher commercial school, in this case Kobe Higher Commercial School, which was founded in 1902 as the second national higher commercial school, the first being the foundation of Tokyo Higher Commercial School.

Kobe Higher Commercial School differed from the other two, however, in that while the higher commercial schools in Tokyo and Osaka evolved from the commercial training schools, founded in the early years of Meiji, Kobe Higher Commercial School had no connection with Shōgyō Kōshūjo of Kobe, founded in 1878 and evolved into Kobe Shōgyō Gakkō, or Kobe Commercial School. As was mentioned earlier, the decision to found the second Higher Commercial School in Kobe, rather than in Osaka, was made by a difference of one vote, a very lucky decision for Kobe as a principle port for foreign trade.

The leading members, including Mizushima Tetsuya, the first head of the school, were graduates of Tokyo Higher Commercial School and were taught by Fukuda Tokuzō. Tsumura Hidematsu, who lectured on the principles of political economy, and Sakanishi Yoshizō, who taught economic history, were among them. In 1906 *Kokuminkeizai Zasshi* (*Journal of Economics and Business Administration*) was published as the first academic journal of political economy in Japan, and the journal was edited jointly by Tokyo Higher Commercial School and Kobe Higher Commercial School. The latter, together with Kyoto Imperial University, was clearly becoming a centre for the study of political economy in the Kansai area.

Of the three schools in Kyoto, Dōshisha started its career the earliest.[36] Unlike all the schools that have been dealt with in this book, Dōshisha started as a mission school and its original name was Dōshisha Eigakkō (Dōshisha School of English Studies), founded by Niijima Jō in 1875. Around the same time it was founded, D. W. Learned, a Ph.D. from Yale University, came to teach political economy and politics as well as theology in Dōshisha. He had great influence on his students, and they translated his political economy writings which were published in two separate forms: *Keizai Shinron* (New Political Economy), 4 vols., 1886, and *Keizaigaku Genri* (Principles of Political Economy), 1891. It is clear from these publications that Learned's political economy was under the influence of the new German Historical School, and was ideologically backed by Christian humanism.

Among those who were strongly influenced by his political economy were Abe Isoo and Ukita Kazutami, who later became professors at Waseda University, and Fukai Eigo, who became the governor of the Bank of Japan.[37]

In 1891, Dōshisha Seihō Gakkō (Dōshisha School of Politics and Law) was opened. The head of the school was Ono Jirō, who had been a student of Learned and received a Ph.D. from the University of Michigan. He learned political economy from H. C. Adams at that university. Seihō Gakkō offered three-year courses on politics and political economy, and the latter course included the history of economic thought, public finance, statistics, bookkeeping, and commercial geography. The school developed into Dōshisha Senmon Gakkō (Dōshisha Advanced School), which was founded in 1904 under the Specialized School Decree, and later became Dōshisha University in 1912. The tradition of political economy was passed over to the Faculty of Politics and Political Economy in that university.

The origin of Ritsumeikan University dates back to 1869 when Saionji Kinmochi opened Ritsumeikan, a private school, in Kyoto, but a clear starting point leading to the present institution was Kyoto Hōsei Gakkō (Kyoto School of Law and Politics), founded in 1900 by Nakagawa Kojūrō, Saionji's secretary.[38] Article 1 of the rules and regulations of this school stated that the purpose of the school was to teach law, politics, and political economy. A three-year course was offered by both the Department of Law and the Department of Politics. The latter course included lectures on political economy (three times a week) for the first year; lectures on political economy (three times a week), public finance (twice a week), and statistics (once a week) for the second year; and lectures on political economy (three times a week) and public finance (twice a week) for the third year. The school developed into Kyoto Hōsei Senmon Gakkō (Kyoto Advanced School of Law and Politics) in 1903 in accordance with the Specialized School Decree, and changed its name to Kyoto Hōsei Daigaku (Kyoto University of Law and Politics) in 1904. At that time the Faculty of Law and the Faculty of Political Economy were set up in that university. It was in 1913 that the university was renamed Ritsumeikan University.

In 1897, three years before Kyoto Hōsei Gakkō was founded, Kyoto Imperial University was founded as a result of the effort of Saionji Kinmochi, the then Minister of Education.[39] In 1899, a Faculty of Law was founded, following the establishment of the Faculty of Science and Engineering. The establishment of Kyoto Hōsei Gakkō was based on the fact that the Faculty of Law was established in Kyoto Imperial University, and most of the lectures in Hōsei Gakkō were by the members of the faculty. For example, Tajima Kinji lectured on political economy and public finance, as did Toda Kaiichi. They were graduates of Tokyo Imperial University and were responsible for lectures on political economy and economic policy in the Faculty of Law of Kyoto Imperial University.

After the foundation of the Faculty of Law in 1899, the number of staff members responsible for the subjects relating to political economy gradually increased. Those who taught subjects relating to political economy in the Faculty of Political Economy of Dōshisha University included Kanbe Masao, Kawakami Hajime, and Kawada Shirō, as well as Tajima and Toda. They were all professors at the Faculty of Law of Kyoto Imperial University. Many of them also lectured at Kansai University in Osaka. In other words, political economy in private universities in Kyoto and Osaka at the end of the Meiji era was taught mostly by the professors at the Faculty of Law of Kyoto Imperial University.

All of the early members of the faculty were graduates of the Faculty of Law of Tokyo Imperial University, and were more or less under the influence of the new German Historical School. Most of them were also members of the Society of Social Policy (Shakai Seisaku Gakkai). It was only after 1915 when some of the graduates of Kyoto Imperial University began to teach at their alma mater that Kyoto began to form its own academic tradition in the field of political economy, independent of, and sometimes in rivalry with, Tokyo Imperial University. The issuing of a scholarly journal of its own, entitled *Keizai Ronsō* (The Economic Review), from 1915 onwards is a clear indication of the academic independence of Kyoto Imperial University.

Part 4

Political Economy Outside Educational Institutions

12

Economists in Government: Ōkubo Toshimichi, the 'Bismarck of Japan', and His Times

Shirō Sugihara

1. Western Economics Books in Governmental Offices

A bibliography entitled *Shokanchō Shozō Yōsho Mokuroku* (Catalogue of Western Books Kept in Government Offices) in two volumes was published in 1882 by Dajōkan Kirokusho (Records Office of the Cabinet). Volume One lists law books and Volume Two economics books.[1] Each volume is divided into three parts composed of English, French, and German books, and books are listed in each part by author in alphabetical order. Volume One contains 5,049 entries, or 10,064 volumes in all, whereas Volume Two for economics books contains only 1,824 entries, or 2,170 volumes in all. The difference seems to illustrate that the government's need for law books was much greater than for economics books.

Most economics books listed in Volume Two are theoretical outlines from which one may presume what kind of political economy the government in those earlier days was interested in and was anxious to introduce into the country. Let us, then, have a look at some notable points related to the kinds of books collected, the quantity, and location of collections.

Out of the 2,170 economics volumes the number of English books is the largest, amounting to 1,394 volumes, followed by French books, amounting to 567, and finally German books, amounting to 209 volumes. In comparison with the proportion of economics books contained in the Shogunate's collection of about 2,300 volumes of Western books, the difference is quite clear; not only because in the later collection the number of economics books is much smaller, but also because the number of English, French, and Dutch books is almost the same.[2] Now Dutch books had completely disappeared and English books had greatly surpassed French books. German books, though smaller in number than English and French books, were to increase rapidly after 1882, a fact clearly reflected in the *Author Catalogue of the Library of Teikoku-Daigaku* (*the Imperial University*), 1891. No doubt this change was caused by the political turnover of 1881 and the consequent inclination on the part of the government towards German studies.

Economics books in English are by English and by American authors, the former being somewhat larger in number. Among the former we find J. S. Mill and Jevons. It may be noted that with Mill, besides *Principles of Political Economy*, his *Essays on Some Unsettled Questions of Political Economy* (1844) is also included, and with Jevons, besides *Money and the Mechanism of Exchange* (1875), his *Theory of Political Economy* (1871) is also included. Among the American books, besides the writings by Francis Wayland, A. L. Perry, and the like, there are as many as seven books by H. C. Carey.

While on law there is about the same number of French books as English, on political economy the number of French books amounts only to one-third of that of English books. Also, the fact that it is Dajōkan (Cabinet), established in the year when the Shogunate was taken over by the Emperor's new government, which kept the largest number of French books, shows that it was in the earliest stage of the Meiji era that great importance was attached to French books. There are two different works by J.-B. Say, but there is only one English version of Bastiat's.

As for German books, the number of economics books for beginners, such as Held's and Contzen's, used as textbooks at Tokyo Gaikokugo Gakkō (Tokyo School of Foreign Languages, established in 1873 as an offshoot of Kaisei Gakkō) is the largest. There are books by Lorenz von Stein, K. H. Rau, W. G. F. Roscher, A. H. G. Wagner but Friedrich List's main work is kept only in English translation. It may be worth noting that such works as A. E. F. Schäffle's *Kapitalismus und Sozialismus* (1870) and Karl Marx's *Das Kapital* (vol. 1, 2nd. ed., 1873) are also kept.

Seventeen governmental establishments held these Western economics books, among which the Imperial University had the largest collection and the Ministry of Finance had the second largest. The reason the ministry held so many Western economics books is that it needed them for reference, and also the ministry served as an institution for educating future economists. The ministry's Department of

Translation, established in 1872 as part of the general policy promoted by Minister Ōkubo Toshimichi and Under-secretary Inoue Kaoru, was engaged, during the two years of its existence, in the education of about twenty students as well as in the translation of Western books, under the charge of the distinguished scholar in English studies, Seki Shinpachi. The department was succeeded by the Department of Banking Affairs in 1874, which again was succeeded by the School of Banking Studies attached to the ministry's Banking Section in 1874. In these educational institutions lectures were given in political economy along with more practical subjects such as bookkeeping, banking business, and the like, as was to be recalled later by Taguchi Ukichi and Shimada Saburō.[3] According to Taguchi, the books by Francis Wayland and A. L. Perry were used as textbooks and Perry's *Elements of Political Economy* (1866) was used in Seki Shinpachi's lectures. The government offices' catalogue shows, among others, that the ministry kept eighteen copies of J. W. Gilbart's *Principles and Practice of Banking*, sixteen copies of J. S. Mill's *Principles of Political Economy*, and eight copies of Perry's *Elements*. These numbers indicate that they must have been used as textbooks.

Some of the books held in the collections of governmental offices were also translated and published by them. It is obvious, from the bibliography appended to this book, that many economics books were translated into Japanese during the Meiji era. In the earlier years of the era many of them were published not privately but by the governmental offices. For example, J. E. Rogers's *Manual of Political Economy*, translated by Takahashi Tatsuo, and W. S. Jevons's *Money and Mechanism of Exchange*, translated by Ōshima Sadamasu, were published by the Ministry of Education; H. D. Macleod's *Principles of Economic Philosophy*, translated by Taguchi Ukichi, was published by the Privy Council; H. C. Carey's *Principles of Social Science*, translated by Wakayama Norikazu, and J. C. Garnier's *Traité de Finance*, translated by Nakayama Shin'ichi, were published by the Ministry of Finance. The 'official publication age' as Honjō Eijirō put it,[4] was nothing but a phase of the 'official enterprise age', in which the government took the initiative in the introduction of the technology and the economic system of the West.

2. The Role Played by Foreign Employees

For the reception of the advanced culture of the West by the newborn government, it was not sufficient merely to educate a small number of young men by means of Western textbooks or to try to spread the newly acquired knowledge by translations of books. In order to make the reception more effective, the government adopted a policy of inviting European and American scholars, technical experts, and businessmen in order to have them in the forefront. In fact it was a policy already practiced by the Shogunate and by Satsuma clan. Following suit, the new government invited a large number of foreigners from the West, paying them very generously, not only in such limited fields as military affairs, medical science, and the spinning industry, but also in a wider range, covering politics, economy, and culture. Here it may be worthwhile to depict briefly the role played by these foreign specialists in the promotion of economic policy or in the education of political economy.

The first foreign employee who played an important part in the new Meiji government was G. H. F. Verbeck. He was a Dutch American who had come over to Japan as a Christian missionary in 1859. In Nagasaki, besides preaching, he taught English and the fundamentals of politics, political economy, and natural sciences to young men of talent, among whom were Ōkuma Shigenobu, Soejima Taneomi, Itō Hirobumi, Ōkubo Toshimichi, Katō Hiroyuki, and some others who were to become the leading figures in the new government. As early as 1869 he became a *yatoi* (a foreigner employed by the government) through the recommendation of Ōkuma and his friends, and worked as a teacher of foreign languages in Kaisei Gakkō (Kaisei School) and at the same time as a legal adviser to the Privy Council. His advice was followed in various ways and put into practice, for example, with regard to conscription, school systems, and, most important of all, the sending of a diplomatic mission to Western countries. Following the advice he gave to Ōkuma in 1869, the Iwakura mission was organized. The significance the mission had in the modernization of Japan will be dealt with below.

But it was as a Christian missionary that Verbeck had come to Japan, so his job as an adviser to the government was only a subsidiary one. The government was in pressing need to employ a number of foreigners who could contribute full-time to the modernization policy in a variety of fields. Thus the *yatoi* increased rapidly from the earliest years of the Meiji era and they totalled over five hundred by 1873. The technological experts who worked for the Ministry of Industry, established in 1870, were the greatest in number, followed by the teachers attached to the Ministry of Education. It is noteworthy that their number reached a peak between 1874 and 1875 when Ōkubo's industry and trade policy was at its height.[5]

Among the *yatoi* there were some who were not specialists in political economy, such as E. von Baelz from Germany, who lectured on physiology at the Imperial University for more than a quarter century, and A. C. du Bousquet from France who contributed to the foundation of the modern army in Japan. However, as already mentioned, there were also men like G. E. Boissonade and K. F. H. Roesler, who introduced European economic thought into Japan through lectures and writings, while being engaged in their major duties in the modernization of the legal system. E. F. Fenollosa was originally invited from the United States to lecture on political economy, politics, and philosophy at the Imperial University. A. A. Shand[6] from the United Kingdom, who entered the Ministry of Finance in 1872, was engaged in teaching and writing about bank bookkeeping methods. W. C. Whitney, who came to Japan from the United States to be a teacher at the Commercial Training School (Shōhō Kōshūjo) and devoted himself to commercial education, was also a foreign employee, though not of the government, to instruct and spread the knowledge on banking and commercial affairs.

There were many foreign engineers who were invited to come for the sake of the advancement of industry. The Ministry of Industry employed many engineers for the industries of mining, telegraphy, civil engineering, shipbuilding, ironworks, railways, and the like. Besides working in industry, they were also engaged in technical education in the Technical College (Kōbu Daigakkō) of the ministry. While there were many Englishmen in railways and telegraphy, there were many Frenchmen in shipbuilding.

In the Industrial Promotion Board (Kangyō Ryō) set up by Ōkubo Toshimichi in 1873 in the Ministry of Home Affairs, there were some foreign employees actively working. In 1879 the number of foreign employees in the Ministry of Home Affairs was the third largest next to the ministries of Industry and Education. The Industrial Promotion Board had three divisions—those concerned with agricultural, commercial, and industrial affairs—but the policy as a whole aimed at an organic unity of the three divisions based on agriculture and a balanced development of all three areas. While in foreign trade and shipping the formation of private capital was encouraged, in agriculture and industry state intervention was more extensive. Public experimental stations, model factories, and educational institutions, built by the state for technical improvement and industrial promotion, initiated and directed industrial activities from above. Hence the need for experienced foreign employees. For example, P. Brunat from France helped establish a silk-reeling factory in Tomioka (1872), the first state-owned factory, and was engaged in technical instruction there. He contributed greatly to the diffusion of the technology of mechanical reeling throughout the country. When he returned to France after five years, the silk-reeling factory in Tomioka was able to run wholly by Japanese people under the Industrial Promotion Board.

The Industrial Promotion Board strove for the modernization of agriculture as well. Following the Naitō Shinjuku agricultural experimental station set up in 1872, the board expanded the Mita breeding station and Komaba Agricultural School (the predecessor of the Faculty of Agriculture of the University of Tokyo) in order to introduce modern farming techniques of the West. The Shimōsa sheep-breeding station and Senju woollen factory were opened to encourage the woollen industry. A number of foreign employees were working in these establishments. Although at Komaba Agricultural School there were old agriculturists like Funatsu Denjihei appointed by Ōkubo, the foreign advisers held the real power. In 1876, five teachers were invited from England to give instruction in English farming, which was quite alien to the existing conditions of Japanese agriculture. No serious efforts were made by either party, and the English teachers returned home when their contracts expired. From 1880, German teachers were invited to replace them. Differing from the English teachers, the Germans did not neglect to investigate the existing conditions of Japanese agriculture. They made an effort to educate in accordance with the real needs of Japanese agriculture, and consequently they were able to found the basis of agricultural science in Japan.

Among the German teachers of Komaba Agricultural School, the greatest achievement was by O. Kellner and M. Fesca.[7] Kellner lectured on agricultural chemistry at Komaba for eleven years. He did not emphasize theory too much, and did some experimental work himself on soil, the components of manure, and also on paddy plants and irrigation. The result of his work, such as proving the need to apply more phosphoric acid in the manure for paddy plants, was useful for the improvement of Japanese agriculture. While lecturing on agricultural science at Komaba, Fesca studied the nature of Japanese soil at the request of the Ministry of Agriculture and Trade, and wrote many articles about Japanese agriculture. While Kellner scientifically analysed Japanese agriculture on the basis of the modern agricultural chemistry established by von J. Liebig in Germany, Fesca tried furthermore to apply the system of modern agricultural management by A. D. Thaer, who was called 'the father of German rational agriculture', to Japanese agriculture.

The major work by Fesca, *Beiträge zur Kenntniss der japanischen Landwirtschaft* (Contributions to the Study of Japanese Agriculture), 1889–94, translated into Japanese by the Geological Institute of the Ministry of Agriculture and Trade, 1891–1894), was the first scientific and systematic study on Japanese agriculture, and it included both natural scientific considerations of agricultural crops, forest products, animal husbandry, sericulture, and social scientific considerations of land-ownership, prices of agricultural products, and management methods. In his work, Fesca insisted that Japanese agriculture should adopt a combination of animal husbandry and farming from the rotation systems in England and Germany, and that for this purpose small farming, suffering from heavy land tax and mounting debts, should be transformed into capital-intensive 'big farming'. It should be noted that his arguments were in touch with Japanese realities, rather than blindly urging the adoption of the modern agricultural system of the West. He attached importance to the gradual improvement of Japanese small-scale farming by offering proper technical advice and by encouraging co-operatives. He also argued that 'big farming' should be created on uncultivated land or in Hokkaido. Fesca was critical of the bold agricultural improvement policy in those days, such as the realization of 'big farming' in one stroke by exchanging the small, dispersed farms for one large block or substituting rice-planting for export-oriented crops. Though a foreigner, Fesca thus developed more realistic arguments than the Japanese.

It was not only at Komaba Agricultural School that the influence of German ideas gained ascendancy over the English or French ones. This tendency beginning in about 1877 grew stronger with the change in government in 1881, after which more Germans were employed in the fields of human and social sciences. In the Imperial University, K. Rathgen lectured on politics and the newly established field of statistics, and U. Eggert taught political economy and public finance. Besides teaching at the university, both were active as advisers to the Ministry of Agriculture and Trade and the Ministry of Finance. They also performed a role in introducing Japan to various foreign countries through their books on the Japanese economy.[8] Of the foreign employees from Germany we must not exclude P. Mayet and G. Wagener. As an adviser to the Ministry of Finance, Mayet presented his views on fire insurance and agricultural insurance. Wagener was active in directing an exhibition for industrial promotion and in expediting the advancement of Japanese traditional arts. In particular, Wagener's arguments in the 'Report on the Domestic Exhibition' of

1881, that the existing policy of state-run model factories should be transformed into a policy for promoting private enterprise, were highly influential in government circles.[9]

3. Ōkubo Toshimichi and the Promotion of Industry

In addition to foreign books and employees there was another source whereby the people were able to obtain information about political economy in Europe and America: by travel or study abroad. From the closing days of the Tokugawa Shogunate to the early days of the Meiji era, many young people went abroad. Among them there were those who were later to make great contributions to economic policy as officers in government. For example, Matsukata Masayoshi, who was to take the leadership in economic policy after the death of Ōkubo, went to France in 1878 and travelled for nine months in England, France, Germany, Holland, etc. Particularly in France, while visiting the Great Exhibition, he met the minister of finance, Léon Say, and the financial expert Paul Leroy-Beaulieu and became informed on financial affairs, an experience which was of use to his later career as minister of finance.

Of the travels abroad by leading government figures, the largest undertaking was the Iwakura mission to the United States and Europe from 1871 to 1873. Among its 106 members, not to speak of Lord Iwakura Tomomi himself, there were included such leading figures as Kido Takayoshi, Itō Hirobumi, and Ōkubo Toshimichi. Their experience during this journey was of great use in their political activities after their return. This was particularly the case with Ōkubo, who was to implement the 'Industry and Trade' policy which prepared the way for the Japanese modernization.

Kido and Ōkubo are, together with Saigō Takamori, said to be the 'three pre-eminent figures of the Meiji Restoration'. Ōkubo, who was the longest-lived among them, shared his views on national development with a friend just before his assassination in May 1878: 'The ten years after the Restoration comprise the first period, that is, the period of starting an enterprise. The next ten years [1878–87] are the second period, which will be the most important. It is during this period that we should settle domestic administration and promote national enrichment, to which work I, for one, will do my best to contribute. The ten years after 1888 will be the third period, that of development to a successful completion, which work is expected to be achieved by our able successors'.[10]

Here we can see Ōkubo's initial ideas. After making a solid foundation for new government during the first ten years and promoting the development and enrichment of the national powers in the second period, he intended to hand over the leadership of the government to his successors in the third period. However, his untimely death abruptly ended his intended plans in the second instead of the third period. Ōkuma, Matsukata, and Itō successfully took over the Ōkubo regime, which they developed into the Meiji constitutional regime. This accomplishment owed much to their outstanding talents and effort, but we must note that Ōkubo had formed the basis and set the direction of the development which they faithfully followed. Ōkubo had also done much work for the promotion of industry in the first period. What, then, were his basic ideas in this respect?

In November 1871 the Iwakura mission set sail from Yokohama and visited twelve countries in North America and Europe, ending in September 1873. The aims of the mission were to conduct preliminary negotiations for the revision of the unequal treaties and to become well informed about the culture and institutions of the advanced countries. The intentions they had for treaty revision proved to be a failure, but the mission brought a plentiful harvest for those men of influence who observed the reality of Western societies, and their personal experiences were of great use in their later work in promoting the modernization of the country. Minister of Finance Ōkubo, who joined the mission as vice-envoy, had so far devoted himself to the political strengthening of the new government, but after his trip showed great enthusiasm in economic policy for the promotion of industry. This change in Ōkubo's attitude apparently reflected his experience abroad. He was highly impressed by the great difference in economic power between the advanced Western countries and Japan, and he was convinced that it was vital to fill the gap.

It was England and Prussia that impressed him most. The mission visited such industrial cities as Liverpool, Manchester, and Sheffield under the guidance of H. S. Parkes, the British minister to Japan, who was then in England. Ōkubo wrote home emphasizing that throughout this tour he felt he had found where the causes of English prosperity really lay. Though the mission's stay in Prussia was short, only one-fifth as long as its stay in England, the members thought that 'it would be more beneficial for Japan to inquire about the politics and customs of Prussia', which, with all its backwardness, pursued the 'wealth and strength' policy in order to catch up with England. It was of great benefit for Ōkubo to meet Bismarck and von Moltke in Berlin and to hear directly from them about their experiences in founding the German Empire. Ōkubo wrote to Saigō about the deep impression made on him by the speech of the 'Man of Blood and Iron'.

Immediately after meeting Bismarck, Ōkubo was recalled by the government, and he returned to Japan in May 1873, four months ahead of the rest of the mission. He set up the Ministry of Home Affairs in order to advance the 'Industry and Trade' policy to the full, and he himself became its first minister. The Ministry of Home Affairs was composed of the Industrial Promotion Board, transferred from the Ministry of Finance, and the Police Administration Board, transferred from the Ministry of Justice. The position of the Ministry of Home Affairs was superior to all other ministries in that its minister was virtually equivalent to the prime minister. This post was very suitable for Ōkubo, who, applying a 'sweets and whip' policy, was a kind of 'Bismarck in Japan'.[11] He occupied the post of president of the Land Tax Revision Office in 1875 as well and thus strove to establish the financial basis of the government. He also showed great ability as president of the first Industrial Promotion Exhibition, which was held in Tokyo in 1877 to instigate economic modernization. His basic ideas underlying these energetic activities are evident in 'Shokusan Kōgyō ni Kansuru Kengisho' (Memorial on the Promotion of Industry and Trade) written in 1874.

The 'Memorial' starts with the following passage: 'In general, the strength or weakness of a nation depends on the wealth or poverty of its people, and the wealth or poverty of the people is due to the plenitude or scarcity of commodities. Even though the plenitude or scarcity of commodities originates in the industry of the people, there has been no case where the government has not executed its power to initiate and encourage it'.

Then Ōkubo explains this theory in the following way: Nothing is more urgent for the government than the promotion of industry and trade. An unsatisfactory state is due partly to the backwardness of the people, but more to an insufficient effort of the government to lead them. From the production of industrial commodities to the means of transport by land and sea, the government should maintain the facilities already established and initiate what has not yet been established. Then Ōkubo turned to the Navigation Acts in the English mercantile system and argued that the acts increased the number of English ships and trained the nation in the art of navigation on the one hand, while it barred foreign commodities from rushing into the country and protected the domestic industry on the other. After this the Navigation Acts were removed and free trade was permitted, which occasioned its present wealth and power. Following the English example, one should encourage and induce the docile nation of Japan to industriousness and endurance in pursuit of trade and industry. This was how the 'Memorial' argued and concluded.

With this firm belief, Ōkubo pursued the course of industrialization chosen and directed by the state. As an example, let us examine the case of Mitsubishi. In his letter of inquiry on the supervision of commercial ships (1875), he argued that Japan should choose a policy in accordance with the stage of the nation's development: Since the Japanese were still of a docile nature, they could not be regarded as capable of walking by themselves without protection from the government. Yet if the shipping industry were to be run wholly by the state and the crews were to be trained only in the governmental school, the gradually rising spirit of the people might be discouraged. The best policy lay in pursuing a middle course. It was therefore essential for the government to aid Mitsubishi company as the most powerful private company, and give it strong support (e.g., by gratuitous transference to the company of government-owned ships, and government subsidy, which lasted for fifteen years, to Mitsubishi's shipping service). This was to encourage the shipping-industry circles to form a kind of united corporation centring around Mitsubishi in order to compete with the powerful foreign shipping industry. In this way Mitsubishi was to lead the way to becoming *zaibatsu* under the government's strong protection based on Ōkubo's ideas.

Thus we see that trade-and-industry promotion policy was the core of the all-round modernization policies of the Meiji government, and it was Ōkubo who laid its foundation to be inherited and developed by those political leaders who succeeded him after his premature death. The teaching of talented young men by means of Western books, the translating and publishing of a number of those books by the government's own hand, the employing of overseas experts in various fields, and the setting up of the Industrial Promotion Board in the newly established Ministry of Home Affairs were part and parcel of such a policy. And it was nothing but the way which led to the Japanese Industrial Revolution.

13

Economists in Parliament: The Fall of Bimetallism in Japan

Norio Tamaki

1. A Metallic Issue

Once the treaty ports had opened in 1859, the financial arrangements of the Japanese government were vulnerable not only to the manoeuvring of the foreign merchants but also to the impact of the international monetary arrangements. Any weakness of the foreign exchange and trade systems in Japan could be exploited by the world outside; this was inevitable and there was no escape.

From the outset, the Meiji government was struggling to achieve a sound financial base. There were two urgent priorities, to secure a regular return of revenue and to create a new stable currency. The reformation of the land tax system, started in 1873, which introduced a money tax instead of a tax payment in rice, gave of course a monetary revenue and took seven years to complete.

The replacing of the old currency by new was also a long and complicated process. It was an urgent necessity to withdraw the old debased coins and *hansatsu*, paper money issued by the local domains, and replace them with the new government currency. Ōkuma Shigenobu, the minister of finance in the 1870s, aimed at economic growth and the withdrawal of inconvertible paper currency. But inflation raged and there was much hardship among those, including samurai, whose dwindling pensions plummeted in value, and peasants, whose taxes were increasingly burdensome. During the power struggle between 1880 and 1881, Matsukata Masayoshi emerged as a tough and uncompromising minister of finance, and Ōkuma went, temporarily, into retirement.

For almost a quarter of a century after the Meiji Restoration in 1868, the arguments raged in Japan between the bimetallists, who wanted a dual metallic system based on gold and silver values, and the monometallists, who insisted that the only way to financial stability for Japan was through the gold standard. In the end, Matsukata and his financial advisers took, as will be explained here, Japan onto the gold standard. The United States, in 1900, followed suit and, then, all world powers, except China which remained tied to silver, were on the gold standard.

The Meiji government proceeded with commendable speed to dismantle the social structure of the old regime. In 1869 the feudal system was abolished and the special status of the samurai was removed, although a new aristocratic class was created. In 1871 the feudal framework of semi-independent domains was replaced by the system of centrally controlled prefectures, each with their own centrally appointed governors. In 1872 the prohibition on the sale of land, a feature of the earlier land-holding system, was removed.

These drastic reforms caused a rapid deterioration of the position of former samurai, which led to the Satsuma Rebellion, ultimately crushed in 1877. This was the last armed resistance to the new regime. But the financial position of the Meiji government as a result of the emergency measures, which had to be taken to finance the war against the rebels, was seriously damaged.

It was particularly unfortunate for the Japanese government to be in such difficulties internally at the same time that great controversy was raging in the world outside over the attempt to establish a bimetallic standard for the currencies of the world in an undertaking to regulate international trade and exchange. Under bimetallism both silver and gold were made standards, the preferred value being 15 1/2 parts of silver to 1 of gold. The establishment of such a standard was sensibly affected by the great gold discoveries of 1848, 1860, and 1870 in California, Australia, and South Africa. Thereafter gold production did not rise considerably while that of silver increased enormously. Under the operation of Gresham's Law, gold value rose and gold coins were quickly exported.

Inevitably those relying on a silver standard, like India, and those producing silver, like the United States, suffered serious losses. Those involved, especially in the United States, exerted great pressure internationally to make the dual standard universal. International conferences were held in 1878 and 1881 in Paris and later in 1892 in Brussels to try to hammer out an acceptable solution. The conferences failed, with Britain and Germany refusing to countenance a bimetallic standard. In the end the problems of bimetallism overwhelmed any advantages. By 1900 America adopted the gold monometallic standard.

By the mid-1880s, the financial positions of the Meiji government had stabilized. The Bank of Japan had been set up in 1882 to serve as the bankers' bank. The remaining financial problem related to the metallic standard to which the Japanese paper money was to be tied. Under Matsukata's strong leadership, the Bank of Japan started to issue silver-convertible bank notes in May 1884, effectively tying the Japanese financial system to the silver standard. Unfortunately other major countries previously on this silver standard had abandoned it by 1880. Even the Latin Monetary Union, formed in 1865 by France, Italy, Belgium, and Switzerland, and later in 1875 joined by Greece, had ceased to operate by 1878. With galloping inflation gone, it was time for Matsukata to examine possible metallic standards which would be conducive to promoting the Japanese economy.

2. The Tokyo Political Economy Club (Tokyo Keizaigaku Kyōkai)

In January 1879, a monthly journal entitled *Tokyo Keizai Zasshi* (Tokyo Economist) was launched.[1] Taguchi Ukichi, the editor of the journal, argued that there were no journals featuring the Japanese economy and that therefore *Tokyo Keizai Zasshi* would undoubtedly be the foremost journal of its kind. As Taguchi explained:

> Some time ago, I had an opportunity to discuss with Mr. Shand, a British banker. At that time glancing at the *Economist* newspaper on the table between us, I told him why Japan should not have this sort of journal. Smiling at me, he said that Japan did not yet have sufficient resources to launch that sort of journal. Alas! Though his words were uttered as a joke, I almost thought that they might have hit the mark. Then I promised him to start a journal of this kind.[2]

Alexander Allan Shand, an important figure for the development of Japanese banking,[3] was thus instrumental in promoting Japanese economic journalism, too. Taguchi's intention was welcomed and financially supported by Shibusawa Eiichi, one of the most influential businessmen and the founder of the First National Bank (Daiichi Kokuritsu Ginkō, 1873) and the Tokyo Chamber of Commerce (1877).

Tokyo Keizai Zasshi reported in the issue of May 5, 1880, that

> the gentlemen who were interested in political economy joined forces to establish a club called the Political Economy Seminar (Keizai Danwakai). The purpose of the seminar was to discuss principles of political economy. . . . Although meetings with speeches and discussions were increasingly prevalent nowadays in the country, we had not heard the establishment of economic clubs. The seminar had to be the first of its kind.

Taguchi was a dominant figure in both *Tokyo Keizai Zasshi* and the seminar, the discussions of which were regularly reported in *Tokyo Keizai Zasshi.*

During the first seven years the seminar met regularly and was influential. The membership was rather narrowly based and applications for entry seemed to be closely scrutinized. The exact number of members is not known. Members came mainly from two sources, the University of Tokyo and Kyōritsu School (Kyōritsu Gakusha). Kyōritsu was set up in Tokyo in 1870 by Seki Shinpachi, a graduate of Shōhei School (Shōheikō), the Shogunate Academy. As early as 1860, he started to learn the English language and became an official interpreter. He was despatched as an interpreter in 1861 to France and in 1862 to the United States. After the Meiji Restoration he was engaged in the duties of interpreter at the American Consulate in Kobe and later was appointed as chief translator at the Ministry of Finance. From 1875 he devoted himself to education at the Kyōritsu School. The school provided the seminar with Taguchi, Noritake Kōtarō, Taguchi's successor as the editor of *Tokyo Keizai Zasshi*, Ishikawa Eisaku, Saga Shōsaku, and other able young journalists at the journal.[4]

The University of Tokyo also provided members, including Tajiri Inajirō, a Satsuma man. Tajiri had attended the Keiō School briefly in 1869, but he soon left there, moving to the South College (Daigaku Nankō, predecessor of the University of Tokyo) and later to the Naval Academy. From the academy he was despatched to New York where he was educated at high schools for six years. He enrolled as an undergraduate at Yale University in 1875, successfully obtaining the first degree in 1878. On his return to Tokyo and at the time of the establishment of the seminar, he was an official at the Ministry of Finance. Later he was appointed to be professor of law at the Imperial University (1886) while at the same time he served as an undersecretary at the Ministry of Finance from 1888 to 1889. Another influential member of the Political Economy Seminar was Amano Tameyuki, who was still a student at the University of Tokyo when he joined. In later life he was distinguished for his part, with Ōkuma Shigenobu, in setting up Waseda University. He also founded another economic journal entitled *Tōyō Keizai Shinpō* (Oriental Economist), which is still in existence.[5] The third man was Sakatani Yoshio. He was the youngest member, a student at the University of Tokyo, and one of the key figures at the Ministry of Finance under Matsukata's regime, as we will discuss later.

During the first seven years, the seminar was very active in holding lectures open to the public. The lecturers were usually seminar members, except on one occasion when Seki Shinpachi, Taguchi's teacher, was invited to speak. In general, members of the seminar were advocates of laissez-faire or free trade, especially Taguchi and Amano. There was no shortage of topics to discuss given the economic problems resulting from Matsukata's deflationary policies. The members of the seminar were studying Western scholars' writings and so had plenty of material for both lectures and discussions.

At the beginning of 1882, the seminar committee displayed another important initiative. *Tokyo Keizai Zasshi* of January 28, 1882 reported that

> the Tokyo Political Economy Seminar will accept subscriptions from 500 people and will publish translated versions of the Western books on which the lectures we give are based. These include: Herbert Spencer, *Principles of Sociology*; Adam Smith, *The Wealth of Nations*; Stanley Jevons, *Money and Mechanism of Exchange*; Henry Fawcett, *Manual of Political Economy.*

Later (May 1882), another four books were added to the publication list. They were F. A. Walker's *Political Economy*, W. Bagehot's *Lombard Street*, H. D. Macleod's *The Elements of Banking*, and J. W. Gilbart's *Lectures on the History and Principles of Ancient Commerce.* The translations were done mainly by the staff under Taguchi. For instance, Spencer's *Principles of Sociology* was translated by Noritake and Smith's *The Wealth of Nations* by Ishikawa. Their translation work doubtless attracted the interest of those concerned with economic problems.

These activities suggested a flourishing seminar which changed the title to the Tokyo Political Economy Club (Tokyo Keizaigaku Kyōkai) in February 1887. In a lecture commemorating the renaming of the club, Taguchi disclosed his private ambition to model the club on the

Political Economy Club, founded by Thomas Tooke in London which boasted David Ricardo, Thomas Robert Malthus, and other notable economists among its members.

It is important to note that shortly after this reorganization Matsukata Masayoshi, the minister of finance, requested the club to investigate the implications for Japan of the fall in the silver value. The club responded immediately by appointing a select committee to consider the silver problem. The members of the committee were Taguchi, Tajiri, Sakatani, Amano, Noritake, Hamada Kenjirō, a graduate of the University of Tokyo and businessman, and Ban Naonosuke, the editor of *Taihei Shinpō* (Pacifist Newspaper), founder of Kyoto Nursing School, and lecturer at the Dōshisha School (Dōshisha Eigakkō). They studied the works of Western scholars, including R. H. I. Palgrave, a British economist, M. G. Mullhall, a British statistician, J. L. Laughlin, a Harvard professor, and A. Sauerbeck.[6]

The committee submitted their report in April 1888 to the minister of finance. The report attributed the cause of the decline of silver price to the fact that gold demands sharply and persistently increased between 1871 and 1883. They argued that silver value, which had itself been constant, was forced to decline relative to the gold value. According to their investigations, there were three reasons for the decrease in the demand for silver. These included increased silver supplies; adoption of a gold standard by Germany in 1871, the United States in 1879, and Italy in 1883; and the collapse of the bimetallic Latin Monetary Union in 1878.[7] The report did not make any recommendation about the monetary standard which Japan should adopt in place of the silver standard. It suggested only that one of the main causes for the decline of the price level in the major countries, particularly Britain, was the gold monometallic standard. They argued that prices in Britain would have been higher if it had been calculated in terms of silver value.

It is clear that Taguchi was a convinced bimetallist. Shortly before the appointment of the committee, he had put forward in *Tokyo Keizai Zasshi* the view that the recent recession in European countries could have been mitigated if they had adopted the bimetallic standard.[8] But his bimetallic arguments did not seem to be reproduced in the report to the minister of finance, perhaps because Matsukata's request for advice stopped short of asking for any recommendation. In addition, there was a strong element in the committee against bimetallism, in the person of Sakatani, a disciple of Matsukata and a radical gold monometallist.

3. Rise of Gold Monometallism

It is not known when Matsukata first began to favour the gold monometallic standard. Perhaps his views on this were of long standing. In 1884, when the Silver Convertible Banknote Decree was promulgated, he had suggested privately that gold was a more stable metal and should be made the standard metal as soon as the gold reserve was sufficient to support the system.[9] Again in 1887 when the silver value relative to the gold was declining sharply, Matsukata sent a letter to Ōyama Iwao, the minister at the War Office, advising him that because of declining silver value much more caution should be used in ordering munitions from foreign countries.[10] But he did not at this stage proceed further towards establishing the gold standard. In August 1892, the Matsukata cabinet, in which he held concurrently the portfolio of finance, resigned. He had to wait one year before he could resume his campaign for the adoption of the gold standard. Meanwhile, disciples of Matsukata and able officials at the Ministry of Finance, Sakatani and Soeda Juichi, took up the job. Soeda had a chequered career. Graduating from the University of Tokyo in July 1884, Soeda entered the Ministry of Finance. But soon in September 1884 he was commissioned to accompany a grandson of his former clan master on his study abroad, mainly in England. This was a splendid opportunity for Soeda. During his stay in Cambridge, Soeda studied political economy under the supervision of Alfred Marshall and befriended J. M. Keynes who later in 1929 wrote an obituary of Soeda in *The Economic Journal.* This Cambridge connection made him a Japanese correspondent of *The Economic Journal* on his return to his former position in the Ministry of Finance. He was an active correspondent, sending articles entitled 'Letter from Japan', chiefly on Japanese economy and finance. A disciple of Marshall, Soeda was undoubtedly one of the right-hand men of Matsukata, but he was too theoretical and academic-minded to push the policy forcibly forward. Thus the task was left to Sakatani.[11]

At the University of Tokyo Sakatani attended Tajiri's and Fenollosa's lectures on political economy and Shibusawa Eiichi's lectures on Japan's public finance. After graduation, he obtained a post in the Ministry of Finance, but continued to work on political economy texts, reading A. H. Wagner's *Finanzwissenschaft*, J. S. Mill's *Political Economy*, Fawcett's *Manual of Political Economy*, L. Cossa's *Guide to the Study of Political Economy*, H. D. Macleod's *The Elements of Banking*, J. W. Gilbart's *The History, Principles and Practice of Banking*, and G. J. Goschen's *The Theory of the Foreign Exchange.* Because of his extramural work, he was asked to serve as an occasional lecturer at the Senshū School. He would have liked to study these matters first hand in Europe, but time did not permit, and he was promoted to be the chief investigator of the Budget Bureau. In this capacity he contributed greatly to the development of Japan's system of public finance. He was commissioned by the minister of finance to prepare a draft of Japan's first Public Finance Bill (Kaikei Hōan), which he delivered to the minister in July 1887 and which was enacted in February 1889. He was also commissioned by the first session of the Diet to give a lecture on the necessity for a national budget before the members of the Diet in November 1890. These Diet members were the first in Japan's history elected only shortly before, in July 1890. Their first job was the national budget for the financial year of 1891–92. It was well known that Sakatani was an extremely able government official. As Matsukata's right-hand man he was one of the most important figures in the making and administration of the so-called Matsukata financial policies.[12]

Eventually Sakatani was instructed confidentially by Matsukata to prepare a draft plan for the adoption of the gold standard. Sakatani worked very hard and produced a series of drafts, entitled 'Draft on the Monetary System', 'Addition to the Draft on the Monetary System', 'Appendix to the Draft on the Monetary System', and 'Replies to Anticipated Questions on the Monetary System'.[13] He was in the forefront of the radical gold metallists. In preparing his drafts he elaborated particularly on two points. How was Japan to cope with the problem that the gold reserve was far smaller than it should be to establish the gold standard? Sakatani devised a system in which, though gold was the standard metal and the free coinage of silver was suspended, silver coins continued to be used under the strict supervision of the Ministry of Finance. This was the so-called limping gold standard.[14] In the second place he also had to prepare efficient and persuasive arguments for the adoption of gold and abandonment of silver. His argument was ingenious:

> I should like to make one particular point. Those who argue for the silver and against the gold are those in the gold-standard countries. They uniformly say that the gold standard is not good and that one should stick to the silver but they remain gold-standard countries. The remaining silver countries are China, Korea, Malaya, and Japan. If silver is good, why do the European and American people desert the silver standard?[15]

When in the summer of 1893, India, the biggest silver-using country, suspended the free coinage of silver, Matsukata immediately stepped forward and pressed for the minister of finance, Watanabe Kunitake, a close friend of Matsukata, to establish a commission to investigate the present problems of the monetary system and hopefully to recommend the adoption of the gold monometallic standard. Watanabe quickly obtained permission to do this. In October 1893, only a few months after the suspension of free coinage of silver in India, the Commission on the Monetary System came into existence.

The commission was composed of twenty-two members. The chairman was Viscount Tani Kanjō, minister of agriculture and trade in Itō Hirobumi's first cabinet. The deputy chairman was Tajiri Inajirō, who then had an additional position of the secretary to the Ministry of Finance. The other members included four governmental officials (one each from the Ministry of Foreign Affairs and the Ministry of Agriculture and Trade and two from the Ministry of Finance), the governor of the Bank of Japan, the governor of the Specie Bank of Yokohama (Yokohama Shōkin Ginkō), the governor of the First National Bank, the president of Mitsui Trading Company, the president of Mitsubishi Corporation, two professors at the Imperial University, the president of Keiō University, a professor of the Tokyo School of Special Studies (Waseda), two senators, four members of Diet, and a journalist. They were commissioned to find answers regarding the following three questions: what were the causes of, and results of, the recent fluctuations in the gold and silver values?; what were their influences on Japanese economy?; and which metallic standard should be adopted: gold, silver, or both?[16]

The commission first opened its proceedings on October 25, 1893. A special committee was appointed to prepare drafts of the report. The members of this committee were Sakatani, Soeda Juichi, Kanai Noburu, professor of political economy at the Imperial University, Sonoda Kōkichi, governor of the Specie Bank, and Taguchi. Chairman Sonoda, the senior-most member, was, like Matsukata, from Satsuma. Graduating from the South College, he entered the Ministry of Foreign Affairs and was soon despatched as a diplomat to England where he stayed for fifteen years. In 1890 he was appointed governor of the Specie Bank. Later he also became the president of the 15th Bank (Dai Jūgo Kokuritsu Ginkō), the so-called Aristocrats' Bank, which was, in effect, controlled by Matsukata. Although Matsukata was out of power at the start of the special committee, the chairman of the drafting committee was his very close friend, Sonoda.

Under the chairmanship of Sonoda, the special committee worked energetically, holding thirty-seven meetings. In March 1895 the interim report was submitted to the general meeting of the commission. Before proceeding to make the final report, the special committee was joined by two additional members, Watanabe Kōki, Diet member and former president of the Imperial University, and Masuda Takashi, president of Mitsui Trading Company. Between August 1894 and April 1895 while the special committee was struggling with its reports, the Sino-Japanese War broke out and, for Japan, was brought to a successful conclusion. Japan anticipated a large amount of indemnity, hopefully in gold, from China. Matsukata also returned during a cabinet reshuffle in March 1895 to be minister of finance. Even with these favourable circumstances, the path to the gold standard was not so smooth as had been expected.

The special committee submitted its final report in May 1895, but the members were not unanimous in their views. Sakatani, Soeda, and Watanabe supported the gold standard, but Taguchi and Kanai preferred silver. Sonoda, the chairman, chose the status quo, i.e., the silver standard. Masuda did not commit himself either way. Excluding Sakatani, the radical gold metallist, the committee members unanimously said No to any immediate change.[17] This result was not what Matsukata wanted. Before the general meeting of the commission in June 1895 he had consulted with Sonoda to try to find a way forward.

At the general meeting of the commission held on June 5, 1895, surprisingly everything was resolved. Sonoda moved that a vote be taken to decide whether any change at some future time would be necessary for the monetary standard. Sonoda and, perhaps, Matsukata thought that if some future change were approved, the path to the gold standard would be smoothed. Someone objected, but when put to vote it was carried by a narrow margin. This was effectively a victory for the gold metallists. By his manoeuvring, Sonoda had ensured that all bimetallists and moderate gold metallists like Soeda had to join the radical gold monometallist Sakatani. Adding the moderate to the radical, the gold metallists were clearly the majority. Indeed, the general meeting of the commission eventually approved the adoption of the gold standard, though the actual transformation of the monetary standard from silver to gold took somewhat longer.[18]

4. Bimetallism: A Lost Dream?

There were seven bimetallists in the commission, but there was only one member, Taguchi Ukichi, who could argue systematically for bimetallism. Taguchi was an enlightened historian, economist, and journalist. In the late 1870s he published two important books, *Nihon*

Kaika Shōshi (Brief History of Japanese Enlightenment, 1877) and *Jiyū Kōeki Nihon Keizairon* (Free Trade and the Japanese Economy, 1878). In history he was strongly influenced by two Western historians, F. P. G. Guizot and H. T. Buckle. He explained in *Nihon Kaika Shōshi* how the law of social progress, formulated by Guizot and Buckle, was explicit in the Japanese history of spirit. *Nihon Kaika Shōshi* extended to six volumes and took five years to complete.

In political economy he was enthusiastic in promoting free trade, as he explained in *Jiyū Kōeki Nihon Keizairon.* As a convinced free trader, he was called the 'Adam Smith of Japan'. Taguchi was also favourably impressed by the British policy of colonization, which he preferred to the Spanish system. He was apparently basing his argument upon Smith's *The Wealth of Nations.* He also introduced to Japan the systematic colonization programme of E. G. Wakefield. As a result of his knowledge of colonization, Taguchi criticized Japan's policy in Taiwan.[19] His free trade and systematic colonization ideas were so remarkable in Japan that his views on bimetallism were sometimes overlooked.

Earlier in 1881 Taguchi had commenced his arguments for bimetallism in *Tokyo Keizai Zasshi.*[20] But of course it was in the report submitted to the Monetary Commission that his arguments were marshalled fully. Opening the discussion, he pointed out that the fall of prices in the gold-standard countries was larger in scale than the rise of prices in the silver-standard countries, in other words, that the degree of the rise in gold value was greater than that of the fall in silver value. From this he insisted that the less-fluctuating silver could be more suitable for the standard metal.

Furthermore, according to Taguchi, there was a fatal defect in the gold monometallic standard which was about to be adopted universally. In his argument, in which he drew upon statistics prepared by the American Mint and other sources, Taguchi calculated there were ¥39 hundred million each of gold and silver in the circulation of countries in the world. This meant, stressed Taguchi, that the silver circulation was even larger than that of the gold before Germany's departure from the silver in 1873. The position of silver metal was thus very stable. Nonetheless, the silver countries were deserting the metal. If all countries adopt the gold monometallic standard and silver would no longer be used as the authorized standard, what would be the result? This was the main thrust of his arguments:

> International trade, which involved ¥78 hundred million, would have to be managed by only ¥39 hundred million. The process will

> undoubtedly result in an enormous rise in the value of gold and an enormous fall in the general prices, which, if these occur, will certainly be a world-wide danger.[21]

And the situation would be more serious in Japan, Taguchi argued. A severe deflation, from which Japan had only recently recovered, would recur and hinder the recovery of economy. Moreover, he believed that Japan was desperately in a shortage of gold stock. If the gold monometallic standard was adopted, Japan would have to buy its bulk of gold in exchange for silver. From these he concluded that the gold monometallic standard was not desirable for Japan as well as for world trade.

How, then, did he see the silver monometallic standard? He strongly opposed the suspension of the free coinage of silver. He insisted that the suspension would raise the domestic value of silver. The rise would bring silver-convertible bank notes current in Hong Kong, Shanghai, and other East Asian ports back into Japan to demand their conversion into the silver species. This would greatly damage Japan's trade in East Asia. Note, however, that Taguchi was not a silver-metallist. He believed that silver, the relative value of which was declining, could not qualify in any case as a standard metal. Taguchi was a typical bimetallist. He believed that if both gold and silver were used jointly as the standard metals, any drawbacks caused by the monometallic standard would be removed. That was the level of sophistication of his arguments for bimetallism, as was his proposal for establishing an international bimetallism. His framework for bimetallism as a national and international system consisted of forming an international agreement among the major countries, that is, no more than a copy of the Latin Monetary Union.

Where did Taguchi find his arguments for bimetallism? We can perhaps find a clue from the publication list of Western writings, prepared by the Tokyo Political Economy Club. Indeed, there was a notable bimetallist among the authors, F. A. Walker. Walker was the president of the Massachusetts Institute of Technology and a prolific writer on economic issues, among which he discussed most enthusiastically international bimetallism. When he was despatched as a delegate to the International Monetary Conference of 1878, Walker proclaimed his adherence to international bimetallism and held to the doctrine ever since. As such, he was 'unquestionably the most prominent and the best known of American writers in the economic field' (*Dictionary of American Biography*) in the mid-1890s.

Walker's arguments for international bimetallism made their first appearance in book form in *Money in Its Relations to Trade and Industry* (New York, 1879) and later in an expanded version in *International Bimetallism* (New York, 1896). In the latter, Walker wrote:

> The system of international bimetallism, —again with free coinage of the metals, at a ratio common to the contracting nations, —such as existed under the Latin Union between 1865 and 1873; such as had been proposed to be constituted between wider groups of nations, in successive international conferences and in a host of treaties, tracts and public addresses. The term would, with due explanation, embrace the monetary system which Professor Alfred Marshall has proposed. (pp. 1–2)

This was his international bimetallism, a typical example of its sort, and an enlarged version of the Latin Monetary Union. Though he used the name of Alfred Marshall, his discussions could not in any way be compared with Marshall's. Perhaps Walker borrowed Marshall's name only for the sake of his own arguments for bimetallism. Walker's arguments were as simple as Taguchi's and their opinions were alike in the fact that both argued for the re-establishment of the Latin Monetary Union and also in the fact that both were defeated.

It is easy to take bimetallists to task for their dreams. The Latin Union, to which they insisted on returning, worked only for a very short time and did not produce any remarkable results. On the contrary, Britain had been basing its prosperity on the gold monometallic standard since 1816. Its capital city, London, was the largest market for gold, and as such other financial centres could not rank with its status. Perhaps it was London's importance which destroyed the Latin Union. It might have been foolish to propose an international bimetallic union in these politically and economically fluctuating circumstances.

However, it was also the case that the international gold standard did not itself survive for long. It started in 1900 when the United States joined the system, but ceased to operate in 1914. In the aftermath of World War I, the major countries conjointly and independently tried hard to re-establish the gold standard system, but they failed. Eventually in 1931 any efforts for the cause of the gold standard were abandoned. Later developments showed that international monetary problems could be solved only by international agreements or unions as was evidenced by the Bretton Woods Agreement of 1944. As far as an international agreement was concerned, the bimetallic dream was worth dreaming.

Finally, we may ask, how is bimetallism regarded by modern monetary economists? J. Niehans, a monetary economist, in explaining the working of bimetallism, has suggested that 'natural and synthetic rubber are perfect substitutes' and has intended to suggest that bimetallism, exemplified by this substitution, would work effectively in tightly controlled conditions, in other words, in a closed economy.[22] Indeed, Niehans's supposition could well be illustrated by many historical incidents. Britain abandoned bimetallism in 1816 when the British economy entered upon a new phase of development, unprecedently open compared with the eve of the Napoleonic Wars. The Latin Union ceased to operate in 1878 when European countries more or less confronted conditions which somewhat resembled those of Britain in 1816. So did Japan and the United States when they adopted the gold standard in 1897 and 1900, respectively.

Using the formula of Niehans, we could assess the validity of the framework of political economy created by the two bimetallists. Taguchi was, as we have seen, a convinced free trader. There are many ways of defining free trade, but it may be safe to say that it means free entry to any country and to any sector of the economy. Taguchi, therefore, incorporated in his framework of political economy both open and closed systems. The bimetallic free trade might have been a self-contradiction. To the contrary, Walker argued against laissez-faire,[23] though it should be noted that laissez-faire has a wider context than free trade does. In this sense, the system of Walker's political economy was more consistent and solid than Taguchi's.

14

Economists in Journalism: Liberalism, Nationalism and Their Variants

Shirō Sugihara

1. Prologue

Like a number of great thinkers in eighteenth-century Western Europe, many Japanese thinkers in the early Meiji era were not just writers, but editors and publishers as well. For example, Fukuzawa Yukichi, who was called the 'Voltaire of Japan', started *Meiroku Zasshi* (Meiji Six Journal) in cooperation with his friends in 1876. He also published *Katei Sōdan* (Journal of Family Life) in the same year (the journal was renamed *Minkan Zasshi* [Popular Magazine] in the following year). In 1882 he published a daily newspaper, *Jiji Shinpō* (Current Affairs Review) in which he wrote most of the editorials himself. Nakae Chōmin, who was called the 'Rousseau of the Orient', started *Tōyō Jiyū Shinbun* (Oriental Liberal Paper) in 1881 and became the editor himself. He also published a journal, *Seiri Sōdan* (Journal of Political Principles, later renamed *Ōbei Seiri Sōdan* [Journal of European and American Political Principles]) in 1882 and introduced J. J. Rousseau's thought to Japan. Tokutomi Sohō started *Kokumin no Tomo* (The Nation's Friend) in 1887, and, while publishing many books from Min'yūsha with the aim of enlightenment, he also started a newspaper, *Kokumin Shinbun* (News of the Nation), from the publisher Kokumin Shinbunsha in 1890 and edited it himself. All these newspapers and journals contributed to the spread of the thoughts of the aforementioned three thinkers, and therefore played an important role in the development of modern thought in Japan.

All three thinkers were very concerned about economic affairs too, and so issues relating to economic affairs frequently appeared in these newspapers and journals. For example, *Jiji Shinpō* contained many articles written by Fukuzawa, commenting on current economic affairs, while the earlier issues of *Kokumin no Tomo* contained many articles which criticized the government's economic policy from the point of view of democratic liberalism. As is well known, Tokutomi changed his ideological stance around the period of the Sino-Japanese War and became a nationalist and supported expansionism. The political tone of *Kokumin Shinbun* was much affected by the change. The effort of Nakae's *Seiri Sōdan* to introduce Western thought to Japan was not confined to Rousseau. It played a significant role in introducing French economic thought, including the work of J.-B. Say.

Along with these aforementioned periodicals of general interest, periodicals specifically concerned with economic matters appeared from the early Meiji era, in Tokyo as well as in other cities. Most of them dealt with information on the supply and demand of major commodities and price fluctuations as well as that on agricultural and industrial technology. However, there also emerged some journals which were not only interested in providing such information, but were also actively involved in the understanding of the national economy as a whole, discussing current economic issues and introducing Western political economy. In this chapter I shall sketch the history of some of these journals, and, by so doing, discuss how Western political economy was received in Japan and was linked to the current issues in the field of journalism.

2. *Tokyo Keizai Zasshi* (Tokyo Economist) and Taguchi Ukichi

The first important economic journal published in Japan was *Tokyo Keizai Zasshi* (Tokyo Economist), started in 1879 by Taguchi Ukichi.[1] Taguchi studied English in a private school in Tokyo and obtained a post in the Department of Translation, Ministry of Finance, in 1873 where he studied bookkeeping and political economy as well as English. Seki Shinpachi taught him political economy, using the textbooks written by F. Wayland and A. L. Perry, while A. A. Shand, a foreign employee of the government, taught him bookkeeping. One day when Taguchi visited Shand's room, Shand showed him a copy of the *Economist* (London) which happened to be on his desk, and, after describing the authority of the journal and pointing out that economists all over the world read it, he commented that Japan would not yet be capable of publishing such an economic journal. Shand's words aroused

Taguchi's nationalistic sentiment, and he promised Shand that he would publish such a journal in his country some day.

It was on January the 29th, 1879, that Taguchi started *Tokyo Keizai Zasshi*, with the support of Shibusawa Eiichi. The journal was published by Keizai Zasshisha which Taguchi had himself founded. The following passage which was written as part of the advertisement of the journal states clearly its nature and aim.

> *Tokyo Keizai Zasshi* is a weekly journal specializing in public finance, banking, and commerce. The journal reports on and discusses political, literary, and all other aspects of current affairs in our society. Every civilized nation has a journal of this kind, for instance, the *Economist* of London, the *Bankers' Magazine* of New York, and the *Economie Française* of Paris.

These Western economic journals contained a variety of statistical information, relating especially to finance and foreign trade, offering basic sources for the objective analysis of economic issues. *Tokyo Keizai Zasshi*, too, devoted many pages to market information on finance and commerce in each issue and placed special emphasis on the importance of this effort.

However, it was the analysis of, and comments on, the current issues written by Taguchi that made the *Tokyo Keizai Zasshi* particularly attractive. Ever since his first book, *Jiyū Kōeki Nihon Keizairon* (Free Trade and the Japanese Economy), was published in 1878, Taguchi had been a persistent advocate of laissez-faire and this continued throughout his life. He never failed to preach the principle that 'trade results in mutual benefit', the principle which he believed to be the eternal 'true theory of political economy'. He persistently criticized the policies which would interfere with free trade and the theories which supported such policies.

An example of this was the debate on free trade versus protectionism which Taguchi opened against *Tōkai Keizai Shinpō* (Tōkai Economist), published between 1880 and 1882. The *Tōkai Keizai Shinpō* was edited by Inukai Tsuyoshi, with the assistance of Toyokawa Ryōhei, his classmate in Keiō Gijuku and a very active leader of the large Mitsubishi concern. In justifying his position, Inukai referred to John Stuart Mill, and pointed out that Mill, in his *Principles of Political Economy*, clearly admitted that protectionism as a policy was inevitable in an undeveloped country. Taguchi, in his reply to Inukai, said, 'Mill is Mill. Taguchi is Taguchi. You cannot refute me by quoting Mill'. For Taguchi it was an unpardonable error to make an exception, as Mill did, to the 'true theory of political economy'.

Taguchi also made use of this journal as an organ for the introduction and diffusion of Western political economy, especially English liberal economic thought. It was not until the early twentieth century that an academic journal specifically devoted to the study of political economy appeared in Japan: *Kokumin Keizai Zasshi* (Journal of National Economy) started in 1906. Therefore during the first half of the Meiji era, journals on economic affairs often acted as journals on economic science. Apart from the *Tokyo Keizai Zasshi*, Taguchi also founded Tokyo Keizaigaku Kōshūkai (Tokyo Economic Lecture Society),[2] and published the Japanese translation of *The Wealth of Nations* by Adam Smith in the form of a textbook for the society. The translator was Ishikawa Eisaku, a staff member of Keizai Zasshisha. Thus Taguchi was called the 'Smith of Japan', but he followed Smith only in his theory of free trade, and did not accept Smith's political economy as a whole. Taguchi's position was quite close to that of the Manchester School, such as R. Cobden, and economists with whom Taguchi was in sympathy included R. Whately, H. D. Macleod, F. Bastiat, and A. L. Perry. Such a position was also shared by Noritake Kōtarō, a friend of Taguchi's, who succeeded to the editorship of the *Tokyo Keizai Zasshi* after Taguchi's death.

The two-hundredth issue of the *Tokyo Keizai Zasshi* (February 9, 1884) contained a section entitled 'How to Study Political Economy'. According to this article, the student of political economy should first read M. G. Fawcett's textbook, then *Rizai Genron* (Elements of Political Economy) by Perry, and go on to *Keizai Tetsugaku* (Economic Philosophy) by Macleod. The article said that the student should understand that the function of political economy was to clarify the principles of nature which exist in the universe and which cannot be changed by any human being. On the basis of this understanding, it continued, he or she should try and discuss advantages and disadvantages of free trade and protectionism. Keizai Zasshisha issued a pamphlet, *Keizaisho Dokuhō* (A Guide to the Literature on Political Economy), consisting of the guidance outlined above and a bibliography, and distributed it among the readers of the journal, free of charge.

Around this time, German protectionist political economy began to gain influence in Japan, conflicting with English and French political economy based on laissez-faire. The German influence was certainly stronger then than at the time when *Tokyo Keizai Zasshi* had a series of controversies with the *Tōkai Keizai Shinpō*. Taguchi felt it necessary to counteract such a trend, and the distribution of the pamphlet was meant to encourage the spread of the political economy of laissez-faire. We shall next look at the protectionist political economy in journalism.

3. Nationalistic Journals and Ōshima Sadamasu

During the second half of the 1880s, the Freedom and People's Rights Movement was at an ebb, and there was a general reaction against extreme Westernization. It was against this background that nationalism began to penetrate into the intellectual world around that time. Such a trend was represented in the journal *Nihonjin* (The Japanese) which Miyake Setsurei started in 1888, and the newspaper *Nihon* (Japan) which Kuga Katsunan started in 1889. On the academic journal front, the Society for German Studies started *Doitsugaku Kyōkai Zasshi* (Bulletin of the Society for German Studies) in 1883, and the Imperial University published *Kokka Gakkai Zasshi* (Journal of the Society for State Sciences) in 1887. They were primarily concerned with German-style social sciences with much emphasis on nationalism and historicism, clearly intending to challenge the existing social sciences based on English and French liberalism and individualism. Among the writers of the bulletin of the German studies society were K. F. H. Roesler and P. Mayet, to whom reference has been made in the Historical Introduction of the present book. Both of them tried to demonstrate the superiority of German state sciences over English and French social sciences. The main writers of the bulletin were professors of the Imperial University, such as Kanai Noburu, who were under the influence of the new historical school then prevailing in Germany.

At this point, it is worth mentioning that there were two economic journals, published independently and unofficially but with an emphasis on nationalism. The first was *Sangyō* (Industry), started by Maeda Masana in 1893, and the second was *Kokka Keizaikai Hōkoku* (Bulletin of the Society for National Economy), started by Tomita Tetsunosuke, Tani Kanjō, and Ōshima Sadamasu in 1890.

When Maeda Masana[3] was an official of the Ministry of Agriculture and Commerce, he was actively engaged in the creation of an economic policy to increase productivity and promote the export of examples of such traditional industries as tea and raw silk, compiling a thirty-volume proposal *Kōgyō Iken* (Proposals for the Promotion of Industry) in 1884.

Maeda, however, relinquished office in 1893, and travelled all over the country as an independent opinion leader, busying himself in the organization of various associations of agriculturalists, industrialists, and merchants. *Sangyō* was published for the same purpose, and Maeda invested his private fortune in its publication. Five thousand copies of the first issue were donated to interested parties all over Japan.

Maeda described his idea in his article in this first issue, taking as an example the tea industry. He argues as follows: The export market for tea at that time was entirely controlled by foreign merchants living in the concessions near the ports, and domestic merchants and producers were so dependent on them that they were unable to make a profit sufficient for the accumulation of funds in order to rationalize and expand their business. This in turn resulted in a lack of large-scale production and eventual stagnation, thus inevitably creating an unhealthy dependency on foreign merchants.

What then would be the way to break this vicious circle? The article 'Danketsu' (Unite!) in the same issue stated, 'In our country today it is absolutely vital for all the agriculturalists, industrialists, and merchants to organize associations of their own'. If through unity they could standardize and improve the quality of their product, it would be possible to 'insist on an equal bargaining position with foreign partners', and to 'trade directly with the country of final consumption'. This was the essence of Maeda's appeal.

Maeda's idea was nationalistic in the sense that it emphasized the importance of traditional industries and their protection, but was not of a reactionary nature, as was the case of Sata Kaiseki who published a unique economic journal, *Saibai Mondō Shinshi* (New Magazine for Vegetation) (1881–82). Maeda differed in his approach from the government's trade and industry promotion policy which tended towards the protection of *zaibatsu* and the military-related industries, but his idea was to supplement and modify the government's policy rather than to contradict it. Maeda's appeal found response, and, for example, resulted in the establishment of the Tea Association of Japan in 1883. *Sangyo* itself, since its thirteenth issue (January 1885), thus became an organ generally representing various nation-wide trade associations, such as the Tea Association of Japan.

Ōshima Sadamasu[4] was the most active critic on economic issues during the emerging current of nationalism in the 1880s and 1890s. He not only contributed to such nationalistic journals as *Nihon to Nihonjin* (Japan and the Japanese), but also wrote a long article, 'Hogo Bōekiron' (On Protectionism), in the liberal *Tokyo Keizai Zasshi* from 1890 to 1891, putting forward his case. Behind his line of thought was *Das nationale System der politischen Oekonomie* by F. List (1841) which he translated, with the encouragement of Tomita Tetsunosuke, as *Rishi Keizairon* (Political Economy of Mr. List, 1889). He also published

Jōseiron (Treatise on the Current State of the Nation) in 1891 in which he systematically developed his ideas. *Jōseiron* begins with (1) 'Kokusei Jijō', (the Current State of the Nation), where Ōshima argues that there is no universal theory in the sphere of politics, law, and political economy, and that 'a national economy can be understood only when its time and place are identified'. The following four chapters show the theoretical basis of protectionism, (2) the balance of trade should be considered as a top priority, (3) the applicability of the theory of the division of labour cannot be extended to international relations, (4) the protection of industrialists leads to the protection of farmers, and (5) all free traders lack foresight. The important thing for a nation is 'not to obtain goods of good quality at a reasonable price, but to foster the capacity to produce such goods itself', and 'a policy of protection and promotion must be adopted to foster such a capacity'. 'The wealth and power of nations have never been automatically acquired'.

The subsequent three chapters, i.e., chapters six, seven, and eight, are devoted to the discussion on the actual protectionist policy that Japan should adopt. In chapter nine, 'Conclusion', Ōshima follows the argument of List and Roscher that the way in which a country should develop its policy is 'freedom first, followed by protection, and eventually back to freedom'. After the opening of Japanese ports to foreign trade, the English idea of foreign trade was introduced to Japan, which, in Ōshima's view, was very effective in breaking up the stubborn and narrow-minded idea of seclusionist and anti-foreign sentiment in the country. However, now that 'the country has been opened up for forty years, the level of knowledge of the people has much improved and there has emerged entrepreneurship in industry and commerce'. We therefore should 'change the tide', and move from freedom to protection. The unequal treaties must be rectified, and Japan should recover tariff autonomy as well as full legal rights. People tend to idealize the concept of freedom, and approve not only of political freedom but also of freedom of foreign trade, but they are two different kinds of freedom. 'Political freedom makes a nation free, while the freedom of foreign trade makes other nations act freely against this nation. We ought to realize that the effects of freedom are not the same'.

Ōshima's efforts to gain acceptance for protectionism was not confined to his writing activities. He founded an organization, the National Economy Society (Kokka Keizaikai), in 1890, with Tomita Tetsunosuke, Tani Kanjō, and Kuga Katsunan. There was already a nationalistic organization called the Japanese Economy Society (Nihon Keizaikai) founded in 1885, the influential members of which included

Wakayama Norikazu, Wadagaki Kenzō, and Shiba Shirō. Indeed, the first edition of Ōshima's translation of List's book was published by this latter organization. The National Economy Society, being a similar kind of organization, became engaged in a survey of and research on the treaty revision and the tariff question. The results were published in *Kokka Keizaikai Hōkoku* which Ōshima had started, acting as editor and publisher himself. The society opposed the abolition of the import duty on raw cotton, from the point of view of protecting the domestic cotton cultivation. Ōshima was particularly active in this issue, and founded the Association for the Promotion of Cotton Cultivation in 1894, calling for the support of the Association of Agriculturalists of Japan (Dai Nihon Nōkai).

In 1899, Ōshima was asked, on the recommendation of Tomita Tetsunosuke, to write a book commemorating the seventieth birthday of a wealthy man in Shizuoka Prefecture to be distributed among his friends, and he published a large volume *Keizai Sanron* (Compendium of Political Economy), a five-hundred-page volume. This volume has forty-five chapters, which are divided into three parts: Production, Distribution, and Exchange. It brings the arguments of various European and American writers together and presents itself as stating the principles of political economy, but its essence is based on Mill's *Principles of Political Economy* with the arguments for protectionism inserted in many places. I shall take an example of Ōshima's presentation in part of the question on population in 'Distribution'.

Ōshima first summarizes the argument of Malthus on population, and, while admitting that it is a great contribution to the study of the subject, comments that if one attributes the poverty of the people of various countries 'totally to the lack of food, it would be a great mistake'. If 'one takes the position that poverty is the fate of the majority of human beings, the government would be able to escape into the position that it is doing everything in its power, the charitable person would feel pity for his fellow human beings, and the owner of the property would have an excuse for overworking his labourers'. In order to show that such a stance is wrong, he describes the Irish question in great detail, and argues that the cause of the poverty in Ireland was that, as a result of the abolition of import duties after the union between England and Ireland in 1801, the manufacturing industry which had been emerging in Ireland was immediately 'ruined'. Thus Ōshima criticizes English scholars as follows: 'The cause of Irish hardship lies in the wrongs of the system. Nevertheless, scholars attribute the cause simply to overpopulation and argue that the present misery in Ireland stems from the fact that ever since the introduction of potatoes the poor have been able to survive, and thus the population suddenly increased. Observing the annual emigration of two to three hundred thousand people, they even say that this is an unprecedented, but the best possible, cure for the Irish illness. How so incredibly wrong can one go in the understanding of the cause of such an illness!'

Among Ōshima's contemporaries I would mention two other nationalistic economists: Tomita Tetsunosuke who was the president of the Bank of Japan and supported Ōshima's activities and asked him to translate List; and Shiba Shirō who was active, together with Ōshima, in the Society for Japanese Economy and the National Economy Society.

It seems that Tomita got to know the nationalistic economic thought during his study in the United States and became an advocate of protectionism. In his preface to the fourth (revised) edition of *Keishi Keizaigaku* (Carey's *Principles of Social Science*, more precisely, its summarized version by Tate McKean), translated by Inukai Tsuyoshi, Tomita tells us that he visited Carey in Philadelphia when the former was vice-consul in New York, and was much impressed by his ideas. Carey apparently warned Tomita not to trust white people too much, and commented as follows: Japan opened the country to Europe and America, but what did the white people bring to Japan with them? 'It would not be in Japan's national interest, nor would it be an increase in national wealth. It would probably be something like strong and harmful spirits'.

Shiba Shirō who came from Aizu went to the United States, too, with the financial support of Mitsubishi, and studied political economy at The Wharton School in Philadelphia, the content of which was in line with Carey's thought. Shiba also contributed a preface to *Keishi Keizaigaku*, in which he described his association with Carey as follows: Although it was after Carey's death that he went to the United States, he was taught by Thompson, Carey's leading disciple, 'visited Carey's house, sat in his library, consulted the books belonging to Carey, and studied in the private school there' for a few years. After Shiba returned to Japan, he became famous as the author of *Kajin no Kigū* (A Beauty's Unexpected Meeting, 1885–97), a political novel written not under his own name as an economist but under the pen name of Tōkai Sanshi. What Shiba wanted to say to the Japanese through this novel, however, was that there was a fear among backward countries of invasion by advanced Western countries, and that the Japanese, too, should realize this danger.

Incidentally it is interesting that the miserable consequences of British rule in Ireland were illustrated in Shiba's novel. As has been mentioned earlier, Ōshima was interested in the Irish question, but he had also planned to do a translation of McKean's summarized version of Carey's work, which was actually translated by Inukai (Ōshima's draft, entitled *Kareishi Kōseigaku* [Principles of Social Science] survives to this day). Both Carey and Thompson came from Ireland, and it is not difficult to see that behind their protectionism there lay a strong nationalistic desire for the independence of their native land. Tomita learned this directly from Carey, Shiba directly from Thompson, and Ōshima through Carey's work, but they were all inspired by protectionism backed by the passionate nationalistic sentiment of the Irish, and cherished nationalistic economic thought in Japan.

4. *Tōyō Keizai Shinpō* and Amano Tameyuki

In November 1895 a new economic journal *Tōyō Keizai Shinpō* (Oriental Economist) (published three times a month) was started by Machida Chūji. The title of the journal indicated that the purpose of the journal was to encourage Japan's future economic development on a scale that would match the scale of the Orient, a sentiment which reflected Japan's victory in the Sino-Japanese War. 'Hakkō no Shushi' (The Aim of the Publication), which Machida wrote in the first issue, said, 'After our victory, this is the right time to make full use of the uplifted national spirit. On the domestic front, rearrange finance, improve transport, and, by so doing, promote industry. In relation to the outside world, expand shipping routes, set up exchange facilities, and, by so doing, keep Oriental trade in our hands instead of letting Western countries snatch it. If we cannot do it now, when can we hope to achieve our commercial supremacy in the Orient?' The editorial 'Kaigun to Jitsugyōka' (The Navy and the Businessman) in the same issue said, 'Trade follows the flag. No other words express better than this just how inseparable military might and commerce are'. This article appealed for the expansion of the navy in order to gain supremacy in Oriental trade, although it also argued that Japan should base its international relations on diplomacy rather than military power. Indeed the basic position of the journal was one of economic liberalism. As the 'Hakkō no Shushi' put it, 'Although it goes without saying that the development of business and the promotion of the national power require government supervision, guidance, protection, and promotion within appropriate limits, a sound economic society must ultimately be based on the developement of sound individuals'. However, it was a liberalism much more realistic than that of Taguchi Ukichi. It did not cross swords with government policy in the sense that it accepted government protection and control 'within appropriate limits', and also in the sense that it sought Japan's commercial supremacy in the Orient, although it did not argue for militaristic territorial expansion.

The first issue contained some new elements which had not been seen in the existing journals; there was an interview with a prominent political and business figure (the first interviewed was Matsukata Masayoshi); there was a column 'Tōyō Shōgyō Jiji' (Current Events of Oriental Commerce), along with 'Ōbei Keizai Jijō' (Economic Affairs of Europe and America); there was a supplement which contained a summary of monthly trade statistics. The last two were to offer relevant information with the object of gaining Japan's supremacy in the Orient.

Tōyō Keizai Shinpō made a good start, thanks to Machida's efforts and the support of the business world, but Machida soon found a post in the Bank of Japan, and moved to Osaka, and the journal had to find a new editor. Had not the change in editorship been successful, the fate of the journal would have been very different. Machida, luckily, found a very suitable successor—Amano Tameyuki,[5] who was lecturing in political economy at Waseda at the time.

Amano's activity as a scholar and educationalist is discussed in Chapter Three. As a scholar of the age of enlightenment, however, he was also interested in the world of politics and journalism. He was a member of the Kaishintō Party, and was elected a member of the Diet in the first election in 1890. He also spent his private fortune which he had gained from the publication of *Keizai Genron* (The Theory of Political Economy), to start, in 1889, *Nihon Rizai Zasshi*[6] (The Japan Economist), of which he became the editor.

Amano wrote in the first issue, 'The aim of the publication of this journal is to clarify the facts in the light of scholarly knowledge on the one hand, and to verify academic principles in relation to its factual foundations on the other, and, by so doing, to make reality and scholarship go hand in hand'. He was not satisfied with the introduction of foreign theories to Japan. The journal came into being with Amano's aim of testing such theories in the actual issues in Japan, and thus combining academic principles with reality. He had two specific goals. Firstly, he wished to make the nation understand the importance of the practice of supervision of finance, which was to follow the enactment of the Constitution and the establishment of the National Diet. In practice he was concerned with regard to the cutting of the fateful bonds between the clan-based government and the 'pseudo-gentleman' type businessman. Secondly, he wanted to promote domestic industries and develop foreign trade, so that the treaty revision at which Foreign Minister Ōkuma was aiming would actually have a positive effect on the Japanese economy. Every issue of *Nihon Rizai Zasshi* contained articles and comments relating to these two matters. It repeatedly emphasized the need for the people to understand not only the Constitution but the Public Finance Act and the local self-government system in order to prevent injustice. It also discussed the economic effects of the impending treaty revision from various angles. An increase in import duty after the revision should be considered, according to the journal, not for the sake of protectionism, but to increase government revenue, just as was the case of import duty in Britain. Such an increase would enable the government to reduce land tax, and farmers would benefit.

There were two more current issues which *Nihon Rizai Zasshi* took up that are worth mentioning here. Firstly, the journal discussed the harmful effects of the concentration of capital and monopoly. Quoting examples in the United States, it warned that monopoly tends to prevent market prices from going down, with the result that the consumer would suffer from higher prices. Secondly, the journal was concerned about the problem of industrial relations which were reflected in strikes. Showing that strikes were causing great social distress and economic loss in Britain and the United States, it criticized the behaviour of the socialist parties which had encouraged the strikes. Considering that it was about ten years later that the problems relating to monopoly and strikes became important issues in Japan, Amano may be said to have had unusual insight in that he identified the importance of these issues so early.

Amano acted as the editor of *Tōyō Keizai Shinpō* for ten years from 1897. The main articles he wrote during that time were all included in his book *Keizaisakuron* (Essays on Economic Policies) published in 1910. Amano's basic position was one of flexible liberalism which was in line with the thought of J. S. Mill. As his article '*Ippanteki Hogoshugi o Haisu*' (Reject General Protectionism) (*Tōyō Keizai Shinpō*, June 1909) shows, Amano believed in 'mild liberalism' which admitted the applicability of protectionism in certain circumstances. As mentioned earlier, this meant that Amano was in conflict with Taguchi Ukichi, a persistent advocate of free trade. Taguchi supported bimetallism, while Amano was a supporter of the gold standard. On the question of the reorganization of exchange, Amano argued for the abolition of all dealings of a speculative nature, and opposed Taguchi who admitted the rationale of speculation to a certain extent. However,

Amano and Taguchi worked together against the nationalists who advocated general protectionism.

On the question of industrial relations, Amano argued, in his article 'Waga Kuni ni okeru Yōsha-hiyōsha Mondai' (The Relationship between Employer and Employee in Japan) (*Tōyō Keizai Shinpō*, Aug. 1897), that the most important way to solve the problem was for workers themselves to work hard and save, so that they could manage large-scale enterprises themselves, for example, in the form of industrial cooperatives. Amano adopted the position of J. S. Mill who sought the real solution to the problem in the spread of industrial cooperatives. In the meantime Amano did not oppose the government policy of increasing armaments around the time of the Russo-Japanese War, but argued that the policy should be in accordance with Japan's economic capacity, and suggested that the period of compulsory military service should be reduced from three to two years (*Tōyō Keizai Shinpō*, Feb. 1906). Such realism was characteristic of both Amano and *Tōyō Keizai Shinpō*.

Amano trained two men, both of whom were students of his at Waseda, as his successors in the world of journalism: Uematsu Takaaki and Miura Tetsutarō. Uematsu first became the editor of *Tōyō Keizai Shinpō* in 1907, succeeding Amano, and occupied the post until 1912 when he was replaced by Miura. In 1924, Ishibashi Tanzan, also a Waseda graduate, assumed office as the editor. All of them followed the liberalistic tradition of the journal, which meant that its ideological stance became increasingly valuable, as the general intellectual atmosphere became more and more inclined towards militarism.[7]

5. *Nihon Keizai Shinshi* and Kawakami Hajime

Kawakami Hajime graduated from the Department of Politics, Faculty of Law of Tokyo Imperial University, in 1902, and studied political economy at the graduate school. He became a lecturer at the Faculty of Law of Kyoto Imperial University in 1908, and lectured in political economy until he resigned from office in 1928. In the 1920s, Kawakami was a leading economist in Japan, his influence equalling that of Fukuda Tokuzō, but around 1924 he began to accept theories of Marxist political economy, and gradually became Marxist. He became involved in Marxist political activities, too, and after his resignation became committed to politics and was eventually imprisoned.

Before he obtained a post in Kyoto, young Kawakami spent some years as a journalist, involving himself in a couple of newspapers and journals, while continuing his study in political economy. His activities during this period are those which we shall be concerned with here.

It was his series of articles entitled 'Shakai Shugi Hyōron' (An Essay on Socialism) which appeared from October to December 1905 in *Yomiuri Shinbun* (Yomiuri Newspaper) that made Kawakami's name well known to the public. The history of the introduction of socialism to Japan dates back to the early Meiji era, but it was not until the end of the nineteenth century that this ideology became a real issue. After the Sino-Japanese War, labour unrest intensified, and the Society for the Promotion of Trade Unions (Rōdō Kumiai Kiseikai) was established in 1897. The government responded to this by enacting the Security Police Act (Chian Keisatsu Hō) in 1900 on the one hand, and by starting a survey on factory labour for the preparation of the enactment of Factory Act (Kōjō Hō) on the other. Against this background, Christian socialists gathered to form the Society for the Study of Socialism (Shakai Shugi Kenkyūkai) in 1898, and in 1901 the Social Democratic Party, Japan's first socialist party, was formed, though it was immediately banned by the government. Abe Isoo, Katayama Sen, and Kōtoku Shūsui were all involved in both activities. In response to the emergence of socialism, the Society for Social Policy (Shakai Seisaku Gakkai), led by some professors from Tokyo Imperial University, issued a statement in 1901, emphasizing that the society had no connections with socialism. Socialists formed Heiminsha (Commoners' Organization) in 1903, and Sakai Toshihiko and Kōtoku Shūsui published *Heimin Shinbun* (Commoners' News) to propagate socialism and pacifism. The translation of *Communist Manifesto* by Marx and Engels was also published, although the fifty-third issue of *Heimin Shinbun* which included it was banned by the government.

Kawakami wrote of the underlying issues of such developments in his article 'Shakai Shugi Hyōron' (An Essay on Socialism),[8] and commented on the stance taken by the Society for Social Policy, Heiminsha, and Christian socialism, calling for the simultaneous reform of the social system and attitudes within it. His argument attracted much public attention, which proved the extent of public concern on the issue.

Around the same time, Kawakami became interested in the agrarian problem in Japan, and wrote on current issues in many agricultural journals as well as a book on Japanese agriculture. Among the journals which published many of his articles was *Nihon Nōgyō Zasshi* (Japan Agricultural Journal), started in 1905. Yokoi Tokiyoshi, the de facto editor of the journal and a professor at Tokyo Imperial University, was his teacher, and Kawakami joined Yomiuri Shinbunsha, the publisher of the journal, in 1906. He argued in one of the articles he contributed to the journal that the government economic policy had been putting too much emphasis on commerce and industry, and appealed to the agriculturalists to voice their interest in initiating change. However, his relationship with this journal became less close from 1907, primarily due to his other commitments. Kawakami became the editor of *Nihon Keizai Shinshi* (New Japan Economist) which started in April 1907, and since devoted his energy to the editorship and management of this semimonthly journal, until he obtained a post at Kyoto Imperial University in August 1908.[9]

The spirit of the journal is reflected both in its title and in the fact that it chose a national holiday in commemoration of the mythical first emperor, Jinmu, as the date of its first publication. 'Hakkō no Shushi' (The Aim of the Publication) on the front page of the first issue was stated to be 'the enhancement of national prestige and the increase in the wealth of the people, placing the national interest as its first consideration'. From this perspective it was to criticize 'extreme individualism according to which laissez-faire was the solution to every issue' on the one hand, and socialism which 'sought to control the economic policy of the national economy with a heavy bias towards the interests of common people' on the other.

As is generally the case with journals taking a definite stance, the editorial column on the opening pages had an important place in this journal. The editorial column in the first issue addressed five topics, including 'Nikkan Kanzei Dōmei no Seiritsu o Nozomu' (Desirability of the Establishment of a Customs Union between Japan and Korea), while that in the second issue discussed eight, including 'Kiito Shijō no Kōkyō' (Boom in the Raw Silk Market). Although only one section in these editorials (The Revision of the Import Duty on Rice) was signed by Kawakami, it is likely that many of the anonymous pieces were also written by him.

The articles which followed the editorial column included, in the case of the first issue, 'Aa Friedrich List' (In Praise of Friedrich List) by Matsuzaki Kuranosuke and 'Nihon Nōgyō no Shōrai o Ronzu' (The Future of Japanese Agriculture) by Yokoi Tokiyoshi. Both writers were Kawakami's teachers in Tokyo Imperial University. Kawakami wrote an article 'Eikoku Konnichi no Keizaiteki Chii' (Economic Position of the United Kingdom Today), emphasizing the way in which the principles of foreign trade at that time led to the decline of British agriculture. He also wrote a note in the 'Miscellaneous' column introducing two foreign works which criticized the principles of foreign trade. It is thus clear that this journal was in favour of protectionism, with an emphasis on agriculture. In the above-mentioned signed editorial, Kawakami supported the customs policy of protecting the farmers' interests, and criticized *Tokyo Keizai Zasshi* which proposed the abolition of import duty on rice. In response to the rejoinder of *Tokyo Keizai Zasshi* (whose editor at that time was Noritake Kōtarō), Kawakami wrote, in the editorial column of the third issue, that the policy of 'sacrificing agriculture, the basis of the prosperity of the nation, for the sake of immediate benefits such as the desire to eat rice at a cheaper price' was unacceptable.

A major task of the Meiji government was to revise the unequal nature of the amity treaties of 1858, so that Japan would become a truly independent nation vis-à-vis foreign countries. Japan, because of the victories in the Sino-Japanese War and the Russo-Japanese War, had enhanced its international status, and had managed to abolish the extraterritorial jurisdiction of foreigners in 1899, and gain tariff autonomy in 1911. Thus the debate on free trade versus protectionism which started in 1880 to 1881 between Taguchi Ukichi and Inukai Tsuyoshi was to have a real impact on the actual policy of the government for the first time.[10]

The debate between Kawakami and Noritake on the taxation of imported rice in this journal actually took place not long before 1911. While Noritake argued that the abolition of import duties would prevent wages from rising, with the result that low wages would promote the export of manufactured goods, Kawakami pointed out that such an abolition would inevitably result in the decline of Japanese agriculture, which would reduce farmers' purchasing power, to the extent that the lack of demand would eventually hamper the development of industry. Thus Kawakami's argument was not one of *nōhon-shugi* (the idea of considering agriculture as the base of the nation) put forward, for example, by Yokoi Tokiyoshi, which totally rejected the idea of basing national development on commerce and industry, but the one with the perspective of 'organic' development of the national economy through the synchronized progress of agriculture, industry, and commerce.

6. Epilogue

Political economy in journalism during the Meiji era was dominated by that based on British liberalism, as was the case with political economy in the groves of academe, but, towards the end of the period, German-style nationalistic political economy such as the Historical School and the Social Policy School gained in influence. The former trend was represented in Taguchi Ukichi's *Tokyo Keizai Zasshi* and Amano Tameyuki's *Nihon Rizai Zasshi*, while the latter was represented in Ōshima Sadamasu's *Kokka Keizaikai Hōkoku* and Kawakami Hajime's *Nihon Keizai Shinshi*. It is worth recalling, in this context, that Taguchi published a translation of Smith's *The Wealth of Nations*, Amano translated Laughlin's edition of J. S. Mill's *Principles of Political Economy*, Ōshima translated List's *Das nationale System*, and Kawakami published a guide to A. Wagner's *Grundlegung der politischen Oekonomie*, specifically the first part of it, 'Grundlage der Volkswirtschaft'.

The ideological stance of *Tōyō Keizai Shinpō* was one of J. S. Mill's liberalism. Unlike Taguchi's persistent liberalism, it was a flexible kind of liberalism which accepted protectionism and the idea of social reform under certain circumstances. It was the path which best reflected the reality in Japan, and, after Taguchi's death, *Tōyō Keizai Shinpō* became the most influential journal, gradually replacing *Tokyo Keizai Zasshi*.

It is interesting that at one time towards the end of the Meiji era, Katayama Sen contributed to this journal. Katayama started a journal, *Rōdō Sekai* (World of Labour), in 1897, thus pioneering socialistic journalism in Japan, but his socialism at that stage was influenced by F. Lassalle of Germany, R. T. Ely of the United States, and C. Kingsley of Britain. It was the kind of socialism which aimed at social reform, in contrast to that of Kōtoku Shūsui who also started with Ely's idea of social reform, but moved his position to Marx's communism and eventually to P. Kropotokin's anarchism. *Shakai Shinbun* (Society News), which Katayama published in 1907, was to criticize Kōtoku's idea of direct action from the point of view of parliamentary reform. Katayama was a close friend of Uematsu Takaaki, the then editor of *Tōyō Keizai Shinpō*, and wrote several articles in that journal, some signed, others not. This reflects the flexibility of *Tōyō Keizai Shinpō* which, while sometimes accepting nationalistic views, agreed at other times to publish socialist views as well. Such a flexibility must have been one of the reasons why this journal survived to the second half of the twentieth century, in a capitalist country which, although a late starter, managed to develop its economy at a very rapid speed.[11]

Part 5

From a Western Point of View

15

'Vain' Learning and the Advent of Political Economy in Meiji Japan

Olive Checkland

1. 'Vain' Learning

The Japanese power structure was in 1868 taken over by a group of thrusting young oligarchs who by acquiring the imperial cachet legitimized their own regime. By this potentially violent and coercive act they succeeded in releasing the pent-up energy of many in Japan hitherto held in the grip of an unyielding and stifling system. The Western study of political economy was one of many disciplines, for which there would have been little use in the closed economy of Tokugawa times, which seemed to offer helpful insights into the economic problems which were exacerbated as Japan tentatively opened its doors to the West.[1]

In 1858 in his letters to his wife, Lord Elgin wrote of the Japanese feudal system[2] as he saw it, 'Everyman from the Emperor (who never leaves his palace) to the humblest labourer, lives under a rigid rule; prescribed by law and custom combined, and the government, through its numerous agents, among whom are hosts of spies, or more properly inspectors (for there is no secrecy or concealment in this proceeding), exercises a close surveillance over the acts of the individual'.[3] Lord Elgin's comments are a reminder of the restraints imposed by such a society in which the maintenance of discipline and the upholding of conservative values became ends in themselves. But as W. W. Rostow has pointed out, change is a necessary concomitant of modern society; a paradigm which could not however have been available to the Japanese under the Tokugawa regime. Rostow, in listing a number of factors which were probably prerequisites for such changes, mentions the need to develop basic science, to accept innovations, to increase consumer demand, to have children, and to apply science to economic ends.[4] It is to this last objective that this book has addressed itself.

The acceptance and discussion of the principles of political economy in modern Japan is the more noticeable because of the attitudes to economic striving and the profit motive held in the consciousness of feudal Japan where commerce and those who practiced it gained no great prestige and officially ranked lower than craftsmen and peasants.[5] Those who espoused the ideas of Western economists were setting aside the priorities of centuries embodied in the ideas of Confucius. It was Tsuda Mamichi who was emboldened to distinguish between Western and Eastern ideas by designating them 'real' and 'vain' learning. By equating civilization with 'real studies', by which he meant Western astronomy, chemistry, medicine, political economy and Greek philosophy, Tsuda was urging the Japanese to take on board another thought system despite the fact that this might in some ways be inconsistent with those ideas and traditions with which they had previously been familiar.

The inconsistency between traditional Japanese thought and that of the West rested on a different understanding and interpretation of nature.[6] In the vocabulary of the West, nature was a system, working regularly and inexorably regardless of man. But because man was the most intelligent of the creatures living on earth, he was bound to use his curiosity to understand, interpret, and control. This interference was considered presumptuous by the Eastern mind trained to accept the laws of nature as immutable, for whom man, being small and vulnerable, was held as fast as any other creature.

If nature was, as in Confucian terms, a 'great parent', then man was but a small part of the universe, bound to uphold the moral principles on which human life, as part of the whole, was based. If, in the idiom of the West, nature was an engine, or machine, which operated according to an established set of rules, then man was bound to endeavour to understand the rules and indeed to use his intelligence to manipulate them to his own advantage. The fundamental difference in concept between the passivity encouraged by Confucianism and the activity demanded by the Western understanding of the universe led Tsuda and others to think of the old Chinese system as 'vain' learning, by which was meant learning which is useless or irrelevant. The difference of approach between these two schools of thought was fundamental and caused considerable stress among those who sought to reconcile them.

Although it was in some senses heretical of Tsuda and others to label Eastern modes of thought as 'vain' learning, it was nevertheless useful. The Japanese had to be encouraged to adopt positive and enquiring attitudes to Western science of which political economy, being a study of the principles by which man arranges his economic affairs, is a part. To shunt long-cherished beliefs onto a siding in this way and to substitute others as preferable to the main line of thought was a difficult although necessary process. The reconciliation of this dichotomy is at the core of this book for each new interpretation of a Western idea, whether of philosophy or political economy or anything else, represented in some senses a departure from the old ways of thought.

Notwithstanding the difficulties of readjustment which faced the Japanese, and led to the West glibly labelling them as imitators rather than initiators, Tsuda, Nishi, and the others were following in a well-hallowed tradition of intellectual borrowing. The themes of Confucianism and much else had come from Japan's great near-neighbour China. That Japan was now borrowing from the West was an extension of rather than a break with an earlier tradition.

Initially, as Western nations threatened their shores, Japanese preoccupations were not with ideas, philosophies, or indeed with political economy but with modern defensive weapons. They believed that with these in place they could fend off the importunate foreigner. Such immediate transfer of new technology was not possible and so the first objective was perforce shelved. Without any serious defences it was easy for the Westerners to intrude. The foreigners' aims were quite simple; with no territorial ambitions, they were eager to exploit profitable trade.

A vivid example of Japan's initial unpreparedness for the commercial onslaught of the Western world comes from Laurence Oliphant, writing of Lord Elgin's mission to Japan in 1858, who described the function of the building in Nagasaki 'devoted to the exchange of foreign money for Japanese paper currency'.

> In an upstairs room, approached by a scrupulously clean staircase, on the upper step of which is a row of Japanese slippers, sit three or four two-sworded officials round a table on which are placed two boxes, one full of metallic, the other of paper currency. It is useless to persuade a Japanese shopkeeper to take a foreign coin, however large or tempting it may be. The government has forbidden him to take anything from the foreigners but the little oblong pieces of card which bear the government stamp, so to this little room every foreigner is compelled to resort to obtain an available circulating medium.[7]

Such a routine designed to hinder and impede rather than encourage was part of a closed system in which taxes were paid in rice and the basic economic processes of distribution and exchange were static and old-fashioned.[8]

During the centuries of closure the Japanese government and its officials knew little of Western business methods or Western economic debate. The seventeenth-century arguments concerning mercantilism, by which each country endeavoured to maintain a favourable balance of trade, counterbalanced by those of Adam Smith with his opposing arguments of 'free trade' were hardly important as long as the Japanese economy remained closed. The currency debates of the Napoleonic wars mounted by Ricardo and others in Europe might, however, have struck a chord in Japan, where the twin evils of inflation and a debased coinage and paper notes were rampant. Indeed, the easy issue of domain paper money (*hansatsu*) accepted locally in the life itself, together with the coinage issued by the Shogunate, sometimes led to a classic manifestation of Gresham's Law,[9] although occasionally clan governments did 'recover and rehabilitate their money supply'.[10]

As it happened, one of the first fruits of foreign intervention taught the Japanese a harsh lesson. When the treaty ports opened in 1859, the foreigners found that gold was seriously undervalued; by exploiting the new exchange regulations the outsiders quickly fleeced the Japanese of their gold reserves.[11] These incidents underlined Japanese weakness and indeed Japanese ignorance and fuelled Japanese determination to learn and to turn disadvantage to advantage.

What Lord Elgin and his entourage could not know, ignorant in their turn as to what was really happening in Japan, was that the port of Nagasaki, in the 1850s, remote from both the spiritual and the secular capital of Kyoto and Edo, thrummed with the bustle of many Japanese who had come from afar to learn more about the West.[12] Nagasaki was also the centre from which a Japanese could arrange to set sail for the West to learn more at first hand of Western education. The many examples, some of which are given in this book, of men who took themselves off to the Netherlands or France or Britain for further learning testify to the great pressures for change which were already building up in Japan before Commodore Perry's black ships appeared.

Within a generation, a handful of Japanese scholars were attempting to teach the principles and theories of political economy in Japan; others as students, often of mature age, were learning theories of economics in Europe and America. Indeed, from 1881, Japanese ministers in government, like Matsukata Masayoshi,[13] had grasped the inflationary nettle and were applying to it firm principles of a deflationary economic policy like any Western statesman. How then were the Japanese able to transform their attitudes and expectations in so short a time?

It goes without saying that the answers are many and complex, but they include the dislike of the Japanese of being at a disadvantage in relation to other nations, the inbred feelings of equality or even superiority, which is allied to a strong sense of nationalism which Japanese have, and a basic human curiosity about how other peoples manage their affairs.

2. The Introduction of Political Economy

Several of the characters who feature in the chapters in this book as pioneers in the introduction of modern economic and political thought in Japan had themselves been residents of Nagasaki during the heady days before 1868.[14] They had learnt from contact with their own compatriots as well as with foreigners the urgent need for the Japanese to know more about Western modes of thought.

The leading figure of this movement was Fukuzawa Yukichi 'who was to be the versatile champion of the Japanese enlightenment' and who consistently declined any government post and remained outside the political arena.[15] By remaining free from political factionalism and the infighting associated therewith, he was able to devote himself solely to propagating his ideas through writing and teaching. Fukuzawa was able to take on the mantle of proselytizer and popularizer because he himself had experienced three overseas journeys, visiting America in 1860, Europe in 1862, and America again in 1867. His extensive travels abroad gave him the edge on most of his compatriots, had a profound effect on his own views, and enabled him to interpret the ideas of the West in the simplest and most readily understood terms.

Perhaps two examples could be given to illustrate Fukuzawa's philosophy and his understanding of what was happening to Japan. At the age of 37, Fukuzawa published the first part of what came in future years to be regarded as his credo. *Gakumon no Susume* (An Encouragement of Learning) appeared in Japan in 1872. This was after the Imperial family had moved from isolation and intrigue in Kyoto to Edo castle in the centre of the new capital of Tokyo, feudal clans had been abolished and prefectures established, and at least in the great urban centres there was an atmosphere of excitement and change.

Section One of *Gakumon no Susume* begins:

It is said that heaven does not create one man above or below anoth-

> er man. This means that when men are born from heaven they all are equal. There is no innate distinction between high and low. It means that men can freely and independently use the myriad things of the world to satisfy their daily needs through the labours of their own bodies and minds, and that, as long as they do not infringe upon the rights of others, may pass their days in happiness.[16]

The remarkable thing about these initial lines is not their originality, but rather the application of these ideals to Japanese society where the Emperor had God-like qualities and where feudal society, hitherto all-powerful, was based on a strict hierarchical system, which made few concessions to the rights and needs of the individual. Fukuzawa's remarks are at least an indication that individual liberty might become a justifiable objective.

The second example of Fukuzawa's practical common sense comes from 'Datsuaron' (On de-Asianization) of March 1885, when he wrote:

> The world-wide facility of communication has allowed the wind of civilization to blow into the East, where not a single grass or tree has been left unswayed by it . . . still to anyone who has seen with his eyes the present state of world affairs . . . there can be no other policy than to move on with the rest of the world and join them in dipping into the sea of civilization joining them in creating the waves of civilization and joining them in the pains and joys of civilization.[17]

Because there is so much in Fukuzawa, including much inconsistency, Sugiyama has suggested that he outlined 'a system of miserable contradictions', but, as Mizuta explains, 'any careful reader will never fail to see between the lines of Fukuzawa's works the figure of an intellectual who was trying hard to create an independent and modernized nation under the seige of Western powers.'[18]

Fukuzawa's recognition of the need for Japan to try to meet the West on equal terms and his championing of basic human rights have resulted in his being thought of as the great popularizer of Meiji Japan. But care should be taken to emphasize not his determination to break with the Japanese past, but rather, his views on the development of ideas as a continuum with what had gone before. Fukuzawa's philosophy can be summed up as 'laissez-faire within the nation and imperialist expansion outside'.

Another figure who made his mark on the academic development of political economy is Ōkuma Shigenobu.[19] Okuma, of the Saga clan, during a long career in which he occupied many government offices, including that of the premiership (in 1898 and in 1914), was something of an outsider. This was partly because he did not belong directly to the then dominant Satsuma/Chōshū group, although he had good friends who did, and partly because he was basically more democratic in his outlook than any other Japanese leader of Meiji times. Even Ōkuma's modest plans to give the Japanese people more say in political matters were distrusted. Although he might be regarded as the forerunner who would have welcomed wholeheartedly Japan's postwar democracy, he never had the chance to test his ideas. Following a great political row in 1880–81, sparked off by possible chicanery in the sale of government properties in Hokkaido, but in reality a power struggle between rival groups, Ōkuma resigned. It was during this interlude that he founded with his disciple, Ono Azusa, Tokyo School for Special Studies (Tokyo Semmon School, later Waseda University). Much of the success of the school must go to Ono who was devoted to the project.

Mori Arinori was another internationally known politician whose interests involved establishing an institution for higher education at which economics was taught.[20] Mori's contribution was to be one of the founders of Hitotsubashi University (Shōhō Kōshūjo) 'in order to promote the economic, social, educational and moral uplift he considered the key to Japan's national survival'.[21]

Godai Tomoatsu, like Mori a Satsuma man, used his early education and travels in the West to good advantage, becoming the leader of the Osaka business community, stimulating and guiding it towards participation in the modern world.[22] One of his initiatives was the founding in 1880 of the Osaka Commercial Training School, now Osaka City University. The emphasis on commercial education for business leaders, which was noticeable at Osaka and Tokyo College of Commerce (Hitotsubashi), is a reminder of how early Japanese leaders recognized the need for properly trained businessmen.

Although these new schools were founded by those motivated by the highest ideals, as institutions they were small, weak, and seriously underfunded. Official government money and support was channelled into one establishment, the University of Tokyo, known for some time as the Imperial University. The Imperial University of Kyoto was established in 1897. The University of Tokyo was founded in 1877 along Western lines primarily to train men to become servants of the new burgeoning Meiji government bureaucracy. Initially it consisted of four faculties, law, medicine, natural science, and liberal arts, but in 1886, to the original four colleges were added those of engineering and agriculture and it was renamed the Imperial University. This university received generous public funding and was fed by students from the five higher middle schools (later higher schools) established in Tokyo and elsewhere in Japan. Political economy was taught in various ways at all these 'colleges', schools, and universities.[23]

How then did these enthusiasts set about introducing Western ideas of political economy into Japan? The first task was for all those engaged, either as students or teachers, to understand a foreign language as thoroughly as possible.[24] Years could be spent in this preliminary preparation before any serious study could be undertaken. Foreign teachers were invited to Japan to teach small groups of dedicated students. As teachers came whose native language was French, German, or English, this led to further complications, students having trained themselves to be proficient in one foreign language could only benefit from teaching in that language. In one sense the Japanese liked having teachers from different nationalities for this lessened their dependence on any one group, but such enrichment was a recipe for disaster in any educational establishment as foreigners quarrelled and jostled to promote their language and themselves.

Nevertheless, the first generation of teachers coming into Japan to teach political economy were foreigners, mostly Americans, from a variety of backgrounds. In the case of Fukuzawa's foundation at Keiō, some of the Americans recommended by the president of Harvard University were Unitarians.[25] Garrett Droppers worked hard at Keiō, teaching political theory as well as economics for nine years. He succeeded in training a group of Keiō students who shortly took over the subjects themselves, teaching directly in Japanese. The University of Tokyo invited a series of American scholars including E. F. Fenollosa. The Japanese who initiated economics teaching at Waseda were originally students of Fenollosa.

Ernest Francisco Fenollosa was a Harvard man who graduated in 1874 and was recruited in 1878 for Tokyo. He taught political economy and politics (1878–80) and logic and philosophy (1880–86).[26] Perhaps his subsequent fame and reputation which rests on his skill and enthusiasm in preserving and exhibiting traditional Japanese art and in bringing a knowledge of Japanese art to America and the West, reflects his real interests. Possibly Tajiri Inajirō, a graduate of Yale, and a German, Professor Rathgen, who also taught economics at the Imperial University, were more involved in teaching and research.[27]

Other universities teaching economics in the late nineteenth century did not themselves employ foreign teachers, although the first generation of Japanese teachers may have studied under foreigners. Apart from the very early years when some non-Japanese were direct interpreters of the writings of political economists, almost all instruction of economics was done in Japan, in Japanese by native teachers. It can only be conjecture, but it seems likely that the Japanese professor, with his background of Confucian thought, would interpret political economy and other things differently from his Western counterpart.

Once the foreign teachers had gone, the Japanese professors of political economy relied on translations into their own language. These they often undertook themselves. In this way most major works of political science and political economy by British, American, French, and German authors were brought to the notice of Japanese students. Translations of a very wide range of texts, including J. S. Mill, *Principles of Political Economy*, Francis Wayland, *Elements of Political Economy*, Adam Smith, *The Wealth of Nations*, W. S. Jevons, *The Principles of Economics*, were used in Japan.

Although these 'great' works were translated into Japanese, many of them were difficult to understand in English, or indeed in Japanese, partly because of the concepts, but also because of the complex quality of the writing. There were also difficulties in finding expressions in Japanese to 'fit' some of the words and phrases used in English. It is especially interesting to note that when Fukuzawa found *Political Economy, for Use in Schools, and for Private Instruction*, published anonymously in 1852 by William and Robert Chambers of Edinburgh, a simple book, which despite its title ranged widely over the fields of political economy, sociology, and international relations, he not only translated it, but also resolved to incorporate some of the writings on 'social economy' into volume 2 (*Gaihen*) of his *Seiyō Jijō* (Conditions in the West). Albert M. Craig of Harvard has undertaken impressive detective work to discover that the author of the book was John Hill Burton, a 'hack' writer who later became well known as an author, biographer, and historian.[28] Burton, an M.A. of the University of Aberdeen (founded in 1494), had received a good grounding in philosophy, science, and arts (classical) subjects.[29] It may be that some of the philosophical ideas of the Scottish Enlightenment were imported into Japan by Fukuzawa through his translation of the work of John Hill Burton.[30] Burton was also acquainted with Henry Dunning Macleod, another political economist whose works were translated into Japanese.[31]

The private schools, recognizing that Germanic ideas were becoming influential in teaching at the Imperial University, preferred to air the ideas on political economy coming from Britain and France. Some of the foreign teachers, including Gustave Boissonade, in Japan from

1873 to 1895, certainly felt that it was their mission to proselytize in this way. The private law schools developed the 'debating meeting', first established in 1888, and initially attracted 1,500 people.[32] Meetings were held every two months, and the proceedings appeared under the imprint of a well-known publisher.

This form of gathering was also important for self-advertisement; many schools were seeking to attract potential students with the range and quality of their teaching. Some of the teachers in these schools were also in the vanguard of the Movement for Freedom and People's Rights.

The proliferation of private law schools alarmed the government, which decided to place them under the jurisdiction of the president of the University of Tokyo. As their teaching and syllabi came increasingly under scrutiny, their graduates were granted the privilege of being accepted into the lower echelons of the government civil service without further examination. In some senses this undoubtedly led to a more uniform system, but it is equally important to recognize that traces of nonconformity still remained. The individuality of the 'private' law schools and universities may be difficult to discern, but it would be foolish to assume that it does not exist.

As well as universities, government departments also taught political economy to their new recruits. Government offices held libraries of foreign books, initially those in English predominating, although after the mid-1880s there was a sharp increase in the number of works in German. Young civil servants were taught law, including commercial and international law, public finance, taxation, and political science. The presence of 18 copies of J. W. Gilbart's *Principles and Practice of Banking* is a reminder of the need to teach such subjects. A man like Alexander Allan Shand, a British banker, who while in the employ of the Finance Ministry wrote *A Detailed Book-Keeping Manual*, published in 1873, trained and influenced a whole generation of young Japanese bankers.

Although the government succeeded in strengthening the control from the centre, there were plenty of serious men outside the system who wished to offer their own ideas on social reconstruction for Japan. They found their outlet through some form of journalism, producing newspapers, magazines, or journals of all kinds. It seems that every literary figure in Meiji Japan either edited or had access to one of the many magazines and journals produced to disseminate the new and existing ideas. The most famous 'journalists' were: Fukuzawa Yukichi, who after early work on *Meiroku Zasshi* (Meiji Six Journal) used the editorials of his daily newspaper *Jiji Shinpō* (Current Affairs Review) as an outlet for his thoughts and ideas; Nakae Chōmin who started the *Tōyō Jiyū Shinbun* (Oriental Liberal Paper) in 1881 which he edited himself; and Tokutomi Sohō, also active with *Kokumin no Tomo* (The Friend of the Nation), 1887.

Apart from these general publications which brought much information and comment to Japanese readers, the professional economists were themselves not idle. A. A. Shand, by showing Taguchi copies of *The Economist*, which although published in London had a worldwide readership, is given the credit for encouraging Taguchi Ukichi to produce *Tokyo Keizai Zasshi* (Tokyo Economist).[33]

During the forty-four years of the Meiji Emperor's reign, there was a proliferation of private educational institutions and newspapers and journals which were run by men anxious to counteract the West's apparent superiority. The institutions with which this book is concerned include in Tokyo, Keiō Gijuku, which became Keiō University, Tokyo School of Special Studies, which became Waseda University, and law schools, which became Shenshū, Meiji, Chūō and Hōsei universities. In Osaka, the Commercial College and the Kansai Law School became important. In Kyoto, Dōshisha University started in 1875 as Dōshisha School of English Studies, Dōshisha Seihō Gakkō (Dōshisha School of Politics and Law) was opened in 1891, and Ritsumeikan University was first opened as a private school in 1869 but is usually dated from 1900 when it became Kyoto School of Law and Politics (Kyoto Hōsei Gakkō). None of these institutions were official government-sponsored bodies. The government created the Imperial University in 1886 and later Kyoto (1897) and Tōhoku (1907) Imperial universities, and it was through these bodies that advanced education was officially funded.[34] In Sapporo, Hokkaido, where the government had created a Development Authority (1869) to expand and strengthen the new Japanese economy there, Sapporo Agricultural College was founded. The other bodies were all privately funded and were in general during the Meiji era poor and weak. Nevertheless, it was in these schools, private and government-sponsored that political economy was first taught. Although there were many foreign teachers involved, the effort was primarily a Japanese one.

3. A Japanese Accommodation

In Japan, the availability of Western or 'real' learning did not go unnoticed, and many regretted the apparent easy acceptance of ideas which had no roots in Japanese soil. From, say, 1881, politically, Western liberal ideas were in retreat. As with so much from the West, ideas, while freely available from a variety of sources, were often contradictory. The Japanese could not themselves remain neutral; they were bound to sift the evidence for themselves and opt for a system which best fitted their background and history.

Fundamental to an understanding of what decisions the Japanese took is an appreciation of what ideas were on offer in the Western shop window. Here the difference between Britain and the countries of mainland Europe must be stressed. As one scholar has noted, 'On the Continent, in France, Prussia, Austria and elsehwere the tradition of state action and surveillance was strong and was never abandoned. By contrast Britain had broken with centralism in the seventeenth century and though there were plenty of mercantilist devices in operation in the later eighteenth century especially as affecting international trade, there was no strong interventionist government at the centre and only the most rudimentary of bureaucracies'.[35]

The American model was different yet again, being in essence a system of checks and balances in which both central government and the states which created it, each jealous of the other, kept a watchful eye on any moves of the other towards self-aggrandizement.

In essence, then, the Japanese had to decide whether to opt for a non-interventionist state, on the British model, or for one in which the state kept a controlling hand on many activities. In this sense, the rivalry between the two models was virtually one of 'no-contest'. The people had been accustomed for centuries to powerful controls from central and local government. It was highly unlikely, given their history, that the rulers of a people newly released from a kind of feudality would choose to offer their people the model of freedom then available in Britain. In any case, some in the United Kingdom, by the end of the nineteenth century, threatened as they were by a variety of economic challenges, had recognized the weakness of their central government and, especially in terms of social welfare, were beginning to strengthen the bureaucracy.

The movement back towards the reinforcement of conservatism in Japan is well known. Itō Hirobumi's position gained increasing authority and influence. During his famous tour of Germany and Austria in 1882 to 1883, he found much in the strong central control exercised by the German government which accorded well with his ideas for Japan. The Japanese state thus developed an attitude of coercive paternalism towards its people. Under this regime there could be no move towards mass proletarianization, for an increasingly nationalistic Japan required the sacrifice of individual personal freedom. This conservative reconstruction movement which had reorganized the

Meiji government on modern lines was, broadly speaking, what the Japanese people wanted. Many who had earlier embraced Western ideas felt in time that perhaps they had earlier been overhasty. Few nationally known figures retained in later life the almost febrile liberalism of their early youth.

Mori Arinori, whose early wild liberalism had outraged his elders, had moved steadily rightwards by the time of his assassination at the age of forty-two in 1889.[36] Tokutomi Sohō, who was a journalist of youthful liberal views, lost all sense of perspective as he hurried to acclaim a government in which nationalistic and militaristic postures became ever more extreme.[37] Even Fukuzawa, who remained liberal in old age, responded to the emotions of nationalism when the Japanese defeated China in the 1894–95 war. Ōkuma, the elder statesman, also remained broad-minded and tolerant, 'as spokesman for non-official Japan, rendered excellent service to the cause of international understanding'.[38]

But however tight the political strait-jacket, the discussion and teaching of the ideas of political economy remained a high priority. To understand this it is helpful to refer back to Sugiyama on Fukuzawa who 'stressed the necessity to learn Western civilization in order to confront Western countries'. Fukuzawa expressed the view that 'there are many among the foreigners since our foreign trade had started, who by impoverishing us, want to enrich themselves. Therefore it would only profit and rejoice foreigners if we continue to engage our interest in Japanese and Chinese classics, preferring old, rather than new, fashion, and thus falling into a state of poverty and stupidity without acquainting ourselves with the circumstances in the outer world. What they fear at this moment is our turning to Western studies. The way to achieve greatness for our country is to became accustomed to the world situation by reading as many books from the West as possible'.[39] Fukuzawa understood much. The Japanese government in encouraging the enthusiasts to study and teach political economy accepted the importance of these subjects.

How then did the Japanese succeed in organizing the teaching of political economy and ensuring that such teaching would educate the young leaders in government, education, and the law along lines which were at once safe and also useful?

The reorganization of the University of Tokyo in 1886 within a structure which owed something to the German tradition, was part of a general movement in Japan towards maintaining strict central control. For the government it was within the walls of the Imperial University in Tokyo that the best officially acceptable education was available. And at Tokyo, it was Wadagaki Kenzō who, after the departure of the American visiting professors, became responsible for the teaching of economics. Wadagaki, influenced by the German Historical School, succeeded in establishing the history of economic thought as a core element in the teaching of political economy. His students, disciples, and ultimately successors as professors were sent by the government to study in Germany before taking up their life's work in Tokyo. At other colleges and places of higher learning, the teaching of political economy continued to flourish. There was a catholicity of views in Japan as scholars considered the many ideas on economics coming in from the West.

The widespread teaching of political economy to a substantial cohort of young men, destined for responsible posts in government, education, and the law, ensured a vigorous debate on matters germane to economics and economic problems.

Nothing was more controversial and likely to produce a heated argument than matters relating to economic liberalism and protectionist theory. The debate in Japan at this time was extraordinarily wide-ranging. Those who argued for protectionism reminded their readers that 'those who clamorously support free trade see Britain flourishing by free trade and believe that we ought to follow suit. But there is nothing common in the trade of the two countries'.[40] Slowly, those who had advocated a freeing of trade in the then-prevailing British mode, were forced on to the defensive.

Even in Britain, which had soared to economic pre-eminence on the wings of free trade, there was a powerful lobby arguing that increasing competition in the international market-place demanded protection for British goods, although the eloquent campaign of Joseph Chamberlain was not sufficient to dislodge the powerful shibboleth of free trade in the United Kingdom. In Japan with centuries of tight control behind it, despite the arguments of some academic economists, free trade could only be a non-starter. When the Japanese achieved tariff autonomy in 1911, they embarked in classic mercantilist style on a protectionist programme guarding their home markets and expanding their foreign trade by exploiting overseas markets, particularly in the Far East.

By the end of the Meiji era, Japan had achieved its independence. The treaty ports[41] and their settlements had been recovered, tariff autonomy had been introduced, and perhaps most important of all, the country had gone on to the gold standard.[42]

Of course the Japanese had relied on intellectual borrowing from the West, and in some senses they felt at home with Germanic institutions. Yet it was with Britain that in 1902 the Anglo-Japanese Alliance was formed.[43] Fukuzawa, who had died the previous year, envisaged a world in which 'it would not be impossible to form a great nation in this far Orient, which would stand counter to Great Britain of the West'.[44] Ōkuma, 'who felt warm predilections for English politics and English institutions'[45] was also delighted to have the links between Britain in the West and Japan in the East strengthened.

The Japanese government, encouraged by most of the educated people, felt strongly the '*fukoku kyōhei* imperative' (to enrich the country and strengthen its arms). With the extraordinary military and naval defeats of China (1894–95) and Russia (1904–5) came a fierce nationalistic pride which burgeoned in the 1920s and 1930s into a harsh militarism. As Fukuzawa commented after the China war ended in 1895, 'This glorious condition of our country cannot but be the fruit of the good inheritance from our ancestors'.[46] Only after 1945 with the end of the Second World War were the Americans able to ensure that Japan adopted parliamentary democracy.

Generations of Japanese scholars have, since 1868, had to create a unity, marrying elements of 'vain' and 'real' learning. All were once students of Chinese learning, all are now scholars in Western studies. As Fukuzawa said, it was like 'living two lives in one body or having two bodies in one person'.[47] But every individual must reconcile opposing forces; to do so successfully gives strength.

The Japanese have succeeded in making a strong nation out of these apparent disparate and contradictory elements. The ideas of political economy were, as has been seen in the pages of this book, successfully introduced into Japan, but the dichotomy is still there. Where else would the free enterprise ideas of Adam Smith flourish within a strictly regulated economic system? In terms of political economy, the Japanese have proved themselves masters of the art of accommodation.

16

From a Western Point of View

A. W. Coats

Viewed as a whole, the contributions to this volume provide a fascinating portrayal of the transfer of economic culture from West to East, and the metamorphosis in the process. While the spread of economic ideas is undoubtedly the central theme, there is much more to it than this, for without an appropriate institutional apparatus—which was lacking initially—the ideas could hardly have taken root.

This apparatus was a good deal more complex than might appear at first sight, for the institutionalization of political economy in Japan did not merely involve the establishment of new schools, colleges, and universities, essential though that was. It also called for a variety of educational and training facilities—the construction of curricula and courses; the provision of teaching materials—especially textbooks, whether imported, translated, or written by native authors; faculties, and departments to administer them, both intra- and extramurally; recruitment procedures and career opportunities for students and teachers; scholarly periodicals and learned societies to facilitate the exchange of ideas and foster the growth of a recognizable 'community of the competent'; and means of communicating with and influencing policy-makers and the general public. All these aspects are considered in the preceding chapters, and while the account is uneven and unavoidably incomplete, it is much richer in detail than is usual in studies of the diffusion of political economy within, say, Europe or the British Commonwealth.

Beyond this, of course, for the Western observer there is the added bonus of fresh insights into Japan's dramatic late-nineteenth-century drive for modernity, a process in which the adoption and assimilation of European and American science and industrial technology have tended to overshadow, if not obliterate, the transfer of economic ideas and institutions. In the study of these matters the intellectual historian is often at a disadvantage owing to the difficulties of identifying ideas clearly and tracing their diffusion and effects precisely. In the present instance, however, there is frequently unambiguous evidence of the transmission processes, including the source of the initiative, the identity of the transmitters and the carriers, and in some cases also the receivers. Most of this evidence directly results from the extraordinary self-consciousness with which the Japanese authorities set about the task of discovering the secrets of Western economic success and applying the results of their investigations to the task of competing with the European powers on equal terms.

For historians of economics, Japan's experience in the Meiji era raises questions of such fundamental importance that it becomes easier to understand why our Japanese colleagues display such a passionate and enduring interest in the field. The tensions resulting from the interaction of two very different, though not necessarily incompatible cultures, is an inescapable central theme. Beyond this, the deliberate and calculated introduction and controlled absorption of Western economic ideas and institutions, especially in the Meiji era, poses the issue of environmentalism—one version of the interrelationship between events and ideas—in an unusually clear form. More broadly, is it true, as many critics have claimed, that orthodox classical and neo-classical economics is essentially and irredeemably culture-bound: that it is not merely the by-product of Western capitalism but also that it is irrelevant, even positively misleading, when applied to the problems and mechanisms of radically different kinds of society? Doubtless that particular formulation is too crude.[1] Yet it will serve the present purpose, for it is directly pertinent to the Meiji era when there was a confluent importation of Dutch, British, French, and American variants of liberalism together with the ideas of the German Historical School—a group some of whose leaders explicitly attacked classical economics for its purported cosmopolitanism and perpetualism (i.e., the claim that the same basic economic theories are equally applicable in all places and at all times). To suggest that Japan's late-nineteenth-century history provides a testing ground for this claim would be too simplistic; nevertheless it is a hypothesis worth bearing in mind when examining the contents of this volume.

In surveying the general relationships between the stages of Japanese economic development and the prevailing economic doctrines, we may begin by noting that the Tokugawa period, which is usually described as feudal, failed to produce a quasi-systematic corpus of mercantilist and policy recommendations of the type widely encountered in early modern Europe prior to the emergence of modern industrial capitalism. Of course the terms feudal and mercantilist are controversial and potentially misleading. Nevertheless, one would scarcely expect to find a coherent body of economic ideas assigning a central place to foreign trade and the activities of merchants in a country such as eighteenth- and early-nineteenth-century Japan, with very limited international contacts, overseas trade in the hands of small, tightly controlled band of foreigners, and an indigenous merchant class which, though slowly growing in importance, was still seriously lacking in social status, influence, and political power.

How far and in what ways the Tokugawa period prepared the ground for post-1868 developments is a matter for debate. According to Michio Morishima,

> Japan was able to form a modern unified nation state immediately after the Meiji Revolution because internal communication and exchange during the 200-odd years of isolation had resulted in the near completion of the foundation work necessary for Japan as a whole to become a single community, namely, the standardisation of language, the acceptance of similar ways of thinking and acting by the people of various provinces and the consequent similarity in social rules and customs, and so forth.
>
> Furthermore, Japanese capitalism . . . was able to function more or less as a market economy from the start.[2]

With respect to economic ideas, J. F. Bell, adopting a narrow interpretation, asserted that 'economic doctrines were first introduced into Japan in the first two decades subsequent to 1860', but Hiroshi Mizuta has demonstrated that 'fragments' of economic doctrine were becoming known to the Japanese at a much earlier date.[3] The distinguished cultural historian Sir George Sansom refers to a 'considerable' but "heterogeneous and unsystematic" body of economic doctrine developed in the Tokugawa period, arguing that the country was 'somewhat better prepared for the critical study of Western ideas in the field of economics than it was in the field of politics'.[4] However he added the significant proviso that

> while Western thinkers in time came to distinguish economics as a separate discipline, the Japanese, imbued with Chinese philosophy, tended to treat their subject as a branch of social ethics and attempt-

> ed to discover how man should, rather than how he does in fact, behave in his environment. It was not until some years after the Restoration that Japan had any scholars who could be regarded as specialists in economic theory.[5]

It was entirely appropriate that the first systematic Japanese encounter with European economics should have occurred with the Dutch, rather than the British, French, or Americans, given the long, if somewhat restricted commercial relations between the two countries. But although one early Japanese commentator described the Dutch ideas as 'more or less Mercantilist',[6] Mizuta has shown that liberal, or even laissez-faire, would be a more suitable characterization. Vissering's contention that the same natural laws of political economy applied equally to the East and the West virtually ensured that his influence was unlikely to prove durable, and there was clear doctrinal continuity between his ideas and the major wave of Western economic and political liberalism imported by such writers as Fukuzawa and Taguchi.[7] Thus in a sense Japan's first serious encounter with European economic doctrines involved leapfrogging over the mercantilist era and direct confrontation with startlingly new theories and policy recommendations that had been gradually evolving in the West for a century or more under radically different economic, social, and ideological conditions. No wonder

> the history of English economic thought in Japan shows very clearly that a well-established culture does not easily absorb even the most persuasive foreign intellectual influences unless they are welcome to the *sette de' tempi*, the prevailing climate of opinion, in the country on which they are exerted.[8]

The pioneers of the Japanese enlightenment faced strong, occasionally even violent, opposition from those who rejected or suspected all things foreign or who feared—not without reason—that the new doctrines would not merely undermine existing beliefs but might even threaten law and order if carried into practice. Some conservatives were outraged when Nishi and others proclaimed the superiority of Western principles.[9] As with other Western innovations, the process of incorporating (rather than merely assimilating) European ideas was extraordinarily rapid, and some of the innovators were undoubtedly carried away by their enthusiasm, perhaps a natural response to the first experience of foreign travel. Their primary aim was to strengthen the nation by narrowing the gap between the East and Europe, and they 'roamed the world of Western ideas in pursuit of a replacement for a tradition from which they were alienated'.[10] Understandably enough, they had considerable initial difficulties in digesting the new ideas, translating (and where necessary inventing new terminology) and communicating them clearly and coherently to domestic audiences and, as seemed appropriate, reconciling them with accepted ways of thinking and action. Within a decade or two 'the earlier adulatory generation of things Western was succeeded by a more culturally conservative breed'[11] sometimes in response to official disapproval. Nevertheless, there was no sharp discontinuity between the early and late Meiji era. The process was more complex and subtle than that. Some clung on to liberal ideas: but by the early 1880s, in politics as in economics, there was a growing awareness that from the various European

> traditions, doctrines, and systems it was possible to make a choice, or a selection, to identify those extraneous elements which would accommodate themselves most fruitfully to the indigenous milieu and, perhaps more important, serve the interests of the ruling oligarchy. The equation that Western influences were liberal, while Japanese reactions were conservative, is based on false premises. Western liberal doctrines found a response among liberal-minded Japanese, whereas Western conservative doctrines met with the approval of conservative-minded Japanese. The fact that many young liberals became old conservatives should not be interpreted as a rejection of the West; Japan could by no means claim a monopoly of young liberals becoming conservatives with age.[12]

In reviewing Japan's incorporation of Western ideas and practices during the Meiji era, one must resist the temptation to dichotomize the relationship between tradition and modernity, since this would simply obscure their symbiotic or dialectical interdependence.[13] The ease and rapidity with which the Japanese adopted, combined, and modified Western ideas is attributable in part to what one author has termed the 'structureless tradition' of Japanese thought, the extreme eclecticism and absence of an organizing principle that made it possible to embrace new and alien concepts while avoiding a direct confrontation with the past.[14] Others refer to 'a venerable Confucian ambivalence'[15] and a tolerant intellectual climate which 'has rejected only those approaches that insisted on consistency and the creation of a set hierarchy of values in relation to all human experience'.[16] In religious affairs, for example, the Japanese were undogmatic,[17] consequently they had avoided the bitter theological conflicts which had racked Europe for centuries. The vigour and persistence of such distinctively Japanese concepts as *kokutai, sonnō jōi, bushidō*, and *tennō-sei*, have caused difficulties both for native and foreign scholars seeking to account for the social and cultural changes following the assimilation of Western ideas and technology, for there was 'a tenacious substratum of social tradition that ran rock-hard under the newer ideological edifices built upon them in the modern period'.[18] According to a distinguished Westernised contemporary Japanese economist, his compatriots had been 'brainwashed and moulded into a specific type of person by their Confucianist education' during the country's long period of isolation,[19] and while this is doubtless an overstatement the remarkable homogeneity of the Japanese—racial, physiological, and cultural—is still a source of surprise to foreign visitors. At the time of Japan's 'take-off' into self-sustained economic growth, the ideological heritage 'had the effect of restricting the possibilities of day-to-day activity within the framework of the activity', and in the secularization of society

> Confucianism and Shintoism collaborated; the former doctrine is perfectly suited to the construction of a constitutional-monarchic regime based on a modern bureaucracy, while the latter can easily serve as a catalyst to promote nationalism. It is therefore not surprising to find that Japanese capitalism was—and still is—nationalistic, paternalistic, and anti-individualistic.[20]

The persistence of the 'emperor system' as a 'spiritual structure', a focus for loyalty and the embodiment of a sense of national unity, yet aloof from politics, was an essential ingredient in the situation, especially in the Meiji era when there were potentially powerful divisive forces of change. Yet this too was enlisted in the modernization process.

> The successful working of the Meiji state depended on a subtle balance between an ideology for public consumption, the *kenkyō*, or exoteric ideology, and an elitist belief in a more restricted definition of imperial power, the *mikkyō*, or esoteric ideology. The exoteric, public, ideology operated to maintain the emperor as absolute monarch with unlimited authority and power. The esoteric canon, on the other hand, placed the authority and power of the emperor in a framework of limitations formed by the constitution and other considerations. The distinction between the two served to mobilize the energy of the people in service to a monarch in whom they could believe without qualification, while the government was

run on the basis of a doctrine of constitutional monarchy—the 'Theory of the Emperor as Supreme Organ of State'.[21]

The urge 'to enrich and strengthen Japan, to put her on an equal footing with the great powers as soon as possible—necessarily resulted in the limitation and, at times, the enforced sacrifice of the modernization of social relations'[22] which proved harder to domesticate than 'the nation-mindedness and civic education that began in the 1880s [and] soon naturalized themselves as elements in the ideological landscape'.[23] Ideology served as an 'integrative mechanism', largely a substitute for force, and there was a strong emphasis on participation and conciliation. Unlike the West, there was no contract theory in Japan, and

> conflicting notions of personal striving and social harmony appear in the ideological contradictions between the sometimes reluctant endorsement of individual economic competition and the always insistent exhortation to place the common welfare of the family or village before that of its individual members.[24]

From the earlier chapters in this volume it is clear that the over-enthusiastic movement towards Western liberalism reached a peak in the 1870s and was forced into retreat during the following decade. Yet while the cultural climate changed markedly between the earlier and later Meiji era the difference should not be depicted as a stark contrast,

> but rather as an evolutionary formation towards a sense of national identity . . . [In both phases] cultural and political discourse took place within a predominantly Western-oriented context. The West might be feared, certain aspects of it might be despised, but nonetheless its power inspired awe and motivation for emulation—which is not the same thing as imitation.[25]

During the 1880s, German economic, political, and legal ideas were eagerly adopted and implemented by the representatives of the ruling oligarchy largely because they seemed less threatening to the status quo than the individualism, egalitarianism, and belief in democracy favoured by the advocates of liberalism and laissez-faire. The use of Herbert Spencer's writings by both sides in the debate is fascinating for they combined individualistic ethics with the theory of social organism.

> In his earlier ideas, the individualistic elements [are] predominant; but in his later thought, the elements of social organism became clearer. . . . In Japan, these two aspects were separated; and each aspect was accepted by a different group. Intellectuals of the popular rights group learned the theory of individual freedom while conservative academicians adopted Spencer's theory of social organism as their own theory.[26]

Needless to say, it was the latter aspect that won favour with the Meiji government. Spencer's doctrine of gradualism—the idea that a different policy and social system is necessary for each stage of social evolution—naturally appealed to conservatives, and was congenial to a society wherein national objectives were given priority over individual interests and goals. Moreover, the compatibility of this approach with the ideas of the German Historical School needs no emphasis.[27]

From the early 1880s there was a series of major steps towards modernization in politics, law, constitutional affairs, and education, as the government sought to strengthen its foundations to withstand the growing economic, social, and political pressures. The new developments in the educational field are clearly the most important from the present standpoint, and as Sansom observes,

> whereas Western influence was strong in the organization of education and the choice of pedagogic methods, educational policy in general was in essence neither enlightened nor progressive by contemporary occidental standards.[28]

In the drive for modernization, education played a strategic role, for 'ultimately . . . Japan's success was derived not so much from financial capital, from technology, but from accumulation and successful formation of human capital'.[29] At the time of the Meiji Restoration the Japanese educational system barely existed, but it was rapidly built up in the next three or four decades through the triple processes of sending students and others abroad, importing substantial numbers of teachers and other experts, and expanding the production of trained personnel. In this era of 'bureaucratic captialism' there was a striking growth of

> a highly capable, efficient, modern elite. Japanese medical doctors, professors of the various disciplines, school teachers, technicians and scientists, foremen of skilled workers, bureaucrats, army and navy officers, industrial managers and financiers provided the high

> quality human resources necessary for the country's development and self-reliance.[30]

Given the increasingly important role of government in economic life, special importance attaches to the emergence of a powerful and influential civil service drawn, inevitably in practice, from the middle and upper income groups who had access to higher education. But it was increasingly open to all men of talent irrespective of their background, selected on the basis of stiff competitive examinations, exhibiting great ability, and enjoying high prestige (but not correspondingly high remuneration). This cadre, whose admission into the elite irrespective of their social background tended to reinforce the existing social structure, played a crucial part in guiding Japan into the twentieth-century industrial world.

The modernizing element in education did not, however, extend throughout the whole of society. Although great efforts were made to ensure that a sizeable proportion of the population acquired the ability to read, write and count, which was essential in an industrializing community, the rapid expansion of basic education coexisted with

> a deeper schism between elementary and higher education than was common in Western countries. This, in turn, resulted in a wide gap between intellectuals and the general public. In Western countries a foundation for learning was provided in elementary schools, while more advanced and specialized knowledge was conveyed in the higher schools. In Japan, however, a priori conclusions were taught unequivocally in elementary schools, while the function of higher education was to convey the variety of methodology and interpretation that underlay these conclusions.[31]

Despite strong and periodically repressive measures by the authorities, and the growing effectiveness of central control and leadership, the Japanese higher educational system did not become monolithic. Indeed, its diversity is still remarkable. While the government exerted a powerful and direct influence on the Imperial University of Tokyo, where a sequence of German-trained economists dominated the teaching of their subject, Western liberal economic ideas continued to flourish in the private universities, colleges, and academies. The development of commercial education is of special interest to American and British observers for a variety of reasons. At the Tokyo Commercial College, later Hitotsubashi University, which began its activities in 1875, six years before the first American university school of business (The Wharton School, at the University of Pennsylvania),[32] the inspiration was clearly and unambiguously American. It was directly modelled on one of the chain of U.S. private commercial and business colleges which have evidently been too humble to deserve the attention of American historians of economics.[33] The fact that these institutions were designed to function at an elementary level may indeed have been an advantage from the Japanese standpoint given their language difficulties, limited background in social science disciplines, and initial lack of suitable teaching materials. The rapidity of the college's subsequent rise to university status suggests that the early handicaps were soon overcome. A curious feature of the situation is that although Tomita, the acting consul in New York, and one of the school's first teachers, had met the outstanding American protectionist and advocate of a 'national' system of political economy, Henry C. Carey, whose views were entirely in accord with 'the nationalized spirit that lay in the basis of the school',[34] which was designed to train merchants, the initial teaching was based on the popularized version of classical political economy, no doubt *faute de mieux*. The richness and variety of the materials in this volume make it impossible to consider the many other educational institutions referred to in this volume or the other manifold aspects of the development of political economy in Japan, such as: the curricula, numbers of students, their career opportunities, the structure and functioning of academic departments, the number and range of publication outlets, the formation of learned societies and clubs, and the impact (if any) of economists on policy and politics. One subject not touched on in the previous chapters may, however, be mentioned, namely: how far did the Japanese develop a distinctive approach to political economy, whether in terms of method, doctrine, or policy?

That is not, of course, the central theme of this study, but the account of institutionalization processes necessarily raises questions about doctrine and theory. How far is it true that Western political economy was incompatible with Japanese culture and habits of thought? Earlier it was noted that American economic books and teachers were welcome partly because of their eminently practical approach; and this focus helps to explain why, at least for most Japanese, doctrinaire liberalism was so difficult to incorporate into their society. Concepts such as atomistic individualism, personal rights, egalitarianism, the uninhibited pursuit of self-interest, profit, and maximum pecuniary returns to enterprise were at odds with accepted ways of thought, as well as potentially subversive politically and socially. The Japanese capacity to blend ingredients from a variety of sources and intellectual traditions into an amalgam which amounted to less than a coherent synthesis, or a single distinctively Japanese approach or point of view, has already been mentioned. This perhaps explains why Japanese historians of economics often seem, to their Western counterparts, as subdivided into specialist groups, each with its own special allegiance or set of intellectual concerns. Perhaps the most distinctively Japanese version of economics—namely, an indigenous form of Marxism without any clear element of class conflict—is an exception, but it is one that had hardly put in an appearance in the period covered by this project.

Appendix 1

Chronological Table

Political Economy in Japan	Other Historical Events
	1853 U.S. Commodore Perry arrives in Uraga, near Edo (now Tokyo)
	1854–55 Amity treaties between Japan and five Western countries concluded
1855 Yōgakusho (School for Western Studies, the forerunner of the University of Tokyo) established in Edo by the Shogunate	
1856 Yōgakusho becomes Bansho Shirabesho (Institute for the Study of Barbarian Books) → Yōsho Shirabesho (Institute for the Study of Western Books) in 1862 → Kaisei-jo (Kaisei Institute) in 1863 → Kaisei Gakkō (Kaisei School) in 1873	
1858 Fukuzawa Yukichi's private school (later Keiō University) established	**1858** Treaties of amity and trade between Japan and five Western countries (U.S.A., Great Britain, Russia, France, and Holland) concluded
1862–66 Nishi Amane and Tsuda Mamichi in Leiden (under S. Vissering)	
1866 Fukuzawa's *Seiyō Jijō* (Conditions in the West), vol. 1 published	

Political Economy in Japan	Other Historical Events
	1868 Meiji Restoration
1871 Ministry of Education established	**1871** Iwakura mission to the U.S.A. and Europe Abolition of clans and establishment of prefectures Yen denomination with nominal gold standard established under the monetary regulations
1872 The Education Decree promulgated Shihan Gakkō (Normal School) established in Tokyo Ōkurashō Hon'yaku Kyoku (Department of Translation in the Ministry of Finance) established	
1872–76 Fukuzawa's *Gakumon no Susume* (An Encouragement of Learning) published	
1873–95 G. E. Boissonade in Japan	**1873** Conscription Decree promulgated Land-tax reform introduced First National Bank established
1874 *Meiroku Zasshi* (Meiji Six Journal) issued	
1875 Fukuzawa's *Bunmeiron no Gairyaku* (An Outline of the Theory of Civilization) published Shōhō Kōshūjo (Commercial Training School, later Hitotsubashi University) established in Tokyo Dōshisha Eigakkō (Dōshisha School of English Studies, later Dōshisha University) established	
1876 Sapporo Nō Gakkō (Sapporo Agricultural College, later Hokkaido University) established	**1876** Mitsui Bank, the first private bank, established
1876–80 Seven Japanese students in Jevons's class at University College London	
1877 Tokyo Daigaku (University of Tokyo) established with four facul-	**1877** Satsuma Rebellion against the government

Political Economy in Japan	Other Historical Events
ties (Law, Science, Arts, and Medicine) Fukuzawa's *Minkan Keizairoku* (Popular Political Economy) published Taguchi Ukichi's *Nihon Kaika Shōshi* (A Brief History of Japanese Enlightenment) published	
1878 Fukuzawa's *Tsūkaron* (On Currency) published Taguchi's *Jiyū Kōeki Nihon Keizairon* (Free Trade and the Japanese Economy) published	**1878** Nominal bimetallic standard adopted Shōhō Kaigisho (Chambers of Commerce) both in Tokyo and in Osaka permitted to be established
1878–88 E. F. Fenollosa's lectures in political economy at the University of Tokyo	
1878–93 K. F. H. Roesler in Japan	
1879 New Education Decree promulgated Taguchi's *Tokyo Keizai Zasshi* (Tokyo Economist) issued D. W. Learned's lectures in political economy started at Dōshisha School of English Studies	
1880 Senshū Gakkō (Senshū School, later Senshū University) established Tokyo Hōgakusha (Tokyo Law Society, later Hōsei University) established Osaka Shōgyō Kōshūjo (Osaka Commercial Training School, later Osaka City University) established Meiji Hōritsu Gakkō (Meiji Law School, later Meiji University) established Keizai Danwakai (Political Economy Seminar) established by Taguchi → Tokyo Keizaigaku Kyōkai (Tokyo Political Economy Club) in 1887	
1881 The law-teaching section of Tokyo	**1881** Political Crisis of 1881

Political Economy in Japan	Other Historical Events
Law Society reorganizes itself as Tokyo Hō Gakkō (Tokyo Law School)	Jiyūtō (Liberal Party) organized Matsukata deflationary policies
1882	**1882**
Tokyo Senmon Gakkō (Tokyo School of Special Studies, later Waseda University) established Taguchi's *Keizaisaku* (Economic Policy) published	Rikken Kaishintō (Constitutional Reform Party) established Nihon Ginkō (Bank of Japan) established
1883	
Doitsugaku Kyōkai Gakkō (school attached to the Society for German Studies) opened	
1884	
Shōhō Kōshūjo (Commercial Training School) in Tokyo becomes Tokyo Shōgyō Gakkō (Tokyo Commercial School)	
1884–86	
Soeda Juichi in Cambridge	
1885	**1885**
Osaka Shōgyō Kōshūjo (Osaka Commercial Training School) developed into Osaka Shōgyō Gakkō (Osaka Commercial School) Igirisu Hōritsu Gakkō (School of English Law, later Chūō University) established	The Cabinet System begins
1886	**1886**
Tokyo Daigaku renamed Teikoku Daigaku (Imperial University) under the Imperial University Decree Kansai Hōritsu Gakkō (Kansai Law School, later Kansai University) established Amano Tameyuki's *Keizai Genron* (The Theory of Political Economy) and *Shōsei Hyōjun* (The Principles of Commercial Legislation) published	Convertible paper currency by the Bank of Japan issued
1886–87	
Nakagawa Tsunejirō's *Keizai Jitsugaku Kōgi* (Lectures in Practical Political Economy) published	
1887	
Tokyo Shōgyō Gakkō (Tokyo Commercial School) becomes Kōtō	

Political Economy in Japan	Other Historical Events
Shōgyō Gakkō (Higher Commercial School) *Kokumin no Tomo* (The Nation's Friend) issued *Kokka Gakkai Zasshi* (Journal of the Society for State Sciences) issued Nakae Chōmin's *San Suijin Keirin Mondō* (Three Drunkards' Dialogue) published Sakatani Yoshio's *Keizaigakushi Kōgi* (Lectures in the History of Political Economy) published	
1889 Amano's *Nihon Rizai Zasshi* (Japan Economist) issued	**1889** Imperial Constitution promulgated
1889–98 G. Droppers's lectures in political economy at Keiō Gijuku	
1890 The Department of Political Economy at Keiō Gijuku established Nihon Hōritsu Gakkō (Nihon Law School, later Nihon University) established Taguchi's *Zoku Keizaisaku* (A Sequel to Economic Policy) published	**1890** Imperial Diet opened
1891 Ōshima Sadamasu's *Jōseiron* (Treatise on the Current State of the Nation) published	
1893 *Osaka Keizai Zasshi* (Osaka Economist) issued Fukuzawa's *Jitsugyōron* (On Trade and Industry) published	
1894 Tokutomi Sohō's *Dainihon Bōchōron* (For the Expansion of Japan) published	**1894–95** Sino-Japanese War
1895 Machida Chūji's *Tōyō Keizai Shinpō* (Oriental Economist) issued	**1895** Treaty of Shimonoseki concluded between Japan and China Triple Intervention Company promotion boom
1896 A study group of social policy or-	

Political Economy in Japan	Other Historical Events
ganized and becomes Shakai Seisaku Gakkai (Society for Social Policy) in 1897	
1897 Kyoto Teikoku Daigaku (Kyoto Imperial University, later Kyoto University) established Tajima Kinji's *Saishin Keizairon* (On Modern Political Economy) published	**1897** Gold standard adopted Society for the Promotion of Trade Unions established Yawata Iron Works, a government-managed iron foundry, established → foundry operation begun in 1901
1898–1910 E. H. Vickers's lectures in political economy at Keiō Gijuku	
1899 Shiritsu Gakkōrei (Private School Decree) promulgated Kobayashi Ushisaburō's *Junsei Keizaigaku* (Pure Political Economy) published	
1900 Kyoto Hōsei Gakkō (Kyoto School of Law and Politics, later Ritsumeikan University) established Taiwan Kyōkai Gakkō (school attached to the Taiwan Society, later Takushoku University) established	
1901 Osaka Shōgyō Gakkō (Osaka Commercial School) becomes Osaka Kōtō Shōgyō Gakkō (Osaka Higher Commercial School)	**1901** Shakai Minshutō (Social Democratic Party) organized but promptly dissolved by the government
1902 Kōtō Shōgyō Gakkō (Higher Commercial School) renamed Tokyo Kōtō Shōgyō Gakkō (Tokyo Higher Commercial School) Kobe Kōtō Shōgyō Gakkō (Kobe Higher Commercial School, later Kobe University) established Kanai Noburu's *Shakai Keizaigaku* (Social Political Economy) published	**1902** Anglo-Japanese Alliance concluded
1903 Senmon Gakkōrei (Specialized School Decree) promulgated Ōnishi Ringorō and Ishimaru Masamitsu's *Keizaigaku Daijiten*	

Political Economy in Japan	Other Historical Events
(Dictionary of Political Economy) published Katayama Sen's *Waga Shakaishugi* (My Socialism) published Kōtoku Shūsui's *Shakaishugi Shinzui* (Essence of Socialism) published *Heimin Shinbun* (Commoners' News) issued	
	1904–5 Russo-Japanese War
1905 Yamaguchi Kōtō Shōgyō Gakkō (Yamaguchi Higher Commercial School) established Nagasaki Kōtō Shōgyō Gakkō (Nagasaki Higher Commercial School) established Kawakami Hajime's *Keizaigaku Genron: Jōkan* (Principles of Political Economy, vol. 1) published	**1905** Treaty of Portsmouth concluded between Japan and Russia
1906 *Kokumin Keizai Zasshi* (later Journal of Economics and Business Administration) issued	**1906** Nihon Shakaitō (Japan Socialist Party) established
1907 Tōhoku Teikoku Daigaku (Tōhoku Imperial University, later Tōhoku University) established The first annual meeting of the Society for Social Policy held Fukuda Tokuzō's *Keizaigaku Kōgi* (Lectures in Political Economy) published Morichika Unpei and Sakai Toshihiko's *Shakaishugi Kōyō* (Elements of Socialism) published	
1907–8 Tsumura Hidematsu's *Kokumin Keizaigaku Genron: Jōkan* (Principles of National Political Economy, vol. 1) published	
1908 Department of Political Economy at Tokyo Imperial University established	
1909 Department of Commerce at Tokyo	

Political Economy in Japan	Other Historical Events
Imperial University established *Mita Gakkai Zasshi* (later Mita Journal of Economics) issued by Keiō University Horie Kiichi's *Zaiseigaku* (Public Finance) published	
1910 Kyūshū Teikoku Daigaku (Kyūshū Imperial University, later Kyūshū University) established Otaru Kōtō Shōgyō Gakkō (Otaru Higher Commercial School) established Amano's *Keizaisakuron* (Essays on Economic Policies) published Tajima's *Keizai Genron: Jōkan* (Principles of Political Economy, vol. 1) published	**1910** Oppression of socialist movements Taigyaku Jiken (High Treason Incident) occurred Treaty of Korean-Japanese annexation concluded
	1911 Autonomy in tariff imposition Factory Act promulgated
1912 Uchida Ginzō's *Keizaishi Sōron* (Outline of Economic History) published Kawakami's *Keizaigaku Kenkyū* (Studies in Political Economy) published Matsuzaki Kuranosuke's *Saishin Zaiseigaku* (Modern Public Finance) published	**1912** Meiji era ended Yūai-kai (Friendship Association) organized → Nihon Rōdō Sōdōmei (Japanese Federation of Labour) in 1921

Appendix 2

Western Economics Books Translated into Japanese, 1867–1912

This is a list of translations published in book form only. Articles that appeared in periodicals have been excluded, as have books by authors then living in Japan. Most places of publication are Tokyo. Books marked with asterisks are abridged translations.

United Kingdom

Bagehot, Walter. *Lombard Street,* 1873. Tr. by Koike Seiichi, 1883; by Kasai Tamotsu, 1911.

Bastable, Charles Francis. * *The Theory of International Trade*, 1887. Tr. by Tsuchiko Kinshirō and Tajima Kinji, 1897; by Kawasaki Naoe, 1901.

———. *The Commerce of Nations*, 1887. Tr. by Hakodate Zeikan (Hakodate Customs House), 1904.

———. * *Public Finance*, 1892. Tr. by Inoue Tatsukurō and Takano Iwasaburō, 1899.

Anon. (Burton, John Hill). * *Chambers's Educational Course: Political Economy, for Use in Schools, and for Private Instruction*, 1852. Tr. by Fukuzawa Yukichi, 1869.

Byles, John Barnard. * *Sophisms of Free Trade and Popular Political Economy Examined*, 1849; American ed., 1872. Tr. by Wakayama Norikazu, 2 vols., 1877.

Cairnes, John Elliot. *The Character and Logical Method of Political Economy*, 1857, 1875 (2nd ed.). Tr. by Ban Naonosuke, 2 vols., 1884; by Komai Shigetada, 3 vols., 1884.

Caldecott, Alfred. *English Colonization and Empire*, 1891 (with a supplementary chapter by F. A. Kirkpatrick, 1901). Tr. by Mizusaki

Motokazu, 1909.

Cunningham, William. *Politics and Economics*, 1885. Tr. by Anon., 1894.

Dawson, William Herbutt. *The Evolution of Modern Germany*, n.d. (1908). Tr. by Azuma Jōzaburō, 1910.

Ellis, William. *Outlines of Social Economy*, 1846 (H. H. Graafland, Groundtrekken der Staathuishoudkunde, 1852). Tr. by Kanda Takahira, 2 vols., 1867; 1 vol., 1868.

Fawcett, Henry. * *Manual of Political Economy*, 1863. Tr. by Nakakuma Keizō, 1884; by * Yano Tsunetarō, 1887; by Amano Tameyuki, 1888.

———. * *Pauperism, Its Causes and Remedies*, 1871. Tr. by Ōno Naosuke, 1887.

———. * *Essays and Lectures on Social and Political Subjects* (with M. G. Fawcett), 1872. Tr. by Shibuya Sōji, 2 vols. 1883.

———. *Free Trade and Protection*, 1878. Tr. by Komai Shigetada, 1880.

Fawcett, Millicent Garrett. *Political Economy for Beginners*, 1870, 1876 (4th ed.). Tr. by Hayashi Masaaki, 4 vols. 1873; by Nagata Kensuke, 5 vols., 1877, 1887; by * Kanezaki Shigeki, 1885; by Suzuki Shigetaka, 1905.

———. *Tales of Political Economy*, 1870. Tr. by Katayama Heizaburō, 1885.

Gibbins, Henry de Beltgons. *The History of Commerce in Europe*, 1891. Tr. by Hayashi Sotokichi, 1892; by Nagata Kensuke, 1896.

Goschen, George Joachim. *The Theory of Foreign Exchanges*, 1861. Tr. by Tajiri Inajirō, 1882; by Komai Shigetada, 1883; by Naruse Masayasu, 1895.

Hobson, John Atkinson. *Problems of Poverty*, 1891. Tr. by Endō Jūrō, 1897.

Ingram, John Kells. *A History of Political Economy*, 1888. Tr. by Abe Toranosuke, 1896.

Jevons, William Stanley. *Money and the Mechanism of Exchange*, 1875. Tr. by Tajiri Inajirō, 1883; by Ōshima Sadamasu, 1883; by * Hayashi Takeichi, 1884.

———. *Primer of Political Economy*, 1878. Tr. by Yasuda Genjirō, 1882; by Watanabe Shūjirō, 3 vols., 1884; by Saga Shōsaku and Furuta Shinroku, 1889; by Sugiyama Shigetaka, 1889.

———. *The State in Relation to Labour*, 1882. Tr. by Suita Tairoku, 1893.

Keynes, John Neville. *The Scope and Method of Political Economy*, 1890. Tr. by Amano Tameyuki, 1897.

Levi, Leone. *History of British Commerce*, 1872. Tr. by Taguchi Ukichi and Fujita Shizuka, 17 vols., 1879; by Tsuchiko Kinshirō, 1887.

Macleod, Henry Dunning. *The Principles of Economical Philosophy*, 2 vols., 1872–75 (2nd ed.). Tr. by Taguchi Ukichi, 2 vols., 1885, 1887.

———. *The Elements of Banking*, 1876. Tr. by Gotō Hiromi, Kanaya Akira et al., 12 vols., 1883–90; by Tajiri Inajirō, 1883.

Malthus, Thomas Robert. *Parallel Chapters from the First and Second Editions of an Essay on the Principles of Population, 1798: 1803*, ed. by W. J. Ashley, 1895. Tr. by Ōshima Sadamasu, 1877; by Mikami Masaki, 1910.

Marshall, Alfred. *The Economics of Industry* (with M. P. Marshall), 1879. Tr. by Takahashi Korekiyo, 2 vols., 1885–86.

———. *Elements of Economics of Industry*, 1892. Tr. by Inoue Tatsukurō, 1896.

Mill, John Stuart. *Principles of Political Economy*, 1848. Tr. by * Hayashi Tadasu and Suzuki Shigetaka, 27 vols., 1875–85; by Amano Tameyuki (Laughlin's ed., 1884), 1891.

Mongredien, Augustus. *Free Trade and English Commerce*, n.d. (1878). Tr. by Nai Keinoshin, 1881; by Yano Jōtarō, 1893.

———. *History of the Free-Trade Movement in England*, 1881. Tr. by Saga Shōsaku, 1889.

Pratt, Edwin A. *The Organization of Agriculture*, 1904. Tr. by Satō Hirotsugu, 1912.

Price, Langford Lovell Frederick Rice. *A Short History of English Commerce and Industry*, 1900. Tr. by Wadagaki Kenzō and Tsuda Kin'ichirō, 1904.

Rogers, James Edwin Thorold. *A Manual of Political Economy for Schools and Colleges*, 1868. Tr. by Takahashi Tatsuo, 8 vols., 1874–78; by Koyama Takashi, 2 vols., 1881.

———. *Social Economy*, 1872. Tr. by Ogasawara Toshitaka, 1878.

Sidgwick, Henry. * *The Principles of Political Economy*, 1883. Tr. by Tsuchiko Kinshirō and Tajima Kinji, 1897.

Smart, William. *An Introduction to the Theory of Value on the Lines of Menger, Wieser and Böhm-Bawerk*, 1891. Tr. by Kiryū Yūyū (Masaji), 1903.

Smith, Adam. *An Inquiry into the Nature and Causes of the Wealth of Nations*, 1776. Tr. by Ishikawa Eisaku and Saga Shōsaku, 12 vols. 1883–88; by Ishikawa Eisaku, 2 vols. (Book IV of *The Wealth of Nations*), 1885–86; by Mikami Masaki (Ashley's ed., 1902), 1910.

Sullivan, Edward Robert. *Free Trade Bubbles*, 1883. Tr. by Suzuki Shigetaka, 1888.

Toynbee, Arnold. *Lectures on the Industrial Revolution (of the Eighteenth Century) in England*, n.d. (1884). Tr. by Yoshida Minosuke, 1908.

Whately, Richard. *Easy Lessons on Money Matters*, 1835. Tr. by Obata Tokujirō, 1870; by Nishimura Shigeki, 1874.

France

Bastiat, Claude Frédéric. * *Sophismes économiques*, 1846–48. (H. White, *Sophisms of Protection*, 1869). Tr. by Hayashi Masaaki, 1878.

———. *Ce qu'on voit et ce qu'on ne voit pas*, 1850 (J. Garnier's ed., 1873). Tr. by Yamadera Nobuaki, 1880.

———. *Harmonies économiques*, 1850 (P. J. Stirling et al., *Harmonies of Political Economies*, 1860–70). Tr. by Tsuchiko Kinshirō, 2 vols., 1887, 1888–89.

Beauregard, Paul. *Eléments d'économie politique*, 1890. Tr. by Yokoyama Masahiko, 2 vols., 1893–94.

Block, Maurice. *Petit manuel d'économie pratique*, 1873, 1880 (8th ed.). Tr. by Nagata Keitarō, 1887; by Ōki Tazō, 1887.

Buffon, Henri Nadauld de. *Notre ennemi de luxe*, 1879. Tr. by Inoue Kowashi, 2 vols., 1885.

Garnier, Joseph. * *Traité de finance*, 1862 (2nd ed.). Tr. by Kusaka Hisashi, 1878; by Nakayama Shin'ichi, 2 vols., 1878; by Takahashi Jirō, 2 vols., 1883.

Gide, Charles. *Economie sociale*, 1900, 1907 (3rd ed.) Tr. by Andō Tadayoshi, 1910.

Jouffroy, Henri. * *Catéchisme d'économie politique*, 1844. English translation by Alexander Siebold tr. into Japanese by Furusawa Shigeru and Tsuchiyama Moriari, 2 vols., 1877–78.

Leroy-Beaulieu, Paul. *Traité de la science des finances*, 2 vols., 1877. Tr. by * Tajiri Inajirō, 1880; by the * Sozei-kyoku (Department of Taxation of the Cabinet), 2 vols., 1882; by the * Ministry of Finance, 2 vols., 1886; by * Tajiri Inajirō, 10 vols., 1882–83; by * Komai Shigetada, 4 vols., 1883; by * Tajiri Inajirō, 1884.

———. *Précis d'économie politique*, 1888. Tr. by Miyako Keizaburō, 4 vols., 1891.

Levasseur, Pierre Emile. *Cours d'économie rurale, industrielle et commerciale*, 1869. Tr. by Nagata Kensuke, 10 vols., 1881–84.

Quesnay, François. *Tableau oeconomique*, 1758 (facsimile, British Economic Association, London, 1894). Tr. by Matsuzaki Kuranosuke, 1902.

Say, Jean-Baptiste-Léon. *Dictionnaire des finances*, 2 vols., * 1883–91,

1889–94, Tr. by Ōkura-shō Shukei-kyoku (Department of the Budget, Ministry of Finance), 1890.

Germany

Bischof, Alois. *Katechismus der Finanzwissenschaft*, 1870. Tr. by Iiyama Masahide, 1887.

Cohn, Gustav. *Finanzwissenschaft* (*System der Nationalökonomie*, II), 1889 (T. B. Veblen, *The Science of Finance*, 1895). Tr. by Amano Tameyuki, 1899.

Fuchs, Carl Johannes. *Volkswirtschaftslehre*, 1901. Tr. by Zaimu Kyōkai (Association for Financial Affairs), 1911.

Golz, Theodor Alexander Ludwig Georg. *Vorlesungen über Agrarwesen und Agrarpolitik*, 1899. Tr. by Takaoka Kumao, 1901.

List, Friedrich. *Das nationale System der politischen Oekonomie*, 1841 (S. S. Lloyd, *The National System of Political Economy*, 1885). Tr. by Ōshima Sadamasu, 2 vols., 1889.

Roscher, Wilhelm Georg Friedrich. *Nationalökonomik des Ackerbaues und der verwandte Urproduktionen* (*System der Volkswirtschaft*, II), 1860 (2. Aufl.). Tr. by Seki Sumizō and Hiratsuka Teijirō, 5 vols., 1886–89; by Hiratsuka Teijirō, 1892.

———. *Nationalökonomik des Handels und Gewerbefleisses* (*System der Volkswirtschaft*, III), 1881. Tr. by Hirata Tōsuke et al., 2 vols., 1896.

Schönberg, Gustav Friedrich von. * 'Volkswirschaftslehre' (in *Handbuch der politischen Oekonomie*), 1882. Tr. by Yoda Masakoto, 1897; by Yoda Masakoto and Kusaka Chōjirō, 1902.

Schulze-Gävernitz, Gerhart von. *Der Grossbetrieb*, 1892. Tr. by Yamazaki Kakujirō, 1903.

Sombart, Werner. *Sozialismus und soziale Bewegung im neunzehnten Jahrhundert*, 1896. Tr. by Kanbe Masao, 1903.

Wagner, Adolf. *Lehr- und Handbuch der politschen Ökonomie*, Hauptabteilung 4: *Finanzwissenschaft*, 4 Bände, 1877–1901. Tr. by the Ministry of Agriculture and Trade, 1895; by Takimoto Yoshio, 1906.

———. *Ibid.* Hauptabteilung 1: *Grundlegung der politischen Oekonomie*, Tl. 1: 'Grundlagen der Volkswirtschaft', 1883. Tr. by Kawakami Hajime, 1906.

———. *Agrar- und Industriestaat. Eine Auseinandersetzung mit den Nationalsozialen und mit Professor L. Brentano über die Kehrseite des Industriestaats und zur Rechtfertigung agrarischen Zollschutzes*, 1901. Tr. by Seki Hajime and Fukuda Tokuzō, 1902.

United States

Adams, Henry Carter. *Public Debts*, 1887, 1893. Tr. by Ono Eijirō, 1896; by Amano Tameyuki, 1900.

Bowker, Richard Rogers. *Economics for the People*, 1886. Tr. by Nakagawa Kojūrō, 1890.

Burton, Theodore Elijah. *Financial Crises and Periods of Industrial and Commercial Depression*, 1902. Tr. by Konisho Yutaka, 1910.

Carey, Henry Charles. *Principles of Social Science*, 1858–59 (K. Mckean's ed., 1864). Tr. by Inukai Tsuyoshi, 4 vols., 1884–88.

Clark, John Bates. *The Philosophy of Wealth*, 1885. Tr. by Hamada Bunji, 1895.

Conant, Charles Arthur. * *A History of Modern Banks of Issue*, 1896. Tr. by Kotegawa Toyojirō, 1896.

Day, Clive. *A History of Commerce*, 1907. Tr. by Mikami Masaki, 1912.

Dunbar, Charles Franklin. *Chapters on the Theory and History of Banking*, 1891. 1901 (2nd ed.). Tr. by Horie Kiichi, 1903.

Ely, Richard Theodore. *French and German Socialism in Modern Times*, 1880. Tr. by Kawakami Kiyoshi, 1897.

———. *The Past and the Present of Political Economy*, 1884. Tr. by Sagane Fujirō, 1888.

———. *Taxation in American States and Cities*, 1888. Tr. by Ienaga Toyokichi and Shiozawa Masasada, 1893, 1894.

———. *An Introduction to Political Economy*, 1889. Tr. by Satō Shōsuke, 1891.

———. *Outlines of Economics*, 1893. Tr. by Yamauchi Masaaki, 2 vols., 1905.

———. *Socialism: An Examination of Its Nature, Its Strengths, and Its Weakness, with Suggestions for Social Reform*, 1894. Tr. by Abe Isoo, 1909.

———. 'A Decade of Economic Theory', in *The Annals of the American Academy of Political and Social Science*, 1900. Tr. by Sasaki Tamon, 1901.

———. *Studies in the Evolution of Industrial Society*, 1903. Tr. by Gotō Osahide, 1910.

Ely, Richard Theodore and George Ray Wicker. *Elementary Principles of Economics, together with a Short Sketch of Economic History*, 1904. Tr. by Ishizawa Kyūgorō, 1909.

Fetter, Frank Albert. * *The Principles of Economics, with Applications to Practical Problems*, 1904. Tr. by Kawakami Hajime, 1911.

Fisher, Irving. **The Nature of Capital and Income*, 1906 (Abridged: *The Rate of Interest*, 1907). Tr. by Kawakami Hajime, 1912.

George, Henry. *The Irish Land Question*, 1881. Tr. by Tsunoda Gōichirō, 1892.

———. *Social Problems*, 1883. Tr. by Eguchi Sansei, 1892; by Takahashi Ten'en, 1893.

Howard, Earl Dean. *The Cause and Extent of the Recent Industrial Progress of Germany*, n.d. (1907). Tr. by Hirata Hisashi, 1908.

Lunt, Edward Clark. *The Present Condition of Economic Science and the Demand for Radical Change in Its Method and Aim*, 1888. Tr. by Mochiji Rokusaburō, 1890.

Mason, Alfred Bishop and John Joseph Lalor. *The Primer of Political Economy*, 1875. Tr. by Makiyama Kōhei, 3 vols., 1877, 1879, 1882.

Perry, Arthur Latham. *Elements of Political Economy*, 1865, 1871 (7th ed.), 1876 (14th ed.). Tr. by * Ogata Tadashi and Mitsukuri Rinshō, 7 vols., 1869–70; by Kawamoto Seiichi, 8 vols., 1876–77, 1880.

Seligman, Edwin Robert Anderson. *Progressive Taxation in Theory and Practice*, 1894. Tr. by Kanbe Masao, 1901; by Mikami Masaki, 1910.

———. *The Economic Interpretation of History*, 1902. Tr. by Kawakami Hajime, 1905.

———. *Principles of Economics, with Special Reference to American Conditions*, 1905. Tr. by Ishikawa Yoshimasa, 1907; 2 vols., 1911–12.

———. * *The Shifting and Incidences of Taxation*, 1892. Tr. by Sekiguchi Ken'ichirō, 1909.

Walker, Francis Amasa. * *The Science of Wealth*, 1866. Tr. by Nagamine Hideki, 3 vols., 1874.

———. *Political Economy*, 1883. Tr. by Kurita Sōji and Yamamoto Junkichi, 1898.

———. * *A Brief Text-book of Political Economy*, 1885. Tr. by Sagane Fujirō, 1894.

Wayland, Francis. *The Elements of Political Economy*, 1837. Tr. by * Ga Hiroyuki, 4 vols., 1870–74; by * Obata Tokujirō, 1870; by Obata Tokujirō, 9 vols., 1871–77.

Wells, David Ames. *Recent Economic Changes and Their Effect on the Production and Distribution of Wealth and the Well-being of Society*, 1889. Tr. by Umekawa Seitarō, 1909.

Italy

Cossa, Luigi. *Primi elementi di economia politica*, 1875 (E. Moormeister, *Die ersten Elemente der Wirtschaftslehre*, 1879 (3 ed., 1896). Tr. by Nagai Naoyoshi, 1901.

———. *Primi elementi di scienza delle finanze*, 1876 (A. H. Gumlogsen, *Taxation: Its Principles and Methods*, 1888). Tr. by Machida Chūji, 1889; Tr. from 3rd ed. by K. Th. Eheberg, *Grundriss der Finanzwissenschaft*, 1888. Tr. by Terada Yūkichi and Hiratsuka Sadajirō, 1891; by Wadagaki Kenzō, 1902.

———. *Guida allo studio dell'economia politica*, 1876, 2 ed., 1878 (*Guide to the Study of Political Economy*, 1880). Tr. by Amano Tameyuki (General Part), 1889; by Sakatani Yoshio (Historical Part), 1887.

Loria, Achille. *La teoria economica della constituzione politica*, 1886 (*Les bases économiques de la constitution sociale*, 1893; *The Economic Foundations of Society*, 1899). Tr. by Hiranuma Yoshirō, 1909.

Belgium

Laveleye, Emile Louis Victor. *Eléments d'économie politique*, 1882 (A. W. Pollard, *Elements of Political Economy*, 1884). Tr. by Chinda Sutemi et al., 1888; by Makiyama Kōhei, 1894, 1897.

Austria

Maurus, Heinrich. *Über die Ursachen der herrschenden allgemeinen Teuerung*, 1875. Tr. by Matsumoto Gozō, 1881; by Tajiri Inajirō, 1882.

Philippovich, Eugen von. *Grundriss der politischen Ökonomie*, Bd. 1, 1893: *Allgemeine Volkswirtschaftslehre*, 1893, 1909. Tr. by Kiga Kanjū, 2 vols., 1903.

———. *Ibid.*, Bd. 2, Tl. 1: *Volkswirtschaftspolitik*, 1899. Tr. by Kiga Kanjū, 2 vols., 1906–8.

———. *Ibid.*, Bd. 2, Tl. 2: *Volkswirtschaftspolitik*, 1907. Tr. by Kiga Kanjū, 1910.

Holland

Pierson, Nikolaas Gerard. * *Principles of Economics* (*Leerboek der Staathuishoudkunde*, 1884–90). Tr. from German by A. A. Wotzel, 2 vols., 1902–12. Tr. by Kawakami Hajime and Kawada Shirō, 1911.

Vissering, Simon. 'Statistiek' (from his lectures, 1863–65). Tr. by Tsuda Mamichi, 1874.

Notes

Chapter 1: Historical Introduction

1. Later, after the Meiji Restoration of 1868, there were some groups of young Christians, including the Kumamoto Band, in Kyushu who tried to accelerate the process of modernization, but it was done under the influence of American Protestants.

2. The Shōgun was originally the supreme military commander under the emperor. However, as chief of the feudal lords he became a regent, ranking beside or above the emperor. Before the Meiji Restoration of 1868, the emperor had nothing to do with the feudal lords and their warriors in either civil or military affairs.

3. I cannot give a full list of those thinkers or anything like a full explanation of their thought. For this summary I relied on the works of Morimoto Jun'ichirō, especially his *Tokugawa Seiji Shisōshi Kenkyū* (History of Political Thought in the Tokugawa Period) (Tokyo, 1978). Incidentally, most Confucianist thinkers are often referred to by their pen names—Tōju, Banzan, etc.—rather than their family names.

4. E. Herbert Norman, 'Andō Shōeki and the Anatomy of Japanese Feudalism', *Transactions of the Asiatic Society of Japan*, 3rd series, Vol. II (1949).

5. Nishi's letter to Matsuoka Rinjirō. All the quotations from Nishi are taken from *Nishi Amane Zenshū* (The Complete Works of Nishi Amane), Ōkubo Toshiaki, ed., 4 vols. (Tokyo, 1960–81).

6. In a latter philosophical manuscript, Nishi mentioned a later edition (1857) of Lewes's book. T. R. H. Havens mentions an 1843 edition which does not exist (T. R. H. Havens, *Nishi Amane and Modern Japanese Thought* [Princeton, 1970], p. 44), misunderstanding the reference in Asō Yoshiteru's *Kinsei Nihon no Tetsugakushi* (History of Modern Japanese Philosophy) (Tokyo, 1942).

7. S. Vissering, *Redevoering over Vrijheid, Grondbeginsel der Staathuishoudkunde* (Leiden, 1850), pp. 17–18.

8. Irene Hasenberg Butter, *Academic Economics in Holland, 1800–1870* (The Hague, 1969), p. 122.

9. S. Vissering, *Handboek van Praktische Staathuishoudkunde*, Part 1 (Amsterdam, 1860); Part 2 (1861) (with continuous pagination). These two volumes were brought home by Nishi and Tsuda and later entered the libraries of Kaiseijo and Fukuzawa's private school (later Keiō University). The Library of Keiō University

also has Tsuda's notes on Vissering's lectures on political economy, but these consist of only the numbers of the sections of the book to which Tsuda was referred.

10. S. Vissering, *Handboek van Praktische Staathuishoudkunde*, Part 3, in two vols. (Amsterdam, 1862–65) (with continuous pagination), p. 429. This third part was sent to them by the author. There is a set of manuscript notes on political economy, perhaps in Vissering's own hand, in the library of Leiden University.

11. I. H. Butter, *op. cit.*, p. 126.

12. S. Vissering, *op. cit.*, pp. 407–8, 412.

13. According to Tsuda's notes, Vissering did not deal with the topic of rent. Boissonade also did not mention differential rent but dwelt on the métayage system, which was nearer to Japanese reality at that time.

14. After abolishing the feudal clan system, the Meiji government issued securities in compensation for feudal stipends. Unemployed warriors had to sell the securities below their face value to merchants or usurers who became the real creditors of the state. In spite of some formal resemblance, this was not the modern system of public debt discussed by Adam Smith.

15. A letter from Matsuki Kōan (later Terashima Munenori) dated August 21, 1862.

16. There was at that time no idea of universal male suffrage, which was to be realized only in 1928. Women's suffrage was left to the new constitution of 1946.

17. Thomas Hobbes revolutionized the concept of natural laws by making them the means of realizing the right of self-preservation as a natural right.

18. Sugiyama Chūhei, 'Fukuzawa Yukichi no keizai shisō' (The Economic Thought of Fukuzawa Yukichi), in *Kindai Nihon no Keizai Shisō* (Economic Thought in Modern Japan), Sugihara Shirō, ed. (Kyoto, 1971).

19. Letter to Kaneko Kentarō, dated August 21, 1892, in H. Spencer, *Life and Letters*, D. Duncan, ed., (London, 1908), p. 319.

20. In contrast to this, the translation of the second part of Hobbes's *Leviathan* was published in 1883 by the Ministry of Education. Among others, the chapters on the natural right of self-preservation were omitted. Apparently the translation was published to advocate the absolute power of sovereignty. An official preface was written by a renegade student of Fukuzawa, Baron Kuki, Under-Secretary of the ministry.

21. 'All legitimate government is republican'. *Du Contrat Social*, liv. 2, ch. 6, *Œuvres Complètes*, tom. 3 (Paris, 1964), p. 380.

22. For the information about these Japanese students, I am indebted to Inoue Takutoshi who traced them in some detail in his article 'Kindai Keizaigaku Dōnyū no Hitokoma' (An Essay on the Introduction of Modern Economics), *Osaka Shōgyō Daigaku Ronshū* (Transactions of Osaka Shōgyō University), no. 54 (1979).

23. For details on factory legislation, see pp. 109–16.

24. Marshall gave his inaugural lecture on January 24, 1885, and started his course on April 24. During the vacancy, Herbert Foxwell and John Neville Keynes taught political economy. Cf. Hashimoto Shōichi, 'A. Marshall no Cambridge e no Kikan' (A. Marshall's Return to Cambridge), *Keizai Ronshū* (The Economic Review of Kansai University) 33, no. 3 (September 1983).

25. See H. Sidgwick, 'Socialistic Interference', Ch. X, *The Elements of Politics*, 4th ed. (London, 1929).

26. R. E. Spiler, W. Thorp, T. H. Johnson, and H. S. Canby, eds. *Literary History of the United States* (New York, 1948), p. 144.

27. J. Dorfman, *The Economic Mind in American Civilization*, vol. 3 (New York, 1959), p. 164.

28. Furuya J., 'Baltimore no Nitobe Inazō' (Nitobe Inazō in Baltimore), *The Journal of International Studies* (Institute of International Relations, Sophia University, Tokyo) 15 (July 1985). I owe this referecnce to Sugihara Shirō.

29. Lecture notes taken by an unidentified student, in the library of Hokkaido

University (Northern Materials Room). Of course it is debatable how reliable they are.

30. Ely's *An Introduction to Political Economy* (1889) was translated by Satō Shōsuke in 1891.

31. His lecture notes are preserved in the University of Grenoble. The first two parts of his course of political economy were published in *Journal des Economistes*, vol. 3 (1872), pp. 7–20. Among his published works, which are mainly legal, the following two may be mentioned as economic: *La Fontaine Economiste* (Paris, 1872), and *Histoire de la Réserve Héréditaire et de son Influence Morale et Economique* (Paris, 1873).

32. Before the appointment of Boissonade, Maurice Block had been retained by the Japanese government to give lectures to Japanese missions and visitors in Paris. With his German background, Block recommended Prussia as a model for Japan. Cf. Yamamuro Shin'ichi, *Hōsei-Kanryō no Jidai* (The Age of Legal Bureaucrats) (Tokyo, 1984), pp. 22–32. Although Block published some work on economic subjects, his influence in Japan seems to have been confined to politics.

33. G. Boissonade, 'L'Economie Politique au Japon', *Supplément de L'Echo du Japon* (Jan. 13, 1876).

34. G. Boissonade, *Keizaigaku Kōgi* (Lectures on Economics), no. 3 (Tokyo, 1876), p. 32.

35. G. Boissonade, *Kodai Keizai Enkaku Ron* (Ancient Economic Development) (in Japanese translation) (1881?), p. 2.

36. In reply to a question by Inoue Kowashi, who helped Itō Hirobumi to draft the constitution, Roesler bluntly rejected the draft on civil law drawn up by Boissonade saying, 'No matter who wrote this, anyone who looks at it thinks, first, that the draft is too theoretically sophisticated to be understood by people and to be practised by courts, and secondly, that the draft . . . is based only on Franco-Roman laws and is of a purely academic character. Therefore, it is very doubtful whether it is really profitable for Japan or not.' Kokugakuin Daigaku Nihon Bunka Kenkyūjo, ed., *Kindai Nihon Hōseishi Shiryō, Roesler Tōgi*, vol. 6 (Tokyo, 1983), Answer 321.

37. K. Kautsky, *Erinnerungen und Erörterungen*, Benedikt Kautsky, ed., (The Hague, 1960), p. 238.

38. G. Nenning, 'Biographie C. Grünberg', *Indexband zu Archiv für die Geschichte des Sozialismus und der Arbeiterbewegung* (Zurich, 1973), p. 24.

39. Kanai Noburu, 'Stein Sensei no Isshūki' (First Anniversary of the Death of Prof. Stein), *Rikugō Zasshi* (Cosmos Journal) (December 1891).

40. *Lectures of Mr. Stein* (Tokyo, 1889). Stein said that the conflict of labour and capital belonged to the future in Japan and recommended no specific policy towards it.

41. The controversy as to whether or not there is any serious contradiction between *Moral Sentiments* and *The Wealth of Nations*, that is to say, between the principle of sympathy and that of self-love.

42. According to Johannes Siemes, the expression 'professorial socialist' (*Kathedersozialist*) was used first by H. B. Oppenheim to criticize Roesler. Siemes, *The Modernization of Japanese State and Roesler*, Japanese translation (1970), p. 20.

43. *Roesler Tōgi*, vol. 1 (Tokyo, 1979), Answer 36; vol. 7 (Tokyo, 1984), Answer 377.

44. *Ibid.*, vol. 4 (Tokyo, 1981), Answers 256, 257.

45. *Doitsugaku Kyōkai Zasshi* (Journal of the Society for German Studies) 21.

46. *Ibid.*

47. *Ibid.* 6. This is almost identical with *Roesler Tōgi*, Answer 256.

48. Sylvia D. Fries, 'Staatstheorie and American politics', *Journal of the History of Ideas* (July-September 1973).

49. If we take into consideration his critical attitude towards Christianity, it is not very difficult to answer the question, but in such a case as this the answer would have been a dangerous one for the government.

50. Obituary in *Tetsugaku Zasshi* (Journal of Philosophy) 260.

51. E.g., Karl Rathgen taught politics and administrative law from 1882 to 1890, Udo Eggert taught public finance from 1887 to 1893, Adolf Wenckstern taught public finance from 1893 to 1895, and Heinrich Waentig taught political economy and public finance from 1909 to 1913. Rathgen seems to have given no lectures on economic subjects while he was in Japan, but later he was appointed professor of political economy and colonial policy in the University of Hamburg, and perhaps he was the first foreign economist to write books on the Japanese economy, i.e., *Japaner und Volkswirtschaft und Staatshaushalt*, 2 vols. (Leipzig, 1891), and *Die Japaner und ihre wirtschaftliche Entwicklung* (Leipzig, 1905). Eggert wrote 'Japans Politik und Wirtschaft im Jahre 1890' for *Beilage zur allgemeine Zeitung* (Munich, 1891), nos. 184–85, 198–201, 222, 224, and 227. Cf. Adolf Freitag, *Die Japaner im Urteil der Meiji-Deutschen* (Tokyo & Leipzig, 1939).

52. As is mentioned in more detail in chapter III, Abe Isoo, lecturer or professor in social problems at Tokyo School of Special Studies and an early Japanese socialist, was one of the students who attended Learned's lectures in political economy at Dōshisha School.

53. Cf. Sumiya Etsuji, *Learned Hakase Den* (Life of Dr. Learned) (Tokyo, 1973).

Chapter 2: Fukuzawa Yukichi

1. *Fukuzawa Bunshū*, 1875; *Fukuzawa Yukichi Zenshū* (The Complete Works of Fukuzawa Yukichi: hereafter *FYZ*) (Tokyo, 1958–64), vol. 4, p. 477.

2. The author and the date of its impression have recently been identified as John Hill Burton and 1852 respectively by: Albert M. Craig, 'John Hill Burton and Fukuzawa Yukichi', *Kindai Nihon Kenkyū* (Journal for the Study of Modern Japan), Tokyo (Keiō Gijuku) I, 1985.

Seiyō Jijō was published in three volumes: the first was *Shohen* (1866), the second *Gaihen* (1868), and the third *Nihen* (1870). All three volumes are translations taken from various sources, and the *Gaihen* volume is mostly a translation of portions of the Chambers book.

3. The phrase repeated here, 'The Japanese Enlightenment', is taken from the title of the book by Carmen Blacker, *The Japanese Enlightenment: A Study of the Writings of Fukuzawa Yukichi* (Cambridge, 1964).

4. *FYZ*, vol. 1, p. 286.

5. Anon. (J. H. Burton), *Chambers's Educational Course: Political Economy*, 1873 ed. (London & Edinburgh, 1852), p. 13.

6. *Ibid.*, p. 12.

7. *Ibid.*, p. 63.

8. *Ibid.*, pp. 13–14.

9. *Ibid.*, p. 49.

10. *Ibid.*, p. 51.

11. *Ibid.*, p. 38.

12. *FYZ*, vol. 3, p. 29.

13. *FYZ*, vol. 1, p. 392.

14. *FYZ*, vol. 3, p. 42.

15. *Ibid.*, p. 44.

16. *Ibid.*, p. 92.

17. *Ibid.*, pp. 93–94.

18. *FYZ*, vol. 4, p. 19.

19. *Ibid.*, p. 207.

20. *FYZ*, vol. 3, p. 107.

21. *Ibid.*, p. 124.

22. *FYZ*, vol. 20, p. 53.
23. *FYZ*, vol. 3, p. 13.
24. *FYZ*, vol. 19, p. 388.
25. *FYZ*, vol. 3, pp. 37–38.
26. *Ibid.*, p. 81.
27. *Ibid.*, p. 111.
28. *Ibid.*, pp. 32–33.
29. *FYZ*, vol. 4, p. 603.
30. *Ibid.*
31. *Ibid.*, p. 608.
32. *Ibid.*, p. 661.
33. *FYZ*, vol. 5, p. 167.
34. *FYZ*, vol. 4, p. 262.
35. *Ibid.*, pp. 289–90.
36. *Ibid.*, p. 290.
37. *Ibid.*, p. 373.
38. For Taguchi's view on railways see: 'On Railways', *Tokyo Keizai Zasshi* (Tokyo Economist), nos. 58 and 60 (5 and 25 April 1881).
39. *FYZ*, vol. 5, pp. 176–77.
40. *Ibid.*, pp. 186–87.
41. *Ibid.*, p. 108.
42. *Ibid.*, p. 167.
43. *Ibid.*, p. 107.
44. *FYZ*, vol. 4, p. 191.
45. *Ibid.*, p. 190.
46. *FYZ*, vol. 20, p. 24.
47. *Ibid.*, p. 53.
48. *Ibid.*, pp. 123–24.
49. *FYZ*, vol. 19, pp. 539–43.
50. *FYZ*, vol. 20, pp. 146–49.
51. *FYZ*, vol. 4, pp. 193–94.
52. *FYZ*, vol. 19, pp. 706–7.
53. For Nishi's and Tsuda's defence of foreigners being allowed to stay and travel anywhere at will, see *Meiroku Zasshi* (Meiji Six Journal), nos. 23 and 24, and for Fukuzawa's refutation *ibid.*, no. 26 (1874–75); also *Minkan Zasshi* (Popular Magazine), no. 6 (1875). These are compiled in *Meiji Bunka Zenshū* (Works on Meiji Culture), revised edition (Tokyo, 1955–74), vol. 5, pp. 166–69, 171–72, 179–82, 291–95. For Fukuzawa's argument, see also *FYZ*, vol. 19, pp. 542–47.
54. *FYZ*, vol. 19, pp. 522–24.
55. *Ibid.*, pp. 521–22.
56. *Ibid.*, p. 518.
57. *Ibid.*
58. Francis Wayland, *The Elements of Political Economy* (New York, 1873), p. 186.
59. *FYZ*, vol. 19, p. 519.
60. *Ibid.*
61. *Ibid.*, pp. 520–21.
62. *FYZ*, vol. 4, p. 435.
63. *Ibid.*, p. 632.
64. *FYZ*, vol. 5, p. 107.
65. *FYZ*, vol. 4, p. 204.
66. *FYZ*, vol. 5, p. 108.
67. *FYZ*, vol. 3, p. 109.
68. *FYZ*, vol. 5, p. 111.
69. *Ibid.*, pp. 111–12.

70. *FYZ*, vol. 3, pp. 19–20.
71. *FYZ*, vol. 4, pp. 268–69.
72. *Ibid.*, p. 258.
73. *Ibid.*, pp. 272–73.
74. *Ibid.*, pp. 270–71.
75. *Ibid.*, pp. 333–34.
76. *Ibid.*, pp. 376–77.
77. *Ibid.*, p. 377.
78. *Ibid.*, p. 122.
79. *FYZ*, vol. 19, p. 634.
80. *FYZ*, vol. 4, p. 489.

Chapter 3: Nishi Amane and Tsuda Mamichi

1. *Nishi Amane Zenshū* (The Complete Works of Nishi Amane: hereafter NAZ) (Tokyo, 1960–81), vol. 1, p. 170.
2. *NAZ*. vol. 1, pp. 282–84.
3. *Ibid.*, vol. 1, pp. 514–15.
4. *Ibid.*, vol. 1, pp. 531–33.
5. *Ibid.*, vol. 4, p. 235.
6. *Ibid.*, vol. 4, pp. 247–50.
7. In Holland in Vissering's time, the political economy of Ellis, Whately, Bastiat, and others were read rather than Smith, Ricardo, and Malthus. See I. H. Butter, *Academic Economics in Holland 1800–1870* (The Hague, 1969), pp. 145–47.
8. *NAZ*, vol. 4, p. 251.
9. *Ibid.*, vol. 3, p. 254.
10. *Ibid.*, vol. 3, pp. 254–55.
11. *Ibid.*, vol. 3, pp. 257–58.
12. *Meiroku Zasshi* (Meiji Six Journal), no. 26 (1875). *Fukuzawa Yukichi Zenshū* (The Complete Works of Fukuzawa Yukichi), vol. 19, pp. 542–47.
13. *Meiroku Zasshi*, no. 8 (1874).
14. *Ibid.*, nos. 14, 25 (1874).
15. *Ibid.*, no. 35 (1875).
16. *Tokyo Gakushikaiin Zasshi* (The Journal of Tokyo Academy), vol. 15, no. 3 (1893); vol. 22, no. 5 (1900).
17. *Meiroku Zasshi*, no. 3 (1874).
18. *Ibid.*, nos. 4–6 (1874).
19. *Ibid.*, no. 6.
20. *Ibid.*, no. 20 (1874).
21. *Ibid.*, nos. 7, 10 (1874).
22. *Ibid.*, no. 24 (1875).
23. *Ibid.*, no. 30 (1875).
24. *Ibid.*, nos. 11, 12 (1874).
25. *Ibid.*, no. 9 (1874).
26. *Ibid.*, nos. 5, 6 (1874).
27. *Minkan Zasshi* (The Popular Magazine), no. 10 (1875).
28. *Meiroku Zasshi*, no. 13 (1874).
29. *Ibid.*, no. 34 (1875).

Chapter 4: The American Professors' Regime

Professor Horie Otoo, formerly at Tōkai University, and Emeritus Professor Masui Ken'ichi, Keiō University, have kindly made available their fathers' invaluable notebooks to me. I am indebted to Professor Nishikawa Shunsaku, Professor Sugiyama Chūhei, the late Professor S. G. Checkland, Mrs. E. O. A. Checkland, Dr. Tomita Masabumi, Emeritus Professor Kiyooka Eiichi, Mr. Higashida Masayoshi and his staff at Keiō for their helpful comments, corrections, and suggestions.

1. Keiō University, *Keiō Gijuku 100 Nenshi* (A Hundred Years of Keiō Gijuku) (*KGH*) (Tokyo, 1958), chapters 1 and 2. For the number of students, see pp. 304–7. The name 'Keiō' came from the name of the Japanese era which preceded Meiji. The term 'Gijuku' reflected the fact that its funding depended on private donations.

2. *KGH*, chapters 1 and 2.

3. Obata Jinzaburō, accompanying his former master Okudaira Masamichi of Nakatsu clan, went to America in 1871 and studied at Rutgers College, New Brunswick, where, sadly, he died in January 1873. His premature death was much regretted by Fukuzawa and his associates. See *Keiō Gijuku Gakuhō* (Keiō School Bulletin) (*KGG*), September 1920.

4. N. W. Senior, *Political Economy* (London, 1850); Keiō's copy is the 1863 edition. H. Fawcett, *Manual of Political Economy* (London, 1863); Keiō's copy is the 1874 edition. J. T. Champlin, *Lessons on Political Economy* (New York, 1868); Keiō's copy is the 1868 edition. F. Bowen, *American Political Economy* (New York, 1870); Keiō's copy is the 1870 edition. F. A. Walker, *Political Economy* (New York, 1883); Keiō's copy is dated 1888. F. Wayland, *Elements of Political Economy* (New York, 1837); Keiō's copy is the 1866 edition.

5. *KGH*, pp. 604–10.

6. *Ibid.*

7. The table of contents is as follows: 'On value', 'On wages', 'Rich and poor', 'On capital', 'On taxes', 'Letting and hiring', and 'Division of labour'.

8. *KGH*, p. 848. Nakayama Kazuyoshi, 'Historical Background of the New Materials', in *Birth of the University Section in Keiō Gijuku*, Kiyooka Eiichi ed. (Tokyo, 1983). Nishikawa Shunsaku, 'Seinansengo Infureki ni okeru Keiō Gijuku to Fukuzawa Yukichi' (Keiō Gijuku and Fukuzawa Yukichi in the Inflation of the post-Satsuma Rebellion), *Mita Shōgaku Kenkyū* (Mita Business Review) (*MSK*) (Keiō University), 1981.

9. University of Tokyo, *Tokyo Daigaku 100 Nenshi* (A Hundred Years of the University of Tokyo (Tokyo, 1984), vol. 2, pp. 59–61.

10. *Ibid.*, p. 60.

11. Knapp to Reynolds 12/2/1889, in Kiyooka, *op. cit.*

12. Knapp to Reynolds 12/2/1889, *ibid.*

13. Knapp to Eliot 14/2/1889, *ibid.*

14. Fukuzawa to Eliot -/4/1889, *ibid.*

15. In order to promote this extraordinary scheme, Keiō despatched a student to Harvard, but there were some unfortunate incidents which eventually destroyed the scheme. See Nishitani Yahei, *Ikeda Seihin Den* (Biography of Ikeda Seihin) (Tokyo, 1954).

16. See S. E. Morrison, *Three Centuries of Harvard* (Massachusetts, 1936), chapter XIV.

17. *Yuniterian* (Unitarian) first appeared in March 1890.

18. *KGH*, p. 872.

19. *Ibid.*, Supplement, pp. 202–4.

20. Nishikawa Shunsaku, 'G. Droppers no Rireki to Gyōseki' (The Career and Achievements of G. Droppers), *MSK*, 1983.

21. Nakajima Tetsuya, 'Aru Keizaigakusha no Omokage (A Portrait of an Economist), *KGG*, July 1900.

22. The author of *A Diplomat in Japan* (London, 1921).

23. G. Droppers, 'Some old Japanese economic theories in the light of modern theories', *Transactions of the Asiatic Society of Japan* (1896).

24. J. S. Mill, *Principles of Political Economy*, abridged by J. L. Laughlin (New York, 1892).

25. Droppers, *Topics and References of Modern Economic History* (Tokyo, 1890).

26. Droppers's 'Lecture Notebook', copied by Horie Kiichi, Keiō University Library.

27. *Ibid.*
28. *Ibid.*
29. J. S. Mill, *Principles of Political Economy* (London, 1891), p. 593.
30. *KGH*, Supplement, p. 211.
31. *Keiō Gijuku Daigaku Shinbun* (Keiō University Newspaper), 8/8/1951.
32. Till then, all the privately established universities in Japan were regarded by the Ministry of Education as professional schools with no right to grant degrees. Legally, only the national universities had the right to call themselves universities. Keiō University was simply a nomenclature assumed privately by Keiō, its students, and alumni.
33. *KGH*, pp. 1092–94, 1126–30.
34. For Droppers' later career, see Nishikawa, *Fukuzawa Yukichi to Sannin no Kōshintachi* (Fukuzawa Yukichi and Three Succeeding Economists) (Tokyo, 1985).
35. Eliot to Kamada 18/10/1898, in Kiyooka, *op. cit.*
36. Koizumi Shinzō, *Koizumi Shinzō Zenshū* (Collected Works) (Tokyo, 1970), vol. 20, p. 166. Takahashi Seiichirō, *Zuisō Keiō Gijuku* (Essays on Keiō Gijuku) (Tokyo, 1970), p. 173.
37. *KGG*, December 1900.
38. In the notebook, the lecture is entitled 'The History of Economic Thought'. The notebook also contains a note on 'The Bank and Industry', but it is not known for which lecture Vickers read this.
39. The original bibliography is as follows (sic): 'Ingram, J. K., *A History of Pol. Econ.*; Cossa, *An Introduction to the Study of Political Economy*; Bonar, *Philosophy and Political Econ.*; Price, L. L., *A Short History of Pol. Econ. in England from Adam Smith to A. Toynbee*; Cannan, *Theories of Production and Distribution*; Rambeau, J., *Histoire de Doctrines Economique*; Eisenhardt, *Geschicht und Nationalökonmie*; Oncken, *Geschicht und Nationalökonomie*; Palgrave, *Dictionary of Pol. Econ.*; Conrad, *Handwörterbuch und Staatswissenschaften*; Schönberg, *Handbuch der pol. Ök*; article by v. Scheel, pp. 85–118'. (Vickers's Notebook copied by Masui Yukio).
40. E. H. Vickers, 'Possible Services of Political Economy to Japan', *KGG*, May 1899.
41. *Ibid.*
42. *Ibid.*
43. Takahashi, *op. cit.*, pp. 370–71.
44. *KGG*, January 1900. *Who's Who in America* (Chicago, 1946). *Transactions of the Asiatic Society of Japan*, 1957, 1958.
45. *KGG*, October 1899.
46. *KGH*, pp. 1127–30.
47. *KGG*, October 1899.
48. *KGH*, p. 1126.
49. *KGG*, October 1900.
50. *Ibid.*
51. *Ibid.*
52. See note 23 above.
53. *KGG*, December 1900.
54. *Ibid.*
55. *Ibid.*, Takenouchi Osamu, 'Mitsui Ginkō ni okeru Keiō Gijuku Sotsugyōsei no Dōkō' (Keiō graduates in the management of the Mitsui Bank), *MSK*, August 1984.
56. *KGH*, Appendix, p. 137.
57. 1) H. C. Adams, *The Science of Finance* (New York). 2) H. A. Miller, *Money and Bimetallism* (New York, 1899). 3) D. F. Schloss, *Money and Industrial Revenueration* (*sic*), 3rd edition (London). 4) W. Sombert, *Socialism and the Social Movement in the 19th Century* (1898). 5) H. B. Russell, *International Monetary Con-*

ference (New York, 1898). 6) F. J. Ford, *The Rise and Growth of American Politics* (New York, 1898). 7) S. F. Van Oss, *Fenn on the Funds*, 16th edition (London, 1898). (*KGG*, May 1899.)

58. Nishikawa, *Fukuzawa Yukichi to Sannin no Kōshintachi*, pp. 127–57.

59. Vol. 5, no. 3, dated April 15, 1912.

Chapter 5: His Majesty's University

Sections 1 through 3 in this chapter were written by Hiroshi Mizuta and sections 4 through 7 by Mikihisa Suzuki.

1. Data taken from *Kyōiku Jiron* (Current Topics in Education), 317 and 318, February 1894. There is a discrepancy between the number of graduates given in this source and that given in the source for Table 1 p. 99, *Tokyo Teikoku Gakujutsu Taikan* (The Outlines of Sciences in Tokyo Imperial University) (Tokyo, 1942).

2. Kanbe Shōichi, 'Nihon Zaiseigakushi no Issetsu' (An Article on the History of the Science of Public Finance in Japan), *Tokyo Teikoku Daigaku Gakujutsu Taikan*, pp. 572–78.

3. For details of Kanai's work, see the books by his son-in-law Kawai Eijirō: *Kanai Noburu no Shōgai to Gakuseki* (Life and Works of Kanai Noburu) (Tokyo, 1939); and *Meiji Shisōshi no Ichidanmen* (One Aspect of the History of Thought in the Meiji Era) (Tokyo, 1941).

4. Nakagawa had been one of Fenollosa's students at Tokyo Imperial University.

5. Nakagawa Tsunejirō, *Keizai Jitsugaku Kōgi* (Lectures in Practical Political Economy) (Tokyo, 1886–87), pp. 10–11.

6. Ministry of Agriculture and Trade, *Ōbei Junkai Torishiribesho* (Report of the Study Tour through Europe and America) (Tokyo, 1888), pp. 5–6.

7. *Kokka Gakkai Zasshi* (Jan.–March, 1891).

8. Yokoyama Gennosuke, *Nihon no Kasō Shakai* (Lower Social Strata of Japan), 1889. The study *Shokkō Jijō* (The Conditions of Labourers), by Kuwata Kumazō and others and Yokoyama's book, despite his standpoint of the labourer in contrast to the government, are regarded together as the two classical works on labour problems in the Meiji era.

9. Katayama Sen (1859–1933) was the son of a substantial farmer. After working as an assistant teacher in a primary school, he went to the United States in 1884 and studied as a working student at Maryville, Grinnell, and Yale universities. Under the influence of Ely's articles in the *Christian Union* and his book *Social Aspects of Christianity* (1889), Katayama became a Christian socialist. He returned to Japan in 1906 and involved himself in labour and socialist movements. In 1914, frustrated by the government's suppression of the socialist movements, Katayama left Japan for the United States. He eventually settled in the Soviet Union, where he went on to hold a position in the Presidium of the Comintern until his death.

10. Rōdō Undō Shiryō Kankō Iinkai, ed., *Nihon Rōdō Undō Shiryō* (Documents for the Labour Movement in Japan), vol. 3 (Tokyo, 1968), p. 184.

11. The translations of the lectures given here are not verbatim. For the full texts, see *Shakaiseisaku Gakkai Shiryō Shūsei* (Collected Documents of the Society for Social Policy), ed. by the Society for Social Policy (Tokyo, 1977–78).

12. Cf. Kanai Noburu, *Shakai Keizaigaku* (Social Political Economics), 10th ed. (Tokyo, 1907), p. 448.

13. Abe Isoo, 'Shakai Seisaku Gakkaiin ni Tadasu' (A Question to the Members of the Society for Social Policy), *Tokyo Mainichi Shinbun* (Tokyo Daily News), (12 July 1901). Abe had been a student under Learned at Dōshisha University.

14. Taguchi Ukichi, 'Shakai Seisaku Gakkai no Benmeisho o Yomu' (On Reading the Apologia of the Society for Social Policy), *Tokyo Keizai Zasshi* (Tokyo Economist), no. 1090 (1901).

15. Apart from Marxist studies on the development of Japanese capitalism, and a few works in economic history, no serious academic work was done in economics

until the decade preceding World War II—for example, one of Fukuda's students translated Marshall's *Principles*, but dropped its mathematical appendix; and in spite of the German Historical School's criticism of Adam Smith for his individualism, there was no serious study of his *Theory of Moral Sentiments* until the late 1930s.

Chapter 6: Domestic Colonization

1. John M. Maki, *W. S. Clark: A Yankee in Hokkaido* (1975), Japanese translation published by Hokkaido University Press (1978).

2. *First (to Sixth) Report of the Sapporo Agricultural College* (Sapporo, 1877–88).

3. The manuscript notes have no date, but it was presumably taken from the course of 1895 since there was a reference to Lorenz von Stein as having 'died five years ago'.

4. Sapporo-shi Kyōiku Iinkai (Board of Education of Sapporo City), ed., *Nitobe Inazō* (1985).

5. These two letters are dated January 7, 1890, and November 5, 1891, respectively. They are quoted here by courtesy of the State Historical Society of Wisconsin.

6. In 1883, that is to say, the year when Satō entered Johns Hopkins, Ely attended a lecture by Johann Most, a rival of Marx, who had been hounded out of Europe. In his paper entitled 'Herr Most in Baltimore' (March 2, 1882), Ely said: 'I considered it of weight that I should hear for myself an exposition of the ideas of a man who was conducting an agitation which aimed at the abolition of existing social institutions. . . . his [Most's] mind has become diseased. He is fanatical and bloodthirsty. . . . [But] the socialism of a man like Wagner . . . differs from that of Most as black and white. Indeed, a man of the stamp of Most rejects the professorial socialist from the start as timid and reactionary'. Rejecting Most, Ely sympathized with Wagner. Cf. B. G. Rader, *The Academic Mind and Reform: The Influence of Richard T. Ely in American Life* (Lexington, Kentucky, 1966), Reprint ed., p. 23.

Chapter 7: Pioneer Economics Department

Facts and figures related to the history of Senshū School are mostly gathered from *Senshū Daigaku Hyakunenshi* (A Hundred Years of Senshū University), 2 vols. (1981), and other relevant sources kept in the Nenshi Shiryōka (The Chronicle Section) of Senshū University. I am indebted to the kind help given by Ms. Fuse Junko and her colleagues in the section. Information concerned mainly with the textbooks and translations collected by the late Professor Morishita Sumio has also been supplied to me by Professor Sugihara Shirō.

1. An independent Faculty of Political Economy was not established in the University of Tokyo until 1919.

2. The trend away from the Anglo-French school to the German school can also be noted in the Keiō School. Professor Howard Vickers, who had a strong German background, stressed the need for historical studies and introduced a new subject, 'Social Problems'.

3. See *Tokyo Teikoku Daigaku 50 Nenshi* (Fifty Years of Tokyo Imperial University) (1932), vol. 2, p. 1095, where the origin of the University Library is related to this practice.

4. When the Economics Department was first instituted within the Law College (later Faculty) of the University of Tokyo in 1909, the Commercial Department was also established alongside it. This parallels the transfer of William Ashley from the Chair of Economic History to the first Chair of Commerce at Birmingham, England, which also took place about this time.

Chapter 8: In the Schools of Law

1. *Godai Hōritsu Gakkō Tōronkai Rengō Zasshi* (Journal of the Joint Meetings of the Five Law Schools).

2. Fukui Atsushi, 'Ōmeisha to Shiritsu Hōritsu Gakkō' (Ōmeisha and Private Law Schools), *Meiji Daigakushi Kiyō* (Transactions of the History of Meiji University), 4 (March 1984).

3. In 1888 'The regulations for Supervising private law schools' were revised as 'the regulations for specially permitted schools', allowing the law department of Tokyo School of French and the department of specialized studies of the school attached to the Society for German Studies to be added to those five private law schools which had already become specially permitted schools. The department of law of Tokyo School of French was amalgamated the following year with Tokyo Law School to become the Franco-Japanese Law School. The school attached to the Society for German Studies was founded in 1883 by the society, which had been established in 1881 and was supported by the government from the very beginning.

4. For the history of the school I have mainly depended on *Hōsei Daigaku 100 Nenshi* (A Hundred Years of Hōsei University) (Tokyo, 1982).

5. *Hōritsu Zasshi* (Law Journal), 133 (September 1880).

6. *Hōsei Daigakushi Shiryōshū* (Collection of Documents for the History of Hōsei University), vol. 1, (Tokyo, 1978), p. 17.

7. For the history of Meiji Law School I have mainly depended on *Meiji Hōritsu Gakkō ni Okeru Hōgaku to Hōgaku Kyōiku* (Law and Legal Education in Meiji Law School), vol. 1, (Tokyo, 1986).

8. Saionji, who graduated from the Sorbonne in 1874, had been deeply influenced by Western liberalism during his study abroad. In later years he was to play a prominent part, almost a 'king-maker' role, in pre-war Japanese politics.

9. See Fukui, *op. cit.*

10. For the history of the school I have mainly depended on *Zusetsu Chūō Daigaku 1885–1985* (Illustrated Chūō University 1885–1985) (Tokyo, 1985); *Chūō Daigaku 100 Nenshi Henshū Nyūsu* (The Editorial News of a Hundred Years of Chūō University), no. 1, 1982; *Chūō Daigakushi Shiryōshū* (Collection of Documents for the History of Chūō University), no. 1 (Tokyo, 1984).

11. Numa Masaya, 'Igirisu Hōritsu Gakkō no Setsuritsu tō ni Kansuru Shojijō' (Circumstances Leading to the Establishment of the School of English Law) (Collection of Documents for the History of Chūō University), no. 1 (Tokyo, 1984).

12. Chūō had been at variance with Tokyo Senmon Gakkō (Waseda) for some time but was soon in cooperation as a member of those five private law schools. For example, it cooperated in holding the debate meeting in 1888 mentioned at the beginning of this chapter, and in 1890, together with the three other private law schools, formed a united front against the Nihon Law School, which was then about to emerge with the support of the government. At the time of the so-called Law Code Dispute since 1890, the school defended the postponement of the enforcement of the civil law against the Franco-Japanese Law School and Meiji Law School which had called for the immediate enforcement. In this case, too, the school was in line with the government and the University of Tokyo.

13. This seems to be for the reason that their lectures were not for the regular-course students and that they wrote only the textbooks for the extramural-course students.

14. Hijikata Naobumi, 'Kengakuseishin o Megutte, Masujima Rokuichirō no Baai' (On the Spirit of the Founding of the School: The Case of Masujima Rokuichirō), *Chūō Daigaku 100 Nenshi Henshū Nyūsu* (Editorial News of a Hundred Years of Chūō University), no. 3 (1983).

Chapter 9: 'Captain of Industry'

1. Thomas Carlyle, *Past and Present*, Book IV, Chap. IV, (London, 1843).

2. Mori Arinori, *Mori Arinori Zenshū* (The Complete Works of Mori Arinori), vol. 3 (Tokyo, 1972), p. 272.

3. *Ibid.*, p. 334.

4. *Ibid.*, p. 386.
5. *Ibid.*, pp. 336–37.
6. *Ibid.*, p. 337–38.
7. *Ibid.*, p. 334.
8. *Ibid.*, p. 352.
9. *Ibid.*, pp. 359–60.
10. *Ibid.*, pp. 363–65.
11. *Ibid.*, p. 17.
12. Fukuzawa Yukichi, *Fukuzawa Yukichi Zenshū* (The Complete Works of Fukuzawa Yukichi), vol. 4 (Tokyo, 1959), pp. 123–25.
13. *Mori Arinori Zenshū*, vol. 1, p. 323.
14. 'Shōhō Kōshūjo Yagaku Ryakusoku' (Simplified Rules of the Evening Course of the Commercial Training School), in *Zusetsu Keiō Gijuku 100 Nen Shōshi 1858–1958* (Illustrated Short History of Keiō University) (Tokyo, 1958), n.p. (p. 37).
15. 'Shōhō Kōshūjo Ryakusoku' (Simplified Rules of the Commercial Training School), original document kept in Tōkyōto Kōbunshokan (Tokyo Prefectural Archives).
16. *Hitotsubashi Daigaku Gakuseishi Shiryō* (The Institutional History of Hitotsubashi University, Selected Documents), vol. 2 (Tokyo, 1982), Introduction; *Hitotsubashi Daigaku 100 Nenshi* (A Hundred Years of Hitotsubashi University) (Tokyo, 1975), chaps. 3 and 4.
17. L. C. Marshall, ed., *The Collegiate School of Business* (Chicago, 1928); W. J. Ashley, 'The Universities and Commercial Education', *North American Review* (Jan. 1903).
18. *Hitotsubashi Daigaku 100 Nenshi*, chap. 3; (British Foreign Office) *Diplomatic and Consular Reports*: 'Report on Commercial Education in Japan' (London, 1899); Sugiyama Kazuo, 'Shōgyō Kyōiku no Hatten to Yano Jirō (The Development of Commercial Education and Yano Jirō), *Seikei Daigaku Keizaigakubu Ronshū* (Seikei University Journal of the Faculty of Economics) (Oct. 1972).
19. *Nihon Kindai Kyōiku 100 Nenshi* (A Hundred Years of Modern Education in Japan), vol. 9, *Sangyō Kyōiku* (Industrial Education) (Tokyo, 1973), pp. 339–402.
20. Sano Zensaku, *Nihon Shōgyō Kyōiku 50 Nenshi* (Fifty Years of Commercial Education in Japan) (Tokyo, 1925), pp. 14, 58.
21. William Layton's article about higher commercial education in Belgium, translated by Ishikawa Bungo as 'Antwerp-fu no Shōgyō Gakkō' in *Kōtō Shōgyō Gakkō Dōsōkai Kaishi* (Magazine of the Alumni Association of the Higher Commercial School), (December 25, 1899).
22. *Hitotsubashi Daigaku Gakuseishi Shiryō*, vol. 1, pp. 28–29 and n. 65; *Mizushima Tetsuya Sensei Den* (The Life of Mizushima Tetsuya) (Tokyo, 1939), pp. 76–79.
23. *Hitotsubashi Daigaku 100 Nenshi*, pp. 143–44; *Nihon Kindai Kyōiku 100 Nenshi*, pp. 413–14; Sano, *op. cit.*, pp. 58–59.
24. *Hitotsubashi Daigaku Gakuseishi Shiryō*, vol. 2, pp. 9–15, 29–30.
25. Kawasaki Misao, 'Wasureraretа Saisho no Berugii Oyatoi Kyōshi' (The First Belgian Teacher in Japan, Now Forgotten), *Josuikai Kaihō* (The Transactions of Josuikai) (Nov. 1970).
26. *Dainihon Kyōikukai Zasshi* (The Journal of the Educational Society of Japan) (May 16, 1887), pp. 191–99.
27. *Hitotsubashi Daigaku Gakuseishi Shiryō*, vol. 2, pp. 124–26.
28. Kawasaki, *op. cit.* See also *Josuikai Kaihō* (April 1931).
29. See Kawasaki, *op. cit.*, pp. 39–40; Itani Zen'ichi, 'Berugii Anvers Shōka Daigaku to Nihon' (The Institut Supérieur de Commerce d'Anvers in Belgium and Japan), *Waseda Shōgaku* (Waseda Journal of the Faculty of Commerce) (March 1974), pp. 20–26.

30. Iida Hatarō, 'Berugii Shōgyō Gakkō no Hanashi' (On the Commercial School in Belgium), *Kōtō Shōgyō Gakkō Gakuyūkai Zasshi* (The Journal of the Friends of the Higher Commercial School) (April 30, 1891), p. 12; an article by Senuma Shigeki on Iida in *Ikkyō Shinbun* (Hitotsubashi News) (June 15, 1965).

31. *Diplomatic and Consular Reports*, p. 3; Iida, *op. cit.* Iida, 'Ryōjiron' (On the Consul), *Kōtō Shōgyō Gakkō Gakuyūkai Zasshi*, (August 18, 1894), pp. 25–40.

32. Iida, 'Berugii Shōgyō Gakkō no Hanashi', p. 19; *Diplomatic and Consular Reports*, p. 4.

33. *Murase Haruo Hakushi no Omoide* (Recollections of Dr. Murase Haruo) (Tokyo, 1964), pp. 3–5.

34. Itani, *op. cit.*, p. 20. See also Itani's article in *Murase Haruo Hakushi no Omoide*, pp. 118–21.

35. See *Murase Haruo Hakushi no Omoide.*

36. *Hitotsubashi 50 Nenshi* (Fifty Years of Hitotsubashi) (Tokyo 1925), pp. 22–23; *Hitotsubashi Daigaku Gakuseishi Shiryō*, vol. 2, Introduction, pp. 10–11.

37. *Hitotsubashi 50 Nenshi*, pp. 32–33.

38. *Koyama Kenzō Den (The Life of Koyama Kenzō)* (Osaka, 1930), pp. 234–44, 278–84.

39. 'Summary of the addresses delivered at the graduating exercises by the director, July 1896 and 1897', *Calendar of the Higher Commercial School for the Year 1896–97 and 1897–98* (Tokyo, 1897–98), pp. 60–61, 74–75.

40. *Shōgyō Sekai* (Commercial World), vol. 1, no. 1, (November 3, 1898).

41. *Koyama Kenzō Den*, pp. 285–87.

42. Koyama Kenzō, 'Shōkōgyōsha no Tokugi' (The Morals of Merchants and Maufacturers), *Kokumin no Tomo* (The Friend of the Nation), vol. 18, no. 284, (1896), pp. 451–53; 'Summary of Addresses, July 1896', *op. cit.*, p. 61.

43. *Ibid.*, pp. 67–71, 80–82.

44. Sano, *op. cit.*, pp. 101–2.

45. Cf. *Calendar of the Higher Commercial School* for each year.

46. Fukuda Tokuzō, 'Ōbei Shōgyō Kyōiku Kinkyō' (The Recent Position of Commercial Education in Europe and America), *Kōtō Shōgyō Gakkō Dōsōkai Kaishi* (December 27, 1898).

47. Cf. articles by Fukuda, Seki, Ishikawa and others in *Kōtō Shōgyō Gakkō Dōsōkai Kaishi* and *Shōgyō Sekai.*

48. R. Beigel, *Der Kampf um die Handelshochschule* (Leipzig, 1898), SS. 31–34; *Koyama Kenzō Den*, pp. 291–94.

49. Beigel, *op. cit.*, SS. 31–34.

50. Fukuda, *op. cit.*

51. F. Redlich, 'Academic Education for Business: Its Development and Contribution of Ignaz Jastrow (1856–1937)', *Business History Review*, vol. 31, p. 57; Fukuda, *op. cit.*

52. 'Recent developments in higher commercial education in Germany' in Board of Education, *Special Reports on Educational Subjects*, vol. 9 (London, 1902), pp. 494–99; F. Redlich, *op. cit.*, pp. 48–67.

53. *Ibid.*, pp. 502–4.

54. F. Redlich, *op. cit.*, pp. 52–53.

55. Michael Sanderson, 'The arts of commerce 1890–1914', in his *The Universities and British Industry 1850–1970* (London, 1972), pp. 184–213.

56. Seki Hajime, *Ōbei Shōgyō Kyōiku no Gaikyō* (The General Position of Commercial Education in Europe and America) (Tokyo, 1899); London Country Council, Technical Education Board, *Report of the Special Sub-Committee on Commerical Education* (London, 1899).

57. Board of Education, *op. cit.*, vol. 8 (London, 1902), pp. 555–67.

58. E. J. Blockhuys, 'To the Editor of *Shōgyō Sekai*, October 28, 1898', *Shōgyō Sekai* (December 5, 1898).

59. *Kōtō Shōgyō Gakkō Dōsōkai Kaishi* (April 30, 1899), pp. 40–43.
60. *Ibid.*, pp. 4–8, 21–25, 39.
61. 'Bankoku Shōgyō Kyōiku Shōreikai no Setsuritsu' (The Establishment of the International Society for the Encouragement of Commercial Education), *ibid.*, (April 30, 1901).
62. *Ibid.* (June 30, 1901), pp. 15–22.
63. *Ibid.* (April 30, 1901); *Hitotsubashi 50 Nenshi*, pp. 48–51.
64. *Hitotsubashi 50 Nenshi*, p. 51; 'Hitotsubashi 40 Nenshi' (Forty Years of Hitotsubashi) (1914), *Hitotsubashi Daigaku Gakuseishi Shiryō*, vol. 4 (Tokyo, 1983), pp. 186–87.

Chapter 10: For Diffusing Economic Knowledge

1. *Waseda Daigaku 80 Nenshi* (Eighty Years of Waseda University) (Tokyo, 1962), p. 34.
2. *Waseda University Bulletin, 1977–1979* (Tokyo), p. 1.
3. *Nihon Kindai Kyōiku 100 Nenshi* (A Hundred Years of Modern Education in Japan), vol. 3 (Tokyo, 1974), p. 1269. It was in 1883 that the University of Tokyo decided to use the native language in its classes. See *Tokyo Daigaku Keizaigakubu 50 Nenshi* (Fifty Years of the Faculty of Economics at the University of Tokyo) (Tokyo, 1976), p. 1195.
4. *Waseda Daigaku 100 Nenshi* (A Hundred Years of Waseda University), vol. 1 (Tokyo, 1978), p. 464.
5. See Sugihara Shirō, *Seiō Keizaigaku to Kindai Nihon* (Western Political Economy and Modern Japan) (Tokyo, 1972), pp. 58–59.
6. Takata Sanae, 'Daigaku toshite no Seijigaku Keizaigaku no Kako o Kangamite Seijikeizai Gakubu no Shimei ni Oyobu' (On the Duty of the Faculty of Political Science and Economics from the Viewpoint of Historical Perspective on Political Science and Political Economy), *Waseda Seiji-Keizaigaku Zasshi* (The Waseda Journal of Political Science and Economics), no. 1 (1925), p. 12.
7. Takata, *op. cit.*, p. 10.
8. *Waseda University Bulletin, 1977–1979*, p. 166. See also *Tokyo Senmon Gakkō Kōsoku Gakkahaitō Shiryō* (School Regulations and Curricula at Tokyo School of Special Studies) (Tokyo, 1978), pp. 14–19.
9. *Waseda University: Its History, Aims and Regulations* (Tokyo, 1936), p. 4.
10. *Waseda Daigaku 100 Nenshi*, vol. 1, p. 494.
11. *Tokyo Senmon Gakkō Kōsoku Gakkahaitō Shiryō*, Document, #1, and pp. 4–5.
12. *Ibid.*, Documents #6 and #7.
13. Teachers of Political Economy at Tokyo School of Special Studies, 1882–97

Name (Term in post)	Main subjects taught
Amano Tameyuki (1882–1917)	principles of political economy, banking, exchange, national debt, international trade, commercial policy, U.S. taxation, economic history, foreign exchange, methods in economic studies, money, public finance, fiscal budget, banking business, applied political economy
Ono Azusa (1882–1886)	public finance
Takata Sanae (1882–?)	money, taxation
Kure Ayatoshi (1884–94)	statistics, principles of statistics
Matsuzaki Kuranosuke (1888–92/1896–?)	public finance, taxation, money
Kiuchi Jūshirō (1888–89)	historical political economy
Aruga Nagabumi (1889?–92)	historical political economy
Soeda Juichi (1888–91)	applied political economy, fiscal budget

Inoue Shinkurō (1890–98)	history of political economy, money, applied political economy, public finance, international trade
Tokonami Takejirō (1892)	taxation, public finance
Tsuchiko Kinshirō (1892–95/1897–99)	exchange, banking
Kotegawa Toyojirō (1895–97)	money
Uchida Ginzō (1898–1903?)	economic history, history of political economy
Takahashi Masaru? (1888–89)	agricultural political economy
Sawayanagi Masatarō (1890–91)	international trade

Source: *Waseda Daigaku 100 Nenshi*, vol. 1, table 22, pp. 1030–41.

14. Matsumoto Yoshitaka, 'Tokyo Senmon Gakkō de Oshieta 16 nin no Gaikokujin Kōshitachi' (Sixteen Foreign Lecturers Who Taught at Tokyo School of Special Studies), *Waseda Daigakushi Kiyō* (Transactions of the Editorial Department of the University History, Waseda), vol. 10, no. 14 (1977), pp. 92–93.

15. *Waseda Daigaku 100 Nenshi*, vol. 1, pp. 479–80. See also *Tokyo Senmon Gakkō Kōsoku Gakkahaitō Shiryō*, pp. 99–100.

16. *Tokyo Senmon Gakkō Kōsoku Gakkahaitō Shiryō*, Document #59 (pp. 218–19).

17. J. S. Mill, *Principles of Political Economy with Some of Their Applications to Social Philosophy*, 1st ed., 1848; *Collected Works of John Stuart Mill*, vol. 2, J. M. Robson, ed. (Toronto, 1965), p. 3.

18. *Tokyo Senmon Gakkō Kōsoku Gakkahaitō Shiryō*, Documents #14, 17, 53.

19. *Ibid.*, Document #22 and *Catalog of the Waseda-Daigaku Toshokwan* (the Library at Waseda University), 'Economics' (Tokyo, 1903), pp. 89–115. We cannot exactly identify the title listed as Roscher's Public Finance in English in the curriculum. It seems to correspond to Volumes I–II (public finance) of his *System der Volkswirtschaft* (1854–94).

20. Jevons's work, which appears in Amano's *Keizai Genron* (Theory of Political Economy), published in 1886, is entitled *The Fundamental Theory of Political Economy*. This seems, however, to be a transcription error, because Jevons himself did not publish anything with that title. Cf. Inoue Takutoshi, 'Bibliographical list of W. Stanley Jevons' writings, etc.', *Keizaigaku Ronkyū* (The Journal of Economics of Kwansei Gakuin University) 39, no. 4, 1986.

21. *Tokyo Senmon Gakkō Nenpō: Meiji 15 Nendo* (Annual Bulletin of Tokyo School of Special Studies in the Academic Year of 1882–83), Reprint (Tokyo, 1982), p. 12.

22. Sugihara, *op. cit.*, p. 171 n. 4, and Asakawa Eijirō and Nishida Taketoshi, *Amano Tameyuki* (Tokyo, 1950), pp. 68–69, 273. Amano seems to have taken charge of instruction of commercial policy, accounting, national debt, and exchange, too. See *Waseda Daigaku 100 Nenshi*, vol. 1, p. 608.

23. Hiranuma Yoshirō was a professor of economic history, the third president of the university (1918–21), and greatly contributed to the development of the Faculty of Commerce. See Irimajiri Yoshinaga, 'Hiranuma Yoshirō: Jiin Monzen Machi no Kenkyū no Kaitaku' (Hiranuma Yoshirō: a Pioneer in Studying the Temple Towns), in *Kindai Nihon no Shakaikagaku to Waseda Daigaku* (The Social Sciences in Modern Japan and Waseda University), and Hori Tsuneo, *Meiji Keizaishisōshi* (History of Economic Thought in the Meiji Era) (Tokyo, 1975), pp. 468–78.

24. *Waseda Daigaku 100 Nenshi*, vol. 1, pp. 579–81.

25. *Ibid.*, vol. 1, pp. 930–33.

26. Sugihara Shirō, *Nihon Keizai Shisōshi Ronshū* (Collected Papers on the History of Economic Thought in Japan) (Tokyo, 1980), p. 89.

27. E. Stuart Kirby, 'The Reception of Western Economics in the Orient', *The Quarterly Journal of Economics*, vol. LXVI, no. 3, 1952, p. 410.

28. Asakawa and Nishida, *op. cit.*, pp. 96–97.

29. Amano Tameyuki, *Keizai Genron* (Theory of Political Economy), 1st ed. (Tokyo, 1886), p. 17.

30. Sugihara Shirō, 'Amano Tameyuki (1861–1938)', *Nihon no Ekonomisuto* (Economists in Japan) (Tokyo, 1984), p. 45.

31. Amano Tameyuki, *Keizaisakuron* (Essays on Economic Policies) (Tokyo, 1910), p. 916.

32. Hirata Tomitarō, 'Amano Tameyuki: Kotengakuha Keizaigaku no Senkusha' (Amano Tameyuki: A Pioneer of the Classical School of Political Economy), *Kindai Nihon no Shakaikagaku to Waseda Daigaku*, p. 147.

33. See Sugihara Shirō, 'Amano Tameyuki to *Nihon Rizai Zasshi*' (Amano Tameyuki and the Japan Economist), *Seiō Keizaigaku to Kindai Nihon*, pp. 164–79.

34. *Ibid.*, pp. 136–37. See also Hori, *op. cit.*, chaps. 2–5.

35. Abe Isoo, *Shakaimondai Kaishakuhō* (Methods for the Interpretation of the Social Problem) (Tokyo, 1901), pp. 5–6.

36. *Ibid.* p. 355.

37. Kubota Akiteru, 'Waseda Daigaku to Keizaigaku' (Waseda University and Economics), *Kindai Nihon no Shakaikagaku to Waseda Daigaku*, p. 131.

38. Kubota Akiteru, 'Shiozawa Masasada,' in *ibid.*, p. 173.

39. *Waseda University: A Photographic History of 100 Years (1882–1982)* (Tokyo, 1982), p. 22.

40. Sugihara, *Nihon no Ekonomisuto*, pp. 133–34.

Chapter 11: In the 'Commercial Metropolis' Osaka

1. Ōshima Kiyoshi, Katō Toshihiko, Ōuchi Tsutomu, *Meiji Shoki no Kigyōka* (The Entrepreneur in the Early Meiji Era) (Tokyo, 1976), pp. 291, 334; Miyamoto Mataji, *Godai Tomoatsu Den* (The Life of Godai Tomoatsu) (Tokyo, 1980), p. 529.

2. Miyamoto, *op. cit.*, pp. 542–64; Tatsuki Mariko, 'Kōgyōka no Riidashippu Godai Tomoatsu' (Leadership in Industrialization: Godai Tomoatsu), in Yui Tsunehiko ed., *Kōgyōka to Kigyōsha Katsudō* (Industrialization and Entrepreneurship) (Tokyo, 1976), pp. 56–58; Ōshima, Katō, Ōuchi, *op. cit.*, p. 355.

3. Miyamoto, *op. cit.*, pp. 556–57.

4. Nakaoka Tetsurō, 'Nihon ni okeru Kōgyōka-shisō no Keisei to Godai Tomoatsu' (The Formation of Ideas on Industrialization in Japan and Godai Tomoatsu), in *Osaka no Rekishi* (The History of Osaka) 18 (1986): 17.

5. Inuzuka Takaaki, *Satsuma-han Eikoku Ryūgakusei* (Satsuma Students to England) (Tokyo, 1974), chaps. 2, 3, 4.

6. Miyamoto, *op. cit.*, pp. 43–56, p. 547. See also *The Times*, Aug. 2, 1865.

7. Kanno Watarō, 'Meiji Shonen Osaka no Suitai' (The Decline of Osaka in the Beginning of the Meiji Era), *Meiji Taishō Osaka Shishi Kiyō* (Bulletin of the History of Osaka City in the Meiji and Taishō Eras) 34 (1931): 2.

8. *Ibid.*, pp. 3–6. Miyamoto Mataji, 'Meiji Ishin to Osaka' (The Meiji Restoration and Osaka), in Miyamoto Mataji ed., *Kamigata no Kenkyū* (Studies in the Kyoto-Osaka Area), vol. 1. (Osaka, 1972), pp. 279–80, 292–96, 301–6.

9. Miyamoto, *Godai Tomoatsu Den*, p. 552.

10. *Ibid.*, pp. 331–41, 382–83. See also *Osaka Shōkōkaigisho 75 Nenshi* (75 Years of Osaka Chamber of Commerce) (Osaka, 1955), pp. 1–10.

11. *Osaka Shōkōkaigisho 75 Nenshi*, pp. 390–95; Miyamoto Mataji, 'Osaka ni okeru Shōgyō Keizai Kyōiku Kotohajime' (The Beginnings of Commercial and Economic Education in Osaka), in *Osaka Daigakushi Kiyō* (Bulletin of the History of Osaka University) 1 (1981): 20–24.

12. *Nihon Kindai Kyōiku 100 Nenshi* (A Hundred Years of Modern Education in Japan), vol. 9, 'Sangyō Kyōiku' (Industrial Education) (Tokyo, 1973), pp. 377–82.

13. Mōri Toshihiko, 'Shiritsu Osaka Shōgyō Kōshūjo no Tanjō to Godai To-

moatsu' (The Birth of the Private Osaka Commercial Training School and Godai Tomoatsu), in *Osaka no Rekishi* (History of Osaka) 18 (1986): 50–52.

14. *Osaka Shōka Daigaku 60 Nenshi* (Sixty Years of Osaka University of Commerce) (Osaka, 1944), pp. 1–7. Katō's article is reprinted therein, pp. 557–61.

15. Mōri, *op. cit.*, pp. 52–56.

16. *Osaka Shōka Daigaku 60 Nenshi*, pp. 7–11; Miyamoto Mataji, *Osaka Keizaijin to Bunka* (Osaka Businessmen and Culture) (Tokyo, 1983), pp. 86–90; *Kirihara Sutezō Ō Tsuikairoku* (Memoirs of Old Kirihara Sutezō) (Osaka, 1930), pp. 18–23.

17. Kataoka Nobuyuki, 'Meiji Shoki no Chūtō Shōgyō Kyōiku oyobi Keiō Gijuku' (Middle-Rank Commercial Education in the Early Meiji Era and Keiō School), *Keizai Keiei Ronshū* (Journal of Economic and Management Studies, Ryūkoku University) 24, no. 1 (1984): 44–46.

18. *Osaka Shōgyō Kōshūjo Hikitsugi Mokurokusho* (The List of Things Transferred from Osaka Commercial Training School), dated August 11, 1881, in *Osaka Shōka Daigaku 60 Nenshi*, pp. 611–19. See also Mōri, *op. cit.*, pp. 61–63.

19. *Osaka Shōka Daigaku 60 Nenshi*, pp. 20–31. Yamamoto's address is therein, pp. 565–66.

20. *Nihon Kindai Kyōiku 100 Nenshi*, pp. 399–405; *Osaka Shōka Daigaku 60 Nenshi*, pp. 44–46, 51–64.

21. *Furitsu Osaka Shōgyō Gakkō Ichiran, 1880–1886* (Calendar of Prefectural Osaka Commercial School, 1880 to March 1886), (1886), pp. 29, 49–50.

22. *Osaka Shōka Daigaku 60 Nenshi*, pp. 67–69, 90–94.

23. *Ibid.*, pp. 70–72, 87–89.

24. *Ibid.*, pp. 94–101, 104–6.

25. *Ibid.*, pp. 106–7, 120. *Shiritsu Osaka Shōgyō Gakkō Ichiran* (The Calendar of the City of Osaka Commercial School), pp. 38–39. According to this latter source (pp. 12–13), the schedule of studies in the principal and superior courses for the academic year of 1893 is as follows:

Principal Course

Subject	Number of hours per week	
	1st year	2nd year
Commercial correspondence	2	2
Commercial arithmetic	4	2
Bookkeeping	5	3
Commercial products	3	
Commercial geography	3	
Commercial history		3
Political economy	3	3
Law	2	3
English	6	6
Commercial practice		6
Gymnastics	5	5
Total	33	33

Superior Course

Subject	Number of hours per week
Bookkeeping	2
Science of commerce	5
Political economy	3
Law	3
English	6
Second foreign language	9
Gymnastics	5
Total	33

26. *Osaka Shōka Daigaku 60 Nenshi*, pp. 110–11, 116–20.
27. *Ibid.*, pp. 108, 112–13; Miyamoto, *Osaka Keizaijin to Bunka*, p. 228.
28. *Osaka Shōka Daigaku 60 Nenshi*, pp. 113–16, 132–33.
29. *Ibid.*, pp. 135–36.
30. *Ibid.*, pp. 136–42.
31. The information on the history of the school derives mainly from *Kansai Daigaku 100 Nenshi* (A Hundred Years of Kansai University) (Osaka, 1986).
32. For details of Tezuka's and Nomura's lectures, see Sugihara Shirō, *Seiō Keizaigaku to Kindai Nihon* (Western Political Economy and Modern Japan) (Tokyo, 1972), pp. 57–103.
33. Sugihara Shirō, *Nihon Keizai Shisōshi Ronshū* (Collected Papers on the History of Economic Thought in Japan) (Tokyo, 1980), pp. 179–99.
34. *Ibid.*, pp. 109–44.
35. For the history of Kobe University, see *Ryōsō 50 Nen* (50 Years of Ryōsō) (Kobe, 1954).
36. For the history of Dōshisha, see *Dōshisha 100 Nenshi* (A Hundred Years of Dōshisha) (Kyoto, 1979).
37. Sumiya Etsuji, *Learned Hakase Den* (The Life of Dr. Learned) (Tokyo, 1973).
38. For the history of Ritsumeikan, see *Ritsumeikan Sōritsu 50 Nenshi* (50 Years of Ritsumeikan) (Kyoto, 1953).
39. For the history of Kyoto Imperial University, see *Kyoto Teikoku Daigakushi* (History of Kyoto Imperial University) (Kyoto, 1943).

Chapter 12: Economists in Government

1. 'Meiji Shoki ni okeru Ōbei Keizaisho no Denrai' (Introduction of European and American Economics Books to Japan in the Early Meiji Era), in Sugihara Shirō, *Nihon Keizai Shisōshi Ronshū* (Collected Papers on the History of Economic Thought in Japan) (Tokyo, 1980), pp. 12–31.
2. For the Western books kept by the Tokugawa Shogunate, see the following catalogues: Rangaku Shiryō Kenkyūkai (Society for the Study of Dutch Literature), ed., *Edo Bakufu Kyūzō Yōsho Mokuroku* (Catalogue of Western Books Formerly Belonging to the Edo Government) (1957); Shizuoka Kenritsu Chūō Toshokan Aoi Bunko (Aoi Collection of Shizuoka Prefectural Central Library), ed., *Edo Bakufu Kyūzō Yōsho Mokuroku* (Catalogue of Western Books Formerly Belonging to the Edo Government) (1967).
3. See Taguchi Ukichi and Shimada Saburō, 'Ōkurashō Hon'yakukyoku no Gakusei' (Students of the Department of Translation, Ministry of Finance), *Kyōiku Hyōron* (Educational Review), no. 635 (Dec. 1902).
4. Honjō Eijirō, *Nihon Keizai Shisōshi Gaisetsu* (Outline of the History of Economic Thought in Japan) (Tokyo, 1946), p. 186.
5. See Umetani Noboru, *Oyatoi Gaikokujin* (Foreign Employees), vol. 1 (Tokyo, 1965), pp. 209–22.
6. See Tsuchiya Takao, *Shand* (in Japanese) (Tokyo, 1966); Tsuchiya Takao, *Oyatoi Gaikokujin* (Foreign Employees), vol. 8 (Tokyo, 1969).
7. For the works of Fesca, Eggert, and Mayet on Japanese agriculture, see Sakurai T., ed., *Meiji Nōgyō Ronshū* (Essays on Agriculture in the Meiji Era) (Tokyo, 1955).
8. Karl Rathegen, *Die Japaner und ihre wirtschaftliche Entwicklung* (Leipzig, 1905). Udo Eggert, *Land Reform in Japan, Specially Based on the Development of Credit Association* (Tokyo, 1890), Japanese translation by Oda H., 1891.
9. See Tsuchiya T., *Nihon Shihon Shugi Shijō no Shidōsha Tachi* (Leaders in the History of Japanese Capitalism) (Tokyo, 1939), pp. 203–26.
10. Mōri Toshihiko, *Ōkubo Toshimichi* (Tokyo, 1969), pp. 192–93.
11. Cf. Masakazu Iwata, *Ōkubo Toshimichi, the Bismarck of Japan* (Berkeley, 1964).

Chapter 13: Economists in Parliament

I am indebted to Professor C. Sugiyama, Professor S. Sugihara, Mrs. E. O. A. Checkland, Professor S. Nishikawa, and Yūichirō Hamada for suggestions and corrections.

1. Shiojima Nikichi, *Tokyo Keizaigaku Kyōkai Enkaku* (A Brief History of the Tokyo Political Economy Club) (Tokyo, 1930), p. 6.
2. *Tokyo Keizai Zasshi*, Jan. 29, 1879.
3. See Mrs. E. O. A. Checkland's forthcoming *Britain's Encounter with Meiji Japan.*
4. Sugihara Shirō, *Nihon no Ekonomisuto* (Japanese Economists) (Tokyo, 1984), p. 39.
5. *Ibid.*, pp. 43–50.
6. *Tokyo Keizai Zasshi*, April 14, 1888.
7. *Ibid.*
8. *Ibid.*, Aug. 7, 1886, Nov. 20, 1886.
9. Tokutomi Iichirō, *Kōshaku Matsukata Masayoshi Den* (Biography of Duke Matsukata Masayoshi) (Tokyo, 1935), p. 673.
10. *Tokyo Keizai Zasshi*, May 7, 1887.
11. Sugihara, *op. cit.*, pp. 63–70; Nishikawa Shunsaku, *Fukuzawa Yukichi to Sannin no Kōshintachi* (Fukuzawa Yukichi and Three Succeeding Economists) (Tokyo, 1985), pp. 96–126. Soeda gave useful explanations on the metallic problem in his 'Letter from Japan' in the 1895 and 1899 issues of *The Economic Journal.*
12. Anon. *Sakatani Yoshio Den* (Biography of Sakatani Yoshio) (Tokyo, 1951) chaps. 2, 3.
13. Ono Kazuichirō, 'Nihon ni okeru Kinhon'isei no Seiritsu, 1' (The Establishment of the Gold Standard in Japan), *Keizai Ronsō* (Economic Review) (Kyoto University) (1963).
14. *Ibid.*
15. *Sakatani Yoshio Den*, pp. 188–89.
16. *Kaheiseido Chōsakai Hōkoku* (Report of the Monetary Commission), in *Meiji Zenki Zaisei Keizaishi Shiryō Shūsei* (Collection of Materials of Economic and Financial History in Early Meiji) (Tokyo, 1931), vol. 12, preface.
17. *Ibid.*, p. 2.
18. *Ibid.*, pp. 4–5; Ono Kazuichirō, 'Nihon ni okeru Kinhon'isei no Seiritsu, 2', *Keizai Ronsō* (Kyoto University), 1963.
19. Sugihara, *op. cit.*, pp. 33–39.
20. See the issues of Jan. 28, 1881 and April 15, 1881.
21. *Kaheiseido Chōsakai Hōkoku*, p. 419.
22. J. Niehans, *The Theory of Money* (Baltimore & London, 1978), pp. 145–55.
23. F. A. Walker, *Political Economy* (London, 1908), p. 390.

Chapter 14: Economists in Journalism

1. For information on Taguchi Ukichi, see Shioshima J., *Teiken Taguchi Ukichi Sensei Den* (Life of Taguchi Ukichi) (Tokyo, 1912).
2. Taguchi formed Keizai Danwakai (Political Economy Seminar) in 1880, which later became the Tokyo Keizaigaku Kyōkai (Tokyo Political Economy Club) in 1887. The club, in contrast to such nationalistic clubs as the National Economy Society and the Japanese Economy Society, was a liberalistic club, similar in spirit to the Political Economy Club in England. In 1923, to commemorate the bicentenary of the birth of Adam Smith, the club held a meeting, which was documented in *Tokyo Keizai Zasshi*, no. 2135 (July 15, 1923). See Sugihara Shirō, *Nihon Keizai Shisōshi Ronshū* (Collected Papers on the History of Economic Thought in Japan) (Tokyo, 1980), pp. 161–64.
3. On Maeda Masana, see Chō Yukio, 'Nashonarizumu to "Sangyō Undō":

Maeda Masana no Shisō to Katsudō' (Nationalism and 'Industry Movement': Thoughts and Activities of Maeda Masana), in *Kindai Nihon Keizai Shisōshi* (A History of Economic Thought in Modern Japan), Chō Yukio and Sumiya Kazuhiko eds., vol. 1 (1969), pp. 85–133.

4. On Ōshima Sadamasu, see Nishida T., *Ōshima Sadamasu: Hito to Gakusetsu* (Ōshima Sadamasu: Profile and Theory) (1945).

5. On Amano Tameyuki, see Asakawa E. and Nishida T., *Amano Tameyuki* (Tokyo, 1950).

6. On this journal, see Sugihara Shirō, *Seiō Keizaigaku to Kindai Nihon* (Western Political Economy and Modern Japan) (Tokyo, 1972), pp. 164–79.

7. On the ideological stance of this journal, see Inoue K. et al., *Taishōki no Kyūshin Shugi* (Radical Liberalism in Taishō Era) (Tokyo, 1972).

8. This article was published in book form in 1906.

9. On the relationship between Kawakami Hajime and *Nihon Keizai Shinshi*, see Ōno Eiji's introduction to *Kawakami Hajime Zenshū* (The Complete Works of Kawakami Hajime), vol. 4 (1982).

10. On the debate on free trade versus protectionism, see Hori T., *Meiji Keizai Shisōshi* (A History of Economic Thought in the Meiji Era) (1975)

11. See Matsuo T., 'Chūgokukan no henka to Katayama Sen' (Katayama Sen and the Change in Japanese Views of China), in Inoue et al., *op. cit.*, pp. 289–301.

Chapter 15: 'Vain' Learning

Professors S. Nishikawa and N. Tamaki have been most kind in giving constructive comments and advice. Tribute should be paid to the valuable conversations over many years not only with Professors Mizuta and Sugiyama but also with my late husband, Professor Sydney George Checkland. Errors of interpretation or fact which remain are my responsibility alone.

1. Political economy has many definitions; very simply 'it is the practical science of the production and distribution of wealth but also the condition of a country as to its material prosperity'. Early works on political economy included Sir James Steuart, *An Inquiry into the Principles of Political Economy* (Edinburgh, 1767), and Adam Smith, *An Inquiry into the Nature and Causes of the Wealth of Nations* (1776). Departments of Economics in the Scottish universities are still called Departments of Political Economy.

2. The term 'feudal' is used for convenience. Fukuzawa (c. 1890) and many others since have argued that the Japanese notion of *hōken-sei* was markedly different from Western feudalism.

3. T. Walrond, *Letters and Journals of James, Eighth Earl of Elgin* (London, 1873), p. 270.

4. See W. W. Rostow, *The Stages of Economic Growth* (Cambridge, 1960), *The Economics of Take-off into Sustained Growth* (London, 1963), and *How It All Began* (London, 1975).

5. See W. G. Beasley, *The Modern History of Japan* (London, 1963), R. Dore, *Education in Tokugawa Japan* (London, 1965); P. Francks, *Technology and Agricultural Development in Pre-War Japan* (New Haven, 1984).

6. See C. Blacker, *The Japanese Enlightenment: A Study of the Writing of Fukuzawa Yukichi* (Cambridge, 1964).

7. L. Oliphant, *Narrative of the Earl of Elgin's Mission to China and Japan in the Years 1857, 1858 and 1859*, 2nd ed. (Edinburgh, 1860), vols. I and II, vol. II pp. 53–54.

8. Comments on the removal of restrictions have been made as follows: 'All check-points on major roads were removed; guilds were dismantled; restrictions on occupational mobility were lifted; and peasants were now permitted to grow any kind of crops they wanted to sell or purchase farm land'. Nishikawa Shunsaku and Saitō Osamu, 'The Economic History of the Restoration Period', in *Meiji*

Ishin: Restoration and Revolution (eds. M. Nagai and M. Urrutia) (Tokyo, 1985), p. 178.

9. The phrase Gresham's Law accepts that 'bad money drives out good', which means that where coins of high and those of low gold or silver content, that is 'good' or 'bad' coins, are circulating simultaneously, people will hoard the 'good' coins leaving the others in circulation.

10. Nishikawa and Saitō, *op. cit.*, p. 183.

11. There are many accounts of what the Japanese government thought of as 'an outrageous act of spoliation'. See R. Alcock, *Capital of the Tycoon* (London, 1863), vol. I, pp. 281–82.

12. A very good picture of the excitement and bustle of life in Nagasaki after 1859 can be gathered from a study of the Jardine Matheson Archives, the University of Cambridge Library, 'Nagasaki Boxes'.

13. Matsukata Masayoshi, *Report on the Post-Bellum Financial Administration of Japan* (Tokyo, 1900). Matsukata had spent time in 1878 in Paris. After his successful efforts to bring inflation under control in Japan in the 1880s he paid tribute to the influence of Léon Say, the French finance minister.

14. C. Sugiyama, 'The Development of Economic Thought in Meiji Japan', *Modern Asian Studies* II, 4 (1968): 325–41.

15. See Blacker, *op. cit.*; Fukuzawa Yukichi, *An Encouragement of Learning*, translated and introduced by D. A. Dilworth and U. Hirano (Tokyo, 1969); *The Autobiography of Fukuzawa Yukichi*, translated by E. Kiyooka, new ed. (1960); *Fukuzawa Yukichi on Education*, translated and edited by E. Kiyooka (Tokyo, 1985).

16. Fukuzawa, *An Encouragement of Learning*, p. 1.

17. Fukuzawa Yukichi, 'On De-Asianization', in *Meiji Japan through Contemporary Sources* (Tokyo, 1972), vol. III, 1869–94, p. 129.

18. H. Mizuta, 'Historical Introduction', p. 15.

19. See J. Iddittie, *Marquis Okuma, a Biographical Study in the Rise of Democratic Japan* (Tokyo, 1956).

20. See I. P. Hall, *Mori Arinori* (Cambridge, Mass., 1973).

21. I. P. Hall, 'Mori Arinori', in *Kodansha Encyclopedia of Japan*, vol. 5, p. 249.

22. See 'Godai Tomoatsu', *Kodansha Encyclopedia of Japan*, vol. 3, p. 39.

23. An interesting but simple contemporary introduction to Japanese education is given in H. Norman, *The Real Japan* (London, 1892), pp. 95–106. See also A. Stead, *Japan by the Japanese* (London, 1904).

24. It may well be that this first generation of Japanese students, who were instructed in a foreign language, were better linguists than their sons who were taught only in Japanese.

25. Unitarianism is a branch of the Presbyterian Non-conformist Christian faith, believing in one God, but not accepting the Trinity. In practical terms, numbers of small active energetic groups made up influential church communities in Europe and America. In the United States they were led at this time by W. E. Channing and Theodore Parker.

26. For E. F. Fenollosa, see V. W. Brooks, *Fenollosa and His Circle* (New York, 1962); W. W. Chisholm, *The Far East and American Culture* (New York, 1963).

27. Tajiri Inajirō was under-secretary to Ōkuma in the Ministry of Finance, and later founded Senshū University (Senshū Gakkō).

28. A. M. Craig, 'John Hill Burton and Fukuzawa Yukichi', *Kindai Nihon Kenkyū* (Studies in Modern Japan) (Fukuzawa Memorial Center for Modern Japanese Studies) 1, Keiō University (Tokyo, 1984).

29. John Hill Burton (1809–81) attended Marischal College and University, Aberdeen. He followed the first three years of the class of 1823–27 and the magistrand year of the class of 1825–29, graduating A.M. in the later year.

30. For a brief, stimulating discussion of the Scottish Enlightenment, see N. E.

Phillipson in *A Companion to Scottish Culture* (ed. D. Daiches) (London, 1981), pp. 340–44.

31. Henry Dunning Macleod (1821–1902), educated at Trinity College, Cambridge, where he graduated B.A. in 1843. His works are held in many university libraries. The National Library of Scotland, Edinburgh, holds a number of his letters. Letters to John Hill Burton 1860–62, MS. 9396, ff. 72–75, 79, 92–95, 110, 136, 172, 229; 1870, MS. 9398, f. 165; 1871, MS. 9399, f. 104; Letters to Blackwoods 1872, MS. 4279; 1892, MS. 4590; Letters to James S. Fleming 1877, Adv. MS. 81. 5. 7., ff. 26–31—about banking history. Macleod particularly remained outside of the establishment, although he would have liked to have the security and status of an academic chair. Macleod applied for the Cambridge Chair of Political Economy in 1863, when Henry Fawcett was appointed and again in 1884 when, after Fawcett's death, Alfred Marshall was elected.

32. The private law schools, Senshū (1880), Hōsei (1881), Meiji (1881), Waseda (1882), and Chūō (1885) later became universities.

33. Although Fukuzawa had already translated material in Western bookkeeping into Japanese and other Japanese translations were used, for example, at Shōhō Kōshūjo, A. A. Shand's involvement with those learning Western business methods was not unimportant, especially as, unlike the Japanese translators, he came to the task from practical experience of bookkeeping problems.

34. After the First World War the Imperial universities of Hokkaido (1918), Osaka (1931), and Nagoya (1939) were set up but without faculty of humanities or social sciences.

35. S. G. Checkland, *British Public Policy* (Cambridge, 1983), p. 2.

36. Mori Arinori's association with Herbert Spencer in the 1880s in London led to Spencer advising Mori to be extremely conservative in introducing any liberal political ideas into Japan. See D. Duncan, *Life and Letters of Herbert Spencer* (London, 1908), p. 161.

37. J. D. Pierson, *Tokutomi Sohō, 1863–1957: A Journalist for Modern Japan* (Princeton, 1980).

38. Idditie, *op. cit.*, p. 355.

39. C. Sugiyama, 'Fukuzawa', p. 44.

40. C. Sugiyama, quoting Nishimura Shigeki, in 'Development of Economic Thought in Meiji Japan, *Modern Asian Studies* II, 4 (1968): 332.

41. See J. E. Hoare, 'The Japanese Treaty Ports 1868–1899, a Study of the Foreign Settlements', Ph.D., University of London, 1971; J. E. Hoare, 'Japan Undermines Extraterritoriality: Extradition in Japan 1885–1899, pp. 125–29, in *European Studies on Japan*, eds. I. Nish and C. Dunn (Tenterden, 1979).

42. See N. Tamaki, 'Economists in Parliament' earlier in this volume, p. 223ff; J. Soyeda (Soeda), 'The Adoption of Gold Monometallism by Japan', *Political Science Quarterly* 8, no. 1 (Boston, 1898): 60–90; E. Foxwell's review of *Report on the Adoption of the Gold Standard in Japan* by Count Masayoshi Matsukata, H.I.J.M.'s Minister of Finance, in the *Economic Journal* 10, no. 38 (June 1900): 232–45.

43. I. Nish, *Anglo-Japanese Alliance* (London, 1966).

44. *The Autobiography of Fukuzawa Yukichi*, p. 334.

45. Idditie, *op. cit.*, p. 334.

46. *The Autobiography of Fukuzawa Yukichi*, p. 335.

47. *Fukuzawa Yukichi on Education*, translated and edited by E. Kiyooka (Tokyo, 1985), p. 104.

Chapter 16: From a Western Point of View

1. E. Stuart Kirby has argued that while classical economics was appropriate to the East, neo-classical marginalism, with its emphasis on individualism and subjective value, was not. See his 'The Reception of Western Economics in the Orient', *Quarterly Journal of Economics* 66 (August 1952): 409–17.

2. *Why has Japan 'Succeeded'? Western Technology and the Japanese Ethos* (Cambridge, 1982), pp. 58–59. Cf. Thomas R. H. Havens, *Nishi Amane and Modern Japanese Thought* (Princeton, 1970) pp. 6–7; also for a penetrating account of the late Tokugawa economy and society see Barrington Moore, Jr., *Social Origins of Dictatorship and Democracy. Lord and Peasant in the Making of the Modern World* (Boston, 1967), especially chap. 5.

3. 'Origins of Japanese Academic Economics', *Monumenta Nipponica* 16 (1960–61): 44. Curiously enough, although Bell appreciated that the Japanese 'had the prerogative of picking and choosing those elements most adaptable to their own peculiar problems', he made no reference whatever to German historical economics which became influential during the later part of the period treated in his article.

4. G. B. Sansom, *The Western World and Japan: A Study in the Interaction of European and Asiatic Cultures* (New York, 1949), p. 437. Cf. Juichi Soyeta [Soeda], 'The Study of Political Economy in Japan', *Economic Journal* 3 (June, 1893): 334.

5. Sansom, *op. cit.* The exclusionist group, which advocated 'expel the barbarians', adopted the slogan 'Eastern morality, Western technology'. Havens, *op. cit.*, p. 18. According to John W. Hall, the absence of a 'recognized separation of the moral order from the actual . . . [is] one of the most fundamental of all Japanese conceptions of the nature of the World.' Cf. 'A Monarch for Modern Japan,' in Robert E. Ward ed., *Political Development in Modern Japan* (Princeton, 1968), p. 29.

6. Soyeta (Soeda), *op. cit.*, p. 334.

7. Mizuta, supra, p. 9.

8. Sansom, *op. cit.*, p. 440.

9. 'The explanations of life's principles in the science "philosophia" are superior even to Sung Confucianism, and the way in which the West has established the basic principles of economics, based on nature and public order, is superior to monarchical government', Havens, *op. cit.*, p. 44.

10. Irokawa Daikichi, *The Culture of the Meiji Period* (Princeton, 1985), p. 264.

11. Jean-Pierre Lehmann, *The Roots of Modern Japan* (London, 1982), p. 214. In some, but not all, cases, the retreat was a response to official disapproval.

12. *Ibid.*, p. 245.

13. 'Modernization appeared to most Japanese who thought about it at all, not as a process in which a life-or-death confrontation of traditional and modern took place, but as a dynamic blending of the two'. Thomas C. Smith, cited by Robert J. Smith, *Japanese Society: Tradition, Self and the Social Order* (Cambridge, 1983), p. 25. Cf. *ibid.*, p. 6; also Lehmann, p. 164; and George Wilson, 'Pursuing the Millennium in the Meiji Restoration', *Conflict in Modern Japanese History: The Neglected Tradition*, Tetsuo Najita and J. Victor Koschmann (Princeton, 1982), especially pp. 117–18n and 194.

14. Irokawa, *op. cit.*, pp. 260–67. He notes that this is an essentially European view of Japanese thought. See also Smith, *op. cit.*, p. 14.

15. Carol Gluck, *Japan's Modern Myths: Ideology in the Late Meiji Period* (Princeton, 1985), p. 259.

16. Maruyama Masao, quoted by J. Victor Koschmann in his *Authority and the Individual in Japan: Citizen Protest in Historical Perspective* (Tokyo, 1978), p. 56. For various supporting views see Smith, *op. cit.*, pp. 58–59. A person who habitually argues with logical consistency is regarded as immature 'and may be called a *rikutsuppoi* (i.e., reason-freak)', p. 58.

17. For example, see Morishima, *op. cit.*, p. 19.

18. Gluck, *op. cit.*, p. 260.

19. Morishima, *op. cit.*, p. 60.

20. *Ibid.*, p. 18.

21. Kuno Osamu, 'The Meiji State, Minponshugi, and Ultranationalism', in Koschmann, *op. cit.*, p. 64. Irokawa, *op. cit.*, remarks that by 1911 'the emperor system was not a compassionate all-enveloping embrace but a tyranny that would

stop at nothing to eliminate heresy, a self-contradicting system that concealed within the shadows of its harmoniousness a brutality that chilled men's hearts', p. 310. This somewhat harsh judgement depicts the situation after the regime had become more firmly established.

22. Nagai Michio, 'Mori Arinori', *Japan Quarterly* 11 (January–March 1964): 105.

23. Gluck, *op. cit.*, p. 34.

24. *Ibid.*, pp. 258–59.

25. Lehmann, *op. cit.*, pp. 244–45. I have drawn heavily on this valuable general history.

26. Yamashita Shigekazu, 'Herbert Spencer and Meiji Japan', in *Japan in Transition: Thought and Action in the Meiji Era, 1868–1912*, Hilary Conroy, Sandra T. W. Davis, Wayne Patterson eds. (London, 1984), p. 78. See also Mizuta supra, pp. 15–16.

27. *Ibid.*, p. 91.

28. Sansom, *op. cit.*, p. 461. In large measure it involved a revival of Confucian ethical purposes in opposition to the earlier tendencies towards utilitarianism and amoralism. *Ibid.*, p. 455.

29. Lehmann, *op. cit.*, p. 198.

30. *Ibid.*, p. 175.

31. Kuno, *op. cit.*, p. 64.

32. See Stephen Sass, *The Pragmatic Imagination: A History of the Wharton School 1881–1891* (Philadelphia, 1982).

33. The existence of these colleges is briefly mentioned in Sass, *op. cit.*, p. 19, and they are enumerated and described in the annual reports of the U.S. Commissioner of Education. Their numbers grew from 60 in 1871 to 222 in 1889.

34. See Sugiyama and Nishizawa, p. 158. They note that the school was for a time governed by Tokyo Prefecture and then taken over by the Ministry of Agriculture and Trade.

Index